Human-Centered Workforce Management in the Age of Digital Work

Ricardo Marcão
https://orcid.org/0000-0003-3277-3078
NECE, University of Beira Interior, Portugal & ISLA Santarém, Portugal

Vasco Ribeiro
NECE, University of Beira Interior, Portugal & GOVCOPP, Portugal & TECH&ART, Portugal & ISLA Santarém, Portugal

Filipa Martinho
ISLA Santarém, Portugal

Isabel Reis
https://orcid.org/0000-0002-2008-9124
ISLA Santarém, Portugal

IGI Global
Scientific Publishing
Publishing Tomorrow's Research Today

Vice President of Editorial	Melissa Wagner
Director of Acquisitions	Mikaela Felty
Director of Book Development	Jocelynn Hessler
Production Manager	Mike Brehm
Cover Design	Jose Rosado

Published in the United States of America by
IGI Global Scientific Publishing
701 East Chocolate Avenue
Hershey, PA, 17033, USA
Tel: 717-533-8845 | Fax: 717-533-7115
Website: https://www.igi-global.com E-mail: cust@igi-global.com

Library of Congress Cataloging-in-Publication Data

LCCN: 2026026429 (CIP Data Pending)
ISBN13: 9798260021781
Isbn13Softcover: 9798260021798
EISBN13: 9798260021804

British Cataloguing in Publication Data
A Cataloguing in Publication record for this book is available from the British Library.

Table of Contents

Detailed Table of Contents

Strategic Human Resource Management (SHRM) has evolved from an administrative support function into a key driver of organizational success and sustainable competitive advantage. This study analyses the strategic alignment between Human Resource (HR) practices and organizational objectives, examining how such alignment supports financial performance, innovation, and sustainability. Based on a systematized literature review, the study identifies core theoretical frameworks, including the Resource-Based View and the Ability–Motivation–Opportunity (AMO) model, which highlight the strategic value of human capital. The findings show that vertical alignment (strategic fit) and horizontal alignment (internal consistency) are essential for positioning HR as a strategic partner that enhances organizational agility and mitigates risk. Overall, these insights improve understanding of how strategically aligned HR systems sustain long-term organizational performance and resilience.

The pace of technological change and digital transformation are also driving the demand of continuous reskilling and agility of the workforce. Conventional, job-based establishments of talent management can no longer be sufficient to support

This chapter examines the strategic role of Human Resources (HR) in managing generational diversity and the effectiveness of onboarding in a municipal organization. Through a case study of "Faz Cultura", a public-sector cultural institution, the research explores challenges and opportunities emerging from the coexistence of different generations in the workplace. The study aims to assess how tailored onboarding strategies and intergenerational management policies influence employee retention, motivation, and overall organizational cohesion. A qualitative case study methodology was employed, utilizing semi-structured interviews, surveys, and document analysis to collect data from employees across different generational cohorts. The study also incorporated a comparative analysis of onboarding programs and HR strategies, identifying patterns of adaptation and resistance among employees from different age groups. This study contributes to the growing body of literature on HR strategies in public-sector organizations by offering empirical insights.

The rapid integration of digital technologies into everyday organizational life has transformed how employees work, process information, and interact. Among the emerging digital habits, doomscrolling, defined as the compulsive consumption of negative online content, has gained attention for its disruptive psychological and behavioral consequences. Generation Z, being highly exposed to digital devices and content, is particularly susceptible to this phenomenon, now that they are entering the workforce. This book chapter examines the implications of digital behaviors such as doomscrolling on Generation Z workplace dynamics. It adopts a human-centred, ethical, and policy-oriented HRM perspective. Drawing on multidisciplinary literature from psychology, digital media, and HRM, the chapter identifies key challenges, risks, and ethical concerns. Building on these nuances, the chapter proposes policy-oriented and governance-based HR interventions designed to promote employee mental health, digital well-being, and sustainable organizational development.

This chapter outlines socio-cultural factors and impact of organizational diversity management strategies and bias-reducing mechanism on recruitment. By relying on case studies and literature, the chapter examines organizational practices like inclusive HR policies, structured recruitment systems, leadership commitment, and technology-enablement of hiring processes for equity in employment outcomes. According to the report, Indian organisations are ramping up their efforts to adopt diversity and inclusion initiatives globally, responding to workplace inequities. D&I initiatives contribute to fairer, more transparent, and more representative workforces. The chapter also shows how organizations adapt global staffing practices to local institutional realities, emphasizing the contextualization of diversity efforts. The finding recommends the integrated commitment by organization; standardized procedure of evaluation and monitoring facilitate recruitment diversity effective management for equitable and inclusive hiring outcome.

The growing adoption of Artificial Intelligence (AI) in organizations creates strategic opportunities while intensifying psychosocial risks, particularly burnout. This chapter introduces the Convergent Emotional Intelligence–Artificial Intelligence–Burnout Model (MCIIB), which integrates Emotional Intelligence (EI), intelligent technologies, and professional exhaustion. Based on an integrative literature review, the model conceptualizes EI as a personal resource moderating the AI–burnout relationship. Organizational factors—AI governance, ethics, emotional culture, and digital maturity—further shape technology's psychosocial impact. Grounded in the Job Demands–Resources theory, Maslach's burnout model, and EI frameworks, the MCIIB advances eight testable hypotheses and provides evidence-based guidance for human-centered HRM. The chapter concludes that emotional sustainability in digital work environments depends on the balanced alignment of emotional competencies, ethical AI, and organizational support.

Preface

The world of work is undergoing one of the most profound transformations in modern organizational history. Digitalization, artificial intelligence, hybrid work models, generational shifts, and evolving employee expectations are redefining how organizations attract, manage, develop, and retain talent. In this rapidly changing landscape, organizations are increasingly challenged to balance technological advancement with the human dimensions of work, well-being, ethics, inclusion, emotional sustainability, and meaningful engagement.

Human-Centered Workforce Management in the Age of Digital Work emerges from this critical moment. This volume brings together scholars and practitioners from diverse academic and professional backgrounds to explore how organizations can remain competitive and innovative while preserving the centrality of people in organizational life. The book advances the idea that technology should not replace the human essence of work, but rather support more inclusive, ethical, agile, and sustainable workplaces.

Across its chapters, the book examines the strategic alignment of human resource management with organizational objectives, the rise of AI-driven talent intelligence, ethical people analytics, leadership and endomarketing practices, hybrid work challenges, generational diversity, digital well-being, inclusive recruitment, emotional sustainability, and employee mental health. Collectively, these contributions provide a multidisciplinary understanding of how organizations can create resilient and human-centered systems in increasingly digital environments.

A recurring theme throughout the volume is the need to integrate technological innovation with empathy, ethical governance, and organizational responsibility. The contributors emphasize that sustainable organizational performance depends not only on operational efficiency and digital capability but also on trust, psychological safety, diversity, emotional intelligence, and employee well-being.

This book is intended for researchers, academics, human resource professionals, organizational leaders, policymakers, and students interested in the future of work and the evolving role of human-centered management. By combining conceptual discussions, empirical insights, practical frameworks, and emerging research agendas, the volume seeks to contribute to ongoing debates surrounding digital transformation and the humanization of organizational practices.

We hope this collection encourages readers to rethink workforce management through a more holistic lens, one that recognizes technology as an enabler of human potential rather than merely a tool for productivity. In doing so, this book aims to inspire organizations to build workplaces that are not only digitally advanced, but also ethical, inclusive, resilient, and deeply human.

CHAPTER OVERVIEW

Chapter 1 Strategic Alignment between Human Resource Management and Organizational Strategy: A Literature Review

This chapter examines the evolution of Strategic Human Resource Management (SHRM) from an administrative function to a strategic organizational partner. Through a systematized literature review, the authors explore how HR practices aligned with organizational goals contribute to financial performance, innovation, sustainability, and long-term resilience. Drawing on frameworks such as the Resource-Based View and the Ability–Motivation–Opportunity (AMO) model, the chapter highlights the importance of both vertical and horizontal alignment in creating agile and strategically coherent HR systems.

Chapter 2 Artificial Intelligence (AI)-Driven Skills Intelligence for Talent Management: Building an Agile and Future-Ready Workforce

Focusing on the increasing importance of workforce agility, this chapter explores how AI-driven skills intelligence is reshaping talent management practices. The authors discuss how machine learning, natural language processing, and predictive analytics enable organizations to identify, map, and forecast workforce capabilities. The chapter further examines applications in personalized learning, career development, succession planning, and employee retention, presenting AI as a strategic tool for building future-ready organizations.

Chapter 3 Responsible AI and People Analytics in HR: Ethical Employer Branding and Human-Centered Talent Management

This chapter investigates the ethical implications of AI and people analytics in HR practices such as recruitment, performance management, and behavioral prediction. Using the Human-Centred Ethical AI (HCEAI) framework, the authors address concerns related to fairness, transparency, accountability, privacy, and bias. The chapter also demonstrates how responsible AI practices strengthen employer branding, foster employee trust, and support inclusive and ethical talent management systems.

Chapter 4 Leading from Within: An Endomarketing-Based Framework

The authors present leadership-driven endomarketing as a strategic approach to strengthening internal employer branding and employee advocacy. This chapter conceptualizes endomarketing as a leadership process that aligns organizational values, communication strategies, and employee experiences. By examining internal campaigns, participatory practices, and leadership communication, the chapter proposes a framework for fostering employee engagement, organizational identification, and voluntary brand advocacy.

Chapter 5 Team Leadership in Human-Centered Organizations

This chapter explores the evolving role of leadership in human-centered organizations. Integrating classical and contemporary leadership theories, the authors discuss how leadership styles, coaching, mentoring, emotional intelligence, and communication practices influence team performance and employee fulfillment. The chapter emphasizes leadership adaptability in digitally transforming and culturally diverse workplaces while encouraging the development of sustainable and inclusive organizational cultures.

Chapter 6 Absenteeism, Internal Marketing, and Productivity in a Hybrid Work Environment: Preliminary Insights

Addressing the growing prevalence of hybrid work, this chapter examines the relationship between internal marketing, absenteeism, and organizational productivity. The authors analyze how organizations have adapted management practices following the COVID-19 pandemic and explore the role of internal communication and employee engagement strategies in maintaining productivity and reducing absenteeism in hybrid environments.

Chapter 7 Managing Generational Diversity: Human Resources and Talent Management Strategies and Onboarding Effectiveness

This chapter investigates the challenges and opportunities associated with generational diversity in the workplace. Through a case study of a public-sector cultural organization, the authors analyze how onboarding programs and HR strategies influence employee retention, motivation, and organizational cohesion across different age groups. The chapter contributes valuable empirical insights into intergenerational management and onboarding effectiveness in contemporary organizations.

Chapter 8 Doomscrolling, Digital Behavior and Gen Z Workplace Dynamics – Policy and Governance Implications for Human-Centered Human Resource Management

The authors examine the emerging phenomenon of doomscrolling and its implications for Generation Z employees entering digitally intensive workplaces. Drawing from psychology, digital media studies, and HRM literature, the chapter explores the psychological and behavioral consequences of excessive negative content consumption. It further proposes governance frameworks and HR interventions aimed at promoting digital well-being, mental health, and ethical organizational practices.

Chapter 9 Human-Centered Recruitment and Selection: Addressing Cultural Diversity in Indian Workplaces

This chapter discusses diversity management and inclusive recruitment practices within the Indian organizational context. Using case studies and literature analysis, the author explores how structured recruitment systems, leadership commitment, inclusive HR policies, and technology-enabled hiring processes contribute to equitable employment outcomes. The chapter also highlights the importance of contextualizing global diversity initiatives within local cultural and institutional realities.

Chapter 10 Emotional Sustainability in Digitized Work Environments

This chapter introduces the Convergent Emotional Intelligence–Artificial Intelligence–Burnout Model (MCIIB), which examines the relationship between AI adoption, emotional intelligence, and burnout. Grounded in established organizational and psychological theories, the chapter argues that emotional intelligence acts as a protective resource in digitally intensive workplaces. The authors also discuss how organizational culture, AI governance, ethics, and digital maturity shape employee well-being and emotional sustainability.

Chapter 11 Fostering Well-Being and Mental Health in Human-Centered Organisations: Employee Well-Being, Burnout, and Mindful Organising

The concluding chapter emphasizes the growing importance of employee well-being and mental health in organizational success. The authors examine how human-centered HR practices, including flexible work arrangements, ethical leadership, wellness programs, and inclusive organizational cultures, reduce burnout and improve employee engagement. By integrating hedonic and eudaimonic perspectives of well-being, the chapter advocates for organizational environments that support both individual flourishing and sustainable performance.

Together, these chapters provide a comprehensive exploration of the challenges and opportunities associated with workforce management in the digital era. The volume underscores that the future of work depends not only on technological innovation, but also on organizations' ability to cultivate ethical, inclusive, emotionally sustainable, and genuinely human-centered workplaces.

Chapter 1
Strategic Alignment Between Human Resource Management and Organizational Strategy: A Literature Review

Ana Isabel Virgolino
http://orcid.org/0000-0002-9914-5861
CeBER-UC, School of Management, Polytechnic University of Tomar, Portugal

Beatriz Batista
http://orcid.org/0009-0004-5602-3639
School of Management, Polytechnic University of Tomar, Portugal

Gizelle Santos
School of Management, Polytechnic University of Tomar, Portugal

ABSTRACT

Strategic Human Resource Management (SHRM) has evolved from an administrative support function into a key driver of organizational success and sustainable competitive advantage. This study analyses the strategic alignment between Human Resource (HR) practices and organizational objectives, examining how such alignment supports financial performance, innovation, and sustainability. Based on a systematized literature review, the study identifies core theoretical frameworks, including the Resource-Based View and the Ability–Motivation–Opportunity (AMO) model, which highlight the strategic value of human capital. The findings show that vertical alignment (strategic fit) and horizontal alignment (internal consistency) are essential

DOI: 10.4018/979-8-2600-2178-1.ch001

for positioning HR as a strategic partner that enhances organizational agility and mitigates risk. Overall, these insights improve understanding of how strategically aligned HR systems sustain long-term organizational performance and resilience.

1. INTRODUCTION

1.1. Background to the topic

Strategic Human Resource Management (SHRM) emerged in the mid-1980s and is now recognised as a vital field of practice and research in business administration (Castro, Araujo, Ribeiro, Demo, & Meneses, 2020). SHRM differs from traditional personnel management in that it adopts a long-term perspective, focusing on workforce planning and skills development aligned with the future needs of the organisation (Dave et al.,2023). This field is based on the premise that human capital is a company's most valuable asset, capable of generating a sustainable competitive advantage that is difficult for competitors to imitate (Jaradat, 2023). In today's business environment, characterised by volatility and uncertainty (VUCA), HR's ability to integrate into the overall strategy becomes a differentiating factor for the survival and growth of organisations (Wash, 2023).

1.2. Relevance to Strategic Management of Organisations

The relevance of HRM lies in its ability to act as a bridge between people management and strategic planning, ensuring that the capabilities, behaviours, and culture of the workforce support business objectives (Jaradat, 2023). HR involvement in the formulation and implementation of organisational strategy allows human capital concerns to be represented from the outset of the decision-making process (Wash, 2023). In addition, HRM contributes to organisational agility, enabling companies to respond quickly to technological changes and market disruptions, such as those observed during the COVID-19 pandemic (Jaradat, 2023).

1.3. Objectives and structure of the work

The **overall objective** of this thesis is to analyse the impact of strategic alignment between human resource management and organisational strategy on the performance and sustainability of organisations. The specific objective is to identify the key success factors and competencies required for HR professionals to act as strategic business partners (HRBPs).

To guide the research, the following research questions are proposed:

1. How does vertical alignment between HR practices and business strategy influence financial and operational performance? (Hossain, Arefin, & Urme, 2025)
2. What is the mediating role of HR outcomes (commitment, satisfaction) in the relationship between HRM practices and organisational performance? (Abualfalayeh, 2025)
3. How does the integration of emerging technologies (AI, RPA) redefine strategic alignment and competitive advantage? (Nastase, Adomnitei, & Apetri, 2025)

The work is structured in seven chapters: introduction, literature review methodology, theoretical framework, strategic alignment, impacts of alignment, discussion, and conclusion.

2. LITERATURE REVIEW METHODOLOGY

2.1. Type of review

This study is based on a systematic literature review, whose objective is to ensure methodological rigour and reproducibility of results (Christina, Alamelu, & Nigama, 2025). This approach allows for the identification, evaluation, and synthesis of empirical and theoretical evidence on GERH in an orderly and transparent manner (Filha, Lima, Oliveira, & Carvalho, 2021).

2.2. Databases used

The bibliographic research was conducted in databases of academic prestige, including Google Scholar (Castro el al., 2020).

2.3. Inclusion/exclusion criteria

The inclusion criteria considered peer-reviewed scientific articles published in English or Portuguese that directly addressed the intersection between HRM, strategic alignment, and organisational performance (Castro et al., 2020). Works that lacked methodological robustness, non-academic sources, and studies that did not focus on the organisational level were excluded (Castro et al., 2020).

2.4. Time period

The analysis focused predominantly on the last 5 years (2020-2025), aiming to capture the most recent trends, such as digital transformation, the impact of remote working, and the integration of the Sustainable Development Goals (SDGs) into people management (Castro et al., 2020).

Table 1. Sources of Strategic Human Resource Management and Organisational Alignment

Year	Author(s)	Thematic Dimension	Study Objectives
2020	Castro et al.	Implementation of GERH in Brazil	Characterise national scientific output on the implementation of strategic HR policies and practices between 1997 and 2017.
2021	Silva, Albuquerque & Costa	Organisational Culture and Alignment	Verify the existence of strategic alignment between organisational culture and people management strategies in Brazilian organisations.
2021	Santos Filha et al.	Communication and Strategic Alignment	Propose a theoretical model of the role of HR in the internal communication process focused on organisational strategic alignment.
2022	Hermansyah et al.	Performance and Human Capital	Review recent articles on HRM to discuss its relationship with business performance, human capital, and competitive advantage.
2022	Yu et al.	Organisational Resilience	Investigate the impact of GERH on organisational resilience and the mediating role of employees' self-efficacy and self-management.
2023	Breaz & Jaradat	Alignment of HR Practices	Investigate the current state of HRM practices and identify how their alignment with business objectives enhances performance and competitiveness.
2023	Wash	Business Partner Competencies	Analyse strategies and skills needed for HRBPs (business partners) to reskill teams for the future of operations.
2023	Boudreau, Ulrich & Buhler	Strategic Interaction in the USA	Conduct a comprehensive review of the conceptual and empirical literature on the interaction between HR strategies and strategic alignment in American organisations.
2023	Storey & Wright	Evolution and Contexts of GERH	Provide an analytical guide on HRM research, addressing new challenges such as COVID-19, remote working, diversity, and sustainability.
2024	Zidan & Al-Loumi	Immunity and Organisational Agility	Measuring the impact of strategic alignment on organisational immunity through strategic agility in the education sector in Iraq.
2024	Kess-Momoh et al.	Innovation and Well-being in the 21st Century	Review trends and innovations in HRM, focusing on technological integration, remote working and prioritising employee wellbeing.
2024	Arora, Malhotra & Ruhil	Effectiveness and Business Objectives	Explore the impact of aligning strategic HR management with organisational objectives on overall effectiveness and performance.

continued on following page

Table 1. Continued

Year	Author(s)	Thematic Dimension	Study Objectives
2024	Mwambela	Performance in Emerging Countries	Examine the impact of HRM components (rewards, training, recruitment) on the performance of profit-oriented companies in Zambia.
2024	Ulrich, Way & Wright	Strategic Human Capabilities	Examine how HR flexibility and strategic management build collective human capabilities that drive organisational performance.
2025	Hossain, Arefin & Urme	Financial Impact and Investment	Quantify the financial impact of HRM practices (training, engagement) on metrics such as ROI and profit margins in Bangladesh.
2025	Prifti et al.	Performance in the Private Sector	Investigate the strategic role of human resource management and its impact on organisational performance in Albania.
2025	Abualfalayeh	Goal and Performance Alignment	Examine how HRM practices influence employee performance through goal alignment in Jordan.
2025	Kashoob et al.	Occupational Psychology and Strategy	Study the alignment of HR practices with business strategy and their impact based on principles of occupational psychology.
2025	Tavares & Vaz	Service Performance Evaluation	Propose a performance evaluation model tailored to the service sector to capture relational and strategic dimensions.
2025	Al-Jaber et al.	Governance and SDGs	Analyse the integration of HR, corporate governance and wellbeing strategies to achieve the Sustainable Development Goals.
2025	Nastase, Adomnitei & Apetri	Digitalisation and Sustainable Advantage	Analyse how HRM practices should evolve to align with technology-driven models such as AI, RPA, and Blockchain.
2025	Christina, Alamelu & Nigama	Sustainability Performance	Synthesise the impact of sustainable HWRM on global corporate sustainability through bibliometric analysis and meta-analysis

Source: Own elaboration

Table 1 presents a general characterisation of the studies included in the literature review of the scientific evolution of HRM, organising key contributions published between 2020 and 2025. This structure allows us to visualise the paradigm shift in HR, which is no longer an administrative support function but has become a strategic business partner focused on vertical alignment and internal consistency of practices. The compiled sources explore the direct correlation between strategic management and organisational performance, quantifying results in terms of ROI, productivity, and profit margins across various global sectors. In addition, Table 1 highlights the integration of emerging technologies, such as AI and RPA, and the urgency of aligning human capital with the Sustainable Development Goals (SDGs) and Industry 5.0 principles. Finally, the mapping reinforces the need to develop strategic human capabilities and organisational resilience to address the volatility and uncertainty of contemporary markets.

3. THEORETICAL FRAMEWORK

3.1. Strategic Human Resource Management

HRM is defined as an integrated set of practices, policies, and strategies through which an organisation manages its human capital, influencing and being influenced by business strategy and socio-economic factors (Hermansyah, Tukiran, Herlina, & Andrianto, 2022). Unlike the traditional model, HRM emphasises the need for HR policies to be consistent with each other and linked to the firm's long-term objectives (Hermansyah et al.,2022). This field has evolved through three main perspectives: universalist (best practices), contingency (context adjustment) and configurational (synergistic action patterns) (Prifti, Vrusho, Toci, Prendi, & Gjuzi, 2025).

3.2. Organisational strategy

Organisational strategy is the plan that defines how a company intends to compete successfully, survive and grow in a given market (Wash, 2023). It involves analysing the internal and external environment (SWOT), defining the mission, vision and values, and formulating SMART (Specific, Measurable, Attainable, Relevant and Time-bound) objectives (Jaradat, 2023). Strategic success depends on the organisation's ability to synchronise its available resources with the requirements of strategy implementation (Dave et al.,2023).

3.3. Concept of strategic alignment (vertical fit)

Strategic alignment, or vertical fit, refers to the congruence between HR practices and the organisation's business strategy (Castro et al., 2020). This concept posits that HR initiatives are most effective when they directly support strategic goals, ensuring that the workforce has the necessary skills to execute the leadership's vision (Jaradat, 2023). A lack of vertical alignment can lead to underutilisation of human capital and hinder the achievement of organisational success (Dave et al.,2023).

4. STRATEGIC ALIGNMENT BETWEEN HR AND ORGANISATIONAL STRATEGY

4.1. Models and theoretical approaches

Several models guide organisations in effective HR alignment. The Harvard Model emphasises the interdependence between HR policies and organisational results, considering the context and interests of stakeholders (JARADAT, 2023). The Ulrich Model proposes that HR should act in four roles: strategic partner, administrative expert, employee champion, and change agent (Jaradat, 2023). Additionally, Resource-Based View (RBV) argues that human capital is a source of competitive advantage when it is valuable, rare, difficult to imitate, and irreplaceable (VRIN) (Hossain et al., 2025). The AMO model suggests that performance is optimised when HR practices increase employees' Ability, Motivation, and Opportunity (Christina et al., 2025).

4.2. Strategic role of the HR function

The HR function has become a business partner (HRBP) that actively collaborates with top management in strategic decision-making (Wash, 2023). This role requires HR professionals to have business literacy, understanding markets, costs and profit indicators (Wash, 2023). HR now acts as a facilitator of change, managing cultural pressure and communicating organisational objectives democratically at all hierarchical levels (Castro et al., 2020). As summarised in Table 2, these objectives are recurrent across the literature and can be grouped into strategic, economic, cultural, and communicational dimensions, reflecting the multidimensional nature of contemporary Strategic Human Resource Management.

Table 2. Objectives by Author and Study Dimension

Author (Year)	General Objective	Specific Objectives	Alignment	Performance	Sustainability/ Innovation
Castro et al. (2020)	Characterise the Brazilian scenario regarding the implementation of strategic HR practices between 1997 and 2017.	Describe methodological and content standards; present the network of researchers and propose a study agenda.	✓		
Silva, Albuquerque & Costa (2021)	Verify the existence of strategic alignment between organisational culture and GP strategies in Brazil.	Identify GP strategies adopted; identify dominant cultural profiles; assess the alignment between the two.	✓		
Santos Filha et al. (2021)	Propose a theoretical model of the role of HR in internal communication with a focus on strategic alignment.	Describe essential factors in communication; identify HR actions that contribute to objectives; define behaviours for alignment.	✓		
Yu et al. (2022)	Investigate the mechanism of GERH's impact on organisational resilience.	Analyse the mediating role of self-efficacy and the moderating role of self-management in their impact on resilience.		✓	✓
Hermansyah et al. (2022)	Review recent articles on HRM to discuss its relationship with management theories and concepts.	Discuss the relationship between human capital and competitive advantage; identify gaps in vertical and horizontal alignment research.	✓	✓	
Breaz & Jaradat (2023)	Investigate the current state of HRM practices and the extent to which they align with organisational goals.	Explore the impact on performance and satisfaction; identify challenges and barriers to implementing alignment.	✓	✓	
Wash (2023)	Advance knowledge about HRM and its implications for business strategies and operations.	Analyse the strategic contribution of HRBPs; identify competencies for future-ready teams; assess operational effectiveness.	✓	✓	
Boudreau, Ulrich & Buhler (2023)	Comprehensive review of the interaction between HR strategies and strategic alignment in the US.	Examine strategies (recruitment, training) in line with goals; analyse impacts on performance, engagement and retention.	✓	✓	

continued on following page

Table 2. Continued

Author (Year)	General Objective	Specific Objectives	Alignment	Performance	Sustainability/ Innovation
Storey & Wright (2023)	Provide a concise analytical guide on the evolution and central themes of research in GERH.	Assess the impact of COVID-19; analyse priorities such as diversity (EDI) and remote working; guide future research.		✓	✓
Zidan & Al-Loumi (2024)	Measuring the impact of strategic alignment on organisational immunity through strategic agility.	Analyse relationships between communication, governance and skills with organisational memory and learning.	✓	✓	
Kess-Momoh et al. (2024)	Review trends and innovations that characterise the evolution of GERH in the 21st century.	Explore technological integration (AI); analyse the impact of remote working and prioritise employee wellbeing.			✓
Arora, Malhotra & Ruhil (2024)	Examine the effect of aligning strategic HR management with business objectives on overall effectiveness.	Explore theoretical frameworks; analyse successful industrial cases; offer recommendations for sustainable growth.	✓	✓	✓
Mwambela (2024)	Examine the impact of GERH components on the performance of for-profit companies in Zambia.	Collect demographic data; analyse the impact of incentives, recruitment and training on performance.		✓	
Ulrich, Way & Wright (2024)	Examine how flexibility and strategic management build collective human capabilities.	Identify capabilities (learning, leadership, culture) that enable strategic differentiation and success.	✓	✓	
Hossain, Arefin & Urme (2025)	Quantify the financial impact of HRM practices on the performance of organisations in Bangladesh.	Examine how investments in training and engagement affect ROI and profit; create evidence-based recommendations.		✓	
Prifti et al. (2025)	Investigate the strategic role of human resource management in the performance of the Albanian private sector.	Examine the chain: Business Strategy → Role of HR → Practices → Results: Organisational Performance.	✓	✓	

continued on following page

Table 2. Continued

Author (Year)	General Objective	Specific Objectives	Alignment	Performance	Sustainability/ Innovation
Abualfalayeh (2025)	Investigate the impact of HRM practices on employee performance in Jordan.	Analyse the alignment of goals as a mediator and organisational culture as a moderator of this relationship.	✓	✓	
Kashoob et al. (2025)	Study the alignment of HR practices with strategy based on principles of occupational psychology.	Determine the influence of work style and years of experience on motivation and organisational effectiveness.	✓	✓	
Tavares & Vaz (2025)	Propose a performance appraisal model (PAS) tailored to the service sector.	Analyse employee perceptions; integrate 360º feedback; design a framework aligned with the organisational mission.	✓	✓	
Al-Jaber et al. (2025)	Analyse the integration of HR, governance and wellbeing strategies to achieve the SDGs in health.	Examine direct/indirect effects on sustainable development; assess mediation of governance and wellbeing.			✓
Nastase, Adomnitei & Apetri (2025)	Analyse how HRM practices should evolve to align with digitally-driven models.	Propose a model linking AI, RPA, and Blockchain to human capital; analyse cases such as IBM and Walmart for competitive advantage.		✓	✓
Christina, Alamelu & Nigama (2025)	Summarise the impact of sustainable WRM on global corporate sustainability.	Map trends and prominent authors; quantify the impact on economic, environmental, and social dimensions via meta-analysis.			✓

Source: Own elaboration

4.3. HR as a source of competitive advantage

When managed strategically, human capital creates unique organisational capabilities that are difficult for competitors to replicate (Jaradat, 2023). HRM enables the accumulation of firm-specific knowledge, promoting innovation and strategic differentiation (Wash, 2023). Through practices such as selective recruitment and continuous training, HR ensures a highly skilled workforce that becomes the main driver of organisational objectives (Jaradat, 2023).

5. IMPACTS OF STRATEGIC ALIGNMENT

5.1. Organisational performance

Studies show a robust positive correlation between strategic alignment and financial metrics such as return on investment (ROI), profitability, and productivity (Hossain et al., 2025). In emerging markets, the integration of HR practices such as reward and training systems directly impacts profit margins and operational efficiency (Strategic human resource management and organisational performance: an investigation of profit-oriented companies in Zambia, 2024). Productivity per employee is significantly higher in organisations with high HRM integration (Al-Jaber, et al., 2025).

5.2. Innovation and sustainability

Strategic alignment fosters a culture of learning and experimentation, which is essential for continuous innovation ((Dave et al.,2023). In addition, sustainable HRM integrates economic, social and environmental dimensions (Triple Bottom Line), aligning the workforce with the UN Sustainable Development Goals (SDGs) (Christinaet al., 2025). Green and socially responsible HR practices legitimise the company's activities in the eyes of stakeholders and promote long-term resilience (Al-Jaber, et al., 2025).

5.3. Commitment and organisational outcomes

Strategic alignment increases employee satisfaction and commitment, as employees understand how their roles contribute to the company's overall vision (Jaradat, 2023). This results in lower turnover rates, a better organisational climate and organisational citizenship behaviours (Castro et al., 2020). Employee´ engagement acts as a critical mediator that transforms HR practices into tangible performance results (Abualfalayeh, 2025). As evidenced in Table 3 and Figure 1, the aggregated results across the analysed studies indicate higher total scores in dimensions related to commitment, engagement, and organisational climate, reinforcing the central role of these variables in linking strategic HRM to organisational performance.

Table 3. Total sums for each dimension

Study Size	Grand Totals (Total Sources)	Relative Frequency (%)
Organisational Performance	16	72,7%
Strategic Alignment	14	63,6%
Sustainability and Innovation	8	36,4%

Figure 1: Relative Frequency Graph (%)

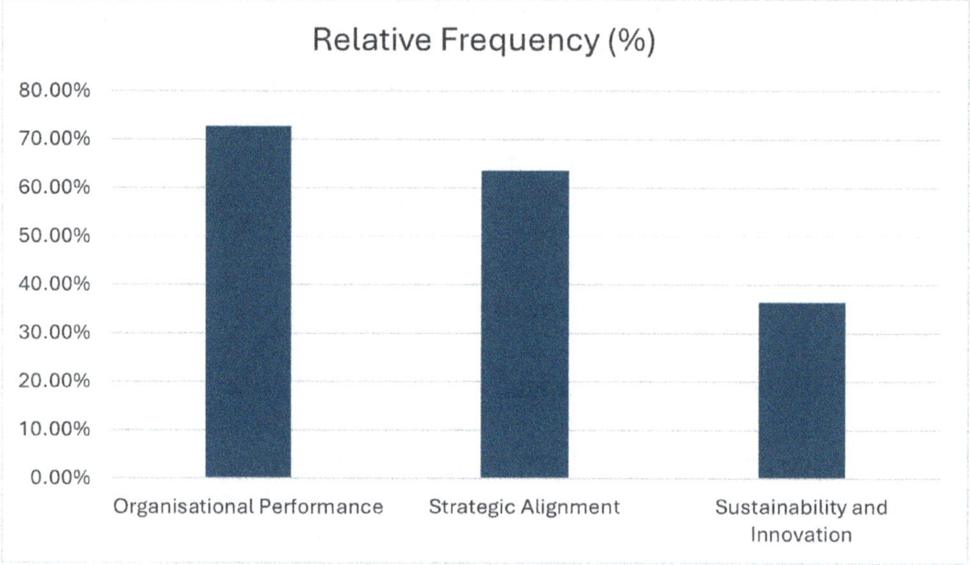

Subsequently, Table 4 provides a more detailed breakdown of these results by disaggregating the total sums for each dimension and identifying the corresponding reference sources. This table allows for a clearer understanding of the empirical and theoretical contributions underpinning each analytical category.

Table 4. Total Sums by Dimension and Reference Sources

Study Dimension	General Totals	Reference Sources (Authors and Years)
Organisational Performance	16	Castro et al. (2020); Yu et al. (2022); Hermansyah et al. (2022); Breaz & Jaradat (2023); Wash (2023); Boudreau et al. (2023); Storey & Wright (2023); Zidan & Al-Loumi (2024); Arora et al. (2024); Mwambela (2024); Ulrich et al. (2024); Hossain et al. (2025); Prifti et al. (2025); Abualfalayeh (2025); Kashoob et al. (2025); Tavares & Vaz (2025).
Strategic Alignment	14	Castro et al. (2020); Silva et al. (2021); Santos Filha et al. (2021); Hermansyah et al. (2022); Breaz & Jaradat (2023); Wash (2023); Boudreau et al. (2023); Zidan & Al-Loumi (2024); Arora et al. (2024); Ulrich et al. (2024); Mwambela (2024); Abualfalayeh (2025); Kashoob et al. (2025); Tavares & Vaz (2025).
Sustainability and Innovation	8	Yu et al. (2022); Breaz & Jaradat (2023); Wash (2023); Storey & Wright (2023); Kess-Momoh et al. (2024); Arora et al. (2024); Nastase et al. (2025); Christina et al. (2025)

Building on this detailed overview, Figure 2 displays the total sums for each dimension, offering an absolute visual representation of the distribution of studies across analytical categories and corroborating the predominance of organisational performance and strategic alignment highlighted in the previous tables.

Figure 2. Total Sums for each Dimension

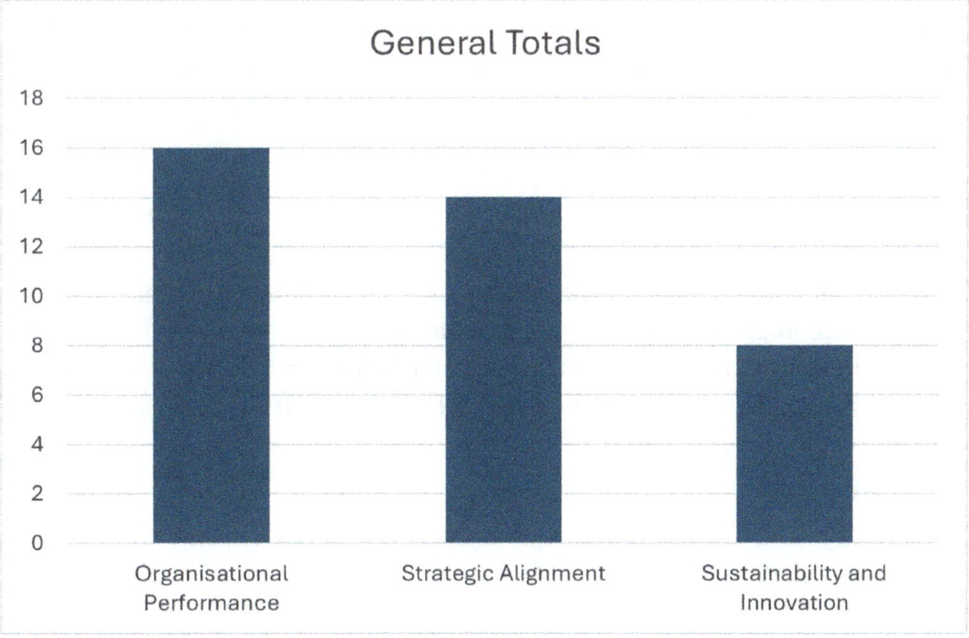

Explanatory Notes on the Sum:

1. **Organisational Performance (16 sources):** This is the most prevalent dimension, focusing on financial impact (ROI, profit), operational impact, and productivity (Castro et al., 2020). Authors such as Hossain et al. (2025) and Mwambela (2024) focus almost exclusively on this metric to validate the effectiveness of HRM (Castro et al., 2020).
2. **Strategic Alignment (14 sources):** Represents the pillar of vertical and horizontal 'fit' (Castro et al., 2020). Studies such as those by Castro et al. (2020) and Boudreau et al. (2023) are fundamental in explaining how HR strategy integrates with business strategy (Dave et al.,2023).
3. **Sustainability and Innovation (8 sources):** Although less frequent, this is the emerging dimension that connects people management to digitalisation (AI, RPA) and the Sustainable Development Goals (SDGs) (Al-Jaber, et al., 2025). Christina et al. (2025) and Al-Jaber et al. (2025) are the main references in this category (Christina et al., 2025).

Final Analogy: These dimensions function as the three pillars supporting a building: Alignment is the architectural design that ensures that the parts fit together; Performance is the solidity of the structure that allows the building to fulfil its function; and Sustainability/Innovation is the technical modernisation that ensures the building remains efficient and relevant in the face of future climate and technological changes. Without any of these pillars, organisational management becomes unstable or obsolete.

6. DISCUSSION

Table 5 presents the analysis of the research questions (RQ) by author, allowing a systematic comparison of how each study addresses the three core issues under analysis: vertical alignment and performance (QI 1), the mediating role of HR results (QI 2), and emerging technologies such as AI and RPA (QI 3).

Table 5. Analysis of Research Questions (RQ) by Author

Author(s) (Year)	QI 1: Vertical Alignment and Performance	QI 2: Mediating Role of HR Results	QI 3: Emerging Technologies (AI/RPA)
Castro et al. (2020)	✓	✓	✓
Silva et al. (2021)	✓	✓	
Santos Filha et al. (2021)	✓		
Yu et al. (2022)	✓	✓	
Hermansyah et al. (2022)	✓	✓	
Breaz & Jaradat (2023)	✓	✓	✓
Wash (2023)	✓		✓
Boudreau et al. (2023)	✓	✓	
Storey & Wright (2023)	✓	✓	✓
Zidan & Al-Loumi (2024)	✓		
Kess-Momoh et al. (2024)	✓	✓	✓
Arora et al. (2024)	✓	✓	✓
Mwambela (2024)	✓	✓	
Ulrich et al. (2024)	✓	✓	
Hossain et al. (2025)	✓	✓	✓
Prifti et al. (2025)	✓	✓	✓
Abualfalayeh (2025)	✓	✓	
Kashoob et al. (2025)	✓	✓	
Tavares & Vaz (2025)	✓		✓
Al-Jaber et al. (2025)	✓	✓	
Nastase et al. (2025)	✓		✓
Christina et al. (2025)	✓	✓	✓

Summary of Observations:

As shown in Table 5, there is a predominance of studies focused on three issues:

QI 1 (Alignment and Performance): This is addressed by all authors (100%), confirming that the basis of HRM is the alignment between practices and business strategy to drive financial and operational results(Castro et al., 2020). This predominance is further confirmed in Table 6, where QI 1 records the highest total score and a relative frequency of 100%, underlining its centrality across all analysed studies.

QI 2 (Mediation of Results): Authors such as Hossain et al. (2025) and Abualfalayeh (2025) highlight the crucial mediating role of engagement and goal alignment in transforming HR investment into tangible performance (Abualfalayeh, 2025). Yu et al. (2022) extend this role to psychological factors such as self-efficacy (Yu, Yuan, Han, Li, & Li, 2022). As summarised in Table 6, this research question appears in 77.3% of the reviewed sources, indicating strong, although not universal, empirical support.

QI 3 (AI and RPA): This represents the fastest-growing issue in recent studies. Nastase et al. (2025) and Kess-Momoh et al. (2024) demonstrate how emerging technologies redefine competitive advantage by automating administrative tasks and enabling HR to focus more strongly on strategic activities and employee well-being (Kess-Momoh, Tula, Bello, Omotoye, & Daraojimba, 2024; Nastase et al., 2025). While less prevalent than the other dimensions, Table 6 shows that QI 3 is already present in 50% of the analysed studies, highlighting its increasing relevance.

The quantitative distribution of these findings is visually synthesised in Figure 3, which presents the total scores for each research question. The figure reinforces the dominance of vertical alignment (QI 1), followed by the mediating role of HR results (QI 2), and the growing importance of emerging technologies (QI 3).

Final Analogy: The three research questions form the organisational propulsion triangle: vertical alignment (QI 1) is the main engine, mediating outcomes such as satisfaction (QI 2) are the fuel that keeps the engine running smoothly, and emerging technologies (QI 3) represent the high-tech navigation and automation system that allows the organisation to move faster and with greater precision than its competitors. Without any of these elements, propulsion loses efficiency or strategic direction.

Table 6. Total Scores for Research Questions (RQ)

Research Question (RQ)	Grand Total (Total Sources)	Relative Frequency (%)	Reference Sources (Selected Examples)
QI 1: Vertical Alignment and Performance (Influence of strategic adjustment on financial and operational performance)	**22**	100%	Castro et al. (2020); Yu et al. (2022); Boudreau et al. (2023); Zidan & Al-Loumi (2024); Hossain et al. (2025).
QI 2: Mediating Role of HR Results (Commitment and satisfaction as links between HRM and performance)	**17**	77,3%	Silva et al. (2021); Ulrich et al. (2024); Abualfalayeh (2025); Hossain et al. (2025).
QI 3: Emerging Technologies (AI/RPA) (Redefining alignment and competitive advantage via digitalisation)	**11**	50,0%	Wash (2023); Kess-Momoh et al. (2024); Prifti et al. (2025); Nastase et al. (2025).

Figure 3. Total QI Scores

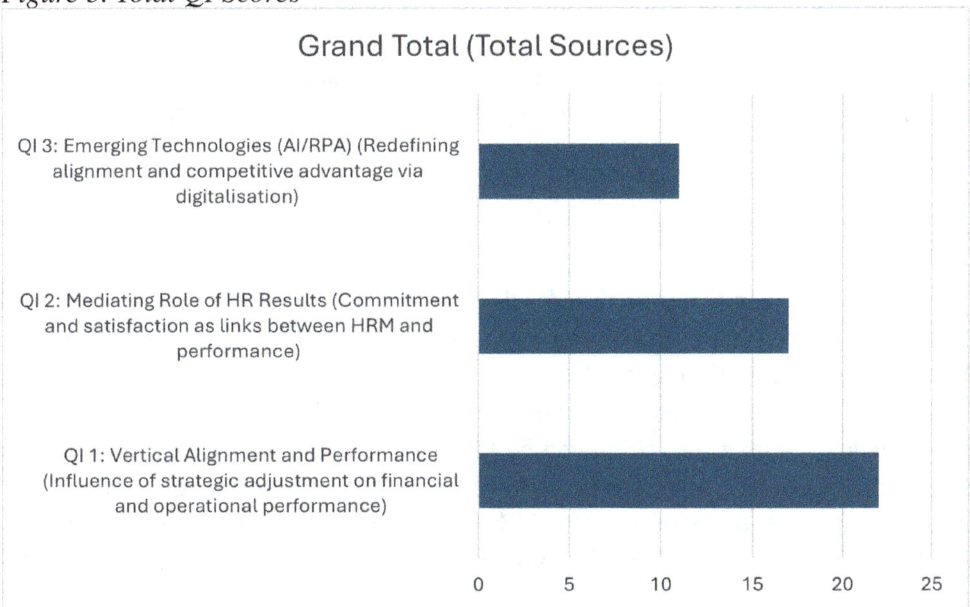

Observations on the Summaries:

1. **Unanimity in QI 1 (22 sources):** All sources consulted confirm that the basis of Strategic Human Resource Management is the vertical connection between

personnel practices and business objectives to generate organisational value (Castro et al., 2020).

2. **Consolidation of QI 2 (17 sources):** There is strong evidence that the impact of HR practices is not purely direct, but mediated by variables such as commitment (Hossain, Arefin, & Urme, 2025), resilience (Yu, Yuan, Han, Li, & Li, 2022), and the alignment of individual goals with those of the company (Abualfalayeh, 2025).
3. **Exponential Growth of QI 3 (11 sources):** Although addressed by half of the sample, this issue focuses on studies published predominantly between 2023 and 2025, highlighting that AI and RPA are now seen as indispensable tools for freeing HR from administrative tasks and enabling strategic focus (Kess-Momoh, Tula, Bello, Omotoye, & Daraojimba, 2024).

Final Analogy: These three research questions function like the components of a high-performance vehicle: Vertical Alignment (QI 1) is the powerful engine that defines strength and direction; Mediating Outcomes (QI 2) are the lubricant and fuel that ensure the parts (employees) work smoothly and energetically; and Emerging Technologies (QI 3) represent the intelligent electronic navigation and automation systems that enable the vehicle to reach higher speeds and adapt to complex terrain (the digital market) much more nimbly than the competition. Without the three elements in harmony, the vehicle loses efficiency or direction.

6.1. Critical literature review

The literature converges on the idea that HRM is indispensable for modern competitiveness, but its implementation faces practical and contextual challenges (Kess-Momoh, Tula, Bello, Omotoye, & Daraojimba, 2024). It is noted that, although HR practices produce positive results in human capital, the direct link to organisational performance is sometimes mitigated by the complexity of the "black box" — the mediating mechanisms that are not always clear or easy to measure (Castro et al., 2020). Digital transformation and the Industry 5.0 paradigm require a new synthesis that balances technological efficiency with human well-being (Castro et al., 2020).

6.2. Convergences and divergences

There is consensus on the effectiveness of models such as RBV and AMO in explaining value creation (Hossain, Arefin, & Urme, 2025). However, there are divergences regarding the universality of 'best practices' (Castro et al., 2020). Some studies suggest that the impact of HR depends heavily on the institutional context, the culture of the country, and the sector of activity, challenging the notion that the same models work equally well in all geographies (Tavares & Vaz, 2025).

Furthermore, counterintuitive results indicate that poorly aligned HR practices can, in certain cases, undermine long-term sustainability goals (Tavares & Vaz, 2025).

6.3. Identified gaps

Three main gaps have been identified:

1. **Lack of quantitative data:** There is still a lack of robust evidence linking specific HR initiatives to concrete financial results, especially in developing economies (Castro et al., 2020).
2. **Technology and Ethics:** The impact of Artificial Intelligence and data analysis on HR ethics and employee privacy has yet to be fully explored (Christina et al., 2025).
3. **Longitudinal Studies:** Most research is cross-sectional, failing to capture how strategic alignment evolves and sustains itself over time in dynamic environments (Castro et al., 2020).

7. CONCLUSION

7.1. Main contributions of the review

This systematic review consolidates the knowledge that strategic HR alignment is a key driver of competitive advantage and organisational resilience (Christina et al., 2025). The work highlights the importance of transitioning from administrative management to a strategic vision that values human capital as a strategic asset (Strategic human resource management and organisational performance: an investigation of profit-oriented companies in Zambia, 2024). It demonstrates that the integration of sustainability and technology objectives in HR redefines performance in the digital age (Nastase, et al., 2025).

7.2. Implications for management

For managers, the main implication is the need to involve HR leaders in all phases of strategic planning (Wash, 2023). Organisations should invest in People Analytics and RPA technologies to free HR from transactional tasks and enable them to focus on value creation (Strategic human resource management and organisational performance: an investigation of profit-oriented companies in Zambia, 2024). In addition, it is crucial to promote an organisational culture that supports the well-being and continuous development of employees to ensure long-term commitment and productivity (Al-Jaber, et al., 2025).

7.3. Suggestions for future research

Future research should focus on longitudinal studies to observe the sustainability of strategic alignment in periods of prolonged crisis (Castro et al., 2020). It is also suggested that 'ethical AI' in HR be explored, as well as how Industry 5.0 will influence employee skills (Christina et al., 2025). Finally, more research is needed in emerging markets and the public sector to validate and adapt HRM models to diverse institutional contexts (Castro et al., 2020).

Limitations and suggestions for the future: The limitations of this study include its reliance on secondary data and the predominance of qualitative or cross-sectional studies in the sample analysed, which may limit statistical generalisation (Castro et al., 2020). Additionally, the focus on high-impact journals may have excluded relevant grey literature or innovative practices in smaller companies (Christina et al., 2025). As a future suggestion, we recommend the application of hybrid models that combine big data analysis with in-depth interviews to capture the qualitative nuances of strategic alignment in the daily practice of organisations (Strategic human resource management and organisational performance: an investigation of profit-oriented companies in Zambia, 2024).

Final Analogy: The strategic alignment between Human Resources and organisational strategy functions like the nervous system of an organism. While strategy defines the 'vision' and direction of the body, HR ensures that all 'members' (employees) are coordinated, motivated, and receive the correct signals to act in harmony. Without this alignment, the organisation is like a body whose organs act independently, resulting in inefficiency and an inability to respond effectively to the challenges of the external environment.

REFERENCES

Abualfalayeh, G. (2025). Strategic HR management: Bridging organizational goals and employee performance. *Journal of Cultural Analysis and Social Change, 10*(2), 4065–4069. DOI: 10.64753/jcasc.v10i2.2232

Al-Jaber, A., Alzghoul, A., Alghizzawi, M., AlFraihat, S. F., Elhawi, R., & Banihani, T. (2025). Integrating HRM strategies to achieve Sustainable Development Goals: The mediating roles of employee well-being and corporate governance. *Administrative Sciences, 15*(12), 474. DOI: 10.3390/admsci15120474

Arora, S., Malhotra, L., & Ruhil, M. (2024). Aligning Strategic HR Management with Business Objectives: Examining the Effect on Organizational Effectiveness and Performance. *ShodhKosh: Journal of Visual and Performing Arts, 5*(3), 31–42. DOI: 10.29121/shodhkosh.v5.i3.2024.1657

Boudreau, D. W., Ulrich, J. S., & Buhler, E. P. (2023). The interplay between Human Resource strategies and strategic alignment: A comprehensive review of conceptual and empirical literature in the United States. *Journal of Strategy and Management, 7*(5), 1–10. DOI: 10.53819/81018102t4170

Breaz, T.-R.-O., & Jaradat, M. (2023). Strategic Human Resource Management: Aligning HR practices with organizational goals. In *Proceedings of the 17th International Management Conference "Management beyond Crisis: Rethinking Business Performance"* (pp. 552–559). Bucharest, Romania.

Castro, M. V. de M., de Araújo, M. L., Ribeiro, A. M., Demo, G., & Meneses, P. P. M. (2020). Implementation of strategic human resource management practices: A review of the national scientific production and new research paths. *Revista de Gestão, 27*(3), 229–246. DOI: 10.1108/REGE-10-2018-0102

Christina, J. L., Alamelu, R., & Nigama, K. (2025). Synthesizing the impact of sustainable human resource management on corporate sustainability through multi method evidence. *Discover Sustainability, 6*(1), 666. DOI: 10.1007/s43621-025-01557-3

da Silva, L. M. T., de Albuquerque, L. G., & Costa, B. K. (2021). O alinhamento estratégico entre cultura organizacional e estratégias de gestão de pessoas. *Revista Eletrônica de Ciência Administrativa, 20*(1), 120–149. DOI: 10.21529/RECADM.2021005

Hermansyah, Tukiran, M., Herlina, E., & Andrianto, M. T. (2022). A review of Strategic Human Resources Management in organization. *Budapest International Research and Critics Institute-Journal (BIRCI-Journal), 5*(2), 14422–14431. https://doi.org/DOI: 10.33258/birci.v5i2.5309

Hossain, M. Z., Arefin, T., & Urme, U. N. (2025). The financial impact of Strategic HRM practices: Linking employee investments to organizational performance. *European Journal of Management. Economics and Business, 2*(2), 25–39. DOI: 10.59324/ejmeb.2025.2(2).02

Kashoob, B.. (2025). Strategic Human Resources Management. *Journal of Posthumanism, 5*(4), 643–650.

Kess-Momoh, A. J., Tula, S. T., Bello, B. G., Omotoye, G. B., & Daraojimba, A. I. (2024). Strategic human resource management in the 21st century: A review of trends and innovations. *World Journal of Advanced Research and Reviews, 21*(1), 746–757. DOI: 10.30574/wjarr.2024.21.1.0105

Mwambela, A. (2024). Strategic human resource management integration and organizational performance: Evidence from profit-oriented companies in Zambia. *Journal of Innovative Business and Management, 16*(1), 2–18. DOI: 10.32015/JIBM.2024.16.1.2

Nastase, C., Adomnitei, A., & Apetri, A. (2025). Strategic Human Resource Management in the digital era: Technology, transformation, and sustainable advantage. *Merits, 5*(4), 23. DOI: 10.3390/merits5040023

Prifti, K., Vrusho, B., Toci, Ç., Prendi, L., & Gjuzi, J. B. (2025). Strategic Human Resource Management and its impact on organizational performance: Empirical insights. *International Journal of Innovative Technology and Interdisciplinary Sciences, 8*(3), 550–594. DOI: 10.15157/IJITIS.2025.8.3.550-594

Santos Filha, A. L., dos, , Lima, F. V. R., & Oliveira, J. F. (2021). Gestão de recursos humanos, comunicação organizacional e alinhamento estratégico: Proposição de um modelo teórico. *Research. Social Development, 10*(8), e22710817224. DOI: 10.33448/rsd-v10i8.17224

Storey, J., & Wright, P. M. (2023). *Strategic Human Resource Management: A Research Overview* (2.ª ed.). Routledge. DOI: 10.4324/9781003364276

Tavares, M. C., & Vaz, M. (2025). Rethinking performance evaluation: Strategic alignment in the service sector through a case-based framework. *Administrative Sciences, 15*(10), 390. DOI: 10.3390/admsci15100390

Ulrich, M. D., Way, S. A., & Wright, P. M. (2024). Building strategic human capabilities that drive performance. *International Journal of Human Resource Management, 35*(20), 3341–3373. DOI: 10.1080/09585192.2024.2408026

Wash, G. L. (2023). Strategy and competencies for future-ready business. *International Journal of Research in Human Resource Management, 5*(1), 11–20. https://www.humanresourcejournal.com. DOI: 10.33545/26633213.2023.v5.i1a.123

Yu, J., Yuan, L., Han, G., Li, H., & Li, P. (2022). A study of the impact of Strategic Human Resource Management on organizational resilience. *Behavioral Sciences (Basel, Switzerland), 12*(12), 508. DOI: 10.3390/bs12120508 PMID: 36546991

Zidan, H. M., & Al-Loumi, A. K. (2024). The impact of strategic alignment in enhancing organizational immunity through strategic agility: A survey study in Kirkuk education directorate - Iraq. *International Journal of Research in Human Resource Management, 6*(2), 167–185. DOI: 10.33545/26633213.2024.v6.i2b.214

KEY TERMS AND DEFINITIONS

Ability–Motivation–Opportunity (AMO) Model: A theoretical framework suggesting that employee performance is maximized when human resource practices enhance individuals' abilities, motivate them to perform, and provide opportunities to apply their competencies.

Horizontal Strategic Alignment: The internal consistency among different human resource practices—such as recruitment, training, performance appraisal, and rewards—so that they operate in a complementary and mutually reinforcing manner.

Human Capital: The collective knowledge, skills, abilities, and experience possessed by employees that represent a critical strategic resource for value creation and organizational differentiation.

Organizational Sustainability: The capacity of an organization to balance economic, social, and environmental objectives through management practices, including human resource strategies that promote well-being, innovation, and long-term resilience.

Strategic Human Resource Management (SHRM): An integrated approach to managing people in which human resource policies and practices are deliberately aligned with organizational strategy to enhance performance, sustainability, and long-term competitive advantage.

Sustainable Competitive Advantage: An organization's ability to achieve superior performance over time by leveraging unique and difficult-to-imitate resources, particularly strategically aligned human resource systems.

Vertical Strategic Alignment: The degree of coherence between human resource management practices and the organization's business strategy, ensuring that employee skills, behaviours, and outcomes directly support strategic objectives.

Chapter 2

Artificial Intelligence (AI)-Driven Skills Intelligence for Talent Management:

Building an Agile and Future-Ready Workforce

Arpita Nayak
http://orcid.org/0000-0003-2911-0492
KIIT School of Liberal Studies, KIIT (Deemed to be) University, Bhubaneswar, India

Ipseeta Satpathy
http://orcid.org/0000-0002-0155-5548
KSOM, KIIT (Deemed to be) University, Bhubaneswar, India

Vishal Jain
http://orcid.org/0000-0003-1126-7424
School of Engineering & Technology, Vivekananda Institute of Professional Studies - Technical Campus, New Delhi, India

ABSTRACT

The pace of technological change and digital transformation are also driving the demand of continuous reskilling and agility of the workforce. Conventional, job-based establishments of talent management can no longer be sufficient to support the growing skill demands. It is in this context that AI-based skills intelligence is emerging as an important instrument in the development of a future-ready workforce. This chapter examines how AI can be applied to bring in skills-based talent management with the continuous identification, mapping and forecasting of the capabilities of the workforce by relying on such AI technologies as machine learn-

DOI: 10.4018/979-8-2600-2178-1.ch002

ing, natural language processing, and predictive analytics. It talks about the way AI-based skills intelligence can crown career journeys, customize learning, map succession and enhance staff maintenance. It proposes a theoretical overview how workforce data is transformed into useable skill information used to make strategic decisions of talent. .

I. INTRODUCTION

The modern era is evolving at a pace that has never been seen before, and it is due to the swift technological development of artificial intelligence, automation, and digital technology. Not only are these innovations transforming the way organizations are structured, but they are altering the types of skills required to remain competitive in a volatile, uncertain, complex and ambiguous world; otherwise known as a VUCA world. As a result, companies are contending with increasing skill gaps, talent shortage, and the accelerating obsolescence of positions already performed in the company-so-called human-resource systems can hardly be used nowadays. This growing disparity between the talent that individuals possess and the talent that is demanded by businesses speak to a critical requirement of a new strategy in talent management (Mancuso et al.,2025).

Traditionally, talent-management has been based on job-based models which focus on preset jobs, competencies and fixed career paths. Even though these models brought some stability in the predictable industrial environment, they prove to be more and more inadequate in the world of accelerated technological change and necessity of competence in skills training. The emergence of AI has exacerbated this issue by continually changing job content, de-jobbing it, and requiring a hybrid combination of skills that cut across the conventional barriers of occupation. Consequently, companies will have to replace the job-centrism with an increasingly dynamic and skills-based workforce management procedure. The shift towards the talent-management system based on skills and not jobs represent a wider assumption that the skills, not titles, are the most valuable part of the workforce. Skills-based systems enable companies to identify, assign, and develop talent in less time by concentrating on capabilities of the individuals, rather than on their official job designation. However, it is difficult to scale a skills-based model in large and diverse organizations. Skills tend to be tacit, in a state of constant flux, and are not well documented, causing a strategy-to-practice gap between what the skills-based models promise and what they will do in practice (Tyskbo & Firtin, 2025).

Skills analysis based on AI has emerged as a revolutionary tool of talent management in the contemporary instance. It identifies, analyzes, and the forecast of the workforce skills on a systematic basis and involves the best, innovative methods of analysis and computation. The AI determines what skills the workers will have by relying on a wide variety of data sources, including resumes, job descriptions, performance records, learning platforms, and project histories. It is an evidence-based and dynamic perspective on the capabilities of workforce that substitutes the introspective constraints of manual skill mapping and fixed competency structures. The intelligence of skills that is based on AI is crucial in particular due to the ability to introduce predictive and adaptation capabilities into talent management systems. Classical HR analytics is based on previous data and descriptive measures, whereas systems powered by AI can predict future demand of skills by analyzing the market trends, technology patterns, and organizational strategy. This proactive strategy enables organizations to develop reskilling and upskilling programs in advance, as opposed to addressing skills gaps when they occur. Consequently, skills intelligence will become a strategic tool that fosters the sustainability of workforce in the long term and organizational stability (França et al.,2023). Besides, integration of AI in skills intelligence can be used to design unique career routes and educational experiences among employees. It aligns personal goals with organizational requirements by suggesting the role change, skill building opportunities and personalized learning paths. This individualization is the point to retention of high-performing talent because the employees are now seeking constant development, employability, and career growth. AI-enabled skills intelligence helps the individual and the organization to be agile by facilitating career Mobility based on data. Alongside a range of personal advantages, AI-driven skills intelligence is also critical to tackling systemic issues in talent management (including succession planning, leadership development, and retention). Predictive analytics has the ability to detect high-potential employees, gauge their preparedness to the critical positions as well as simulate the future leadership situations under varying strategic conditions. Such strength enhances effectiveness of succession planning, which has always been a subjective and biased exercise. Consequently, strategic workforce planning undergoes more open, fair, and forward-looking decision-making due to AI-based talent knowledge (Pavlakou et al.,2025).

Although AI-based skills intelligence has the potential to change some facets of life, it presents gravitational ethical, governance and trust challenges. The skills inference algorithms are prone to reinforce bias accidentally in case they are trained on historical data that is based on the existing inequalities within the labor market. The constant surveillance of the employee skills and performance data also introduces complicated privacy, consent, and data ownership concerns. All these issues should be addressed to ensure that AI-based talent systems are effective and equally socially responsible and in accordance with the principles of ethical AI. As a manager, the emergence of AI-based intelligence of skills alters HR functions and leadership positions. HR specialists are required to divest themselves of the more administrative to become more strategic personalities who merge AI-informed decisions with human decisions. This change needs data literacy, ethical thinking, and change management expertise and cultural shift towards lifelong learning and experimentation. Managers should strike the balance between algorithmic suggestions and social consciousness, understanding, and organizational principles to not become excessively dependent on automated decisions (Floridi n.d.,).AI-related skills intelligence is a conceptual area that is currently at the intersection of HRM, information systems, and organizational research. The current body of research has concentrated on the idea of AI in recruitment where it is utilized, performance management, and learning analytics, but little or nothing has been done to reference the overall scope of skills intelligences in talent management. This vacuum explains the necessity of structured conceptual models and empirical studies that evaluate the impacts of AI-facilitated systems of skills on organizational agility, employee performance, and organizational performance. It is important in terms of theoretical development and practical enhancement in digital talent management to advance such research.

Considering the advances of technologies, the chapter can be viewed as a thorough, evidence-based perspective on AI-based skills intelligence as the keystone of creating a nimble and future-proof workforce. Skills intelligence is framed in the chapter as a strategic ability that engages organizations to manage the development of talent in line with transforming business ecosystems. Combining the knowledge of AI technologies, skills-based HRM, and strategic talent management, the chapter contributes to the knowledge of how organizations may pilot the transformation of the workforce in the era of AI. Finally, the chapter emphasizes that the future of talent management is conditional not only on the implementation of AI-tools, but the adoption of the rethinking of the interaction of skills, technology, and human potential in intelligent organizations.

II. RESEARCH QUESTIONS

- How does AI-driven skills intelligence enable the transition from job-based to skills-based talent management in building an agile and future-ready workforce?
- What is the impact of AI-enabled skills mapping and predictive analytics on personalized career pathing, talent mobility, and strategic workforce planning outcomes?

III. RESEARCH OBJECTIVES

- To examine the role of AI-driven skills intelligence in facilitating skills-based talent management by identifying skills gaps, enhancing workforce agility, and aligning employee capabilities with evolving organizational demands.
- To analyse how AI-enabled skills mapping, personalized career recommendations, and predictive talent analytics influence career progression, talent retention, succession planning, and long-term workforce sustainability.

IV. EVOLUTION OF SKILL BASED TALENT MANAGEMENT

The development of the skills-based talent management has been influenced by the fundamental transformation in the essence of work, organizational structure, and technology. With businesses shifting towards more flexible, project-based forms of structure instead of laid-back and hierarchical ones, a new challenge is being brought to traditional methods of talent management. This transformation is accelerated by digital transformation and automated work with AI, which constantly changes job descriptions and decides under what skills a person can be successful. Because of this, talent-management systems should change and become more dynamic, skills based, instead of the role-based models that are used (Babashahi et al.,2024).

Traditional competency frameworks have traditionally been used as instruments of managing talents since they outline the knowledge, skills, abilities, and behaviors that should be applied to particular job positions. These frameworks were created to facilitate recruitment, performance reviews, training and career development in the comparatively predictable organizational situations. Nevertheless, with the increasingly dynamic environments of work places, the fixed its nature has come out as the major constraint to competency models. Competency frameworks usually presume that the job content remains the same hence they do not capture the dynamic nature of job that occurs owing to changes in technology and the market. Besides, conventional competency models are often formulated using the expert judgment and managerial decision and subjectivity and bias can be added to the skills estimation. This dependency on human interpretations contributes to the fact that tacit, emerging and cross-functional skills that do not neatly fit into pre-existing categories are hard to capture. Consequently, organisations find it difficult to have a real-life time and granular picture of the capabilities of work force and making suboptimal decisions in the deployment and development of talent. These limitations reduce the usefulness of competency frameworks to proactive workforce planning in the high change environment (Kaliannan et al.,2023). The old structures are hard to expand in large organizations which are diverse. The cost and process of updating competency models after the company increases is expensive and ineffective. The process of updating the framework is painfully slow and thus before capturing the skills they are rendered redundant. Such delays in updating skills and models make competency-based talent management less strategic.

Compensated by the inadequacy of competency-based models, the use of skills taxonomies and ontologies has become more flexible and dynamic as a talented management tool in organizations. Skills taxonomy organizes skills in an organized manner, allowing companies to bring definitions together and develop a usage cross-functional, and cross-role common language. In contrast to the traditional competency frameworks, taxonomies are based on explicit, visible competencies that could be measured separately and revised on a continuous basis. This design of modules allows organizations to adjust to new skills fast. Skills ontologies extend taxonomies with relational and contextual layers of the representation. Ontologies identify the relationship between skills, roles and tasks, career moves and learning paths and provide a more comprehensive picture of the capabilities of the workforce. Ontologies assist in the promotion of advanced analytics and AI-led insights by demonstrating how skills are altered, recombined and relocated between roles. This hierarchy is particularly effective when it comes to identifying similar talents and encouraging internal mobility of the talent (Aman, 2024).The development of skills taxonomies and ontologies has been directly associated with the development of AI, specifically machine learning and natural language processing. These technologies can automatically mine and categorize unstructured sources of data, including resumes, job descriptions, learning materials, and project documentation, into skills. Due to this, organizations are able to have dynamic and data-driven repositories of skills that mirror the real-time workforce capabilities. This kind of technological integration is a huge departure when it comes to manually managed and immobile talent management systems (Just,2024).

Workforce agility will help to see the strategic significance of skills-based talent management. Workforce agility refers to the capability of an organization to redesign skills, roles and teams promptly when there is a change in the business requirements. Agility is an essential factor of performance and stability in dynamic, technologically active markets. Skills-based systems enable agility by liberating talent under job title, and enable a more seamless redeployment. Through skills intelligence, firms are able to identify its internal talent that are ready to work in new projects or strategic tasks. These saves using an outside recruitment firm, decreases recruitment expenses, and decreases the speed to productivity. Permit us to refer to skills-based agility, which further drives continuing learning through the alignment of reskilling and upskilling initiatives to the impending skills demands. Employees remain workable and the company does not lose its competitive advantage. Workforce agility enhances innovation and flexibility of a firm on a strategic level. Skills-based talent management allows leaders to identify capability gaps and other benefits of talent management include workforce simulation and maintaining talent plans in line with long-term objectives. This change makes talent management more than an everyday operation; it makes it a strategic position. Talent management shift towards skills-based is, in other words, not only a technical adjustment, but rather a more fundamental reorganisation of the ways in which companies think, build and deploy human capital in the era of AI (Tessarini et al.,2021).

V. AI-DRIVEN SKILLS MAPPING AND WORKFORCE ANALYTICS

Introduction of AI-based skills mapping and talent management analytics both represent a significant move towards operationalizing skills-based talent management. With a transition of the companies with fixed job designs to dynamic skill ecosystems, a precise identification, measurement and analysis of the workforce skills become vital to strategic advantage. Conventional HR analytics that are primarily based on historical data and job-specific measures are not sufficient to reflect the dynamics and subtlety of modern skills demand. On the other hand, AI-based workforce analytics can provide a factual base to see the present and the future of an organization (Rožman et al.,2022).

The issue of determining the absence of skills is crucial, but the traditional approaches tend to focus more on current weaknesses as well as ignore the future needs. This limitation is handled through skills mapping with AI by incorporating the employee profile, learning management systems, performance information, project assignments, and external trends in the labor-market. Machine-learning algorithms not only deduce latent skills but also measure competence more thoroughly and more precisely, giving a real-time perspective of the existing state of the skills environment of the organization. In addition to diagnosing the current capabilities, the AI-based analytics take the workforce planning to a more foreseeable space. Based on technological trends, benchmarking in the industry, and strategic goals, predictive models are used to determine the requirement of skills in the future. Comparing the existing stocks to the estimated requirements, organizations will be able to identify the case of the gaps prior to them turning into limiting factors in their operations and implement proactive reskilling and upskilling programs to minimize the chances of unexpected shortages and excess capacity mismatch. Additionally, AI-based gap analysis serves to facilitate the evidence-based decision making because it focuses on the skills that can produce the most strategic effect. Instead of the blanket strategy of one size fits all, efficient allocation of resources is directed to the high value skills and those that are future oriented. This prioritization in strategy improves responsiveness and also makes the investments with regard to workforce in accordance with the long-term objectives of the business (Rodgers et al.,2023).Internal marketplace brings in AI to find the skills of employees with internal opportunities. They align the profiles of employees with their skills in short-length projects, gig jobs, and vacancies within the company. Such marketplaces liberalize the talent deployment by shifting the title emphasis towards abilities. The outcome is the more appropriate utilization of inner talent and wider availability to development prospects. AI talent marketplace relies on skills mapping and recommendation engine. Machine learning and natural-language processing use the skills, career objectives and training history of a worker and propose personalized opportunities. Simultaneously, the system also considers what the organization requires, project needs, strategic objectives, etc., to ensure that there is a perfect match. The two-way fit between the employee capacity and what the organization requires enhances the effectiveness of internal labour markets. Internal talent markets enhance an organization in terms of retention and engagement because they provide employees with a clearer insight into their career paths. When the company provides their employees with a clear goal at developing their skills and changing roles, the former are more likely to remain in their positions. In addition, internal mobility reduces the cost of recruitment, decreases the time of onboarding and thereby makes talent marketplace a cost-effective and strategic solution to the workforce (Heger, 2024).

Talent mobility and role transition is an effective talent management within skills-based talent management. Work environment is changing rapidly and this results in employees swapping jobs, functions, and projects. Workforce analytics with AI assistance can assist organizations in identifying transferable and adjacent skills and finding a path to smooth transition and reduce turnover friction within the company in addition to minimized risk of misaligning skills. AI systems aid the purpose of role transition, implying that they propose individualized learning courses to close the distance between the skills possessed now and those required. These provisions keep on changing continuously and they are based on real time evaluation and performance statistics. The employees are constantly guided and this increases their employability and career resilience. This individualized style cultivates organizational culture of lifelong learning and adaptability. Tactically, talent mobility can be better to achieve organizational resilience as it can be adjusted to fast workforce organization. This is better in a response to the disturbances in the market so that companies can reposition the internal talent rather than having to use external hiring taking it as the only option. This pliability drives creativity, accelerates strategic plans and strengthens sustainability of the workforces. Therefore, AI-powered skills mapping and workforce analytics will become the important facilitator of agile talent ecosystems, which will place organizations at the center of an ever-changing environment (Hussaini et al.,2019).

V. PERSONALIZED CAREER PATHING USING AI

Customized career interactive has found its way to being a necessity in present talent management. Employees are now seeking meaningful, flexible and sustainable journeys. The conventional models of the career envision a clear ladder and job up the hierarchy. As a matter of fact, careers are quite shifting, skills expand and learning is on-going. The ever-evolving technology at high speed alters the job descriptions and the required skill. An AI-adept career pathing provides an evidence-based, dynamic method of aligning individual desires and corporate demands (Salvadorinho et al.,2024).

Career recommendation systems are based on AI and employ the sophisticated analytics to provide substantial employee-specific recommendations. They examine numerous kinds of data- skill, experiences, performance records, learning patterns as well as career preferences. When this information is applied by comparing with organizational skill requirements and labor action trends, AI models identify a good career match, which is realistic and strategically important. Such alignment makes decisions better, minimizes the reliance on subjective managerial judgment, and minimizes informal network prowess. Machine-learning algorithms also narrow down the suggestions by identifying trends in career progressions that have succeeded in the company. These patterns assist in discovering complementary or related roles that require similar or different same skills to widen the career possibilities of employees. As a result, employees recognize evident pathways into cross-functional and non-traditional jobs, which would remain inaccessible. This openness facilitates equality in career development as well as reduced structural blocks in mobility. In terms of organization, AI based suggestions would contribute to the strategic deployment of talent within the organization by promoting internal mobility rather than external recruitment. Companies can bridge the talent gap can eliminate the talent deficits and bolster pipelines, by assigning staff to the roles that fit their skill requirements in the future. Therefore, career guidance assisted by AI is useful to personal growth as well as to general workforce planning (Yadalam et al.,2020).Adaptive learning solutions are algorithms that build upon AI-based career suggestions to facilitate career objectives into action. AI tools are able to identify skill deficits when personalized learning interventions are advised based on setting the desired roles or trajectories. These can include training of formal type, micro-credentials, project work, mentoring or practical assignments. Since the pathways are dynamic, learning materials are changed with changes in skill requirements and individual developments. Learning systems powered by AI monitor activity, accuracy, and the development of skills and update the suggestions accordingly. The feedback loop ensures that pathways are always relevant and effective due to the continuous feedback loop. Unlike typical training, adaptive pathways consider the speed of every learner, interests, and objectives. This individuality enhances results and gives superior ROI on development of talents. Strategically, the adaptive learning paths help to increase organizational agility by accelerating reskilling and upskilling. As new technology or business models come to the scene, firms are able to readjust learning strategies accordingly in a short time with new skills requirements. This flexibility enhances labor preparedness and reduces the distance between the new skills and competencies (Herrera et al.,2026).

The waves of continuous employability change the concept of job security to skill security. With these models, the focus is on a constant growth of transferable and future relevant skills, which maintain the individual as valuable in all aspects and positions. This is operationalized through AI-based career pathing by providing real-time information about the value of various skills and what an effective career should be like. AI systems predict the demand with skills in the future and determine the future sustainability of careers. Through this information, employees make decisions on making an investment in their development of skill abilities and when to change jobs. Organizations boast of a strong, flexible workforce that puts it in line with strategic priorities. This will generate a win-win situation and enforce the psychological contract in uncertainty. Sustainable talent management is also facilitated by continuous employability as lessening the chances of skills becoming obsolete and unintentional job losses. Through integration of employability in career pathing tools, the companies focus on long-term growth in capabilities and not immediate performance. The strategy creates a culture of life-long learning and collective accountability towards career growth and development, making AI-based pathing a pillar of future-proof talent systems (Khuntia, 2025).

VI. PREDICTIVE TALENT MANAGEMENT OUTCOMES

Another modern trend in the sphere of AI-based predictive talent-management results is the incorporations of skills intelligence with workforce analytics that represent the most recent development in the modern sphere of organizational activities. Since the talent-management systems move away to describe and diagnostic to predictive and prescriptive, the firms are able to see the workforce dynamics coming instead of just responding to them. This is important in situations where there is scarcity of talent, leadership is dynamic and strategy is fast evolving. By using prediction analytics, organizations can be proactive in managing the succession, retention, and workforce make-up as solutions to the long-term objectives (Onyekachi et al.,2025). Historically, succession planning has been based on biased decisions, it does not provide a good exposure into talent, and it has remained stagnated in fixed leadership standards. A predictive model that uses AI overcomes these deficiencies using the skills information, performance history, the learning agility markers, and career-advancement trajectories. Organizations can identify high-potential employees and assess their leadership potential more precisely with the help of machine-learning algorithms. This is an evidence-based approach that enhances openness and reduces discrimination when it comes to defining leaders. Predictive analytics enables firms to model numerous successional scenarios, all of which represent varying strategic or environmental scenarios. An example of this is that they are able to test the strength of a leadership pipeline when it falls under conditions of growth spikes, technology changes or when the attrition increases. The simulations that are the result of this identify the possible areas of weak implementation and direct targeted leadership-development efforts. Thus, succession planning becomes a fluid administrative process rather than a one-time administrative assignment. Besides, AI can be used to enhance leadership pipes by identifying career trajectories and skills that are non-traditional. This wider perspective increases talent pool and enhanced succession plans. Predictive succession planning, in its turn, enhances the continuity, and long-term strategic stability of organization (Gunda et al.,2025).Talent retention and engagement attracts organizational performance particularly in knowledge-based and innovation-based industries. Predictive analytics can be used to reinforce retention policies to identify early indications of disengagement and risk of attrition. Using trends in performance, engagement in learning, internal moves, and worker feelings, the AI models can accurately forecast turnover. These understandings enable the companies to act before disengagement becomes a case of attrition. Personalized retention actions are also possible with the use of AI-powered engagement analytics. Firms can design strategies according to their preferences, career goals and development requirements rather than adopting a one-size-fits-all program. This specific strategy enhances the efficiency of retention measures and makes employees more committed. Open communication regarding career opportunities and skill-development chances is also an additional indication of organizational support, which is one of the motivational factors of engagement. On an organizational level, the predictive retention analytics directs the workforce-stability planning procedure; that is, identifying roles and skill areas that are most prone to losing to the competitors. Knowledge of this helps the companies to make priority in key talent and make strategic resource allocation. In turn, predictive retention analytics facilitate the continuity of the operations and the sustainability of talent over the long perspective (John & Hajam, 2024).One of the major outcomes of predictive talent management is strategic workforce planning. It will bring the expertise in the workplace to the future strategies of the company. The AI-based planning integrates both in-house skill data with external data on the labor market to forecast demand and supply of talents. Such predictions enable the organizations to know the realism of their strategic plans and change their workforce approaches.

What comes out is a reactive to a proactive headcount exercise to strategic decision-making process. The use of predictive models will assist the planners to consider the impacts of various strategic options on the workforce. As an example, a company can analyze the implications that automation, entering new markets, or a shift in regulation will have on skills requirements and workforce composition. These insights provide data to make better decisions on hiring, reskilling, outsourcing, and automation spending. Through this, companies are able to minimize risks on workforce and invest better in talents. Resilience is also enhanced through strategic workforce planning as it enables an individual to respond promptly to any emerging circumstance. Companies maintain an effective image of the workforce trends by continually updating predictive models using real-time data. This helps to make prompt decisions and align talent strategies with the changing business needs. Predictive talent management will assist the businesses to create a sustainable, future workforce, which can withstand the changing forces in the long term.

VII. ETHICAL AND GOVERNANCE CONSIDERATIONS

The increase in the utilization of AI-based Intelligence in talent management brings forth a question of ethics and governance that extends beyond technical usage of the technology. Savings in time, scalability, and improved predictions come along with the threats of fairness, accountability, and employee rights with AI. Such risks of particular concern are in the area of talent management, where artificial intelligence-based decisions have a direct impact on career opportunities, hire ability, and professional identity. Thus, responsible AI-based skills intelligence deployment requires ethical and governance concerns (Zuiderwijk et al.,2021).

One of the primary ethical issues when using AI to manage talents is talent-inference-bias. Such systems are typically trained on past workforce data which most of the time captures inequalities that exist, including those related to gender, age, education, or job assignments. Determined by this prejudiced information entering a machine-learning algorithm, the prescribed algorithm may pay accidentally impressive attention to the perpetuation or exacerbation of the structural inequalities. The risk is critical in particular where the inferred skills influence high stakes choices such as promotions, the allocation of roles, or the choice of leadership. Inequality and partiality may also be a result of lack of homogeneity in data among employees. Individuals, whose abilities are not formally recorded, or whose functions are associated with tacit, interpersonal work, can be intentionally under currented by AI. This underscores the epistemic issue of attempting to construct all the capabilities of humans using computational models. Unless deliberate efforts are employed, skills-inference algorithms are inclined to prefer characteristics than can be measured easily to complex and context-specific skills. Controlling algorithmic bias requires powerful leadership. That consists of bias audit, the utilization of a variety of training data and the constant assessment of the functioning of the model. To control the outcomes of algorithms and their conformity to organizational values and equity objectives, human control is crucial. Organizations will minimize ethical risks associated with AI-based skills inference by ensuring fairness of how they design and deploy such systems (Varsha et al.,2023).The second principle of trust creation in AI-driven talent management is transparency. As AI influences career guidance, education direction, and movement decisions, the workers might feel insecure or distrustful towards the decision-making process. The black-box algorithms might undermine trust since they conceal the processes that predict career success. Such ambiguity may decrease perceptions of fairness and decrease interaction. Explainable AI (XAI) provides the means of making decisions more transparent and providing understandable insights into the decision-making process. Once the employees understand how the skills are gauged and where the ideas to be given to emerge, they will likely perceive AI as helpful and not authoritative. Honest information on data usage, decision requirements and system scope also develop trust and sense of psychological safety. The concept of trust also relies on the feeling of agency and control that employees have towards AI -enabled systems. Giving the ability to review, confirm, and update skill profiles will enable the staff to own their career data. This participatory approach means that AI talent management is associated with empowerment and collective responsibility. Therefore, transparency is not a technical fact, but rather a socio-organizational requirement that ensures long-term adoption of AI (Ghoneim, 2024).In talent management using AI, continuous skills monitoring is one of the most notable features that would offer real-time data on the capabilities of the workforce. However, employee's privacy and data protection are a serious concern when it concerns the continuous gathering of data. Learning activities, work on projects, collaboration tools, and performance metrics can provide the required skilled data and can make it difficult to distinguish between the professional development and surveillance. In the absence of a definite governance, such monitoring might be intrusive and coercive. The more, the bigger, and sensitive the skills data, the greater the privacy concerns. The illegal usage, data breach, or misuse of personal information might negatively affect the well-being of employees and the reputation of a specific organization. The laws on data protection emphasize the concept of informed consent, data minimization, and purpose limitation. The companies have to gather and process the skills data according to these principles. Skills data should be governed well beginning with clear policies on the ownership, permission of access and time scales of retention. An ethical stewardship must place the consent of employees and the transparency in the second position and it also meets the analytics and planning requirements within an organization. Companies can create AI-based skills intelligence that honours individual rights and becomes trustful by integrating privacy-by-design and effective cybersecurity. The most important aspect of capability of turning AI-based talent management into the sustainable and human-centred development of workforce is ethical governance (Mir,2024).

VIII. MANAGERIAL IMPLICATIONS

Implications on the managerial practice beyond technology include integrating AI-based skills skills intelligence into talent management systems. The rise of AI in making decisions regarding skills evaluation, career growth, and the staffing processes forces the managers to reconsider their roles, skills, and decision making. These changes imply that HR activities, workforce practices, internal culture, etc. all require strategic re-alignment so that they could maximize the values of AI-based talent intelligence without compromising the human-focused ethics.

Intelligent skills via AI adoption necessitate a complete redefinition of the abilities of HR. The traditional HR functions that had previously been characterized by the administrative efficiency and compliance are required to transform into the strategic and analytical ones. The role of HR professionals is becoming more and more demanded to read between the lines of intricate information, apply the insights generated by AI to the strategy creation process, and align talent programs with organizational objectives. This change requires more skills in data literacy, systems thinking and ethical reasoning. Talent management has also transformed the use of managerial authority because of AI-icated decision-making. Instead of reactionary and less predictive analytics, managers can now enjoy the services of predictive and prescriptive analytics giving them evidence-based advice. Nevertheless, this enhancement of the decision-making authority needs more responsibility and critical assessment. Managers need to be taught how to challenge, authenticate and frame AI outputs to ensure that they conform to organizational values and created realities. Consequently, the decisions will be more informed, transparent and strategic (Murugesan et al.,2023).

AI provides strong analytical data, but to implement talent management effectively, it is necessary to mix these analytical data with human instincts. Robots are able to scan through a large amount of knowledge and identify patterns, yet they do not have any background, empathy or ethical thinking. Managers can fill this gap through reliance on their experiences and emotional intelligence to decipher AI suggestions. The collaboration between human beings and AI enhances quality and perceived legitimacy of talent decisions. Sams collaboration with human analysis also helps to reduce the chances of algorithmic bias and too much automation. When monitored by humans, the managers are able to identify any deviations, challenge unjust outcomes, and ensure that personal circumstances are considered. Such an equal approach makes employees feel fair and procedural justice. Consequently, AI is being used as a decision-supporting tool but not a decision-' (Căvescu & Popescu, 2025). The knowledge of artificial intelligence skills depends on the learning culture in order to use AI responsibly. The advent of technology and transformation of business models require organizations to cultivate life long learning, experimentation, and flexibility. Managers are key enablers. They share the importance of learning as a strategy and promote reskilling and upskilling among employees. Managers promote developing talents by exemplifying learning patterns and supporting growth prospects and make continuous growth a fundamental priority. This process is further increased by AI tools. They identify the gaps in skills automatically, monitor the process of learning, and evaluate the outcome of development programs. These ideas enable managers to customize the learning and career-track of individual employees. Alignment of learning opportunities with individual objectives and the needs of the organization enhances involvement, motivation and a sense of reinforcement. It is this alignment that creates a greater psychological contract that is founded on trust and a communal need to grow and stay employable in the long term. The learning culture enhances agility and innovation. It allows the labor force to acquire new capabilities and adjust in a short time. Resilience and providing the organization with a sustained competitive advantage is enhanced by managers who introduce AI insights in the process of making learning and talent decisions. Concisely, leaders should be technologically balanced and inclusive as well as ethical. They apply AI as a strategic talent mechanism, which has human judgment as its support rather than successfulor (Tusquellas et al.,2024).

CONCLUSION & FUTURE RESEARCH DIRECTIONS

Future efforts within AI driven skills intelligence will need to consider aspects beyond individual organizations in an attempt to understand emergent skill ecosystems and emerging dynamic, AI facilitated labor markets. In such markets, skills of firms, digital platforms, and industry networks have mobility. The study can investigate the impact of AI technologies on the significance of skills in signaling, employee valuation, and mobility. This involves the ways in which skills are identified, their prices, and conflicts with the opportunities in the interrelated labor systems. The redefinition of the historic employment relationships as creating more fluid, project-based, and platform-oriented employment relationships will also be made visible by such work. There is also the anthropo-artificial co-evolution of capabilities that should be given permanent consideration. The constant communication between intelligent systems and human beings will change the learning process, decision-making process and professional identity with time. Longitudinal research can reveal how the human capabilities respond to the AI augmentation and the way AI systems can change under the influence of human knowledge and feedbacks. This is the key to the interpretation of the long-term implications of the human-AI cooperation in the aspects of maintaining careers, leadership formation and development, as well as the generation of knowledge within the organization. Lastly, the studies ought to please come up with sustainable talent-management paradigms that are efficient in technology, embracing ethical governance, employee welfare, and employability in the long-term perspective. These paradigms have to be concerned with fairness, transparency, and data privacy and make AI-based talent systems more resilient to workforce and socially sustainable. Together, AI-enabled skills intelligence can serve as a strategic point to shape future workforces allowing flexible talent mobilisation, career path individualisation and proactive workforce planning. Organizations can become responsible, adaptive, and future-ready in the constantly changing business ecosystems by aligning their potential with the changing needs.

REFERENCES

Al-Hussaini, S. H., Turi, J. A., Altamimi, A. N., Khan, M. A., & Ahmad, M. (2019, March 26). Impact of talent management strategies on employee performance behaviour with the mediating role of talent management outputs. *Archives of Business Research*, *7*(3).

Aman, A. (2024). A review on e-learning and employability skills. *International Research Journal of Multidisciplinary Scope.*, *5*(3), 682–698. DOI: 10.47857/irjms.2024.v05i03.0782

Babashahi, L., Barbosa, C. E., Lima, Y., Lyra, A., Salazar, H., Argôlo, M., Almeida, M. A., & Souza, J. M. (2024, June 16). AI in the workplace: A systematic review of skill transformation in the industry. *Administrative Sciences*, *14*(6), 127. DOI: 10.3390/admsci14060127

Căvescu, A. M., & Popescu, N. (2025, August 5). Predictive analytics in human resources management: Evaluating AIHR's role in talent retention. *AppliedMath.*, *5*(3), 99. DOI: 10.3390/appliedmath5030099

Floridi, L. (2023). The ethics of artificial intelligence: Principles, challenges, and opportunities.

França, T. J., São Mamede, H., Barroso, J. M., & Dos Santos, V. M. (2023, April 1). Artificial intelligence applied to potential assessment and talent identification in an organisational context. *Heliyon*, *9*(4). PMID: 37035361

Ghoneim, M. (2024). Strategic integration of Explainable AI in Recruitment: Towards a framework for Ethical decision-making and Stakeholder confidence.

Gunda, V. N., & Muzira, J. (2025). *Leveraging Predictive Analytics for Workforce Planning*. Succession Planning, And Organizational Development.

Heger, B. (2024). Enabling Strategic Workforce Planning Through Skills, Artificial Intelligence, and Internal Talent Marketplace. Strategic Workforce Planning: Best Practices and Emerging Directions, 164.

Hernández-Herrera, J. R., Ortiz-Bejar, J., & Ortiz-Bejar, J. (2026). Adaptive and Personalized Learning in Higher Education: An Artificial Intelligence-Based Approach. *Education Sciences*, *16*(1), 109.

John, A. S., & Hajam, A. A. (2024). Leveraging Predictive Analytics for Enhancing Employee Engagement and Optimizing Workforce Planning: A Data-Driven HR Management Approach. *International Journal of Innovation in Management. Economics and Social Sciences*, *4*(4), 33–41.

Just, J. (2024). Natural language processing for innovation search–Reviewing an emerging non-human innovation intermediary. *Technovation*, *129*, 102883. DOI: 10.1016/j.technovation.2023.102883

Kaliannan, M., Darmalinggam, D., Dorasamy, M., & Abraham, M. (2023, March 1). Inclusive talent development as a key talent management approach: A systematic literature review. *Human Resource Management Review*, *33*(1), 100926. DOI: 10.1016/j.hrmr.2022.100926

Khuntia, R. (2025, April 1). From Job Security to Skill Security: Embracing Adaptability in India's Evolving Job Market. *Splint International Journal of Professionals.*, *12*(2), 261–266. DOI: 10.5958/2583-3561.2025.00022.0

Mancuso, I., Petruzzelli, A. M., Panniello, U., & Vaia, G. (2025, May 1). The bright and dark sides of AI innovation for sustainable development: Understanding the paradoxical tension between value creation and value destruction. *Technovation*, *143*, 103232. DOI: 10.1016/j.technovation.2025.103232

Mir, A. I. (2024, November 30). Application of AI in talent management: A systematic review of benefits, challenges, and prospects. *Academy of Education and Social Sciences Review.*, *4*(4), 612–630. DOI: 10.48112/aessr.v4i4.941

Murugesan, U., Subramanian, P., Srivastava, S., & Dwivedi, A. (2023, June 1). A study of artificial intelligence impacts on human resource digitalization in industry 4.0. *Decision Analytics Journal.*, *7*, 100249. DOI: 10.1016/j.dajour.2023.100249

Onyekachi, A., Okoro, U., & Iqbal, Z. (2025). Predictive Analytics in Talent Management: Enhancing Recruitment and Retention through AI.

Pavlakou, E., Katsarou, M., Misiou, M., Nakou, M., Papakosta, M. A., & Papavasilopoulos, V. (2025). The Impact of Artificial Intelligence on Learning and Development-Case Studies in Companies of Different Sectors. *Current Res. J. Soc. Sci. & Human.*, *8*(1), 49–66. DOI: 10.12944/CRJSSH.8.1.05

Rodgers, W., Murray, J. M., Stefanidis, A., Degbey, W. Y., & Tarba, S. Y. (2023, March 1). An artificial intelligence algorithmic approach to ethical decision-making in human resource management processes. *Human Resource Management Review*, *33*(1), 100925. DOI: 10.1016/j.hrmr.2022.100925

Rožman, M., Oreški, D., & Tominc, P. (2022). Integrating artificial intelligence into a talent management model to increase the work engagement and performance of enterprises. *Frontiers in Psychology, 13*, 1014434. DOI: 10.3389/fpsyg.2022.1014434 PMID: 36506984

Salvadorinho, J., Ferreira, C., & Teixeira, L. (2024, June 1). A technology-based framework to foster the lean human resource 4.0 and prevent the great resignation: The talent management lift. *Technology in Society*, *77*, 102510. DOI: 10.1016/j.techsoc.2024.102510

Tessarini, G.Junior, & Saltorato, P. (2021, September). Workforce agility: A systematic literature review and a research agenda proposal. *Innovar (Universidad Nacional de Colombia)*, *31*(81), 155–167. DOI: 10.15446/innovar.v31n81.95582

Tusquellas, N., Palau, R., & Santiago, R. (2024, November 1). Analysis of the potential of artificial intelligence for professional development and talent management: A systematic literature review. *International Journal of Information Management Data Insights*, *4*(2), 100288. DOI: 10.1016/j.jjimei.2024.100288

Tyskbo, D., & Firtin, C. E. (2025, August 8). Contextualizing talent management: A practice-based study of Turkish SMEs and large organizations. *Journal of Small Business Management*, , 1–41.

Varsha, P. S. (2023, April 1). How can we manage biases in artificial intelligence systems–A systematic literature review. *International Journal of Information Management Data Insights*, *3*(1), 100165. DOI: 10.1016/j.jjimei.2023.100165

Yadalam, T. V., Gowda, V. M., Kumar, V. S., & Girish, D. (2020, June). Career recommendation systems using content based filtering. In 2020 5th International Conference on Communication and Electronics Systems (ICCES) (pp. 660-665). IEEE.

Zuiderwijk, A., Chen, Y. C., & Salem, F. (2021, July 1). Implications of the use of artificial intelligence in public governance: A systematic literature review and a research agenda. *Government Information Quarterly*, *38*(3), 101577. DOI: 10.1016/j.giq.2021.101577

Chapter 3
Responsible AI and People Analytics in HR:
Ethical Employer Branding and Human-Centered Talent Management

Aadhya Rajput
http://orcid.org/0009-0007-9975-2956
Christ University, Bengaluru, India

Sadashiva Tandur
http://orcid.org/0000-0003-4662-0582
Christ University, Bengaluru, India

ABSTRACT

HR practices such as recruitment, performance management and prediction of employee behaviors are changing as AI and people analytics are used more widely within organizations. Although these practices enhance efficiency they have their ethical challenges, which include bias, opacity, privacy and a lack of accountability. The HCEAI (Human-Centred Ethical AI) framework, based upon the principles of fairness, transparency, accountability and human primacy, helps to support the governance of responsible AI. Research evidence also shows that ethical AI is related to employer branding, employee trust, outcomes and diversity and performance.

1. INTRODUCTION

The adoption of artificial intelligence across the Human Resource Management (HRM) function is occurring on a scale and at a level of sophistication that challenges

DOI: 10.4018/979-8-2600-2178-1.ch003

the underlying theoretical assumptions that have guided scholars and practitioners in understanding people management for decades. What began in the earlier decades as administrative automation-payroll calculations, benefits management, compliance record-keeping-has grown into a dense ecosystem of machine learning applications which now dictate the terms of some of the most pivotal points in a person's professional life: will my CV be seen by a human recruiter, how will my performance evaluation be rated, will my manager be alerted that I am a 'flight risk', and which developmental path will an algorithm recommend for me and for whom? (Vrontis et al., 2022; Kellogg et al., 2020). The HR tech market is estimated to be over USD 62 billion in 2023 with the fastest growing segment being AI-driven HR tools (Vrontis et al., 2022). The reasons why this technology is gaining widespread adoption among organizations are clear and empirically documented: HR tech can potentially offset human bias, extract predictive insights that humans are unable to match in speed or scale, and offer individually tailored experiences to a large number of employees that one human cannot manage (Cappelli & Tavis, 2018; Guenole et al., 2017).

The decade that has now passed since the beginnings of AI's application in HRM complicates this positive narrative in ways that we can no longer responsibly downplay. As Barocas and Selbst (2016) show using precise technical rigor, machine learning models built from data accumulated in HR departments historically reproduce and amplify structural inequalities already present in the data-creating a phenomenon they call disparate impact by design. Amazon's infamous decision to reject female candidates based on their own algorithm trained on years of historically male hiring demonstrates this issue at the organizational level where it was predicted at a theoretical level (Dastin, 2018). Evidence exists of performance management systems in HR leveraging racially inflected proxies that disproportionately disadvantage workers belonging to underrepresented ethnic groups (Green, 2019). Asynchronous video interviews, which employ computer vision and sentiment analysis in order to evaluate candidates, have shown to be less accurate and favorable for individuals with darker skin tone, older age, neurodiversity or non-normative communication style (Langer et al., 2019; Tippins et al., 2021). These are not aberrations, but structurally predictable outcomes which can be observed when attempting to create optimization systems using data from HR that has been informed by decades of structural disadvantage and discrimination.

Ethical concerns extend beyond algorithmic bias to areas like transparency, privacy, accountability, and the legitimacy of the employment relationship itself. Pasquale (2015) highlighted how the lack of clarity associated with algorithmic decision-making poses a structural threat to fairness and autonomy, a phenomenon he termed 'black box society,' where outcomes affecting individuals of paramount importance are dictated by unseen and misunderstood systems. Zuboff (2019) describes the infiltration of behavioral surveillance into the workplace as a transformational change of the employment relationship, which erodes worker autonomy, dignity, and the relational trust which form the basis of a sustainable employment relation, a phenomenon she terms 'surveillance capitalism.' The tension between the commercial interest of the providers of AI solutions and the fundamental right of users to have a transparent and explainable rationale behind decisions that shape their professional futures has been clearly articulated by Wachter et al. (2017). Moreover, the deployment of algorithmic management systems in organizations shapes the organizational environment to the point that managerial control extends in novel ways, altering the existing power dynamics of the employment relation (Kellogg et al., 2020). All this evidence leads to the conclusion that AI in HR cannot be viewed merely as a technological issue; it is an inherently political, sociological and ethical issue.

This chapter will argue that these are at once governance issues, issues of employer branding, and Human Centered organizational design issues that can, and should, no longer be separated. An organization that utilizes opaque or biased algorithms in its HR processes is not only morally compromising its values; it is creating a gap between what it professes outwardly and how it conducts itself inwardly-a phenomenon known as organized hypocrisy (Brunsson, 1989)-with the predictable reputational consequences in talent markets that are increasingly informed by transparent information (Backhaus & Tikoo, 2004; Cable & Turban, 2003; Van Hoye & Lievens, 2009). In turn, an organization that develops and invests in clear and equitable governance mechanisms around AI use is signaling itself as a trustworthy employer brand, a valuable differentiator in informationally imbalanced labor markets (Spence, 1973). In summary, ethically sound AI use in HR should be viewed not as a cost, but rather as a strategic imperative, yielding benefits for employee retention, trust, DEIB and reputation.

The chapter makes four significant scholarly contributions. First, it integrates the disparate and fragmented fields of AI ethics, people analytics, employer branding, stakeholder theory, DEIB scholarship, organizational trust and psychological contract theory into a comprehensive framework that identifies the strategic links between these fields that are not apparent in a fragmented academic discourse. Second, this theoretical framework will be grounded with qualitative data from 12 case organizations in five different industries to understand the particular HR governance challenges that current HR professionals face and the various strategies leading organizations are adopting in response. Third, an integrated framework, the practice types typology ranging from a Minimalist Approach to a Compliant Approach, to a Proactive Governance to an Integrated Governance approach will be presented to provide a roadmap to organizations at varying levels of maturity in their efforts towards ethically sound AI use in HR. Finally, this paper presents the Human-Centered Ethical AI (HCEAI) framework-a four-component structure for

AI governance, designed to translate theoretical ethical principles into operational mechanisms that include structure, processes, communications, and metrics. The subsequent chapters are organized as follows: section 2 provides a detailed literature review across five domains. Section 3 constructs the Integrated Theoretical Framework. Section 4 provides information on the methodology utilized in the research, followed by Sections 5 and 6 which lay out the empirical findings of the research. Section 7 presents the HCEAI framework in full and Section 8 is dedicated to discussing theoretical and practical implications, while Section 9 addresses limitations and future research directions. Section 10 will then conclude the chapter.

2. LITERATURE REVIEW

2.1 The Evolution of People Analytics and AI in HRM

People analytics has been classically conceptualized by Marler and Boudreau (2017, p. 15) as 'a HR practice enabled by information technology that employs descriptive, visual and statistical analyses of data related to HR processes, human capital, firm performance and external economic measures to define business impact and inform data-driven decisions.' This definition encapsulates the epistemic ambition of the field-to leverage the evidentiary standards and analytical bandwidth of data science to explain and optimize aspects of organizational life which were previously managed largely through managerial fabrications, institutional wisdom, and practitioner custom. Angrave et al. (2016) charted the evolution of the field starting with fundamental workforce reporting and population identification in the 1970s and 1980s, followed by the advent of predictive attrition models in the early 2010s, to the current age of augmented, real time behavioral analytics enabled through artificial intelligence. Guenole et al. (2017) outlined the development stages of descriptive, predictive and prescriptive analytics, finding much practice lags behind vendor discourse when it comes to comprehensive prescriptive use.

Today's AI forms of HRM capitalize on the full range of the employee life cycle with a level of intensity and specificity that would have been technically infeasible a decade ago. In talent attraction and employer branding, programmatic advertising platforms leverage machine learning algorithms to determine where to serve employer brand messages across multiple digital channels, personalize content to individual passive candidates based on online behavior, and adjust message profile in real time using engagement metrics (Cappelli & Tavis, 2018). Natural language processing systems analyze the text of job descriptions to flag exclusionary wording that could dissuade qualified candidates from underrepresented backgrounds (Bogen & Rieke, 2018). Candidate search, filtering, and ranking in talent acquisition is enabled through applicant tracking systems that compare resumes to semantic models of target job positions, process hundreds of thousands of applications beyond human capacity and identify 'best-fit' candidates (Kochling & Wehner, 2020). Conversational AI chatbots automate asynchronous phone and video interviews, utilize validated psychometric assessment instruments, respond to candidate questions, and book subsequent interviews without involving a recruiter. In talent development and performance management, AI systems recommend personalized development content based on the applicant's competency gaps relative to role benchmarks and competency models, previous individual learning patterns (Guenole et al., 2017). Multi-source feedback, continuous performance and behavior data collection and analysis are fed into algorithms that predict job performance and create alternative performance rating reports to traditional manager appraisal forms. Finally, predictive attrition models utilizing internal HRIS, social listening, collaboration, survey, and engagement data and external labor market signals allow managers to intervene with at-risk workers before disengagement snowballs (Kellogg et al., 2020).

The scientific support for the predictive validity and practical operational value of these applications is extensive and, in some cases, conclusive. The original psychometric research would more than meet meta-analytic standards of evidence, showing that an actuarial, mechanical combination of predictor scores is superior to clinical, intuitive judgment at predicting later job performance-a finding which has been replicated across cultures, job types, and job performance criteria (Schmidt & Hunter, 1998; Highhouse, 2008; Oswald & Putka, 2016). The 'actuarial advantage,' as Highhouse (2008, p. 27) calls it, exists because humans are prone to cognitive

However, and this caveat is comprehensively analytical, the actuarial benefit holds only when several assumptions are met, assumptions which are invariably shattered by the reality of HR AI applications. Foremost among them is the assumption that the use of training data is free of reference to the very cohorts the model is to serve, and free of the organizations it was trained within. This is structurally impossible when models, in the real world, are derived from and optimized to historical HR outcomes of organizations in societies defined by inequality (Barocas & Selbst, 2016). When a promotion model is trained in an organization whose leadership has been, historically and predominantly, male, the model seeks to optimize out (predict success with the characteristics that predict success in organizations in historic organizations with systematic inequality). This is not because gender is coded into the model as a factor but because the indicators of success the model identifies in fact coded (indirectly) for femaleness. Barocas and Selbst (2016) spell out precisely the formal paths through which gender neutral algorithms engender gender inequality: selecting indicators-attributes of people and performance that are themselves the fruits of oppression-selecting optimized labels-attributes of women and men that reflect the sexist information women have to contend with. Sampling datasets that distort sample sizes of women and men existing at the domain level, with implicit allusions to, characters of, and associations with the categories delineated. And aggregating data at the aggregate level, which, even in domains where outcome variables can be fully observed, homogenizes individual variation.

A second key concern relates to construct validity of the behavioral and physiological signals newer AI applications use to supposedly measure These issues have been scrutinized in an empirical paper by Langer et al. (2019) who took the claim that some of the major commercial video interview analysis platforms could accurately assess personality, cognitive ability, and fit to the culture from behavioral signals such as facial micro-expressions, vocal prosody, verbal word choice, and discourse structure. The authors found serious problems with the own reliability of claimed assessments at different assessment time points and with models' ability to consistently assess across different demographic groups (especially race, gender, and age). Tippins et al. (2021) extend this critique to AI-enabled selection tools more generally, arguing that they are held to lower psychometric standards and falling short of standards required of traditional selection tools of comparable stakes despite the greater severity of at-scale deployment of automated decision making. They end with a formal 'call to action' that applied psychology develop requirements and enforce standards of reliability and fairness in AI-enabled selection reflecting the maturity of these tools.

2.2 The Ethics of Algorithmic Decision-Making: A Multi-Dimensional Framework

The AI ethics academic and policy literatures have grown exponentially over the last decade, resulting in a wealth of principles, frameworks, and analytical methods that establish the normative coverage of responsible AI development and use. Jobin et al.'s (2019) systematic review of 84 AI ethics documents released by governments, inter-governmental organizations, technology companies, and civil society organizations uncovered general agreement in most of the examined documents on five central principles: transparency, justice and fairness, non-maleficence, responsibility, and privacy. Principles of beneficence, autonomy and freedom, dignity, solidarity, and sustainability appeared in important subsets. The EU Ethics Guidelines for Trustworthy AI (European Commission, 2019) and the OECD AI Principles (OECD, 2019) offer influential institutional declarations of these commitments in the most relevant jurisdictions to HR practitioners in multilevel, multinational organizations doing business in or for European markets.

Despite this apparent convergence, numerous scholars have pointed out an enduring and growing 'operationalization gap' between the framing of principles for AI ethics and the implementation of those principles into organizational processes and technical decisions (Mittelstadt et al., 2016; Whittlestone et al., 2019; Raji et al., 2020). Mittelstadt et al. (2016) highlight a litany of structural elements characteristic of algorithmic ethics that make its operationalization more complicated than the medical, research and professional ethics traditions that provide the vocabulary for the bulk of AI ethics frameworks: algorithmic systems are rolled out in marketized situations where dialectical, corporate and competitive interests systematic pressure toward the ethics principles underweight of consideration; where they have statistically significant aggregate effects that

Theoretically and analytically, the idea of algorithmic fairness has attracted the most scholarly emphasis. Chouldechova (2017) and Kleinberg et al. (2016) independently established that some of the most commonly utilized mathematical formulations of fairness are logically incompatible with each other in real-world settings. They showed that no algorithm can achieve demographic parity (equalized positive prediction rates), equalized odds (equalized false positive and true negative rates), and calibration (equalized true/false prediction accuracy) in the presence of differing base rates across demographic groups; which is a condition that real life HR data artificially imbues to almost always be the case. This 'fairness impossibility theorem' has significant yet insufficiently recognized pragmatic consequences: fair machine learning is not inherently a technical challenge with a necessarily clear solution, but a normative challenge where the 'correct' decision should be one that reflects established explicit agreements about who is most affected and what variables are more versus less desirable as predictions; a challenge that face organizations and developers of it is that responsible decisions about those agreements can only be made in a dialogic and transparent process that is overseen by senior leadership.

Algorithmic transparency, as defined in the literature, encapsulates multiple notions that are sometimes implicitly subsumed as one in policy discussion, with negative implications on governance mechanism design. Wachter et al (2017) distinguishes between: ex ante transparency about the fact of AI use and its general nature; process transparency about the features, criteria and optimization goals used and; ex post decision transparency-the ability to produce intelligible, decision-specific explanations to impacted persons. Each dimension of transparency fulfills different ethical functions and necessitates specific technical and organizational measures. Goodman and Flaxman (2017) analyzed the 'right to explanation' embodied in the GDPR and found it to be meaningful but insufficient to the establishment of strong procedural justice-aligned

The accountabilit y aspect of algorithmic governance is also affected by the phenomenon of "the problem of many hands" as van de Poel et al. (2012) have described it-the observation that in situations in which harm is caused by a complex socio-technical system with many contributing actors, it is important challenge to assign material moral responsibility because each actor is contributing too little to cause the harm. In the context of HR AI, the chain of contributing actors is very long-and invariably crosses organizational boundaries: AI researchers creating foundational model structures; vendors taking these models and turning them into deployed technology; HR technology procurement teams selecting from vendor solutions; HR data scientists and engineers configuring, complementing, and integrating these solutions into company context; HR business partners interpreting and acting upon AI-generated output in particular organizational decisions; line managers ultimately making employment decisions based on these outputs; and company leadership establishing company culture and incentive structures for all actors. Raji et al. (2020) explicitly addresses this issue with their concept of internal algorithmic auditing, which they characterize as a set of process elements for parts of an organization to consider observed AI features or behaviors, document decisions about those observations and outputs, and assign accountability for those decisions. The resulting framework is by far the most practically implementable governance model I have yet seen.

Regulation around the use of AI in employment contexts is no less bi-polar than elsewhere and increasingly material for HR practice. Currently the most comprehensive regulation of AI in place is the EU Artificial Intelligence Act (European Parliament and Council, 2024), which regulates AI systems used in employment, management of workers, and access to self-employment as 'high-risk' applications. These must be subject to a comprehensive conformity assessment prior to use, with a lengthy set of post-market monitoring obligations; one of a set of transparency obligations requiring notice of AI use to individuals; requirements for accuracy and robustness; human

2.3 Employer Branding Theory: Identity, Authenticity, and the War for Talent

Artist and colleagues: 1 According to Ambler and Barrow (1996, p. 187), employer branding is 'the package of functional, economic and psychological benefits provided by employment, and identified with the employing company', which laid the conceptual foundation for a research agenda that has flourished over the past thirty years. Backhaus and Tikoo (2004) presents a more comprehensive conceptual model that differentiates employer brand identity-the values, attributes, and associations that the organization attempts to project to the talent marketplace-and employer brand image-the actual perceptions held by existing and potential employees. Managing the congruence between the two or managing the gap between them has since become one of the most important practical issues in employer branding, especially in the digital world in which the difference is constantly uncovered, published, and debated by reviewsites, social networks of professionals, and social media (Van Hoye & Lievens, 2009).

The EVP is the centerpiece of the employer brand: the myriad of instrumental, symbolic, and experiential rewards that an organization provides to and receives from employees or prospective employees in exchange for their skills, capabilities, and commitment (Edwards, 2010). Numerical data and meta-analyses of employer branding studies founded to date demonstrate the triple conditions under which EVP effectiveness can be ascertained: it has to be attractive in relation to the degrees of importance sought-by or provided to-talent segments (the EVP has to offer specific blue benefits to prospective employees); it has to be differentiated from competing organizations (the EVP has to shape perceptions in terms of leadership, among the various alternative options); and as well that the EVP has to be authentic-that is rooted in the actual lived experience of

More recently, Cable and Turban (2003) tested a conceptual framework derived from job information processing theory and social identity theory in their employer brand research, again providing strong evidence that prospective employees develop employ er brand knowledge structures that blend cognitive perceptions of ageneral-ized"organization-related attributes, such as size, financial position, industry, and practices, with positive affectively labeled social identity associations based on the perceived fit ofthe organization's values and identity with the individual's own values and identity. This line of research provided an important contribution to the field by establishing that employment brand perceptions not only carry implications for intention to apply, but also for applicant quality and thematic self-registration. The degree to which an organization possesssa strong, distinctive, andunique"employer brand draws a higher volume of self-selected applicants who pursue a better fit, triggering a virtuous cycle in which employer branding potency increases practice and cultural fit. Edwards (2010) extended this evolutionary analysis of employer branding by merging organizational identification theory (Dutton & Dukerich, 1991) with employer branding, providing evidence that employer brand must serve not only as a signal of externally perceived attraction, but also as an internalizing guides to behavioral contribution, job performance and retention through the lens oforganizational identification.

The concept of organizational authenticity is especially relevant to modern-day employer branding research. Gilmore and Pine (2007), inspired by extensive observations of contemporary consumer culture, contend that in modern markets characterized by an overabundance of choice and information technology-enabled information sharing, authenticity has eclipsed quality and value as the benchmark that people use to judge their organizations. Morhart et al. (2015) have generalized this argument to the realm of talent markets with their proposed model of brand authenticity, which consists of four components: continuity (the organization remains in line with its history), originality (the organization is not copying others), reliability (the organization always

The association between employer branding and organizational reputation has been conceptualized in terms of Fombrun's (1996) model of corporate reputation, which conceptualizes organizational reputation as the collective perceptual assessment of an organization by its multiple stakeholder constituencies over time. Using the employment market, the impact of employer reputation on applicant attraction, offer acceptance percentage, and applicant pool quality has been explained in terms of signaling (Spence, 1973) and social proof (Van Hoye & Lievens, 2009). In the digital labor market, both the velocity of transferring information regarding employer reputation and the nature of reputation damage has been accelerated. Data shows that more negative than positive emotion is conveyed through negative user experiences regarding AIHR processes on employer review sites and professional social media platforms-thus the online emitter of employer brand content evinces a culturally negative valence that an organization must work hard to address through practice change, not simply messaging (Van Hoye & Lievens, 2009).

2.4 Organizational Trust, the Psychological Contract, and AI-Mediated Employment

Organizational trust, as a multidimensional construct, has been modeled as comprising at least two recognizably distinct components. McAllister (1995) conceptualized cognition-based trust, derived from rational evaluation of an actor's trustworthiness based on assessment of their competence, reliability and given history and affect-based trust, derived from the emotional sense that the actor's actions are motivated by genuine concern for the trustee's interests and wellbeing. Both types of trust are relevant to AI governance in HR, and the processes by which different types are shaped by AI use appear to differ somewhat. Cognition-based trust appears to be shaped

The literature on procedural justice is particularly germane for understanding how humans in organizations respond to AI-mediated HR decisions. Lind and Tyler (1988) establishednot only theoretically but also empirically"the dominance of procedure in processes of influence and control" over outcomes in all sorts of organizational and institutional contexts: the organization and administration of justice, police work, corporate governance, labor management relations. They established the primacy of procedural justice-the extent to which individuals perceive the processes of influence to be fair-over distributive justice-the extent to which individuals perceive the final outcomes to be fair-in determining not only trust in, but also satisfaction with, the organization in question. These results were newly examined and confirmed by Folger and Konovsky (1989) within an organization-specific sample of employees. The findings have an immediately counterintuitive but nonetheless valuable practical implication for designing AI-mediated processes within HR: if one wishes to increase employees' trust in one's organization, in addition to changing the effects the decisions produce, one should change the AI system's transparency and explainability to center on creating the perception of fairness by controlling for perceivedprocess controls (e.g., its consistency, neutrality, accuracy, ability to be remedies, representation, and morally groundedness (Leventhal, 1980).

In addition to the organizationemployment relationship considering exchange obligations, also the employeeemployer relationship grounded in the psychological contract-a set of individual's beliefs about reciprocal exchange terms between on the one hand, that person, and an external party, on the other hand-can be used as a complementary theoretical perspective to assess AI governance in HR. As Rousseau (1989, p. 123) would define it, the psychological contract says that"an individual's beliefs concerning the terms and conditions of the exchange arrangement it has with another party". Unlike formalized contractual exchange obligations, the psychological contract frames offices as informal, unwritten obligations of relation-based exchange, including the transfer of respect, good information sharing, investment of development, and organization concern for employee welfare. Morrison and Robinson's (1997) model of psychological contract violation-the perception that one's employment provider(provider here meaning any organizations or individuals to which the psychological contract registers), has failed to deliver on these implicit relational obligations-was found to exert broad negative effects oforganizational commitment, extra-role performance, norms of reciprocity, and departition commitment. This perspective is particularly relevant for the coming technology-driven workplace: employment relationships will be shaped and held accountable for violations through the experience of AI-enabled HR systems that were disrespectful of individual (namely, digitalized, automated and standardized) identities and results (through the illusion of personalized, contextualized HR decisions), and failed to fulfill its organization-sponsored job to communicate those changes (by monitoring and auditing activity without clear purpose).

Self-determination theory (Deci & Ryan, 2000) offers a third key theoretical framework for framing the wellbeing consequences of AI management in HR. The theory argues that motives and wellbeing are fundamentally derived from satisfying three basic psychological needs: autonomy-the feeling of self-endorsement and freedom of action, competence-the feeling of mastery and impact, and relatedness-the feeling of genuine connection and care. Van den Broeck et al. (2016) offer a broad meta-analytic survey of self-determination research applied to workplace settings, showing strong, robust effects of need satisfaction on positive employee outcomes across a wide range of cultural and organizational contexts. In HR, AI applications that restrict agency through algorithmic employee specification and observation, undermine competence through non-transparant, uncontestable performance assessment and feedback, or damage relatedness through the substitution of mere algorithmic efficiency for human relationships threaten the psychological need satisfaction that sustainable employee motivation rests upon-constructing wellbeing and performance costs that myopic ROI-focused organizations systematically overlook.

2.5 DEIB, Power, and the Politics of Algorithmic HR

The DEIB literature has also argued that organizational design can be too superficially 'neutral' and 'non-discriminatory' yet reproduce and institutionalize the very inequities that we wanted to unlearn (Shore et al., 2011; Nkomo & Hoobler, 2014).The critical insights provided by these studies are especially pertinent for AI governance in HR, which exactly runs into this dilemma: systematic, well-intentioned machine learning designs that seek to 'operate' in a 'neutral' space can still exacerbate inequalities through the processes ultimately described by Barocas and Selbst (2016).Shore et al. (2011) powerful model of inclusion in organizations offers a framework to understand this potential: belonging exists when individuals perceive that they are an appreciated and fully welcomed participant of the organizational world; and uniqueness exists when individuals feel validated when their idiosyncratic identities are acknowledged and tolerated, in contrast to the pressure of assimilation and elimination.We see that algorithms that seek to categorize employees as data points to be optimized, to construct workers who conform to a uniform behavioral expectation, or to recommend careers based on the statistical norms of identical past high performers threaten both the belonging-ness and the uniqueness-ness of the inclu18sion process in organizations even while the 'demographs' of the organization appear adequate.

Nkomo and Hoobler (2014) call for a more power-aware approach to DEIB that more directly attends to the ways that the seeming universality and objectivity of organizational practices mask the contributions that dominant groups-typically educated, white, male, and economically-privileged- make to the configuration of AI systems. This dimension is of particular relevance to AI governance because the theorized democratization of the conception, procurement, configuration, and deployment of AI systems in the HR context is in practice determined overwhelmingly by the members of dominant organizational groups who, by virtue of their social position, are typically less likely to be directly impacted by the biases encoded in their AI systems and are less likely to recognize when their systems operate in biased ways. In their extensive review of AI use in hiring, for instance, Bogen and Rieke (2018) highlight how lack of affected employee and candidate voice translated into a systematic giving of less weight to equity issues than efficiency issues during the compilation of an optimal AI system, ultimately leading their authors to conclude that the pathway toward actual equitable AI in the HR context is not technical

The notion of intersectionality (Crenshaw, 1989) affects how one conceptualizes and operationalizes notions of algorithmic bias in human resources (HR). Fairness testing that looks at algorithmic fairness along individual demographic axes - race, gender, age, disability - might find no algorithmic unfairness on any one of those axes and yet fail to encapsulate the many harms incurred by those at the intersection of multiple axes of oppression. The Black women with disabilities who work in this industry, like all marginalized workers in this industry, experience unique historical marginalizations that span multiple demographic axes - only a governance structure that asks how the algorithm treats those at the intersection of withhold justice.

3. THEORETICAL FRAMEWORK

The theoretical framework developed within this chapter is constructed from the combination of four compatible theoretical approaches, which cumulatively serve to elucidate the strategic, ethical, organizational, and communication aspects of governing AI within HR. Each theoretical perspective provides analytic insight into a discrete, though related dimension of the phenomenon, whose integration yields a framework with explanatory and practical utility beyond the mere sum of its parts.

3.1 Stakeholder Theory: Mapping the Obligation Landscape of HR AI

Freeman's (1984) foundational conceptualization of stakeholder theory-that organizations have duties to all groups that are impacted significantly by organizational actions, not simply to shareholders-has since been richly elaborated upon. Donaldson and Preston (1995) offered three justifications for stakeholder theory: descriptive (how organizations behave), instrumental (stakeholder management contributes to organizational performance), and normative (organizations should attend to stakeholders on grounds of their intrinsic value); they considered the normative dimension to be primary. Mitchell, Agle, and Wood (1997) constructed a model of dynamic stakeholder saliency that prioritizes stakeholders according to power (the capacity of a stakeholder to impose his will upon the organization), legitimacy (the extent to which the claims

Applied to HR AI governance, the stakeholder analysis highlights a complex of parties whose interests must be aligned. Job candidates, though primary stakeholders of AI recruiting systems and endowed with high legitimacy (as the subjects whose data will be used and whose futures will be shaped by algorithms) and high urgency (as algorithmic decisions directly shape future employment opportunities), have little power, as they lack formal organizational status and the means to question algorithmic recommendations (Mitchell et al., 1997). While employees (who have slightly more leverage due to their employment contract) share the same high levels of legitimacy and urgency vis-a-vis the AI systems that will determine their career development, evaluation, and retention, they remain economically subordinate to the employer (Rousseau, 1989). Technology vendors hold power derived from contractual arrangements and their proprietary systems, have some legitimacy (as business entities providing valuable services), but hold little urgency regarding ethical impacts on end users. Regulatory agencies possess legitimate power based upon their mandate to oversee public safety, and significant institutional power; however, constraints of resources and expertise limit their capacity for sustained, in-depth oversight of real-time AI use in practice. This stakeholder map reveals a structural imbalance: those who are most immediately affected by HR AI systems (candidates and employees) hold the least power within the HR AI ecosystem, creating an inherent potential for systematically biased consideration of their interests, absent deliberate intervening action (Mitchell et al., 1997).

3.2 Signaling Theory: AI Ethics as a Credible Employer Brand Signal

Spence's (1973) groundbreaking work on signaling in labor markets, which explains how observable educational credentials can serve as valid indicators of otherwise unobservable attributes of job applicants, also helps to explain the signaling potential of HR AI governance practices for an organization's employer brand. According to Spence's (1973) theory, informationally asymmetric markets cannot rely on an assessment of intrinsic product quality and thus require some "signal" – some observable characteristic of the product or provider that can serve as a proxy for quality – that can be acquired at a certain cost; if this signal is positively related to the product or provider's intrinsic quality, and sufficiently costly for substandard providers to replicate, then low-quality providers are dissuaded from attempting such imitation and the signal serves as a reliable indicator of higher quality.

HR AI ethics practices can be framed as employer brand signals to the extent they fulfill these conditions. The act of committing to and executing comprehensive pre-deployment diversity impact assessments for all AI recruitment tools, making assessment results available on demand to candidates and candidates on demand-and to follow through by making a subset of findings public-carries intrinsic costliness to execute and maintain that makes it difficult to simulate. Similarly, a public promise to explain algorithmic assessment logic on demand to candidates whose applications are screened out communicates genuine dignity and a willingness to attend to individual circumstances, the fulfillment of which necessarily requires substantial internal resource allocation, which is impossible to duplicate at scale and low cost by less sincere firms. These signals differ from perfunctory declarations of "we care about AI ethics", which carry negligible cost and information value because anyone can make them.

3.3 Institutional Theory: Regulatory, Normative, and Mimetic Pressures

Neo-institutional theory offers three mechanisms for how organizations tend to convergence in their behavior within an institutional field: coercive isomorphism, where organizations adopt similar practices due to regulation and power influence; normative isomorphism, where professionals within an industry strive to adhere to similar standards and practices based on shared values and expertise; and mimetic isomorphism, where uncertainty drives organizations to copy successful practices from other companies. All three mechanisms of isomorphism appear to be operating simultaneously, and with accelerating force, in the institutional field of HR AI governance, thereby creating pressures for the development of standardized, rigorous forms of HR AI ethics governance. The European Union's forthcoming Artificial Intelligence Act (European Parliament and Council, 2024), for instance, provides detailed compliance requirements that are specifically targeted at high-risk AI in employment. Meanwhile, multiple U.S. State and local jurisdictions have begun to implement detailed and specific HR AI regulatory frameworks that provide a new layer of legal pressure for adherence to particular operational, transparency, and notification practices. Normative pressures also play an increasingly significant role, as professional organizations like the Society for Human Resource Management are developing explicit guidance documents for responsible AI in HR that define best practices for HR practitioners. Mimetic pressures have been fueled by high-profile reputational losses suffered by organizations that deployed AI without adequate governance, increasing the attractiveness and

3.4 Organizational Identity Theory: AI Governance as Values-in-Practice

Albert and Whetten's (1985) influential conception of organizational identity as the attributes that its members perceive as central, distinctive, and enduring provides a theoretical lens through which to analyze how an organization's values are embedded in its practices. Research since Albert and Whetten has advanced a more dynamic view of organizational identity; Dutton and Dukerich (1991) established that organizational identity acts as a mechanism of organizational governance because members strive to align external events and organizational actions with existing identity perceptions, seeking to reaffirm and protect their organizations' identities when they are threatened. Gioia, Schultz, and Petroselli (2000) extended this notion by arguing that organizations maintain a "label" for their identity, which may remain constant over time, while the "meaning" of that label is able to evolve in response to external pressures, allowing for organizational adaptation while preserving identity continuity. From an HR AI governance standpoint, this framework of dynamic identity is invaluable because organizations today face immense pressure to renegotiate their identities as human-centered institutions within a context where they are implementing the very AI systems that most profoundly affect human workers and jobs. The degree to which organizations can demonstrate through their AI governance practices that their stated values are in practice-"walk the walk", as is often said-is directly consequential both for internal and external organizational members. Internally, strong alignment between perceived identity and implemented HR AI practices leads to higher levels of employee commitment, identification with the organization, and willingness to engage in discretionary behavior (Dutton & Dukerich, 1991). Externally, the perceived match between the candidate's and investor's expectation of organizational values and the behavior evidenced through HR AI governance practices strongly influences trust formation, by establishing credibility on dimensions such as benevolence and integrity (Mayer et al., 1995). Conversely, when an organization's identity claims are mismatched with the realities of its AI governance practices (i.e., when there is an 'identity-practice gap'), the result is organizational hypocrisy, which has demonstrably negative impacts on identification and reputation (Brunsson, 1989).

4. METHODOLOGY

4.1 Research Design

This study employed a qualitative, interpretive, multi-case design (Yin, 2018). The choice of a qualitative methodology was motivated by the belief that the complex phenomena that it aims to uncover-the organizational adoption of AI in HR, the management of associated ethical issues, the resulting governance mechanisms, and the influence of these dynamics on employer branding and DEIB-are not well suited to the production of decontextualized causal relationships favored by large-N quantitative studies (Eisenhardt, 1989). A multi-case research design was selected for a number of reasons. First, it enabled cross-case comparisons to identify patterns that occur in the phenomenon, allowing for higher confidence in theoretical generalization than single-case designs could afford (Eisenhardt &

Graebner, 2007). Second, its interpretive, in-depth approach provided the necessary access to meaning-making processes and participant experiences that are crucial to understanding how individuals perceive and experience the complexities of HR AI governance (Strauss & Corbin, 1998).

4.2 Case Selection and Organizational Context

This study recruited twelve organizations as cases for in-depth analysis. Purposive theoretical sampling (Strauss & Corbin, 1998) was used to ensure variation across: (a) industry sector (financial services (n=3), healthcare (n=2), technology (n=3), professional services (n=2), and retail (n=2)); (b) organizational size (ranging from 850 to 94,000 employees; median 12,400); (c) geographic scope (four were national, five were multinational with a presence in several continents, and three were regional with a presence in a single country); and (d) level of HR AI adoption maturity (determined through pre-study questionnaire that gauged the extent to which AI was deployed within HR, the formality of governance structures, and the degree of perceived organizational awareness regarding AI ethics). The goal of theoretical sampling was to gain a range of variation that would illuminate the phenomenon across its natural spectrum of variation (Eisenhardt & Graebner, 2007) rather than to ensure representativeness of the organizational universe.

4.3 Data Collection

Data were collected through three methods between January 2023 and November 2024. First, 74 semi-structured interviews were conducted with a diverse array of key informants from each of the twelve organizations. These informants included: Chief HR Officers (n=12), People Analytics Directors/Managers (n=9), Employer Branding Specialists (n=8), AI Engineers and Data Scientists (n=11), HR and Employment Counsel (n=7), line managers (n=15), and employee representatives/works council members (n=12). Interviews were recorded with consent and averaged 64 minutes in duration. In cases where English was not the participants' native language, the interviews were conducted in their native tongue and translated; all were professionally transcribed. The interview guide, informed by the theoretical framework and piloted in two exploratory interviews, explored the organization's uses of AI in HR, perceived benefits and disadvantages of such technologies, any ethical issues and mitigation strategies employed, the existence and formality of AI governance structures and processes, and how these factors related to the organization's employer brand and its employees' trust. Second, 18 focus groups were conducted-12 with employees and 6 with recent job candidates who had previously interviewed using AI-driven technology. Focus groups were selected for this phase to provide access to group-based meaning-making processes that often produce insights and dynamics difficult to elicit through individual interviews (Morgan, 1997). The discussions explored employees' and candidates' experiences with AI-driven HR processes, focusing on the degree to which the processes felt fair, transparent, and respectful, and the type of information participants felt they lacked and would have wanted. Third, a thorough document analysis was undertaken, comprising a total of 213 organizational documents including: HR AI technology governance policies (n=24), AI ethics guidelines or codes of conduct (n=18), DEIB strategy documents (n=22), employer branding materials such as website content and advertisements (n=47), social media data (n=156 posts on LinkedIn, Twitter/X, and Glassdoor), and publicly filed reports and audits (n=14).

4.4 Data Analysis

Data analysis employed a reflexive thematic approach based on Braun and Clarke's (2006) methodology, which unfolded in six distinct phases. The researchers first immersed themselves in the data through repeated readings of all transcripts and documents, annotating relevant passages and writing reflexive memos throughout the process. This stage was followed by the generation of initial codes based on interesting or relevant passages and the systemization of these codes across the entire dataset. Candidate themes were then clustered and refined based on similarities and theoretical relevance to create final, distinct themes. Each theme was defined clearly with its defining characteristics, and the entire dataset was reviewed to ensure that the themes captured the essence of the data and did not overlap unfairly. Finally, an analytic narrative was created to explain the identified themes in relation to the overall research questions. Data management and comparison across cases was supported by Atlas.ti (v. 23) software, and theoretical sensitivity was maintained throughout the analysis process by continuously referring back to the relevant literature (Strauss & Corbin, 1998). Rigor in analysis was bolstered by researcher triangulation (two analysts independently coded a portion of the data and met to reconcile any disagreements), data triangulation (drawing evidence from interviews, focus groups, and documents in support of claims), and member-checking (a summary of preliminary findings was shared with six HR leaders in four of the participating organizations, who provided feedback that was integrated into the final report).

5. FINDINGS: AI IMPLEMENTATION, BENEFITS AND EMERGENCE OF ETHICAL COMPLEXITY

5.1 The scope and depth of AI adoption throughout the employee lifecycle

AI-driven HR tools were utilized across all twelve cases with a degree of depth and breadth that supports industry assessments of their rapid adoption (Vrontis et al., 2022). AI-powered tools were adopted across eleven of the twelve case organizations for applicant tracking and resume ranking; eight organizations implemented conversational AI to handle initial candidate screening; six had adopted programmatic, AI-driven job advertising; four had incorporated asynchronous video interview platforms featuring automated scoring; three case organizations had introduced AI-assisted candidate assessment through gamified tasks or psychometric tests delivered via an AI intermediary. When looking at performance management and development, eight organizations used AI-enabled systems for ongoing feedback, seven had deployed recommendation engines for personalized learning and development, and five organizations had implemented organizational network analysis tools to map unofficial influence patterns and identify bottlenecks in collaboration. For retention, seven case organizations were employing predictive attrition models with varying degrees of sophistication ranging from basic regression based risk scoring to complex ensemble models based on real-time behavior signals.

Organizations saw and reported substantial operational benefits which aligned well with research into the value of people analytics (Guenole et al., 2017). For talent acquisition mature, AI-enhanced screening at scale reported reductions in time-to-fill by 35-65 percent for roles with high

The most significant finding from our study was however the near universality of the retrospective discovery of unforeseen ethical complexities. All case organizations experienced what we termed an 'ethics lag' – a period between the deployment of a particular AI system and its ethical implications becoming apparent and requiring organizational intervention. This lag occurred in different ways depending on the specific AI application and organizational context. In four cases, unexpected demographic imbalances in selection or outcomes were discovered through internal audits or customer complaints; in three, employee relation incidents related to perceived surveillance triggered governance reevaluation; in five, candor surfaced from employer review sites indicating worker frustration with automated hiring processes being perceived as impersonal, opaque, and unfair; in two, regulatory questions prompted the study of ethical issues. What was analytically interesting was that this patterns of lag persisted across diverse organizations – organisations with high investment in AI capability seemed systematically underinvested in governance capability and the consequences were becoming increasingly apparent and material to the business.

5.2 Five domains of ethical challenge: empirical evidence

5.2.1 Algorithmic bias: structural reproduction of historical inequality

Algorithmic bias was perceived as a key concern in eleven of twelve case organizations and four had provided evidence of discriminatory outcomes on human metrics derived from AI systems-identified through post-deployment auditing, examination of individual candidate complaints, or systematic pipeline analysis. In the most compelling case, an 18,000 person professional services firm had deployed a third party CV ranking tool for its 2,000 person graduate recruitment program. A DEIB analyst reviewing the initial hiring pipeline (not a member of the HR tech group) noticed systemic underperformance of candidates from non-elite universities, individuals with gaps in their employment records possibly associated with caretaking duties, and candidates with names statistically linked with South Asian and Black African origins. This was despite candidates possessing objectively comparable qualifications. Upon deeper examination, the algorithm was discovered to have weighted completion of education at a set group of 12 specific universities and non-interrupted employment history, neither being legitimate criteria in this case, extremely positively based on eight years of previous hire data. While the vendor had provided a fairness certification before the hire date of this analysis, the certification tested for direct discrimination against protected classes rather than indirect, proxies for discrimination, based on features such as university prestige or continuity of employment. The finding illustrated Barocas and Selbst's (2016) concept of bias emergence through facially neutral variables correlated with protected characteristics through historical structures of inequality.

This case yielded key governance implications. The immediate organizational response was to technically adjust algorithm weighting to ameliorate the documented disparate impact of educational and employment history factors on the selection process, a move that yielded partial success but did not entirely eliminate measured differences. More importantly the organisation then recognised the importance of internal and independent audit not vendor certification as the appropriate form of bias assurance, given the differences between testing and implementation contexts and the limited ability of a vendor to truly understand the internal use context (Tippins et al., 2021).This change in perspective highlights the practical impact on resources, with HR leaders in multiple case organizations highlighting lack of internal data science capability as a key barrier to realizing fully responsible governance that does not depend on vendors for a complete guarantee of fairness.

5.2.2 Transparency and Explainability: rights, relationships and the architecture of accountability

Transparency and explainability emerged as the second biggest area of ethical challenge in the context of talent acquisition, where candidates who had been unsuccessful were challenging algorithmic selection outcomes. Seven of twelve cases reported widespread candidate desire for explanation and all of these expected that to continue and grow, driven by increasing public awareness of AI use in recruitment and also increasing candidate assertiveness regarding data rights. A clear mismatch between candidate expectations and organisational capacity was highlighted by one of the employer branding managers at a large technology firm: 'Candidates are already aware we are using AI to rank candidates… they want to know what the AI looked at, how it weighted these various features, and what could have been done differently to pass. The first of those we can approximate, but we truly cannot tell them the latter two, as we are legally prohibited from doing so by contract. This is a very bad situation legally, ethically and for the brand.'

This demonstrates what we have described elsewhere as 'accountability laundering' whereby the reliance on a vendor system that prohibits organisation knowledge of the precise workings of the algorithm makes it impossible to hold either party accountable for adverse selections. This phenomenon was described as a systemic element of the commercial applications of AI by Pasquale (2015) but this analysis shows it within the specific domain of people analytics and employer brand harm. The forthcoming EU AI Act directly addresses this governance gap by establishing that providers of high-risk AI systems must make available technical documentation that can be accessed by using organisations and informs individual-level explanations, making commercial confidentiality less of a barrier.

5.2.3 Privacy, Surveillance and the Psychological contract

Privacy issues dominated the discourse for case organizations with significant employee behavioral monitoring installed during the COVID-19 pandemic and not rolled back or adjusted after it. In three cases the scope of this monitoring which included things like communication metadata, activity patterns and even in two cases content based sentiment analysis, had exceeded what employees had anticipated and it led to immediate loss of organizational trust and harm to the employer brand (measured through Glassdoor rating changes and employee retention).

Zuboff's (2019) framework of surveillance capitalism offers a strong theoretical basis for this problem of monitoring. In essence it means treating employee behavioural data as a raw material and processing it for the purpose of creating organisational value and prediction rather than individual betterment; this exactly parallels the pursuit of people analytics for some purposes and employees clearly feel this process when they describe feeling 'watched', 'monitored' or like they are 'just data points'. This psychological violation directly correlates to the notion of the psychological contract (Rousseau, 1989), whereby the tacit promise to the employee of fair treatment and genuine relationships appears to be violated when organizations undertake invasive surveillance without any real indication that they truly care about their employees.

5.2.4 Accountability diffusion and the governance vacuum

Accountability was diffused in virtually all of the 12 case organisations as is consistent with van de Poel et al. (2012) on complex socio-technical systems. When participants were asked to specify who in their organization was actually accountable for AI assisted decisions, disparate answers indicated lack of clear chain of command, with vendors saying it was HR, HR tech saying it was Legal/Data Scientists, Legal saying it was HR/Managers and Managers saying it was the AI system itself, what Kellogg et al. (2020) call 'humanisation of technology', a key component of flawed governance and what could easily develop into accountability gaps. These gaps are often exacerbated by the dynamic nature of technology, as many AI systems were upgraded by their vendors on an ongoing basis, without corresponding updates or re-audits of organisational governance structures to reflect technical changes. This 'governance erosion under technical change' requires an adaptive, and not static, approach to governance with a view to ongoing, real-time, monitoring of AI systems (Raji et al., 2020).

5.2.5 The displacement of relational human judgment

The final major ethical concern related to the displacement of genuine human judgment, by a relationship driven interaction to management; this was most vocal among experienced HR business partners, employee relations officers, and employee representatives. They raised concern about AI-mediated interventions failing to engage with specific human circumstances and, consequently, being interpreted as uncaring or manipulative management, rather than thoughtful care. The well-documented case of a nurse being flagged by a predictive model for flight risk who then resigned as a direct result of a scripted manager conversation that was perceived as an invasion of her privacy (in addition to lacking genuine interpersonal connection) is one example, of a myriad of examples in the study, that illustrate a potential disconnect between algorithmic objectives and their human implications. The core of the issue here, supported by work on relatedness and autonomy (Van den Broeck et al., 2016), is the failure of a purely computational model to appreciate that human intervention will always carry social meaning for the recipient, and in this case, the nurse's need for relatedness and a sense of being valued as an individual was met by behavior, which she perceived correctly as being driven by surveillance not connection.

6. FINDINGS: AI ETHICS, EMPLOYER BRAND, AND THE TRUST ECOSYSTEM

6.1 Candidate Experience, Procedural Justice, and Employer Brand Formation

The focus group data collected with recent job candidates revealed consistently that candidate experience in AI-mediated recruitment contexts significantly shapes their perceptions of the employer brand through procedural justice evaluations (Lind & Tyler, 1988; Folger & Konovsky, 1989). Candidates consistently reported on three dimensions of perceived procedural justice in the AI-mediated interaction that inductively arose from the data and correlate to existing literature on procedural justice: whether the process afforded an appropriate mechanism and relevant criteria for demonstrating ability (process fairness), whether they were informed accurately and in a timely manner about how the process worked and what was being assessed (informational justice), and whether they felt they were treated with respect (interpersonal justice). These three dimensions of candidate experience map onto Colquitt's (2001) influential four-factor model of organizational justice that conceptually separates procedural justice from its distributive, informational, and interpersonal dimensions.

For candidates who perceived positively the dimensions of procedural justice in their interactions with an AI recruiter, the experiences were linked to significantly more favorable employer brand perceptions, higher acceptance intentions, and greater likelihood of word-of-mouth referrals to colleagues (Cable & Turban, 2003; Van Hoye & Lievens, 2009). Candidates with negative experiences- particularly those who felt unfairly dismissed by a system without any meaningful human interaction or feedback regarding negative assessments, or candidates who believed the system judged them based on irrelevant criteria-reported a significantly more durable and recalcitrant level of brand damage that could not be easily corrected through subsequent human

Special consideration must be given to the intersectionality of candidates' experiences. Candidates from underrepresented ethnic groups, candidates with breaks in employment, those from non-elite universities, and self-identified neurodivergent individuals reported systematically more negative informational and interpersonal justice experiences in AI-mediated recruitment contexts than their counterparts who did not hold such identities, even when the final outcome of selection remained the same. This observation suggests that because an AI treats candidates with identical, uniform logic, it can be differentially inequitable in terms of procedural justice outcomes for varying groups of people, and such differential procedurally unjust experiences cannot be observed through aggregate analyses of outcome data alone (Crenshaw, 1989). This may mean that organizations assessing the fairness of their AI tools in recruitment only through outcome data will consistently underestimate the procedurally unjust experiences generated by their systems.

6.2 Employee Trust, AI Transparency, and the Organizational Trust Ecosystem

For current employees, the connection between perceptions of the transparency with which the organization isgoverning AI systems and two types of trust established in previous research--affect-based and cognition-based trust in organizational integrity-- emerged consistently (McAllister, 1995). When employees felt their organization was communicating honestly about the use of AI systems in HR, the amount of data being collected, how it was analyzed, which decisions would be impacted, and what employee rights applied, both forms of trust were significantly higher than among employees who stated the organization was using AI "behind their back" without them being aware or given opportunity for meaningful consent. In our analysis, this relationship between transparency and trust was mediated by "benevolence"-an organizational attribute of not intending harm or exploitation. Organizations that were open about AI's capabilities, and those that candidly discussed limitations and ongoing governance challenges, signaled to employees that their best interests are protected, thereby increasing organizational trust.

Important to thisfinding is the qualification of an authenticity prerequisite for such an effect. When organizations offered communication in overly generalized or generic language that did not articulate the specific operational realities, the scope of governance, and dedicated resources or specific promises related to AI use, it did not result in significant improvements in employee trust. Instead, employees stated the generic communications revealed an intent to obscure rather than share substantive governance work, reinforcing the results of other research that shows that consistent behavioral integrity is more persuasive than communication alone in building trust (Dirks & Ferrin, 2002) and that authenticity is composed of reliability-that is, that an organization does what it says it will do (Morhart et al., 2015).

6.3 A Practice Typology: Four Governance Orientations

Our cross-case analysis revealed that organizations varied systematically across four types of governance practices related to AI ethics, based on the extent of integration and depth of commitment to ethical deployment. This typology follows the developmental stages often discussed in corporate social responsibility (CSR) literature (Carroll, 1979; Matten & Crane, 2005) and offers a practical framework for assessment and development planning.

Three organizations fell into the category of Minimalist Compliance. These organizations viewed AI ethics purely as a legal and technical exercise of satisfying regulations and minimal employer/candidate expectations. They utilized external vendor assurances without internal checks for fairness or algorithmic validity beyond what was stipulated in vendor contracts and generally provided minimum disclosures required by law, only addressing ethical breaches once they resulted in legal trouble or formal complaints. The organizations lacked formal roles or committees dedicated to AI ethics, and had not historically conducted impact assessments when evaluating HR technology purchases. While two organizations in this category had experienced algorithmic bias in the past, neither had implemented significant process changes to avoid similar occurrences in the future.

Four organizations demonstrated Reactive Ethics governance. Although these organizations had more in-depth responses than the Minimalist Compliance organizations, these responses tended to be after-the-fact and primarily in response to crises rather than through forward-looking governance planning. They had the capacity for some internal testing, had established clear response plans after events, and were starting to formalize cross-functional oversight committees. Communication around AI ethics with employees/candidates was often limited to standard disclaimers in employment terms, reflecting the gaps between aspirations and realities.

Three organizations demonstrated Proactive Governance.These companies have robust pre-deployment due diligence processes for assessing AI tools, ongoing monitoring programs to evaluate algorithm fairness and impact, and have invested in creating cross-functional oversight bodies with authentic advisory capacity and the power to delay deployment. These organizations tend to require extensive testing data from vendors, conducted their own additional tests, and have built significant internal capacity in data science devoted to assessing algorithmic integrity. Their external communication tends to be somewhat more specific, though still predominantly focused on Risk Mitigation rather than framing ethical AI governance as a proactive source of positive brand value.

Two organizations-large global multinational corporations with established public employer brands-achieved Integrated Governance.These organizations have fully embedded AI ethics considerations across HR strategy, their branding and public narrative, DEIB initiatives, and overall organizational identity. These organizations have dedicated, authority-carrying AI Ethics Committees empowered to delay or halt any system deployment found to be problematic; provide AI explanations to candidates about the information processed by a system; have secured vendor contract clauses allowing for mandatory bias auditing; and have integrated explicit and verified commitments related to AI ethics into their employer brand messaging. For these organizations, AI ethics is not merely about avoiding harm, but a way to express core organizational values and a tangible source of organizational differentiation-a behavior signaled effectively according to Spence's (1973) signaling theory of expensive, visible, and verifiable organizational commitments.

7. THE HUMAN-CENTERED ETHICAL AI (HCEAI) FRAMEWORK

The Human-Centered Ethical AI (HCEAI) framework synthesized findings from across the domains investigated to produce an integrated model of governance over the lifecycle of AI deployment in HR. The HCEAI framework's four key pillars address discrete, although interconnected, aspects of governance. The normative core commitment is that AI in HR should not solely optimize organizational efficiency at the expense of human flourishing; it should serve the goals of enhancing human potential and well-being.

7.1 Pillar One: Foundational Principles

Six foundational ethical principles guide every AI-related decision and process in HR. These principles, based on the literature cited above in AI ethics, stakeholders, and human-centered design, function not as aspirational ideals, but as specific, practical criteria by which actual system choices and organizational processes are evaluated.

Human Primacy: It is incumbent on the organization to ensure that AI is deployed in ways that augment human capacity and improve work processes without detracting from human dignity, autonomy, and overall well-being (Shneiderman, 2020). An organization must be able to articulate a justification for its use of AI beyond claims of mere efficiency that does not demonstrably sacrifice individual interests, and this human-in-the-loop design implies a substantive role for humans, beyond mere algorithmic decision validation, where human judgment, empathy and context are incorporated into each decision (Kellogg et al., 2020).

Substantive Fairness: AI systems deployed in HR must avoid generating unfair or biased outcomes on the basis of protected categories, and they must undergo rigorous testing and monitoring to ensure they comply with this standard. Acknowledging the impossibility of perfect fairness (Chouldechova, 2017; Kleinberg et al., 2016), the framework requires that explicit and meaningful multi-stakeholder decisions are made to identify which particular fairness definition(s) apply to specific applications; that these choices be communicated openly to stakeholders; that the criteria are explained; and that it can be verified by external auditors. Moreover, it requires that HR apply an intersectional approach to assessing fairness, one which recognizes that combinations of protected characteristics may produce uniquely disadvantaged outcomes that are overlooked in single-axis testing (Crenshaw, 1989).

Meaningful Transparency: The organization must employ a graded approach to disclosure about AI, which ranges from a basic notice of the system's existence for any HR AI application, to providing criterion transparency (explanation of the variables the system is using to make decisions) for any system impacting job assessment, performance appraisal, promotion or development, up to individualistic explanation of adverse outcome criteria, upon request, for high-stakes selection and employment-related decisions (Wachter et al., 2017; Goodman & Flaxman, 2017). Importantly, the level of detail of each form of transparency should be geared towards an employee audience rather than technical jargon, and each type of disclosure must contain a human-readable explanation of the information.

Privacy and Proportionality: Data must only be collected if it serves a necessary, legitimate, organizational purpose that cannot be fulfilled by less invasive means, and that it should be retained only for as long as needed. Intensity of surveillance needs to be in proportion to the recognized value of collecting that data, relative to its risk to privacy (Zuboff, 2019). The temptation organizations feel to expand data collection simply because it is feasible must be resisted in favor of the rule that any data collected for HR AI systems be tied to a specifically identified and disclosed purpose and employees must have readily accessible rights to access, rectify and delete their own personal data.

Accountability and Traceable Human Oversight: This principle directly targets the fragmentation of responsibility often seen when AI systems are employed by various parties in an organization. A clear chain of command is established, ensuring that specific individuals bear responsibility for decisions made at every point in the AI system lifecycle, such as design, acquisition, implementation and sunsetting; all actions and decisions must be documented such that evidence can be used to understand what occurred if something went wrong (Raji et al., 2020). Override capability for human decision-makers must be built into each system; there must be reporting, analysis of these overrides and any significant fluctuations in override rates monitored as a governance indicator, and human actions taken to override must be rigorously documented with accompanying explanations.

Continuous Improvement and Adaptive Governance: Organizations must recognize that AI systems are not static, that contexts and circumstances evolve, and that new harms may arise as systems are used in ways that were not predicted at deployment. Regular auditing (annual, but more frequent if the application is very high volume or its use is rapidly changing) and clear mechanisms for raising complaints and implementing revisions based on those inputs, audit findings and new external requirements such as updated regulations, ensure a dynamic, responsive system (Mittelstadt et al., 2016).

7.2 Pillar Two: Multi-Level Governance Architecture

This pillar establishes a three-part hierarchy of responsibility designed to streamline the governance of AI in HR without diffused ownership.

Executive Sponsorship (Strategic Tier): Each organization must have an individual leader-preferably the Chief Human Resources Officer-who owns AI ethics in HR. The Executive Sponsor will advocate for resources, foster an organizational culture of ethical compliance, ensure that AI ethics is integrated into overarching organizational risk management strategies, and maintain ultimate accountability for adherence to the HCEAI framework. Executive sponsorship is a crucial element in overcoming resistance from operational leaders who prioritize efficiency over fairness or from external vendor pressures.

Cross-Functional AI Ethics Committee (Operational Tier): A committee of representatives from HR, legal, data science, DEIB, employee relations, and crucially, from the employee body, will provide ongoing evaluation and guidance for AI implementation. With real authority to halt deployment and demand modifications when ethical concerns are identified, this committee will convene at regular intervals to monitor compliance, evaluate proposals, and respond to incidents. The inclusion of employees is essential, drawing upon the stakeholder theory to give voices to individuals who will be most affected by the systems in question (Mitchell et al., 1997).

AI Governance Protocols (Process Tier): For each HR AI application, a dedicated, written protocol will detail its usage, the types of data collected and analyzed, fairness metric selection rationale, internal testing results, disclosures to individuals and oversight mechanisms. These protocols serve as contractual documents for both internal operations and vendor partnerships. They function as formal mechanisms of internal control and also as evidence in cases of internal or external auditing.

7.3 Pillar Three: Operational Lifecycle Practices

These are specific, day-to-day processes to ensure adherence to the principles and structure laid out above, extending throughout the entire lifecycle of an AI system.

Pre-Deployment Ethical Impact Assessment: Every AI system to be used for HR applications must undergo a rigorous ethical impact assessment before deployment.

This assessment must consider the business purpose, data implications, fairness criteria and findings, transparency and disclosure levels, human oversight requirements and an analysis of regulatory compliance. If these criteria are not met, deployment is automatically blocked and is not subject to any human decision unless an entirely new system meeting all criteria is developed.

Continuous Fairness Monitoring: The outcomes of all AI-driven HR decisions are tracked and continuously analyzed over time. Monitoring processes should be rigorous, allowing for detection of unintended discriminatory effects at the outset through the measurement of key HR metrics by relevant demographic subgroups. Any identified deviations are addressed with corrective action plans.

Human Override and Contestation Mechanisms: There must be clear guidelines on how to override AI decisions at every point in a workflow. The reasoning for each override must be clearly documented, and there must be an escalation process for when override frequency or patterns suggest systematic problems in the algorithm. Individuals who interact with HR AI should also have the ability to formally contest an outcome, appeal to human decision-makers, and provide additional information that may not have been accounted for in an automated assessment. These procedures are presented as a sign of good HR practice and positive employer brand value.

Vendor Governance Integration: Contracts for AI tools must clearly stipulate the organization's expectations for the tools, including disclosures, rights to audit, and vendor accountability for algorithm fairness, performance and impacts on diverse user groups. Vendor selection processes prioritize those who willingly comply with such demands, moving beyond simple technology features to consider ethical performance of partners.

7.4 Pillar Four: Communication, Employer Brand Integration, and External Accountability

This pillar acknowledges that the demonstrable practice of responsible AI ethics creates tangible employer brand value that must be actively communicated and continuously reinforced through consistent behavior.

Internal Communication: Employees must be fully informed in accessible terms about how AI is being used in HR, what specific systems are involved, the types of data that are being collected, and their rights and appeal mechanisms. Authentic communication of these facts, including candor about challenges and ongoing governance efforts, will foster greater employee trust and engagement, unlike vague or superficial statements that have been shown to reduce credibility (Dirks & Ferrin, 2002).

External Employer Brand Communication: Organizations must be able to link their claims about responsible AI use to specific, verifiable organizational processes and behavior that meet Spence's (1973) conditions for signaling-that the practice is specific, costly to replicate, and consistently enacted. Employer brand communications should highlight specific governance practices rather than generic value statements and must be demonstrably aligned with the actual candidate and employee experience of using the organization's AI systems. Periodic external audits and public disclosure of aggregate findings related to those audits can also be powerful mechanisms of external accountability.

8. MANAGERIAL IMPLICATIONS AND ACADEMIC CONTRIBUTIONS

8.1 Theoretical Contributions

In several ways, this chapter contributes to the theoretical bodies of literature it draws on and combines. To the literature on AI ethics, by empirically tracing the "ethics lag" (the systemic temporal gap between AI adoption and organizational acknowledgement of the ethical complexity it entails) we are adding a longitudinal perspective to the literature on the operationalization gap (Mittelstadt et al. 2016; Whittlestone et al. 2019) and implying that static governance assessments at the point of deployment understate the governance requirements for AI systems as their ethical implications unfold during their deployment into complex organizational environments. For the literature on employer branding, by showing empirically that AI governance impacts employer brand perceptions through procedural justice perceptions rather than simply via an evaluation of outcome level results, we are extending prior models on the formation of employer brand perceptions (Cable & Turban, 2003; Backhaus & Tikoo, 2004) and recommending that procedural justice theory (Lind & Tyler, 1988) be integrated more prominently into the literature on employer branding. To the organizational trust literature, by demonstrating that AI governance transparency impacts affect based trust (i.e., perceived organizational benevolence) more than cognition based trust (i.e., perceived organizational competence) we are extending the two component model on trust to AI governance (McAllister, 1995) and arguing that organizations wanting to use AI governance as a source of trust in the organization need to focus on authenticity rather than the technical sophistication of their communication.

The practice typology developed in this chapter – minimal compliance, reactive ethics, proactive governance, integrated governance – is a capability maturity model contribution to the literature on governance maturity, parallel to capability maturity models in other fields (Raji et al. 2020). It provides a practical and theoretically grounded framework with which to discuss AI ethics governance development.

Critically, it also shows empirically that governance orientation is associated with significant differences in employer brand perceptions, levels of employee trust, and DEIB outcomes – providing an evidence base that complements the theoretical articulation of the business case for investing in AI ethics that exists in prior literature.

8.2 Managerial Implications for HR Leaders

The main managerial implication of this chapter for HR leaders is that establishing effective AI governance competence is now a critical HR core competency rather than a niche, technical or legal domain expertise. HR leaders cannot effectively discharge their responsibilities in an AI-empowered HR environment if they lack a functional ability to engage with the ethical considerations of AI system design-e.g. If they cannot ask pertinent technical questions of vendors, interpret the findings of fairness audits, or articulate the inherent normative assumptions that distinguish alternative fairness approaches. To this end, HR must invest strategically in developing AI literacy among HR practitioners at all levels, beyond just the functions of HR technology and people analytics (Tippins et al. 2021).

The HR procurement function is another critical but underappreciated leveraged point for governance. Demanding detailed fairness testing data from vendors, treating transparency and explainability as essential vendor selection criteria, and stipulating contractual governance provisions (including rights to independent testing and notification of system updates), build accountability mechanisms into vendor behavior that will not emerge on the market in response to market-level dynamics alone. Many HR technology leaders we interviewed for this study noted that implementing these rigorous procurement level governance requirements profoundly altered the competitive landscape by pushing previously less transparent vendors towards greater transparency, once the organizations demonstrated to vendors that transparency was no longer a mere preference but a fundamental condition of purchase. This implies that when HR leaders implement rigorous procurement-stage governance requirements, they not only manage organizational risk but contribute to creating the organizational landscape conditions that facilitate responsible AI adoption in HR (Raji et al. 2020).

8.3 Managerial Implications for Employer Branding Professionals

Employer branding professionals operate at the crossroads of AI governance and talent communication. The critical challenge and opportunity stems from the authenticity imperative that runs throughout this chapter: in a fast-paced and amplified digital labor market, communications about AI governance that fall short of organizational reality risk significant and asymmetric reputational damage, even with the best of intentions (Van Hoye & Lievens, 2009). In turn, organizations that actually possess substantive AI governance practices have a distinctive competitive differentiator that is likely to become increasingly attractive as more talent (particularly young, digitally-savvy talent among whom many organizations compete for priority access) begins to prioritize ethical alignment in their employers.

The principal managerial recommendation for employer branding professionals is thus to become highly informed about the reality of the organization's AI governance practices before engaging in external communications about these efforts, and to prepare to refrain from external communication altogether if the reality does not align with the message. The employer brand equity that can be generated through credibly managed AI ethics communications can be substantial and lasting (Fombrun, 1996); the damage that can result from communicated aspirational positions is equally substantial and far more enduring. Disciplined grounding of communications about AI governance in actual organizational processes thus serves not only the ethical imperative of truthfulness but also the strategic imperative of protecting the organization's reputation over time.

8.4 Managerial Implications for Policy Makers

The regulatory approach underpinning the EU Artificial Intelligence Act (European Parliament and Council, 2024) which places binding obligations on high-risk employment AI, requiring conformity assessment, transparency standards and human oversight obligations, is supported by our empirical results. The evidence that governance orientation is powerfully shaped by regulatory constraints (coercive isomorphism) means that voluntary standards and industry self-regulation alone will likely not be sufficient to achieve adequate governance quality given the stakes involved in employment AI. Organizations investing in ethical AI governance in an un regulated market would compete for talent and contracts against less responsible organizations, leading to a structural market failure that will only be overcome through regulation. Our results are consistent with extending the EU AI Act to other jurisdictions and developing sector-specific implementation guidelines that detail specific actions for HR AI governance.

9. LIMITATIONS AND FUTURE RESEARCH

The theoretical propositions and empirical insights presented in this chapter should be considered in light of its limitations. Being a qualitative multi-case study, the work is able to analytically generalize its findings (Yin, 2018), providing new conceptual developments and illumination of important mechanisms and patterns rather than the establishment of statistical prevalence in a clearly defined population. The sample, predominantly comprising organizations located in Europe and North America, may therefore not translate to AI governance in other geographic locations, such as Asia, Africa, or Latin America, given differing market structures, regulatory environments, and cultural values relating to privacy, employee voice, and transparency. In

In terms of specific avenues of future research, several domains seem particularly critical. Firstly, the use of experimental methods to compare candidate and employee perceptions and reactions to various specific mechanisms of transparency and explainability – from procedural information about system workings and counterfactual descriptions to granular algorithmic transparency reporting – is needed to provide clear and causally identifiable guidance for how to shape communications about AI governance (Wachter et al. 2017). Secondly, international comparative research into how cultural variables (power distance, individualism-collectivism, uncertainty avoidance, long-term vs short-term orientation etc.) mediate between AI governance practices and subsequent effects on organizational trust, perceptions of the employer brand, and DEIB outcomes will substantially generalize the theoretical framework outlined here. Thirdly, quantitative research on AI governance maturity that validates a measurement scale for the four stage practice typology introduced here is necessary to determine the size and significance of the association between governance maturity and the organization's outcomes on a large scale, providing the statistically evidenced arguments for investments in AI ethics that organizations need. Fourthly, research on the assessment of intersectional bias is sorely needed for development and validation of rigorous methodologies of intersectional algorithmic fairness testing within the HR domain (Crenshaw, 1989), highlighting and beginning to address an important area of concern in both literature and practice. Lastly, the use of vendor ecosystem research can provide insights into how governance requirements on the part of HR organizations cascade down through the vendor market for HR technology, and what changes that necessitates in vendor practice.

10. CONCLUSION

In this chapter, we have argued on both theoretical and empirical grounds that responsible AI governance is essential not only as a moral and regulatory imperative but also as a source of strategic competitive advantage for organizations aiming to embrace a human-centered identity. The theoretical arguments are built by drawing on stakeholder theory (Freeman, 1984; Mitchell et al., 1997), signaling theory (Spence, 1973), institutional theory (DiMaggio & Powell, 1983), and organizational identity theory (Albert & Whetten, 1985; Dutton & Dukerich, 1991) to establish that AI governance decisions are essentially identity expressers, signals, and stakeholders affecters. They impact perceived employer brand, levels of trust within the organization, and the overall quality of the employment relationship in a way that is directly linked to organizational performance.

The evidence presented from the multi-case study reveals five distinct categories of ethical concerns-algorithmic bias, transparency gaps, privacy violations, accountability diffusion and erosion of meaningful human judgment in relation to automated decision-making-and details the organizational mechanisms by which they result in negative consequences for the employer brand, employee trust, and DEIB outcomes. The framework's typology of four different governance orientations, which empirically distinguishes organizations that are managing these concerns successfully from those that are not, provides organizations with a developmentally-informed map of what it takes to achieve the appropriate level of governance maturity.

The framework presented here-the Human-Centered Ethical AI (HCEAI) framework in section 7-synthesizes these findings into four integrated pillars: Foundational Principles (human supremacy, substantive fairness, meaningful transparency, proportionality and privacy, accountability and traceable human oversight, and continuous learning); Multi-Level Governance Architecture (top-down sponsorship, mid-level AI Ethics Committee, and process-level Governance Protocols); Operational Practices (pre-deployment impact assessment, ongoing monitoring for fairness and bias, mechanisms for human challenge and override of algorithmic decisions, and inclusion of vendor governance considerations); and Integration with Communications and Employer Branding (transparent internal messaging and credible external signals regarding the organization's ethical use of AI). What distinguishes the HCEAI framework from independent initiatives in related domains (e.g., separate efforts around AI ethics, employer branding, DEIB, procedural justice, and human-centered organizations) is its interconnectedness, creating a governance logic that is more coherently ethical and organizationally effective than any approach addressing these dimensions in isolation.

The changes that AI will bring to human resources management are irreversible and are fundamentally desirable in their potential to improve evaluation processes, customize employee experiences, predict turnover risk and expand access to talent pools-but they require a new framework for realizing their positive potential: one that recognizes that responsible governance, rather than simply speed or efficiency, is the foundation upon which the ethical realization of these benefits rests. The demand for these features of responsible AI in HR is mounting from stakeholders, including employees, the regulatory community, and clients. The evidence in this chapter suggests that organizations can either meet these expectations head-on by proactive adoption of ethical AI governance, or they will eventually be forced to do so; proactive adoption is far more likely to lead to sustained competitive advantages through improved talent attraction, deeper employee trust, better DEIB outcomes, and an enhanced organizational reputation. Now is the time for meaningful, proactive and integrated AI ethics governance in HR.

REFERENCES

Albert, S., & Whetten, D. A. (1985). Organizational identity. *Research in Organizational Behavior*, *7*, 263–295.

Ambler, T., & Barrow, S. (1996). The employer brand. *Journal of Brand Management*, *4*(3), 185–206. DOI: 10.1057/bm.1996.42

Angrave, D., Charlwood, A., Kirkpatrick, I., Lawrence, M., & Stuart, M. (2016). HR and analytics: Why HR is set to fail the big data challenge. *Human Resource Management Journal*, *26*(1), 1–11. DOI: 10.1111/1748-8583.12090

Backhaus, K., & Tikoo, S. (2004). Conceptualizing and researching employer branding. *Career Development International*, *9*(5), 501–517. DOI: 10.1108/13620430410550754

Barocas, S., & Selbst, A. D. (2016). Big data's disparate impact. *California Law Review*, *104*(3), 671–732. DOI: 10.15779/Z38BG31

Bogen, M., & Rieke, A. (2018). *Help wanted: An examination of hiring algorithms, equity, and bias*. Upturn.

Braun, V., & Clarke, V. (2006). Using thematic analysis in psychology. *Qualitative Research in Psychology*, *3*(2), 77–101. DOI: 10.1191/1478088706qp063oa

Brunsson, N. (1989). *The organization of hypocrisy: Talk, decisions and actions in organizations*. Wiley.

Cable, D. M., & Turban, D. B. (2003). The value of organizational reputation in the recruitment context: A brand-equity perspective. *Journal of Applied Social Psychology*, *33*(11), 2244–2266. DOI: 10.1111/j.1559-1816.2003.tb01883.x

Cappelli, P., & Tavis, A. (2018). HR goes agile. *Harvard Business Review*, *96*(2), 46–52.

Carroll, A. B. (1979). A three-dimensional conceptual model of corporate performance. *Academy of Management Review*, *4*(4), 497–505. DOI: 10.2307/257850

Chouldechova, A. (2017). Fair prediction with disparate impact: A study of bias in recidivism prediction instruments. *Big Data*, *5*(2), 153–163. DOI: 10.1089/big.2016.0047

Colquitt, J. A. (2001). On the dimensionality of organizational justice: A construct validation of a measure. *The Journal of Applied Psychology*, *86*(3), 386–400. DOI: 10.1037/0021-9010.86.3.386

Crenshaw, K. (1989). Demarginalizing the intersection of race and sex: A Black feminist critique of antidiscrimination doctrine, feminist theory and antiracist politics. *University of Chicago Legal Forum, 1989*(1), 139–167.

Dastin, J. (2018, October 10). Amazon scraps secret AI recruiting tool that showed bias against women. Reuters.

Deci, E. L., & Ryan, R. M. (2000). The 'what' and 'why' of goal pursuits: Human needs and the self-determination of behavior. *Psychological Inquiry, 11*(4), 227–268. DOI: 10.1207/S15327965PLI1104_01

DiMaggio, P. J., & Powell, W. W. (1983). The iron cage revisited: Institutional isomorphism and collective rationality in organizational fields. *American Sociological Review, 48*(2), 147–160. DOI: 10.2307/2095101

Dirks, K. T., & Ferrin, D. L. (2002). Trust in leadership: Meta-analytic findings and implications for research and practice. *The Journal of Applied Psychology, 87*(4), 611–628. DOI: 10.1037/0021-9010.87.4.611

Donaldson, T., & Preston, L. E. (1995). The stakeholder theory of the corporation: Concepts, evidence, and implications. *Academy of Management Review, 20*(1), 65–91. DOI: 10.2307/258887

Dutton, J. E., & Dukerich, J. M. (1991). Keeping an eye on the mirror: Image and identity in organizational adaptation. *Academy of Management Journal, 34*(3), 517–554. DOI: 10.2307/256405

Edwards, M. R. (2010). An integrative review of employer branding and OB theory. *Personnel Review, 39*(1), 5–23. DOI: 10.1108/00483481011012809

Eisenhardt, K. M. (1989). Building theories from case study research. *Academy of Management Review, 14*(4), 532–550. DOI: 10.2307/258557

Eisenhardt, K. M., & Graebner, M. E. (2007). Theory building from cases: Opportunities and challenges. *Academy of Management Journal, 50*(1), 25–32. DOI: 10.5465/amj.2007.24160888

European Commission. (2019). *Ethics guidelines for trustworthy AI.* High-Level Expert Group on Artificial Intelligence.

European Parliament and Council. (2024). *Regulation (EU) 2024/1689 laying down harmonised rules on artificial intelligence (Artificial Intelligence Act).* Official Journal of the European Union.

Folger, R., & Konovsky, M. A. (1989). Effects of procedural and distributive justice on reactions to pay raise decisions. *Academy of Management Journal, 32*(1), 115–130. DOI: 10.2307/256422

Fombrun, C. J. (1996). *Reputation: Realizing value from the corporate image*. Harvard Business School Press.

Freeman, R. E. (1984). *Strategic management: A stakeholder approach*. Pitman.

Gilmore, J. H., & Pine, B. J. (2007). *Authenticity: What consumers really want*. Harvard Business Review Press.

Gioia, D. A., Schultz, M., & Corley, K. G. (2000). Organizational identity, image, and adaptive instability. *Academy of Management Review*, *25*(1), 63–81. DOI: 10.2307/259263

Goodman, B., & Flaxman, S. (2017). European Union regulations on algorithmic decision-making and a 'right to explanation.'. *AI Magazine*, *38*(3), 50–57. DOI: 10.1609/aimag.v38i3.2741

Green, B. (2019). The false promise of risk assessments: Epistemic racism and the limits of fairness. *Proceedings of the 2019 ACM Conference on Fairness, Accountability, and Transparency*, 337–344. DOI: 10.1145/3287560.3287591

Guenole, N., Ferrar, J., & Feinzig, S. (2017). *The power of people: How successful organizations use workforce analytics to improve business performance*. Pearson FT Press.

Highhouse, S. (2008). Stubborn reliance on intuition and subjectivity in employee selection. *Industrial and Organizational Psychology: Perspectives on Science and Practice*, *1*(3), 333–342. DOI: 10.1111/j.1754-9434.2008.00058.x

Jobin, A., Ienca, M., & Vayena, E. (2019). The global landscape of AI ethics guidelines. *Nature Machine Intelligence*, *1*(9), 389–399. DOI: 10.1038/s42256-019-0088-2

Kellogg, K. C., Valentine, M. A., & Christin, A. (2020). Algorithms at work: The new contested terrain of control. *The Academy of Management Annals*, *14*(1), 366–410. DOI: 10.5465/annals.2018.0174

Kleinberg, J., Mullainathan, S., & Raghavan, M. (2016). Inherent trade-offs in the fair determination of risk scores. *Proceedings of the 8th Innovations in Theoretical Computer Science Conference*. DOI: 10.4230/LIPIcs.ITCS.2017.43

Kochling, A., & Wehner, M. C. (2020). Discriminated by an algorithm: A systematic review of discrimination and fairness by algorithmic decision-making in the context of HR recruitment and HR development. *Business Research, 13*(3), 795–848. 1. DOI: 10.1007/s40685-020-00134-w

Langer, M., Konig, C. J., & Papathanasiou, M. (2019). Highly automated job interviews: Acceptance under the influence of stakes. *International Journal of Selection and Assessment*, *27*(3), 217–234. DOI: 10.1111/ijsa.12246

Leventhal, G. S. (1980). What should be done with equity theory? In Gergen, K. J., Greenberg, M. S., & Willis, R. H. (Eds.), *Social exchange: Advances in theory and research* (pp. 27–55). Plenum Press. DOI: 10.1007/978-1-4613-3087-5_2

Lind, E. A., & Tyler, T. R. (1988). *The social psychology of procedural justice*. Plenum Press. DOI: 10.1007/978-1-4899-2115-4

Marler, J. H., & Boudreau, J. W. (2017). An evidence-based review of HR analytics. *International Journal of Human Resource Management*, *28*(1), 3–26. DOI: 10.1080/09585192.2016.1244699

Matten, D., & Crane, A. (2005). Corporate citizenship: Toward an extended theoretical conceptualization. *Academy of Management Review*, *30*(1), 166–179. DOI: 10.5465/amr.2005.15281448

Mayer, R. C., Davis, J. H., & Schoorman, F. D. (1995). An integrative model of organizational trust. *Academy of Management Review*, *20*(3), 709–734. DOI: 10.2307/258792

McAllister, D. J. (1995). Affect- and cognition-based trust as foundations for interpersonal cooperation in organizations. *Academy of Management Journal*, *38*(1), 24–59. DOI: 10.2307/256727

Mitchell, R. K., Agle, B. R., & Wood, D. J. (1997). Toward a theory of stakeholder identification and salience: Defining the principle of who and what really counts. *Academy of Management Review*, *22*(4), 853–886. DOI: 10.2307/259247

Mittelstadt, B. D., Allo, P., Taddeo, M., Wachter, S., & Floridi, L. (2016). The ethics of algorithms: Mapping the debate. *Big Data & Society*, *3*(2), 1–21. DOI: 10.1177/2053951716679679

Morgan, D. L. (1997). *Focus groups as qualitative research* (2nd ed.). Sage. DOI: 10.4135/9781412984287

Morhart, F., Malär, L., Guèvremont, A., Girardin, F., & Grohmann, B. (2015). Brand authenticity: An integrative framework and measurement scale. *Journal of Consumer Psychology*, *25*(2), 200–218. DOI: 10.1016/j.jcps.2014.11.006

Morrison, E. W., & Robinson, S. L. (1997). When employees feel betrayed: A model of how psychological contract violation develops. *Academy of Management Review*, *22*(1), 226–256. DOI: 10.2307/259230

Nkomo, S. M., & Hoobler, J. M. (2014). A historical perspective on diversity ideologies in the United States: Reflections on human resource management research and practice. *Human Resource Management Review*, *24*(3), 245–257. DOI: 10.1016/j.hrmr.2014.03.006

OECD. (2019). *Recommendation of the Council on Artificial Intelligence (OECD/LEGAL/0449)*. OECD.

Oswald, F. L., & Putka, D. J. (Eds.). (2016). *Statistical methods for personnel research*. Society for Industrial and Organizational Psychology.

Pasquale, F. (2015). *The black box society: The secret algorithms that control money and information*. Harvard University Press. DOI: 10.4159/harvard.9780674736061

Raji, I. D., Smart, A., White, R. N., Mitchell, M., Gebru, T., Hutchinson, B., Smith-Loud, J., Theron, D., & Barnes, P. (2020). Closing the AI accountability gap: Defining an end-to-end framework for internal algorithmic auditing. *Proceedings of the ACM Co* DOI: 10.1145/3351095.3372873

Rousseau, D. M. (1989). Psychological and implied contracts in organizations. *Employee Responsibilities and Rights Journal*, *2*(2), 121–139. DOI: 10.1007/BF01384942

Schmidt, F. L., & Hunter, J. E. (1998). The validity and utility of selection methods in personnel psychology: Practical and theoretical implications of 85 years of research findings. *Psychological Bulletin*, *124*(2), 262–274. DOI: 10.1037/0033-2909.124.2.262

Shneiderman, B. (2020). Human-centered artificial intelligence: Reliable, safe & trustworthy. *International Journal of Human-Computer Interaction*, *36*(6), 495–504. DOI: 10.1080/10447318.2020.1741118

Shore, L. M., Randel, A. E., Chung, B. G., Dean, M. A., Holcombe Ehrhart, K., & Singh, G. (2011). Inclusion and diversity in work groups: A review and model for future research. *Journal of Management*, *37*(4), 1262–1289. DOI: 10.1177/0149206310385943

Spence, M. (1973). Job market signaling. *The Quarterly Journal of Economics, 87*(3), 355–374. DOI: 10.2307/1882010

Strauss, A., & Corbin, J. (1998). *Basics of qualitative research: Techniques and procedures for developing grounded theory* (2nd ed.). Sage.

Tippins, N. T., Oswald, F. L., & McPhail, S. M. (2021). Scientific, legal, and ethical concerns about AI-based personnel selection tools: A call to action. *Personnel Assessment and Decisions, 7*(2), 1–22. DOI: 10.25035/pad.2021.02.001

van de Poel, I., Royakkers, L., & Zwart, S. D. (2012). *Moral responsibility and the problem of many hands*. Routledge.

Van den Broeck, A., Ferris, D. L., Chang, C.-H., & Rosen, C. C. (2016). A review of self-determination theory's basic psychological needs at work. *Journal of Management, 42*(5), 1195–1229. DOI: 10.1177/0149206316632058

Van Hoye, G., & Lievens, F. (2009). Tapping the grapevine: A closer look at word-of-mouth as a recruitment source. *The Journal of Applied Psychology, 94*(2), 341–352. DOI: 10.1037/a0014066

Vrontis, D., Christofi, M., Pereira, V., Tarba, S., Makrides, A., & Trichina, E. (2022). Artificial intelligence, robotics, advanced technologies and human resource management: A systematic review. *International Journal of Human Resource Management, 33*(6).

Wachter, S., Mittelstadt, B., & Russell, C. (2017). Counterfactual explanations without opening the black box: Automated decisions and the GDPR. *Harvard Journal of Law & Technology, 31*(2), 841–887.

Whittlestone, J., Nyrup, R., Alexandrova, A., & Cave, S. (2019). The role and limits of principles in AI ethics: Towards a focus on tensions. Proceedings of the 2019 AAAI/ACM Conference on AI, Ethics, and Society, 195–200. DOI: 10.1145/3306618.3

Yin, R. K. (2018). *Case study research and applications: Design and methods* (6th ed.). Sage.

Zuboff, S. (2019). *The age of surveillance capitalism: The fight for a human future at the new frontier of power*. PublicAffairs.

Chapter 4
Leading from Within: An Endomarketing-Based Framework

João Reis
http://orcid.org/0009-0007-2098-3584
ISLA Santarém, Portugal

Carlos Galveias
ISLA Santarém, Portugal

João Farinha
http://orcid.org/0000-0002-4193-8914
ISLA Santarém, Portugal

Maria de Fátima Pina
http://orcid.org/0000-0003-3738-1153
ISLA Santarém, Portugal

Christian Zhelev
University of National and World Economy, Sofia, Bulgaria

Nuno Nogueira
http://orcid.org/0000-0003-2400-3567
ISLA Santarém, Portugal

ABSTRACT

This chapter examines leadership-driven endomarketing as a core mechanism for building internal brand advocacy and strengthening employer branding. It conceptualizes endomarketing as a strategic, leadership-led internal marketing process that promotes organizational vision, brand values, and employee experience to transform employees into credible brand ambassadors. The proposed framework links leadership communication, internal campaigns, and participatory practices with outcomes such as employee engagement, identification, and voluntary advocacy on digital and offline channels. By articulating the interplay between internal employer branding, endomarketing tools, and human-centered organizational culture, the chapter formulates propositions and a research agenda for empirical studies in diverse sectors and cultural contexts.

DOI: 10.4018/979-8-2600-2178-1.ch004

1. Introduction

Internal employer branding and endomarketing have gained growing attention as organizations seek to build sustainable competitive advantage through people in increasingly turbulent markets (Staniec, 2021). Grounded in the internal marketing tradition, which conceptualizes employees as internal customers and jobs as internal products, endomarketing reframes internal communication and people management as a strategic marketing process directed toward employees (Berry, 1981; Grönroos, 1990). From this perspective, leadership-driven internal marketing is not merely a set of communication tactics, but a philosophy that aligns employee experience, organizational culture, and brand promise.

Classical internal marketing research emphasizes that effective service quality and external brand delivery depend on motivated, informed, and engaged employees who understand and internalize the organization's vision and values (Berry, 1981; Grönroos, 1990). Endomarketing extends this logic by positioning leaders as central actors in orchestrating internal campaigns, symbolic actions, and participative practices that translate the external brand into meaningful, lived experiences for employees (Bekin, 2004). In human-centered organizations, such practices are particularly salient because they seek not only compliance but genuine identification and advocacy.

The link between internal employer branding, engagement, and performance is increasingly supported by empirical studies showing that internal branding activities and perceived organizational support reinforce the employee value proposition and employee engagement (Staniec, 2021; Zhang, 2024). Building on Kahn's (1990) seminal work on psychological conditions of personal engagement, this chapter conceptualizes leadership-driven endomarketing as a mechanism that shapes the cognitive, emotional, and behavioral dimensions of employee engagement, thereby fostering internal brand advocacy (Kahn, 1990; Saks, 2006). Social identity theory further suggests that when employees perceive alignment between their own values and the organizational brand, they are more likely to define themselves in terms of their organizational membership and to act as active brand ambassadors (Tajfel & Turner, 1979).

Against this backdrop, the present chapter examines leadership-driven endomarketing as a core mechanism for building internal brand advocacy and strengthening employer branding in human-centered organizations. The main objective is to propose a conceptual framework linking leadership communication, endomarketing tools, and organizational culture to employee engagement, identification, and advocacy outcomes. A secondary objective is to formulate theoretically grounded propositions that can guide future empirical research across sectors and cultural contexts. Accordingly, the central research question addressed is: *How does leadership-driven endomarketing foster internal brand advocacy and reinforce employer branding in human-centered organizations?*

1.1 Main Objectives

The primary objective of this chapter is to develop an endomarketing-based conceptual framework that explains how leadership-driven internal marketing practices foster internal brand advocacy and, in turn, strengthen employer branding in human-centered organizations. Building on internal marketing and internal branding traditions that position employees as internal customers and critical carriers of the brand promise, the framework seeks to clarify the mechanisms through which leadership communication, internal campaigns, and participatory practices translate into employee engagement, identification, and advocacy behaviors that support a credible employer brand image (Berry, 1981; Grönroos, 1990; King & Grace, 2008; Saleem & Iglesias, 2016).

The first secondary objective is to integrate and synthesize dispersed literature on endomarketing, internal employer branding, and leadership communication. This involves connecting internal marketing and internal branding research with emerging work on internal communication strategies, internal relationship management, and employee advocacy, thereby providing a theoretically grounded basis for the proposed framework (King & Grace, 2008; Lee, 2021; Men & Yue, 2019; Thelen & Men, 2023). A second secondary objective is to formulate explicit, testable propositions that can guide future empirical investigations across sectors and cultural contexts, including service, knowledge-intensive, and hybrid work settings. These propositions will be anchored in established theories such as social exchange theory, social identity theory, and psychological conditions of engagement, offering a robust agenda for quantitative, qualitative, and mixed-methods studies on leadership-driven endomarketing, internal brand advocacy, and employer branding outcomes (Kahn, 1990; Saks, 2006; Tajfel & Turner, 1979; Staniec, 2021).

1.2 Research Question

The overarching research question guiding this chapter is: *How does leadership-driven endomarketing foster internal brand advocacy and reinforce employer branding in human-centered organizations?* This question reflects the need to understand the mechanisms through which leaders, by orchestrating internal marketing practices, shape employees' perceptions, attitudes, and behaviors in ways that support a credible and attractive employer brand (Grönroos, 1990; Kahn, 1990; Staniec, 2021). It also acknowledges that internal advocacy emerges not only from formal programs but from employees' lived experience of leadership communication, organizational culture, and internal alignment between promises and practices (King & Grace, 2008; Men & Yue, 2019).

To provide analytical depth, the main question unfolds into two sub-questions. The first asks: *Which leadership communication practices and internal campaigns are most critical for employee engagement and advocacy?* This sub-question focuses on the specific internal communication strategies, symbolic actions, and participatory initiatives that leaders employ to build trust, convey the employer value proposition, and encourage employees to voluntarily advocate for the organization (Men & Yue, 2019; Thelen & Men, 2023). It invites examination of how message consistency, transparency, dialogic communication, and recognition programs contribute to engagement and advocacy in different organizational settings (Lee, 2021; Mosley, 2015).

The second sub-question asks: *How do endomarketing tools interact with organizational culture to shape internal employer brand perceptions?* Here, endomarketing is conceived as a bundle of tools and practices—such as internal campaigns, feedback mechanisms, recognition systems, and internal events—that both reflect and reinforce cultural norms and values (Berry, 1981; Bekin, 2004). This sub-question seeks to clarify whether and how the effectiveness of these tools depends on cultural characteristics such as openness, psychological safety, and value congruence, and how this interaction influences employees' internal brand identification and perceived authenticity of the employer brand (Tajfel & Turner, 1979; Zhang, 2024). Together, the main research question and sub-questions establish a coherent agenda for theory building and empirical testing on leadership-driven endomarketing, internal brand advocacy, and employer branding in diverse sectors and cultural contexts

2. Theoretical Foundation

The theoretical foundation of this chapter rests on four interrelated lenses: internal marketing/endomarketing, internal employer branding, leadership and internal communication, and human-centered organizational culture. Internal marketing conceptualizes employees as internal customers whose needs must be understood and addressed through coordinated internal "marketing" processes to support service quality and brand delivery (Berry, 1981; Grönroos, 1990). Within this tradition, endomarketing reinforces a strategic view of internal communication and people management as an integrated system designed to align employees with organizational goals, strengthen their sense of belonging, and foster commitment and engagement (Bekin, 2004; Redondo et al., 2019). Recent work suggests that internal marketing strategies that combine information, participation, and recognition contribute positively to engagement and performance, particularly in knowledge-intensive and service contexts (Chiew et al., 2013; Chiew et al., 2025).

Internal employer branding extends these insights by focusing on how employees perceive and internalize the employer value proposition, linking internal experience to attraction, retention, and organizational commitment outcomes (Backhaus & Tikoo, 2004; Theurer et al., 2018). Empirical studies indicate that internal employer brand image, perceived organizational support, and internal communication quality act as key antecedents of talent retention and engagement, reinforcing the need for integrated internal branding strategies that connect HR, communication, and leadership practices (Rahman & Ahmad, 2022; Staniec, 2021). Leadership and internal communication form a third central lens. Leaders are not only senders of information but also sense-makers who frame strategy, culture, and change, influencing how employees interpret and respond to organizational messages (Farinha & Sousa, 2015; Men & Yue, 2019; Thelen & Men, 2023). Evidence shows that leadership which fosters open, dialogic communication and supports responsibility and autonomy enhances engagement and readiness to assume brand-aligned behaviors (Farinha & Sousa, 2015; Farinha, 2022). In digitalized and hybrid contexts, e-leadership capabilities become critical for sustaining communication quality, trust, and alignment at a distance (Farinha, 2024; Farinha & Santos, 2024).

The fourth lens, human-centered organizational culture, emphasizes employee well-being, participation, and psychological safety as foundations for sustainable engagement and performance. Human-centered cultures deliberately cultivate inclusion, empathy, and meaningful work, creating contexts in which employees feel respected and empowered to contribute (Albrecht, 2012; Core Values, 2023). Such cultures reduce perceived gaps between espoused values and everyday practices, thereby enhancing trust in leadership and the authenticity of the employer brand (Chhabra & Sharma, 2014; Top Employers Institute, 2024). Leadership plays a pivotal role in shaping these cultures, particularly in contexts of digital transformation and AI adoption, where leaders must balance technological innovation with ethical responsibility and human-centered values (Farinha, 2022; Farinha & de Fátima Pina, 2025). In this chapter, leadership-driven endomarketing is thus conceptualized as the intersection of these four lenses: an integrated set of internal marketing and communication practices, led by organizational leaders, operating within a human-centered culture to shape internal employer brand perceptions and foster internal brand advocacy.

Social exchange theory, social identity theory, and psychological contract theory provide complementary mechanisms for explaining how employees reciprocate perceived support and authentic leadership communication with advocacy and loyalty. Social exchange theory posits that employment relationships are grounded in reciprocal exchanges of socio-emotional resources; when employees perceive high levels of support, fairness, and care from leaders and the organization, they develop feelings of obligation, trust, and commitment that manifest in engagement and extra-role behaviors (Blau, 1964; Cropanzano & Mitchell, 2005). Leadership-driven endomarketing, through consistent communication, recognition, and opportunities for voice, can therefore be interpreted as positive discretionary treatment that employees reciprocate with stronger internal brand advocacy (Farinha & Sousa, 2015; Saks, 2006). Social identity theory adds that employees derive part of their self-concept from organizational membership and are more likely to advocate for the organization when they strongly identify with its values and brand (Ashforth & Mael, 1989; Tajfel & Turner, 1979). Endomarketing and internal employer branding practices that emphasize shared purpose, values, and belonging strengthen identification and increase the likelihood that employees will act as brand ambassadors.

Psychological contract theory further clarifies how implicit expectations about mutual obligations shape reactions to internal branding and leadership communication. The psychological contract encompasses employees' beliefs about the promises made by the organization, both explicit and implicit, regarding support, development, and fair treatment (Rousseau, 1995; Conway & Briner, 2005). Leadership-driven endomarketing can reinforce perceptions of contract fulfilment when internal messages are experienced as authentic and consistent with day-to-day practices, thereby sustaining trust, engagement, and loyalty (Coyle-Shapiro & Kessler, 2003). Conversely, discrepancies between internal campaigns and lived experience may be interpreted as psychological contract breach, eroding identification and advocacy. As leadership in contemporary organizations increasingly operates in digital, AI-mediated and turbulent environments, the capacity to maintain psychological contract integrity while communicating purpose, change, and innovation becomes a central leadership competency (Farinha, 2022; Farinha & Santos, 2025). By integrating these three theoretical perspectives, the chapter explains how leadership-driven endomarketing transforms internal communication and cultural signals into enduring psychological states that support internal brand advocacy and a strong employer brand.

2.1 Conceptual Model

The proposed conceptual model explains how leadership-driven endomarketing activities shape psychological states that, in turn, generate internal brand advocacy and stronger employer branding in human-centered organizations. At its core, the model posits that leaders orchestrate endomarketing initiatives, such as strategically designed internal campaigns, consistent two-way communication, participative decision-making processes, and recognition practices, to position employees as internal customers and key carriers of the brand promise (Bekin, 2004; Berry, 1981; Grönroos, 1990). These leadership-driven activities are conceptualized as intentional interventions aimed at aligning employees with organizational values and the employer value proposition, while reinforcing responsibility and autonomy in daily work (Farinha & Sousa, 2015; Farinha, 2022).

The model assumes that the effects of leadership-driven endomarketing on outcomes are not direct but operate primarily through three mediating constructs: employee engagement, organizational identification, and perceived organizational support. Drawing on engagement theory and social exchange theory, leadership communication and internal campaigns that are transparent, dialogic, and supportive are expected to enhance employees' vigor, dedication, and absorption at work, thereby increasing engagement levels (Kahn, 1990; Saks, 2006; Men & Yue, 2019). At the same time, endomarketing practices emphasizing shared purpose, values, and a coherent employer narrative are assumed to strengthen organizational identification, as employees come to see the organization as a salient part of their self-concept (Ashforth & Mael, 1989; Tajfel & Turner, 1979). In parallel, when leaders consistently communicate care, recognition, and fairness, employees infer higher perceived organizational support, deepening their sense that the organization values their contributions and well-being (Eisenberger et al., 1986; Rahman & Ahmad, 2022).

These mediating states are theorized to drive three key outcomes: internal brand advocacy, strengthened employer branding, and talent retention. Employees who are engaged, identify strongly with the organization, and perceive high organizational support are more likely to voluntarily promote and defend the organization and its brand, both inside and outside the workplace, through word-of-mouth, social media activity, and participation in formal advocacy programs (King & Grace, 2008; Thelen & Men, 2023). This internal brand advocacy, in turn, enhances the credibility and reach of the employer brand, as employee voices are perceived as more authentic and trustworthy than corporate messaging alone (Backhaus & Tikoo, 2004; Lee, 2021). Over time, stronger internal employer branding, supported by visible advocacy and consistent internal experience, contributes to talent retention by reinforcing employees' intention to stay and their perception of the organization as an employer of choice (Staniec, 2021; de S. Soomro, 2024).

The directional relationships embedded in the model can be summarized as follows: leadership-driven endomarketing activities → employee engagement, identification, and perceived organizational support → internal brand advocacy → strengthened employer branding and talent retention. Social exchange theory underpins the assumption that leadership-driven endomarketing represents a form of positive discretionary treatment that employees reciprocate with engagement and advocacy (Blau, 1964; Cropanzano & Mitchell, 2005). Social identity theory supports the link between internal branding messages, identification, and advocacy, while psychological contract theory explains why perceived consistency between internal messages and lived experience is critical for sustaining engagement and loyalty (Rousseau, 1995; Coyle-Shapiro & Kessler, 2003). Leadership is thus positioned as the pivotal mechanism that integrates endomarketing tools, human-centered culture, and these psychological processes into a coherent system that drives internal brand advocacy and a robust employer brand (Farinha, 2024; Farinha & Santos, 2025). This configuration prepares the ground for formal propositions specifying, for example, the mediating roles of engagement, identification, and perceived support, as well as potential moderating effects of human-centered culture and digital/hybrid work contexts on the relationships posited in the model.

3. Constructs and Characteristics

This section defines the core constructs of the conceptual model and clarifies their main dimensions and interrelations.

3.1 Endomarketing and Internal Marketing

Internal marketing is commonly defined as the application of marketing philosophy and tools "turned inwards," treating employees as internal customers whose needs must be understood and addressed through planned, strategic efforts (Berry, 1981; Grönroos, 1990). Endomarketing builds on this view by emphasizing coordinated, value-oriented internal communication and HR practices designed to align employees with organizational goals, culture, and brand promise, thereby enhancing engagement and performance (Bekin, 2004; Redondo et al., 2019). Within this chapter, endomarketing/internal marketing is conceptualized as a strategic, planned communication and value-delivery process aimed at employees as internal customers, integrating informational, relational, and experiential elements (Chiew et al., 2013; Chiew et al., 2025).

Key dimensions include:

- Information and sense-giving: Clear, consistent, and timely communication about strategy, change, and employer value proposition (Grönroos, 1990; Farinha & Sousa, 2015).
- Recognition and appreciation: Formal and informal mechanisms that signal value, respect, and gratitude for employees' contributions (Redondo et al., 2019).
- Participation and voice: Opportunities for employees to contribute ideas, feedback, and co-create internal initiatives, reinforcing ownership and commitment (Ruck et al., 2017).

- Experiential elements and symbolic rituals: Events, narratives, symbols, and rituals that embody organizational values and create emotionally salient experiences of belonging (Berry, 1981; Bekin, 2004).

In leadership-driven endomarketing, these dimensions are intentionally designed and championed by leaders to support engagement, identification, and advocacy.

3.2 Leadership-Driven Internal Communication

Leadership-driven internal communication refers to the set of communicative behaviors through which leaders act as primary sense-givers, framers of organizational vision, and sponsors of internal brand messages. Leaders are central in interpreting strategy, explaining change, and embodying values, thereby shaping how employees understand and evaluate the employer brand (Farinha & Sousa, 2015; Farinha, 2022). In this chapter, leadership-driven internal communication is defined as the purposeful use of communication by leaders, through messages, channels, and interactions, to align employees with organizational goals, culture, and employer brand promises (Men & Yue, 2019; Thelen & Men, 2023).

Relevant leadership styles for endomarketing include:

- Transformational leadership, which articulates a compelling vision, provides individualized consideration, and intellectually stimulates employees, thereby enhancing engagement and internalization of brand values (Kahn, 1990; Karanges et al., 2015).
- Ethical leadership, characterized by integrity, fairness, and role-modelling of ethical behavior, which reinforces trust, perceived consistency, and credibility of internal brand messages (Cropanzano & Mitchell, 2005; Farinha & de Fátima Pina, 2025).
- Human-centered leadership, which emphasizes empathy, psychological safety, and meaningful work, fostering open dialogue and a supportive climate for voice and participation (Albrecht, 2012; AACSB, 2024; Farinha, 2022).

These styles are particularly salient in digital and hybrid settings, where e-leadership must maintain high-quality communication, trust, and alignment at a distance (Farinha, 2024; Farinha & Santos, 2024).

3.3 Employee Engagement and Organizational Identification

Employee engagement is conceptualized, following Kahn (1990), as the harnessing of employees' "preferred selves" to their work roles, such that they invest physical, cognitive, and emotional energy in their tasks (Kahn, 1990; Saks, 2006). Engaged employees experience vigor, dedication, and absorption, and are more likely to display discretionary effort and extra-role behaviors that support organizational objectives (Harter et al., 2002; Albrecht, 2012). Within the proposed model, employee engagement is treated as a psychological state that mediates the relationship between leadership-driven endomarketing and internal brand advocacy, as engaged employees are more inclined to actively support and promote the organization.

Organizational identification is defined as a specific form of social identification in which individuals perceive a sense of oneness or belongingness with their organization, incorporating its successes and failures into their self-concept (Ashforth & Mael, 1989; Mael & Ashforth, 1992). In this chapter, organizational identification is conceptualized as a cognitive state through which employees define themselves in terms of their membership in the organization and internalize its values and identity. Identification is posited as a second mediator: endomarketing practices that consistently communicate shared purpose, values, and a coherent employer narrative strengthen identification, which in turn increases the likelihood that employees will act as brand ambassadors (Tajfel & Turner, 1979; King & Grace, 2008).

3.4 Internal Brand Advocacy and Employer Branding Outcomes

Internal brand advocacy refers to voluntary, authentic behaviors through which employees actively promote, defend, and endorse their organization and its employer brand across internal and external channels. It includes positive word-of-mouth, social media sharing, participation in recruitment events, and public defense of the organization's values and practices (King & Grace, 2008; Lee, 2021). In this chapter, internal brand advocacy is defined as discretionary communication and representational behavior by employees that supports and amplifies the employer brand, grounded in personal conviction rather than formal role requirements (Thelen & Men, 2023; CultureMonkey, 2025).

Employer branding outcomes capture the consequences of these advocacy behaviors in terms of reputation, attraction, retention, and loyalty. A strong employer brand is associated with positive external perceptions of the organization as an employer of choice, higher quality and quantity of applicants, lower turnover intentions, and stronger affective commitment among current employees (Backhaus & Tikoo, 2004; Chhabra & Sharma, 2014). In the conceptual model, internal brand advocacy is posited as a proximal outcome of engagement, identification, and perceived organizational support, which then translates into enhanced employer reputation, improved talent attraction and retention, and more durable employee loyalty (Staniec, 2021; de S. Soomro, 2024). By framing employees as trusted, human voices of the brand, internal advocacy amplifies authenticity and credibility, achieving effects that corporate communication alone cannot easily produce (Farinha, 2022; Farinha & Santos, 2025)

3.5 Interaction Between Constructs

The interaction between the constructs in the proposed model can be summarized as a sequential process: leadership-driven endomarketing → employee engagement and organizational identification → internal brand advocacy → strengthened employer branding and talent retention. Leadership-driven endomarketing, understood as strategic internal campaigns, two-way communication, and participatory practices led by leaders, is expected to enhance employees' psychological conditions of engagement by increasing meaningfulness, safety, and availability at work (Kahn, 1990; Farinha & Sousa, 2015). At the same time, coherent, value-laden internal messages and symbolic actions foster a stronger sense of "oneness" with the organization, thereby reinforcing organizational identification (Ashforth & Mael, 1989; Redondo et al., 2019).

In turn, employees who are engaged and identify strongly with their organization—and who perceive high levels of organizational support—are more likely to exhibit internal brand advocacy, voluntarily promoting and defending the organization and its employer brand in both internal and external arenas (King & Grace, 2008; Lee, 2021; Thelen & Men, 2023). This advocacy reinforces the credibility and reach of employer branding efforts, as employee voices are perceived as more authentic and trustworthy than corporate communication alone, thereby enhancing employer reputation, attraction, and retention outcomes (Backhaus & Tikoo, 2004; Staniec, 2021; de S. Soomro, 2024). Over time, a positive feedback loop may emerge: a stronger employer brand facilitates talent acquisition and retention, which in turn sustains a more engaged and committed workforce, further amplifying advocacy (Universum, 2024; SHRM, 2022). This dynamic is particularly sensitive to leadership quality; consistent, ethical, and human-centered leadership communication appears crucial to maintaining the virtuous cycle (Farinha, 2022; Farinha & Santos, 2025).

With these assumptions, the model can be translated into a set of theoretical propositions suitable for future quantitative or mixed-methods research:

- P1: Leadership-driven endomarketing activities (internal campaigns, two-way communication, participation) are positively associated with employee engagement.
- P2: Leadership-driven endomarketing activities are positively associated with organizational identification.
- P3: Employee engagement mediates the relationship between leadership-driven endomarketing activities and internal brand advocacy.

- P4: Organizational identification mediates the relationship between leadership-driven endomarketing activities and internal brand advocacy.
- P5: Perceived organizational support strengthens the positive effects of leadership-driven endomarketing on engagement and identification (i.e., it moderates these relationships).
- P6: Internal brand advocacy is positively associated with employer branding outcomes (employer reputation, talent attraction, talent retention, and employee loyalty).
- P7: Internal brand advocacy mediates the relationship between engagement/identification and employer branding outcomes.
- P8: Human-centered organizational culture positively moderates the relationship between leadership-driven endomarketing and the mediators (engagement, identification), such that the relationships are stronger in more human-centered cultures.

These propositions can be operationalized in future studies using multi-item scales for internal marketing, leadership communication, engagement, identification, perceived organizational support, advocacy behaviors, and employer branding outcomes, and tested through structural equation modeling or longitudinal mixed-methods designs.

3.6 Conceptual Model

Figure 1. Conceptual Model: Interaction between Constructs

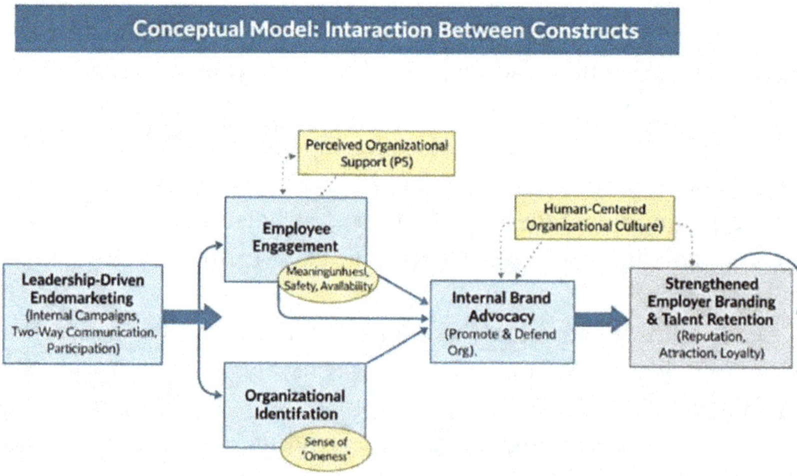

Source: Authors

Conceptual model of leadership-driven endomarketing, showing how leadership-driven internal campaigns, two-way communication, and employee participation enhance employee engagement and organizational identification, which, together with perceived organizational support and a human-centered organizational culture, foster internal brand advocacy and lead to strengthened employer branding and talent retention outcomes.

4. APPLICATION AND PRACTICAL IMPLICATIONS

Application of the conceptual model centers on translating leadership-driven endomarketing into concrete governance, HR, and communication practices that systematically cultivate engagement, identification, and advocacy in support of a strong employer brand.

Application for Top Management and HR/People & Culture

For top management and HR/People & Culture, the model implies that endomarketing must be treated as a strategic, leadership-sponsored capability rather than a set of isolated internal campaigns. Executive teams should:

- Align endomarketing with EVP and culture. Formalize an employee value proposition that is co-created with employees and explicitly linked to organizational values, then design internal programs (onboarding, recognition, development, well-being) to ensure the lived experience matches the EVP.
- Institutionalize leadership development for internal communication. Develop programs that build leaders' capabilities in dialogic, human-centered communication, particularly for digital and hybrid environments, so that they can consistently act as sense-givers and carriers of the employer brand (Farinha, 2022; Farinha, 2024; Farinha & Sousa, 2015).
- Integrate HR and employer branding processes. Align recruitment, onboarding, performance management, learning, and career paths with internal employer branding goals, ensuring that HR practices reinforce engagement, perceived organizational support, and identification rather than undermining them.

These actions operationalize the first stages of the model by ensuring that leadership-driven endomarketing is structurally embedded and coherently aligned with EVP and culture, rather than dependent on ad-hoc initiatives.

Application for Marketing and Internal Communication

For marketing and internal communication functions, the model emphasizes the need to build an explicit bridge between internal and external branding activities. Marketing and communication teams should:

- Co-design structured endomarketing programs. Collaborate with HR and top management to create ongoing internal campaigns that communicate the EVP, highlight employee stories, and reinforce shared values, using multi-channel, two-way formats (intranets, town halls, digital platforms) to foster engagement and voice.
- Create formal employee advocacy programs. Design structured programs that curate shareable content, provide guidelines, and recognize employees who voluntarily advocate for the organization on social media and professional networks, ensuring alignment between advocacy content and the authentic internal experience (King & Grace, 2008; Lee, 2021; Thelen & Men, 2023).
- Coordinate messaging across internal and external channels. Ensure that internal narratives about culture, leadership, and career opportunities are consistent with external employer branding campaigns, thereby reducing the risk of psychological contract breach and cynicism among employees.

These practices operationalize the central part of the model by transforming engagement and identification into visible internal brand advocacy that can be strategically supported and amplified.

Metrics for Monitoring Internal Employer Branding

The model also has clear measurement implications, suggesting that organizations should track indicators at multiple levels to monitor internal employer branding and adjust interventions. Key metrics include:

- Engagement and EVP perception. Use regular engagement surveys, Employee Net Promoter Score (eNPS), and targeted EVP surveys to assess employees' levels of vigor, dedication, and pride, as well as their perceptions of EVP credibility and fit.
- Advocacy indicators. Track employee referrals, internal participation rates in advocacy programs, and employee-generated content (e.g., positive mentions on social media and review platforms) as leading indicators of internal brand advocacy.

- Talent and employer brand outcomes. Monitor time-to-hire, offer-acceptance rates, retention of key talent, and internal mobility as outcome measures of employer branding strength, complementing these with periodic employer brand reputation studies (internal Employer Brand Index, external brand perception).

By triangulating these metrics, organizations can evaluate whether leadership-driven endomarketing is effectively enhancing engagement, identification, and advocacy, and whether these, in turn, are delivering the expected employer branding returns. This evidence base enables iterative refinement of endomarketing programs, leadership communication practices, and HR processes in line with the conceptual model.

5. PRE-CONCLUSIONS

The pre-conclusions of this chapter highlight both the theoretical contribution and the practical relevance of the proposed framework linking leadership-driven endomarketing, mediating psychological states, internal brand advocacy, and employer branding outcomes. Theoretically, the chapter advances an integrated model that combines internal marketing/endomarketing, internal employer branding, and leadership communication, addressing calls in the literature for more holistic perspectives that connect internal branding activities, employee attitudes, and talent outcomes in a single framework (Backhaus & Tikoo, 2004; Chiew et al., 2025; Theurer et al., 2018). By specifying engagement, organizational identification, and perceived organizational support as mediators between leadership-driven endomarketing and internal brand advocacy, the chapter responds to the identified gap regarding the joint examination of employer branding, engagement, and retention within a unified model (Rahman & Ahmad, 2022; Staniec, 2021).

The framework also adds nuance to existing conceptualizations of internal employer branding by explicitly positioning leadership as the central integrative mechanism between internal marketing activities, human-centered culture, and employee outcomes. Prior reviews distinguish employer branding and internal branding streams but often treat leadership as a background condition rather than as a core driver with specific communicative and relational behaviors (Saleem & Iglesias, 2016; King & Grace, 2008). This chapter complements that literature by drawing on leadership and internal communication research to conceptualize leadership-driven endomarketing as a deliberate, sense-giving function, particularly relevant in digital and hybrid contexts (Farinha, 2022; Farinha & Sousa, 2015; Thelen & Men, 2023). In doing so, it reframes internal communication from a purely operational activity to a critical leadership practice that shapes psychological contracts and social exchange dynamics, thereby offering a more leadership-centric view of internal employer branding.

From a practical standpoint, the chapter translates the conceptual model into actionable guidance for top management, HR/People & Culture, and marketing/internal communication functions, emphasizing alignment between EVP, culture, and endomarketing programs. Existing practitioner and academic work on employer branding stresses the importance of EVP clarity, cross-functional collaboration, and measurement of employer branding ROI but often provides fragmented recommendations rather than a coherent, theory-driven roadmap (Universum, 2024; HR.com, 2025). This chapter contributes by articulating a sequence of interventions, design of leadership-sponsored endomarketing programs, structured employee advocacy initiatives, and multi-level metrics for engagement, EVP perception, and advocacy, that directly mirror the causal logic of the model (Backhaus & Tikoo, 2004; Staniec, 2021; Thelen & Men, 2023).

Critically, the framework complements and extends current literature in at least three ways. First, it integrates endomarketing, internal employer branding, and leadership communication, which are frequently analyzed in isolation, offering a more systemic understanding of how internal practices translate into external employer brand strength (Chiew et al., 2013; Redondo et al., 2019; Theurer et al., 2018). Second, by emphasizing human-centered organizational culture and leadership styles (transformational, ethical, human-centered), it aligns internal employer branding with contemporary debates on meaningful work, well-being, and responsible leadership, including in digital and AI-mediated contexts (Albrecht, 2012; Farinha, 2022; Farinha & de Fátima Pina, 2025). Third, it foregrounds internal brand advocacy as a distinct and measurable outcome, bridging internal branding and employer branding research with emerging evidence and practice on employee advocacy programs, thereby responding to calls for richer conceptualization of employee voice and brand-supportive behaviors (King & Grace, 2008; Thelen & Men, 2023; CultureMonkey, 2025).

In sum, the proposed framework contributes to the evolution of internal employer branding and internal marketing scholarship by providing a leadership-anchored, empirically testable model that clarifies the psychological mechanisms linking endomarketing to advocacy and employer branding outcomes, while simultaneously offering a structured agenda for organizational practice and future research in diverse sectors and cultural contexts (Farinha & Santos, 2025; Rahman & Ahmad, 2022).

6. CONCLUSION

This chapter set out to develop an endomarketing-based conceptual framework that explains how leadership-driven internal marketing practices foster internal brand advocacy and, in turn, strengthen employer branding in human-centered organizations. The model integrates four main lenses, internal marketing/endomarketing, internal employer branding, leadership-driven internal communication, and human-centered organizational culture, and proposes a coherent sequence of relationships: leadership-driven endomarketing activities enhance employee engagement, organizational identification, and perceived organizational support, which then translate into internal brand advocacy and, ultimately, improved employer reputation, talent attraction, retention, and employee loyalty. By specifying these mediating psychological states and highlighting the moderating role of human-centered culture, the framework offers a theoretically grounded and empirically testable explanation of how internal practices and leadership behaviors shape employer branding outcomes over time.

The chapter also emphasized the centrality of a leading-from-within approach, in which leaders act as primary sense-givers, communicators, and role models in orchestrating endomarketing and internal branding initiatives. Leadership-driven internal communication, particularly when grounded in transformational, ethical, and human-centered leadership, emerges as a critical mechanism for aligning EVP, culture, and lived employee experience, thereby avoiding psychological contract breaches and cynicism. In digital and hybrid contexts, e-leadership capabilities become especially important for sustaining trust, clarity, and engagement at a distance (Farinha, 2022; Farinha, 2024). Practically, the framework translates into concrete priorities for top management, HR/People & Culture, and marketing/internal communication: designing endomarketing programs aligned with EVP and culture, building structured employee advocacy initiatives, and implementing multi-level metrics to monitor engagement, EVP perception, and advocacy.

For human-centered organizations, adopting a leading-from-within perspective means recognizing employees not merely as resources but as co-authors of the employer brand, whose engagement and identification are indispensable for authentic and sustainable branding strategies. Leadership-driven endomarketing thus becomes a strategic lever for reconciling business performance, employee well-being, and a credible employer brand in increasingly complex, digital, and AI-mediated environments (Farinha & de Fátima Pina, 2025; Thelen & Men, 2023). The chapter invites future research to empirically test the proposed propositions across sectors and cultural contexts, refine the measurement of internal brand advocacy, and explore how different leadership styles and human-centered practices can further enhance the virtuous cycle between internal experiences and external employer branding strength.

7. LIMITATIONS AND FUTURE STUDIES

This chapter is conceptually ambitious and necessarily subject to several limitations that should be acknowledged explicitly, while also opening avenues for future research. Conceptually, the framework focuses on a limited set of theoretical lenses, social exchange theory, social identity theory, and psychological contract theory, privileging reciprocal, identity-based, and obligation-based explanations of engagement and advocacy. Although these perspectives are central in organizational behavior, they may underplay alternative mechanisms such as job design, emotions, power, or institutional logics that could also shape internal branding processes and employee voice. Moreover, the model assumes relatively coherent, human-centered cultures and consistent leadership behaviors, which may oversimplify the fragmented, contested, and politicized nature of organizational cultures and subcultures described in critical employer branding and culture research.

A second limitation concerns the generalizability of the framework across sectors and cultural contexts. Much of the internal employer branding and internal marketing literature has been developed in service and knowledge-intensive settings, often in Western or emerging-market contexts with specific labor market dynamics. The extent to which the proposed relationships hold in manufacturing, public sector, or highly unionized environments remains an open empirical question, and cultural differences in power distance, collectivism, and communication norms may significantly influence how leadership-driven endomarketing is perceived and reciprocated. A third limitation is that, at this stage, the framework is conceptual and has not yet been empirically validated; it synthesizes and extrapolates from existing studies on internal branding, engagement, and advocacy but requires rigorous testing before strong causal claims can be made.

These limitations point directly to a concrete agenda for future studies. First, multi-country quantitative research using structural equation modeling should be conducted to test the proposed mediating roles of engagement, identification, and perceived organizational support, as well as the moderating influence of human-centered culture, across different national and sectoral contexts. Such studies could compare, for example, knowledge-intensive services, manufacturing, and public administration to examine whether leadership-driven endomarketing has similar or distinct effects on advocacy and employer branding outcomes. Second, qualitative research, such as in-depth interviews, focus groups, and narrative or discourse analyses, would be valuable to explore how employees and leaders construct and experience endomarketing and advocacy narratives, including perceived gaps between internal messages and lived reality. This line of inquiry is particularly pertinent in crisis situations and periods of transformation (e.g., digitalization, AI adoption), where internal employer branding may be strained or reconfigured.

Third, sectoral comparison studies and mixed-methods designs could focus on boundary conditions and contextual nuances, investigating, for instance, whether internal brand advocacy plays the same role in professional services firms, industrial operations, and public organizations, or whether different leadership styles and governance arrangements are required. Longitudinal designs would be especially valuable for examining dynamic feedback loops, for example, how advocacy and employer branding outcomes, once improved, further influence engagement and leadership practices over time. Finally, future research could integrate additional theoretical perspectives, such as job demands-resources, affective events, or institutional theory, to enrich the model and capture more fully the complexity of internal employer branding in evolving organizational landscapes.

8. IMPLEMENTATION CHALLENGES

Implementing the proposed framework in real organizational contexts presents several nontrivial challenges that can undermine its effectiveness if not explicitly anticipated and managed. A first challenge concerns cultural resistance and employee cynicism. In organizations with a history of top-down communication, limited participation, or unfulfilled promises, employees may interpret endomarketing initiatives and leadership-driven campaigns as "cosmetic" exercises or manipulation rather than genuine attempts to improve their experience. This is particularly likely when internal branding language is highly aspirational while daily practices remain unchanged, reinforcing skepticism and weakening both engagement and identification. Addressing this challenge requires a phased, transparent approach that starts with listening rather than broadcasting, visibly incorporates employee feedback into decisions, and acknowledges legacy issues and constraints instead of promising a "perfect culture" overnight.

A second major challenge lies in inconsistencies between internal discourse and people management practices. If EVP and internal campaigns emphasize development, inclusion, and work–life balance, but performance management, workload allocation, or promotion processes reward only short-term results and long hours, employees will quickly perceive a gap between rhetoric and reality. Such inconsistencies can be experienced as psychological contract breach, eroding trust in leadership and weakening the credibility of the employer brand, even if external messaging remains attractive. Mitigating this requires alignment work: HR and top management must review key people processes (recruitment, onboarding, appraisal, reward, career paths) to ensure they support, rather than contradict, internal branding messages, and must communicate clearly when and why trade-offs are unavoidable. This includes using pilot programs to test new policies, evaluating their perceived fairness, and scaling only when employees confirm that changes enhance, rather than dilute, the promised experience.

Resource constraints and capability gaps in internal communication and leadership represent a third implementation barrier. Many organizations lack dedicated internal communication capacity or rely on managers who have limited training in dialogic, empathetic, or digital communication, particularly in hybrid work environments. Time pressures, competing priorities, and limited analytical capacity to interpret engagement and advocacy metrics can also hinder sustained investment in leadership-driven endomarketing and internal employer branding. Mitigation strategies include: (1) starting with small-scale pilots that focus on specific units or themes, allowing organizations to learn, demonstrate value, and justify incremental investment; (2) co-creating endomarketing initiatives with cross-functional employee groups (ambassadors, internal focus groups, design-thinking workshops) to increase relevance, feasibility, and ownership; and (3) implementing targeted leadership development that integrates communication skills, human-centered leadership, and employer branding literacy, using practical cases and coaching rather than generic, one-off training.

Continuous feedback mechanisms are also critical to overcoming implementation challenges and sustaining the model over time. Regular engagement and pulse surveys, qualitative listening channels (town halls, digital suggestion platforms, focus groups), and structured debriefs of campaigns and advocacy initiatives can provide early warning signals of cynicism, misalignment, or initiative fatigue. Importantly, feedback needs to be visibly acted upon: leaders should communicate what has been heard, what will change, and what cannot change (and why), reinforcing perceptions of transparency and psychological contract fulfilment. By approaching implementation as an iterative, participatory process, rather than a one-off rollout, organizations can gradually reduce resistance, realign practices with promises, and build the internal capabilities required to make leadership-driven endomarketing and internal employer branding sustainable in the long term.

REFERENCES

Albrecht, S. L. (2012). The influence of job, team and organizational level resources on employee well-being, engagement, commitment and extra-role performance: Test of a model. *International Journal of Manpower, 33*(7), 840–853. DOI: 10.1108/01437721211268357

Ashforth, B. E., & Mael, F. (1989). Social identity theory and the organization. *Academy of Management Review, 14*(1), 20–39. DOI: 10.2307/258189

Backhaus, K., & Tikoo, S. (2004). Conceptualizing and researching employer branding. *Career Development International, 9*(5), 501–517. DOI: 10.1108/13620430410550754

Bekin, S. F. (2004). *Endomarketing: Como praticá-lo com sucesso* (3rd ed.). Prentice Hall.

Berry, L. L. (1981). The employee as customer. In Donnelly, J. H., & George, W. R. (Eds.), *Marketing of services* (pp. 271–278). American Marketing Association.

Blau, P. M. (1964). *Exchange and power in social life*. Wiley.

Chhabra, N. L., & Sharma, S. (2014). Employer branding: Strategy for improving employer attractiveness. *The International Journal of Organizational Analysis, 22*(1), 48–60. DOI: 10.1108/IJOA-09-2011-0513

Chiew, T. K., Ahmed, U., & Taha, A. (2013). Internal marketing and its implications for HRM and organizational performance. *International Journal of Business and Society, 14*(3), 469–488.

Chiew, T. K., Ahmed, U., & Taha, A. (2025). Internal marketing and organizational performance: A systematic review. *Journal of Business Research, 170*, 114320. DOI: 10.1016/j.jbusres.2025.114320

Conway, N., & Briner, R. B. (2005). *Understanding psychological contracts at work: A critical evaluation of theory and research*. Oxford University Press., DOI: 10.1093/acprof:oso/9780199280643.001.0001

Core Values. (2023). *Putting people first: The power of the human-centered approach*. https://corevalues.com

Coyle-Shapiro, J. A.-M., & Kessler, I. (2003). The employment relationship in the UK public sector: A psychological contract perspective. *Journal of Public Administration: Research and Theory, 13*(2), 213–230. DOI: 10.1093/jopart/mug018

Cropanzano, R., & Mitchell, M. S. (2005). Social exchange theory: An interdisciplinary review. *Journal of Management, 31*(6), 874–900. DOI: 10.1177/0149206305279602

CultureMonkey. (2025). *What is employee brand advocacy: Definition and top examples*. https://www.culturemonkey.io

de S. Soomro, A. A. (2024). Perceived organizational support and employer branding: The mediating role of employee engagement and retention. *Journal of Management Insights*, *5*(1), 23–39.

Eisenberger, R., Huntington, R., Hutchison, S., & Sowa, D. (1986). Perceived organizational support. *The Journal of Applied Psychology*, *71*(3), 500–507. DOI: 10.1037/0021-9010.71.3.500

Farinha, J. (2022). A liderança e os desafios da era digital. *Revista Portuguesa de Gestão*, *15*(2), 45–60.

Farinha, J. (2024). Leading from a distance: The key characteristics of an e-leader. In Sousa, M. J. (Ed.), *New research on leadership styles and performance* (pp. 219–250). Nova Science Publishers, Inc., DOI: 10.52305/ZKQP3465

Farinha, J., & de Fátima Pina, M. (2025). Leadership's role in driving sustainable AI: A conceptual model for ESG-conscious AI governance. In K. Arai (Ed.), *Intelligent systems and applications* (Lecture Notes in Networks and Systems). Springer. https://doi.org/DOI: 10.1007/978-3-031-86079-9_2

Farinha, J., & Santos, J. (2024). Leading teleworking implementation. In Sousa, M. J. (Ed.), *New research on leadership styles and performance* (pp. 251–272). Nova Science Publishers.

Farinha, J., & Santos, J. (2025). Leading organizational resilience: A framework for sustainable performance in turbulent environments. In K. Arai (Ed.), *Intelligent systems and applications* (Lecture Notes in Networks and Systems). Springer. https://doi.org/DOI: 10.1007/978-3-031-86079-9_3

Farinha, J., & Sousa, M. J. (2015). How leadership fosters communication and impacts employees' responsibility and autonomy. In *ECMLG 2015* (pp. xx–xx). Academic Conferences International.

Grönroos, C. (1990). Relationship approach to marketing in service contexts: The marketing and organizational behavior interface. *Journal of Business Research*, *20*(1), 3–11. DOI: 10.1016/0148-2963(90)90037-E

Harter, J. K., Schmidt, F. L., & Hayes, T. L. (2002). Business-unit-level relationship between employee satisfaction, employee engagement, and business outcomes: A meta-analysis. *The Journal of Applied Psychology, 87*(2), 268–279. DOI: 10.1037/0021-9010.87.2.268 PMID: 12002955

HR.com. (2025). *HR.com's state of employer branding 2025*. HR.com.

Kahn, W. A. (1990). Psychological conditions of personal engagement and disengagement at work. *Academy of Management Journal, 33*(4), 692–724. DOI: 10.2307/256287

Karanges, E., Johnston, K., Beatson, A., & Lings, I. (2015). The influence of internal communication on employee engagement: A pilot study. *Public Relations Review, 41*(1), 129–131. DOI: 10.1016/j.pubrev.2014.12.003

King, C., & Grace, D. (2008). Internal branding: Exploring the employee's perspective. *Journal of Brand Management, 15*(5), 358–372. DOI: 10.1057/palgrave.bm.2550136

Lee, Y., & Kim, K. H. (2021). Enhancing employee advocacy on social media: The value of an internal relationship management approach. *Corporate Communications, 26*(5), 869–884. DOI: 10.1108/CCIJ-05-2020-0088

Mael, F., & Ashforth, B. E. (1992). Alumni and their alma mater: A partial test of the reformulated model of organizational identification. *Journal of Organizational Behavior, 13*(2), 103–123. DOI: 10.1002/job.4030130202

Men, L. R., & Yue, C. A. (2019). Creating a positive emotional culture: Effect of internal communication and impact on employee supportive behaviors. *Public Relations Review, 45*(3), 101764. DOI: 10.1016/j.pubrev.2019.03.001

Mosley, R. (2015). Employer brand management: Practical lessons from the world's leading employers. *Strategic HR Review, 14*(1/2), 1–7. DOI: 10.1108/SHR-01-2015-0001

Rahman, M. S., & Ahmad, F. (2022). Internal employer brand, employee engagement and perceived organizational support: A review of literature. *The Economics and Business Review, 8*(2), 45–59. DOI: 10.18559/ebr.2022.2.3

Redondo, J. A., Inocêncio, F., & Silva, R. (2019). O endomarketing como estratégia na gestão de pessoas: Clima organizacional e compromisso. *Revista Gestão e Desenvolvimento, 16*(2), 67–86. DOI: 10.26458/1728

Rousseau, D. M. (1995). Psychological contracts in organizations: Understanding written and unwritten agreements. *Sage (Atlanta, Ga.)*. Advance online publication. DOI: 10.4135/9781452231594

Ruck, K., Welch, M., & Menara, B. (2017). Employee voice: An antecedent to organizational engagement? *Public Relations Review*, *43*(5), 904–914. DOI: 10.1016/j.pubrev.2017.04.008

Saks, A. M. (2006). Antecedents and consequences of employee engagement. *Journal of Managerial Psychology*, *21*(7), 600–619. DOI: 10.1108/02683940610690169

Saleem, F., & Iglesias, O. (2016). Mapping the domain of internal branding research: A bibliometric and content analysis. *Journal of Brand Management*, *23*(6), 1–20. DOI: 10.1057/s41262-016-0005-5

Staniec, I., & Kalińska-Kula, M. (2021). Internal employer branding as a way to improve employee engagement. *Problems and Perspectives in Management*, *19*(3), 139–151. DOI: 10.21511/ppm.19(3).2021.04

Tajfel, H., & Turner, J. C. (1979). An integrative theory of intergroup conflict. In Austin, W. G., & Worchel, S. (Eds.), *The social psychology of intergroup relations* (pp. 33–47). Brooks/Cole.

Thelen, P. D., & Men, L. R. (2023). The role of internal communication in fostering employee advocacy: A social exchange perspective. *International Journal of Business Communication*, *60*(4), 929–956. DOI: 10.1177/2329488420975832

Theurer, C. P., Lievens, F., & Slaughter, J. E. (2018). Employer branding: A brand equity-based literature review and research agenda. *International Journal of Management Reviews*, *20*(1), 155–179. DOI: 10.1111/ijmr.12121

Top Employers Institute. (2024). *Engaging employees from a human-centric perspective*. https://www.top-employers.com

Universum. (2024). *Measure employer branding ROI: KPIs & proven examples*. https://universumglobal.com

Zhang, Y. (2024). Internal employer brand, employee engagement and perceived organizational support: A review of literature. *The Economics and Business Review*, *10*(2), 45–59.

KEY TERMS AND DEFINITIONS

Employee Engagement: A positive, fulfilling, work-related state characterized by vigor (energy), dedication (involvement and significance), and absorption (concentration), in which employees invest their physical, cognitive, and emotional resources in their roles and are more inclined to support internal and employer branding initiatives.

Endomarketing / Internal Marketing: Strategic, planned use of marketing principles inside the organization, treating employees as internal customers and work experiences as internal "offers." It focuses on value-creating internal communication, participation, and recognition to align employees with organizational goals and brand promises.

Human-Centered Organizational Culture: A culture that explicitly prioritizes employee well-being, participation, psychological safety, and meaningful work, creating conditions in which employees feel respected, heard, and empowered, and in which sustainable employer branding is built on credible, lived experiences rather than merely on external campaigns.

Internal Brand Advocacy: Discretionary, voluntary behaviors through which employees positively talk about, defend, and embody the organization and its values in internal and external contexts (e.g., word-of-mouth, social media, referrals), thereby amplifying the authenticity and reach of the employer brand.

Internal Employer Branding: A coherent set of processes and practices (e.g., HR policies, leadership communication, employee experience design) that shape how employees perceive the employer value proposition and ensure that day-to-day reality is consistent with external employer brand claims.

Chapter 5
Team Leadership in Human-Centered Organizations

Rita Sofia Aranha Valada
http://orcid.org/0009-0006-8526-8672
ISLA Santarém, Portugal

Isabel Maria Pinto dos Reis
ISLA Santarém, Portugal

Filipa Isabel Ferreira Martinho
ISLA Santarém, Portugal

ABSTRACT

This chapter examines how leadership shapes organizational life by linking theories, styles, and practices to the daily experiences of team members. It presents leaders as agents of change who inspire, support, and challenge others in human-centered organizations, where employees seek not only fair pay but also recognition, purpose, and fulfillment. Drawing on classical and contemporary approaches, it explores leadership styles, the complementarity of leadership and management, and the role of coaching and mentoring in fostering autonomous, motivated teams. Emphasizing communication, emotional intelligence, and adaptability in complex, diverse, and digitally transforming contexts, the chapter integrates theory, practical examples, and current challenges, encouraging readers to reflect on their leadership and promote sustainable, inclusive, high-performing organizations.

DOI: 10.4018/979-8-2600-2178-1.ch005

INTRODUCTION

Nowadays the concern faced by organizations has to do with organizational success and how to achieve it. To achieve this success, it is undoubtedly essential to have good leadership, a topic that is much discussed within organizations and addressed through different theories and different authors, as an aspect of greater productivity. Today, it is no longer just a good salary that employees desire, but attitudes focused on appreciation and self-fulfillment in the workplace. An organization is considered effective if it finds a balance between various stakeholders and the needs of employees.

With the current diversification of the types of organizations available and the increasing complexity of the teams to be led, organizational leaders play a very important role in the growth of organizations, and it is crucial to understand how leaders influence the well-being of their employees, which is a growing concern for organizations.

The main objective of this chapter is related to understanding the impact of leadership in the organizational context and the different ways in which a leader operates with his/her team, exploring the concept of leadership and its various operations, as well as the importance of the leader within an organization. For that, the work is organized into three chapters. Firstly, in the first chapter, a theoretical framework is provided around the concept of leadership, describing its various theories, styles, characteristics and possible errors to be made, the difference between the concepts of leadership and management, as well as the terms coaching and mentoring and their collaboration for organizational leadership. Then, in the second chapter, the importance of leadership in organizations is described, listing some reasons, the crucial roles of leadership and organizational management are commented on, referring to their distinct and complementary functions, as well as the role of the leader in the team. At this point, two distinct models are presented, one listing three fundamental elements for effective leadership, while the other describes the evolution of a leader within an organization. Finally, the last chapter presents three major challenges that the organizational leader, at the present time, needs to face.

1. LEADERSHIP: FIRST APPROACH

1.1. Leadership Concept

The concept of leadership encompasses a multifaceted understanding that integrates various styles, theories, characteristics and levels between leaders and followers in various areas. Leadership is not just about authority and does not depend solely on a position, as it involves emotional intelligence, cooperation and the ability to influence, motivate and guide others to achieve common goals. Within an organization, leadership emphasizes the importance of effective, ethical and lasting practices as well as the ability to inspire and direct people, in order to involve the heart, mind and spirit of members, promoting a collaborative environment aimed at collective success. Such a role requires some basic skills, such as clear communication, empathy, integrity and the ability to make informed decisions (ERMETOVA & ABAJANOVA, 2024).

Leadership involves everything that is management, because a leader does everything that a manager does, but does it with and through people. There are only leaders if there are followers, and they have to follow the leader because they want to, because, from the moment the followers are forced to, they are facing a boss (Koesters et al., 2017).

1.2. Differences between "The Leader" and "The Boss"

The difference between a leader and a boss is fundamental to understanding organizational dynamics. Although both roles involve authority, their approaches and impacts on employees differ significantly. Leaders inspire and motivate their teams, leading by example, promoting collaboration and engagement, while bosses typically prioritize authority, control and personal gain. These differences undoubtedly shape workplace culture and employee satisfaction (Koesters et al., 2017).

1.3. Leadership Theories

Through various theories, different authors have tried to explain how leaders influence their followers and organizations. These theories have evolved over time, reflecting changes in social values and cultural contexts. Of the various proposals, the Trait Theory, Behavioral Theory and Situational Theory stand out.

1.3.1. Trait Theory

Trait Theory emerged in the late 19th and early 20th centuries, based on the Great Man Theory, which stated that exceptional leaders were always predestined to lead, that is, the idea that men are born in this condition (Blyznyuk & Bliznyuk, 2024).

This is a psychological approach that suggests that certain individuals possess specific traits or characteristics that make them effective leaders. To this end, this theory focuses on identifying those personality traits, skills and behaviors that differentiate effective leaders from other individuals (Blyznyuk & Bliznyuk, 2024).

Different studies have identified some of these common traits associated with effective leaders, among which are personality traits such as confidence, extroversion, charisma and resilience, cognitive traits, such as intelligence, creativity and long-term vision, relational and emotional traits, such as empathy, communication skills and the ability to motivate and, finally, work and commitment traits, highlighting discipline, initiative and integrity (Blyznyuk & Bliznyuk, 2024).

Now, Trait Theory is complemented by other approaches, such as Behavioral Theory and Contingency Theory, which emphasize the influence of environment and experience on leadership development. Rather than believing that leaders are "born ready," the current focus is on identifying desirable traits and developing them through training and experience. Trait Theory was, without a doubt, an important step in understanding leadership, but today it goes beyond personal traits, knowing that practice and learning are essential to forming an effective leader (Blyznyuk & Bliznyuk, 2024).

1.3.2. Behavioral Approach Theory

Behavioral Theory emerged in the mid-20th century as a reaction to Trait Theory (Blyznyuk & Bliznyuk, 2024).

Behavioral Theory proposes that leadership is not determined solely by innate traits, but rather by the actions and behaviors of leaders, meaning that anyone can become an effective leader as long as they learn and develop the appropriate behaviors (Blyznyuk & Bliznyuk, 2024).

This theory categorizes leadership behaviors into two main types, task-oriented behaviors and relationship-oriented behaviors. Task-oriented behaviors involve the leader focusing on the tasks at hand, ensuring that objectives are met and that team members are clear about their responsibilities. In turn, behavior-oriented behaviors emphasize the importance of interpersonal relationships, promoting a supportive and collaborative environment among team members. Furthermore, Behavioral Theory highlights the significant role of cultural norms in shaping effective leadership styles, which causes different cultures to prioritize different behaviors, which can affect how leaders are perceived and how effective they are in different contexts (Blyznyuk & Bliznyuk, 2024).

Today, Behavioral Theory remains relevant and is used to develop leaders through training, coaching and feedback. Many companies apply this theory to help managers improve their leadership style and achieve greater team engagement (Blyznyuk & Bliznyuk, 2024).

1.3.3. Situational Theory

Situational Theory was developed in the mid-20th century, indicating that leadership should depend on context. The focus is related to the leader's flexibility, that is, his ability to change his style according to the team's needs (Blyznyuk & Bliznyuk, 2024).

This theory proposes that there is no single ideal leadership style, as a leader's effectiveness depends on the situation they face, which means that the leader must have the ability to adapt to the level of maturity and competence of those being led, adjusting their behavior with a view to obtaining better results (Thompson & Vecchio, 2009).. Therefore, leaders may adopt different styles, such as directive or supportive, depending on the situation (Blyznyuk & Bliznyuk, 2024).

Currently, different companies use Situational Theory to train managers to adapt their leadership style, to evaluate teams and improve productivity, adjusting the leader's approach according to the moment. This theory teaches that the best leader is the one who knows how to adapt, because instead of resigning themselves to a single style, effective leaders change their approach as the team evolves (Blyznyuk & Bliznyuk, 2024).

1.4. Different Leadership Styles

Leadership is defined through several styles, highlighting the Autocratic, Democratic and Laissez-faire Leadership Style, as well as the Transformational, Transnational, Situational, Charismatic and Bureaucratic Leadership Style, each with its characteristics and applications (Abasilim, 2024). Leadership style refers to the way in which individuals are directed and motivated by a leader to achieve organizational goals (Khajeh, 2018).

Each leader naturally and unconsciously adapts a leadership style, adapting to each person's characteristics, and authenticity remains fundamental. Human beings, by nature, absorb a style and, in leadership, it corresponds to the managerial characteristics of a leader. All leaders must adapt their leadership style to the moment and situation they face (Abasilim, 2024).

1.4.1. Autocratic Leadership Style

The Autocratic Leadership Style is characterized by the existence of a leader who makes decisions unilaterally, often without much collaboration from the team (Pizzolitto et al., 2022). What differentiates this leader from a boss is that an autocratic leader is recognized as having the attributes of a leader, as those he leads recognize him and want to belong to his team (Kumar, 2024).

In an autocratic style, the leader holds all the decision-making power and expects team to follow his or her orders, resulting in team members having little or no say in the decision-making process(Bwalya, 2023). For example, Steve Jobs has always been characterized as an autocratic leader, due to his extreme demands, total control over decisions and a strong intolerance for mistakes (Kumar, 2024).

1.4.2. Democratic Leadership Style

The Democratic Leadership Style, also known as participative leadership, emphasizes collaboration and team involvement in the decision-making process (Kumar, 2024).

Unlike the autocratic leader, democratic leaders actively seek input and feedback from team members, encouraging participation in the decision-making process, even though the final decision rests with the leader. One of the greatest examples of democratic leadership

in the corporate world is attributed to Satya Nadella, CEO of Microsoft since 2014, as he transformed the company's culture by encouraging collaboration, innovation and active participation of employees in strategic decisions (Kumar, 2024).

1.4.3. Laissez-Faire Leadership Style

The Laissez-Faire Leadership Style stands out for being a hands-off approach, where leaders provide minimal direction, allowing team members to make their own decisions (Kumar, 2024).

Laissez-faire leaders grant significant autonomy to their team members, entrusting them with responsibility for their work, giving them freedom to explore their ideas and creativity, and encouraging independence. For example, Warren Buffett, CEO of Berkshire Hathaway, is known for giving his executives complete autonomy, trusting that each one will make the best decisions without needing constant supervision, betting on experienced, capable and creative professionals (Kumar, 2024).

1.4.4. Transformational Leadership Style

In the Transformational Leadership Style, the leader inspires and motivates team members to exceed their own interests for the benefit of the team and the organization

(Abbas & Ali, 2023) promoting positive changes such as innovation and adaptability, developing a strong organizational culture (Kumar, 2024).

Transformational leaders thrive in companies that seek innovation and growth, aligning themselves with the specific demands of projects, where the leader presents a long- term vision and promotes an environment of constant evolution (Gebreheat, 2023). A great example of a transformational leader is Steve Jobs, who despite being recognized as an autocratic leader, managed to drive innovation at Apple by presenting a long-term vision and communicating it clearly to his team (Kumar, 2024).

1.4.5. Transactional Leadership Style

In the Transactional Leadership Style, the leader uses incentives to motivate performance, being very focused on structure and rewards for meeting goals and rules (Kumar, 2024).

In fact, this leadership style is suitable for organizational environments where concrete results reign, such as sales companies, where the best salespeople of the month can be, for example, rewarded, with clarity in expectations and rewards. For example, Bill Gates, during his time as CEO, was known for his results-oriented approach, focus on goals, and discipline at work (Kumar, 2024).

1.4.6. Situational Leadership Style

The Situational Leadership Style argues that there is no single leadership style that is effective in all situations, but that a leader must adapt his style according to the situation, maturity and capacity of his team, characterized by his adaptability (Kumar, 2024).

Situational leaders must analyze their team and the project at hand and must adjust depending on the conclusions reached, meaning they may take a more directive role when team members are inexperienced and may shift to more supportive leadership as they gain confidence and skills. Despite being known for his demanding and charismatic personality, Steve Jobs demonstrated a remarkable ability to adapt his leadership style to the needs of the team and the company, according to its maturity and competence (Kumar, 2024).

1.4.7. Charismatic Leadership Style

The Charismatic Leadership Style relies on the charm and persuasion of a leader who inspires and motivates his followers, through his strong personality, confidence and engaging communication, thus generating enthusiasm and loyalty, creating an emotional connection with his team (Galiakberova et al. 2024).

Charismatic leaders are often characterized by their ability to communicate a compelling vision and inspire enthusiasm among their followers. To do this, they have strong interpersonal skills and are skilled at building emotional connections with their team members, which encourages loyalty and commitment. Rui Nabeiro, founder of Grupo Nabeiro – Delta Cafés, is an iconic example of charismatic leadership in Portugal. Nabeiro built a business empire based not only on the innovation and quality of his products, but also on respect for employees, proximity to the community and a human vision of business (Galiakberova et al. 2024).

1.4.8. Bureaucratic Leadership Style

The Bureaucratic Leadership Style is characterized by strict adherence to rules, procedures, and hierarchy within an organization (Galiakberova et al. 2024).

A bureaucratic leader's leadership is defined by his or her adherence to established policies and procedures, where he or she ensures that all team members follow organizational rules and regulations, aiming to maintain order and awareness within the organization. An example of bureaucratic leadership is Henry Ford, founder of the Ford Motor Company, known for innovation in the automobile industry, especially for the implementation of the assembly line. Ford was also very strict with processes and rules, focusing heavily on operational discipline and efficiency within his company (Galiakberova et al. 2024).

1.5. Leadership Characteristics

Leadership encompasses a series of characteristics that allow the leader to influence, motivate and direct their teams to achieve common goals in various contexts. That said, effective leaders often exhibit traits such as intelligence, responsibility, integrity, and the ability to delegate, which are essential characteristics for guiding organizations and influencing those they lead. Additionally, attributes such as emotional intelligence, empathy, and strong communication skills are crucial to fostering collaboration and managing team dynamics. Consistent, leaders with a clear vision of the future, creativity, and decision- making and problem-solving skills can navigate uncertain environments and drive organizational change. Finally, a growth mindset, adaptability, resilience, inspiration and intrinsic motivation are vital for personal development and for mentoring others (Fleshman, 2020).

Several authors consider that these are the necessary skills that a leader must have to be a good leader, and these characteristics can be developed and improved over time. Furthermore, although these characteristics are widely recognized, some authors argue that leadership effectiveness may also depend on situational factors and the specific context in which a leader operates, suggesting that adaptability may be as important as inherent traits (Gutterman, 2023).

1.5.1. Vision

In the context of leadership, the leader's vision plays a fundamental role in guiding and inspiring others. This refers to your ability to create a clear and compelling picture of the future, with challenging but achievable goals, serving as a roadmap for both the leader and his or her followers, providing direction and purpose in their endeavors. For example, Jeff Bezos founded Amazon in 1994 as a simple online bookstore, but from the beginning he had a clear vision, that of transforming Amazon into the largest retail and technology company in the world. Your ability to plan long-term, communicate this vision and invest in innovation was fundamental to the company's exponential growth (Machynska et al., 2024).

1.5.2. Communication

Effective communication from a leader is vital to shaping the organizational environment, so leaders must have the ability to convey ideas in a clear, objective and motivating way, so that all stakeholders understand, as well as the ability to listen and give constructive feedback. Steve Jobs is widely recognized as one of the greatest corporate communicators in history, having revolutionized the way corporate leaders communicate through his ability to simplify messages, tell engaging stories and convey passion, which helped him consolidate Apple as one of the most influential companies in the world (Machynska et al., 2024).

1.5.3. Empathy

Empathy is one of the most important characteristics for an effective leader, allowing a leader to understand and connect emotionally with their team, therefore it concerns the ability to put oneself in the other person's shoes, with a view to understanding their emotions, challenges and needs. To do this, it is necessary to actively listen and demonstrate a genuine interest in employees, as well as creating a safe and respectful environment, where employees feel that their opinions and feelings are valued. For example, Satya Nadella transformed Microsoft's once rigid and highly competitive culture into a more collaborative, innovative, and people-centric environment. His empathetic leadership, with prioritizing people, promoting an environment of inclusion and learning, and valuing well-being, helped the company grow significantly, both in innovation and in market value (Machynska et al., 2024).

1.5.4. Emotional Intelligence

Emotional intelligence in leadership corresponds to the ability to control emotions under pressure and to make balanced decisions, not acting on impulse. Leaders with high emotional intelligence have the ability to motivate and inspire their team with empathy and confidence, as well as the talent to resolve conflicts and develop a positive work environment (Korakis & Poulaky, 2025). Without a doubt, emotional intelligence is not an innate talent, but a skill that can be learned and improved over time. Typically, leaders who invest in self-knowledge, empathy and communication strengthen these skills and become more effective (Nwagwu & Henry.. For example, Tim Cook, who took over leadership of Apple in 2011 after the death of Steve Jobs. Unlike Jobs' visionary and intense style, Cook is a leader known for his highly developed emotional intelligence, through his self-awareness and self-control, empathy and rapport with the team, clear and inspiring communication, and motivation and resilience (Machynska et al., 2024).

1.5.5. Decision making

Decision-making in leadership involves developing strategic thinking, considering the short, medium and long-term impact, assessing risks and opportunities, analyzing data and information, the ability to make decisions under pressure, the existence of consensus and team participation, listening to opinions and team involvement, and the ability to adapt and constantly learn, as a leader must understand that not all decisions made will be perfect, learning from mistakes, being ready to adjust or change strategy when necessary. For example, when Satya Nadella took over Microsoft at a time when the company was in decline and managed to turn it into a technology giant again, his ability to make strategic decisions was essential to this turnaround. This was achieved because we knew how to analyze the market, identify opportunities and make strategic choices (Machynska et al., 2024).

1.5.6. Motivation and Inspiration

Motivation and inspiration in leadership comes down to defining a clear and inspiring vision of the future, which inspires action and enthusiasm, and must be realistic and achievable, but also challenging, recognizing achievements and efforts and being an example, as a model of behavior and attitude motivates others to follow it, providing personal development and growth. For example, Richard Branson, founder of the Virgin Group, is a classic example of a leader who cultivates motivation and inspiration in his team. These are achieved by defending a positive organizational culture, in which it is believed that happy and motivated employees are the key to business success, by leading by example, being known for being an approachable person who practices what he preaches, by valuing innovation and entrepreneurship and by prioritizing well-being and work-life balance, as it is believed that motivated employees are those who have a balance between their professional and personal lives (Machynska et al., 2024).

1.5.7. Responsibility and Integrity

Leaders must demonstrate responsibility for their decisions and actions, being ethical and honest, because by assuming responsibility for their choices they set a standard for their team, encouraging them to adopt similar responsibility in the future. Furthermore, integrity is essential to building trust between leaders and their employees, because when leaders act with honesty and transparency, they foster an environment where employees feel safe to express their ideas and creativity. Tim Cook has been an example of leadership based on responsibility and integrity, guiding the company with a strong commitment to transparency, ethics and social impact, defending values such as privacy, human rights and diversity (Machynska et al., 2024).

1.5.8. Adaptability and Resilience

Adaptable and resilient leaders are those who adjust quickly to change, overcome challenges with determination, and find opportunities where others see obstacles. They stay calm under pressure, are constantly learning and instill confidence in their teams. Satya Nadella is an example of an adaptable and resilient organizational leader, having transformed Microsoft from a stagnant company to a global leader in innovation, proving that the ability to quickly adapt to change and overcome challenges is essential for success (Machynska et al., 2024).

1.5.9. Ability to delegate

The ability to delegate is an essential trait of a successful leader, as knowing how to trust the team, distribute tasks strategically, offer support and allow autonomy are aspects that make a leader not only efficient, but also a talent developer within the organization. For example, Warren Buffett, CEO of Berkshire Hathaway, has a leadership style based on strategic delegation, allowing his managers to have autonomy and responsibility over their areas, since he chooses his managers well, gives them freedom to make decisions, defines clear objectives and focuses on the strategic growth of the organization (Machynska et al., 2024).

1.6. Common Leadership Mistakes

Without a doubt, even the best leaders can make mistakes. A few slip-ups within leadership can significantly harm employee effectiveness and retention. The most common pitfalls include micromanagement, lack of clear communication and lack of recognition. That said, knowledge about these issues is crucial to promoting a productive work environment and maintaining high morale among employees.

1.6.1. Micromanagement

Micromanagement refers to a leadership style characterized by excessive control over employees' work, where the leader oversees every little detail, ultimately suffocating the team. Such a situation can lead to several negative results for both leaders and their teams, from reducing creativity and autonomy to generating frustration among employees (Westover, 2024).

Micromanagement can hinder organizational change and employee engagement. Therefore, leaders must strive to empower their teams by setting clear expectations, promoting collaboration, and allowing autonomy in decision-making. This approach can lead to a more motivated and productive workforce (Westover, 2024).

1.6.2. Lack of Clear Communication

When leaders fail to communicate clearly or fail to encourage team members to share their ideas and experiences, employees may not see their roles, responsibilities, or the organization's goals. This ambiguity can lead to confusion and frustration, as well as distrust and uncertainty, making it difficult for employees to perform effectively. Clear communication is essential to setting expectations and aligning team efforts with organizational goals, so leaders should prioritize clear, consistent, and open communication with their teams. By doing so, they can create a culture of trust and support that encourages top talent to remain committed to the organization for the long term (Westover, 2024).

1.6.3. Lack of Recognition

A common mistake made by leaders is related to not recognizing and praising their employees for their contributions, which can reduce motivation and increase turnover rates, as people clearly need recognition to continue delivering good results.

Therefore, it is essential that leaders implement regular praise and recognition, and that they can develop mechanisms and strategies for this purpose (Westover, 2024).

While mistakes can negatively impact an organization's well-being, without being a bad thing, some authors argue that they can also serve as learning opportunities for leaders to improve their practices and develop their leadership skills over time.

1.7. Coaching and Mentoring

Coaching and mentoring are integral parts of effective leadership, particularly in promoting professional development and inclusion in various fields. These practices not only enhance individual capabilities, but also contribute to organizational success by aligning personal and institutional goals (Westover, 2024).

In relation to the concepts of leadership, coaching and mentoring, in leadership, the leader inspires, guides and influences a team, in coaching, the coach seeks to develop skills and achieve specific goals for those receiving coaching and in mentoring, the mentor intends to share knowledge and experience to guide those receiving mentoring (Westover, 2024).

In fact, coaching and mentoring help a lot in the leadership role. Coaching applied to leadership helps to develop specific skills in employees, encouraging self-knowledge and professional growth, using techniques such as structured feedback, reflective questions and setting goals. For example, a leader might use coaching to help an employee improve specific aspects, such as communication or leadership skills. In leadership mentoring, the mentor shares real-world experiences and lessons learned throughout his or her career, providing strategic insight and long-term guidance, enabling employees to make better decisions based on the mentor's experience and wisdom. For example, a CEO may act as a mentor to an inexperienced manager, helping him or her grow within the organization (Westover, 2024).

Therefore, a leader can act as a leader-coach, encouraging autonomy, asking reflective questions and focusing on team development or as a leader-mentor, sharing knowledge, giving practical advice and directing the careers of employees, combining elements of coaching and mentoring to form more prepared and motivated teams (Westover, 2024).

2. TEAM LEADERSHIP IN ORGANIZATIONS

2.1. The Importance of Leadership in Organizations

Leadership is one of the most critical factors for an organization's success. A good leader not only sets strategic directions, but also motivates, inspires and develops teams, ensuring that objectives are achieved efficiently and sustainably (Anyanugo et al., 2024).

2.1.1. Key Benefits of Effective Leadership

Effective leadership, through its multiple styles and characteristics, can bring numerous benefits to an organization, such as increased productivity, as it has the ability to create a motivating work environment, where employees feel valued, resulting in greater efficiency and better results. Furthermore, good leadership allows for the improvement of the organizational climate, promoting an environment of trust, respect and collaboration, reducing internal conflicts and increasing employee well-being, talent development and employee retention, investing in employee growth, promoting training, mentoring and opportunities for professional advancement and strategic decision-making by evaluating scenarios, identifying risks and making assertive decisions. Finally, a competent leader promotes a culture of constant innovation, encouraging the sharing of new ideas and creative solutions (Anyanugo et al., 2024).

2.2. The Importance of Leadership and Management for Organizations

2.2.1. Differences between Leadership and Management

Although the concepts of management and leadership are related, they both have distinct functions within an organization. This distinction is crucial to organizational effectiveness, as both roles have complementary functions. Leadership focuses on inspiring and motivating individuals, while management emphasizes planning, organizing, and controlling resources. Understanding these differences can improve organizational performance and employee satisfaction (Toor & Ofori, 2008).

Among the main differences between leadership and management, the distinctions related to philosophical foundations, functions, problem-solving approaches and behavioral differences stand out. In terms of philosophical foundations and functions, leaders and managers play different roles within an organization, as leaders are often seen as visionaries who motivate and inspire their teams and managers are responsible for planning, organizing and executing tasks to achieve specific goals. Furthermore, the way leaders solve problems varies significantly, as leaders tend to take a more innovative and flexible approach, encouraging creativity and new ideas, while managers often rely on established processes and procedures to solve problems. Finally, both exhibit different behaviors due to their intrinsic and extrinsic motivations, because leaders are typically more focused on influencing and guiding people, while managers focus on maintaining order and efficiency within the organization (Toor & Ofori, 2008).

Some authors argue that organizations need to cultivate leaders who can also possess management skills. This dual capability is essential to fostering a competitive advantage in the future, as leaders must not only inspire but also understand the operational aspects of their organizations. Despite their differences, the terms leader and manager are often used interchangeably, leading to confusion. It is important to recognize that all leaders can be managers, but not all managers are necessarily leaders (Toor & Ofori, 2008).

2.2.2. Reconciliation between Leadership and Management

Although leadership and management have distinct roles and functions, they also share some important similarities (Gradinarova, 2021).

Both share common ground in their influence, goal orientation, team motivation, task accomplishment, relationship management, and adaptability. That said, both leaders and managers have the power to influence others, playing crucial roles in guiding their teams toward achieving organizational goals, leveraging their authority to motivate and direct their team. Therefore, both roles are focused on achieving specific goals, where leaders inspire their teams to pursue a vision and managers ensure that the necessary processes are in place to achieve those goals. Both are responsible for motivating their teams, that is, encouraging team members to engage in tasks and work collaboratively to solve problems, fostering a sense of unity and purpose within the group. Both are concerned with the successful completion of tasks, working to ensure their teams have the resources and support they need to accomplish their goals, albeit through different approaches. Both roles involve managing relationships within a team, so leaders focus on informal personal relationships and managers also need to maintain official relationships to ensure smooth operations. Finally, both leaders and managers must be adaptable to changing circumstances because they need to respond to new challenges and adjust their strategies to maintain team performance and achieve organizational goals (Gradinarova, 2021).

2.3. Organizational teams arising from Leadership

Leadership plays a critical role in shaping team dynamics and performance in organizations, where effective leaders not only motivate their teams but also create an environment conducive to collaboration and innovation (Lubis et al., 2024).

Leaders are essential to promoting motivation among team members, and must go beyond traditional incentives such as salary to include personal fulfillment and appreciation. To do so, they must use effective communication, positive feedback and recognition, which are essential to motivating teams and improving performance. Furthermore, leaders are responsible for creating a supportive work environment characterized by trust and collaboration, as well as cultivating an atmosphere that encourages growth, innovation and collective learning, which directly impacts creativity (Lubis et al., 2024).

Finally, leaders must adapt to future trends by developing skills in emotional intelligence, sustainability and inclusion to navigate the ever-evolving business landscape, as well as emphasizing human-centered work design and digital enablement, which are crucial to fostering creativity and team agility. (Lubis et al., 2024).

2.4. Conceptual Model: The Impact of Leaders Communication on Employee Accountability and Autonomy

A study developed by Farinha (2019) explores how the concepts of leadership, communication, autonomy and responsibility can be drivers of organizational success, arguing that effective leadership in organizations depends on a balance between them. These elements form an interconnected conceptual model, in which each factor directly influences the other.

Initially, the leader delegates autonomy and this ability to delegate corresponds to the ability to let go and trust others. This act of delegating is achieved through communication, which is the basis of the process, which must be clear, transparent and objective in order to avoid noise and misalignments. Therefore, the leader empowers his employees, promoting their autonomy, which is fundamental for innovation and development within an organization, where the leader delegates tasks. Autonomy leads to a feeling of responsibility on the part of those targeted, making them want to show that they deserve such trust. That said, the leader automatically gives more motivation, responsibility and autonomy to the team, working more efficiently, causing greater productivity, making him a better leader, this being an inverted spiral model (Farinha, 2019).

2.5. Maxwell's Five Levels of Leadership

John C. Maxwell, one of the world's leading experts on leadership, developed the Five Levels of Leadership Model, which describes the evolution of a leader within an organization, providing a framework for understanding and developing leadership skills. These levels, which range from basic positional authority to the pinnacle of leadership influence, emphasize the progression and growth necessary for effective leadership. Each level builds on the previous one, creating a comprehensive path for leaders to increase their impact and effectiveness. However, it is important to note that this model does not only cover "first-time" leaders, as a leader may be at the top, but when changing companies, he or she goes back to square one (Maxwell, 2011).

The different levels progress in the following order:

Level 1: Position

Position is the lowest level of leadership, the basic one. The only influence that the individual has is based solely on the authority granted by a title or position that he holds. In this case, the team follows the leader because they are obliged to (Maxwell, 2011).

People who do not go beyond the first level can be bosses, but never leaders, having team and not members of a team. They use rules, regulations, procedures and organizational charts as means to control the team, who follow the leader only within the established limits of his authority and do only what is their responsibility. When positional leaders ask for extra effort or time, they rarely get positive responses (Maxwell, 2011).

Level 2: The Permission

Level 2 is based entirely on relationships and the premise that people follow the leader because they want to. When a leader likes people, he treats them with value, begins to develop influence over them, establishing bonds of trust (Maxwell, 2011).

The priority at Level 2 is not for the leader to maintain his position, but for him to know his people and figure out the best way to deal with the group. Here, leaders discover who the people who work for them are, just as their followers discover who the leader is, and solid, lasting relationships are born from there. In fact, it is possible to like people without leading them, but it is impossible to lead well without liking people (Maxwell, 2011).

Level 3: The Production

Indeed, upon reaching the Permission Level there is a risk that the leader will be tempted to stop there. However, good leaders do not limit themselves to simply creating a pleasant work environment, and for this very reason, they must move on to Level 3, which is based on results. At the Production Level, the leader gains influence and credibility and people begin to follow him because of what he does for the organization (Maxwell, 2011).

At this stage, results are seen, team mood improves, profits rise, turnover drops and goals are achieved. Additionally, leaders become agents of change by solving complex problems and making difficult decisions (Maxwell, 2011).

Level 4: The Person

Level 4 leaders use their position, relationships, and productivity to invest in their followers and develop them into leaders themselves. The result is reproduction, as in this phase the leader reproduces (Maxwell, 2011)

At Level 4 two situations always occur. First, teamwork reaches a very high level, because strong investment in people deepens relationships, helps them get to know each other better and strengthens loyalty. Second, team performance improves as there are more leaders on the team who help improve the performance of all team members (Maxwell, 2011).

In fact, Level 4 leaders change the lives of the people they lead. Likewise, people follow leaders because of what they have done for them personally. These relationships sometimes last a lifetime (Maxwell, 2011).

Level 5: The Person Plus Purpose (Pinnacle)

The highest and most difficult level of leadership is the Pinnacle. Although most leaders are capable of reaching Level 4, Level 5 not only requires effort, expertise and intentionality, but also enormous talent, where only natural leaders reach this stage (Maxwell, 2011).

Here, with their leadership, the leaders created a legacy. People follow the leader because of who he is and what he represents, so his leadership style gains a good reputation. In this way, Level 5 leaders often transcend their position, their organization, and sometimes their industry (Maxwell, 2011).

For example, Commander Rui Nabeiro, founder of the Nabeiro-Delta Group, is recognized beyond borders, having been considered one of the most relevant leaders with the best reputation in Portugal, thanks to his effort, dedication and relationship with others (Barroso, 2012).

3. CHALLENGES OF CONTEMPORARY LEADERSHIP

Contemporary leadership faces numerous challenges shaped by globalization, technological advances, and evolving workforce dynamics. Leaders must, in the first phase, know and understand these challenges and then adapt to them, responding to the diverse needs of stakeholders. From an endless list of challenges that 21st century leadership must face, the following stand out:

3.1. Adapting to Change

The role of leaders has transformed significantly over time. As society continues to evolve, leadership is no longer seen as a simple act of influencing others, but encompasses a much broader range of elements, including the dynamics between leaders and their followers, the processes of leading and following, and the context in which these interactions occur. Understanding this complexity is essential for leaders to effectively adapt to change ("Leadership - Advancing Great Leaders and Leadership", 2023).

The business world is very dynamic, requiring agile leaders to adapt to new technologies, regulations and market trends, as well as to crises and uncertainties, which have been quite noticeable in recent years, as the world has witnessed the emergence of pandemics (such as Covid-19 and the emergence of teleworking), global conflicts and economic crises that demonstrate the importance of resilient leadership capable of acting quickly in the face of adversity ("Leadership - Advancing Great Leaders and Leadership", 2023).

3.2. Diversity and Inclusion Management

Contemporary leadership faces numerous challenges shaped by globalization, causing leaders to navigate a complex global landscape due to the interconnectedness of economies, cultures and societies around the world, requiring an understanding of diverse cultural perspectives and practices (Chowdhury et al., 2024).

In this "global village", cultural sensitivity and inclusion are essential for organizational leaders, involving the recognition and respect for differences in values, beliefs and practices, encouraging companies to opt for more diverse and inclusive environments, providing equitable opportunities for all, allowing them to understand and respect the diverse backgrounds of their employees. This understanding fosters an inclusive environment where all stakeholders feel valued, supported and heard (Chowdhury et al., 2024).

However, such diversity is not only observed from a global perspective, of different cultures and nationalities, but leaders also face the great challenge brought about by the increase in average life expectancy, that is, managing teams made up of different generations (Baby Boomers, Generation X, Millennials and Generation Z), which requires knowledge of the different perspectives, values and motivations of each group, with a view to promoting an inclusive environment and encouraging the exchange of knowledge between generations (Cahyono, 2024).

3.3. Digital Transformation and Innovation

Rapid technological advances require leaders to be adaptable and innovative, using technology to increase organizational effectiveness (Chowdhury et al., 2024). A culture of continuous improvement is crucial for leaders to remain relevant and have a competitive advantage in a rapidly evolving market, achieved through regular evaluation and updating of technological tools and strategies to meet new needs. To this end, companies and organizations must be guided by the use of data analysis, with a view to identifying trends, evaluating performance and making informed choices that align with institutional objectives and the needs of stakeholders (Chowdhury et al., 2024).

To successfully implement technological adaptations, leaders must provide adequate training and support to their employees, ensuring that all stakeholders are equipped to effectively use new technologies, fostering a more inclusive and productive operating environment (Chowdhury et al., 2024).

CONCLUSIONS

The current business environment is highly dynamic and competitive, increasingly demanding quick and effective responses from companies through high-quality performances, which has increased the pressure felt among organizational leaders and managers. Combating and understanding current challenges, such as adapting to change, managing diversity and inclusion, and digital transformation and innovation, is only possible through effective leadership, someone who takes the reins and walks alongside team members towards success. Leadership and its practice are, today, factors of enormous impact on organizational life, being decisive for the performance and effectiveness of organizations and the achievement of defined objectives.

Organizational leadership is an essential factor for the success and sustainability of companies, as it directly influences motivation, productivity and organizational climate. An effective leader not only defines strategies and directs the team, but also inspires, develops talent and promotes a culture of innovation and collaboration, and may resort to coaching and mentoring. These are essential tools for team development and organizational growth.

Therefore, it is important to recognize the role of leadership and understand that there is no fixed prototype of a good leader, as the way in which leadership is exercised can vary according to the context, challenges and needs of the company, with different styles and characteristics that a leader can adopt, which impact the performance of the team and the organization in different ways, as well as different theories to explain the different types of leadership. Furthermore, it is essential to understand that no leader is perfect, as even the most experienced make mistakes throughout their career. The important thing is to learn and correct mistakes quickly, with a view to continuing to evolve and guide the team efficiently.

In today's corporate environment, both managers and leaders play critical roles in the success of an organization. Although these terms are often used interchangeably, they represent distinct and complementary roles, as managers ensure operational efficiency, while leaders inspire and direct teams toward innovation and sustainable growth.

However, it is not just the leader and the manager who make the company. For a long time now, workers have not only longed for a good salary, but also for attitudes focused on appreciation and self-fulfillment in the workplace, which means that a good leader constantly faces the difficult challenge of gaining the unconditional support of his team. Leadership at the organizational level is only possible if employees, of their own free will, choose to adopt their leaders and the organization's goals. This characteristic corresponds to the difference between a leader and a boss.

Ultimately, investing in leadership development becomes a strategic necessity for any organization, as well-prepared leaders contribute to a healthy work environment, a more motivated team and sustainable results in the long term, continuing to be one of the main competitive differentiators for companies.

REFERENCES

Abasilim, D. U. (2024). *Exploring the concept of leadership*. Humanities and Social Sciences., DOI: 10.7862/rz.2024.hss.01

Abbas, M., & Ali, R. (2023). Transformational versus transactional leadership styles and project success: A meta-analytic review. *European Management Journal, 41*(1), 125–142. DOI: 10.1016/j.emj.2021.10.011

Anyanugo, M. O., Ololube, N. P., & Okuru, C. L. (2024). Establishing the basis for organizational success through effective leadership. *SAR Journal of Humanities and Social Science, 6*(4), 156–169. DOI: 10.36346/sarjhss.2024.v06i04.003

Barroso, D. C. P. (2012). *O perfil de um líder – O futuro da Delta Cafés* (Dissertação de mestrado, ISCTE – Instituto Universitário de Lisboa). Repositório ISCTE. https://repositorio.iscte-iul.pt/bitstream/10071/5428/1/Tese_Daniela%20Barroso.pdf

Blyznyuk, T., & Bliznyuk, O. (2024). Contemporary theories of leadership: Cross-cultural analysis. *Economy and Society*, (66). Advance online publication. DOI: 10.32782/2524-0072/2024-66-42

Bwalya, A. (2023). Leadership styles. *Global Scientific Journal, 11*(8).

Cahyono, N. D. (2024). The role of emotional intelligence in HR leadership: Building strong teams in a multigenerational context. *The Journal of Applied Organizational Studies*. http://thejoas.com/index.php/thejoas/article/view/114/152

Chowdhury, T. I., Saeedi, A. S., Karim, A. M., Ahmed, A. R., & Karim, A. M. (2024). Effective contemporary leadership in tertiary education: Global stakeholders' viewpoint. *International Journal of Academic Research in Business and Social Sciences*. https://hrmars.com/index.php/IJARBSS/article/view/20466

Ermetova, Z., & Abajanova, G. (2024). Leadership in modern organizations. https://journalsnuu.uz/index.php/1/article/view/1215/464

Farinha, J. (2019). *O impacto da comunicação dos líderes na responsabilidade e autonomia dos colaboradores* (Tese de doutoramento). Repositório Científico de Acesso Aberto de Portugal. https://comum.rcaap.pt/bitstream/10400.26/31064/1/Dissertação%20de%20Doutoramento%20em%20Gestão%20-%20Joao%20Farinha.pdf

Fleshman, J. W. (2020). How to develop a leadership training program. *Clinics in Colon and Rectal Surgery, 33*(5), 305–310. DOI: 10.1055/s-0040-1712975 PMID: 32624715

Galiakberova, A. A., Mukhametshin, A. G., Dyrin, S. P., Asratyan, N. M., Kornilova, I. V., & Galiev, R. M. (2024). Tipologia dos estilos de liderança em função do processo de tomada de decisão e da orientação para a tarefa/pessoa [Типология стилей руководства в зависимости от характера принятия решений и ориентации на дело/человека]. *Management Science*. Advance online publication. DOI: 10.26794/2304-022X-2024-14-3-135-146

Gebreheat, G., Teame, H., & Costa, E. I. (2023). The impact of transformational leadership style on nurses' job satisfaction: An integrative review. *SAGE Open Nursing*, *9*, 23779608231197428. DOI: 10.1177/23779608231197428 PMID: 37691720

Gradinarova, N. (2021). *Leadership vs. management: Understanding the key differences and similarities*. https://typeset.io/papers/leadership-vs-management-understanding-the-key-differences-gfslxdyfvx

Gutterman, A. S. (2023). *Leadership traits and attributes. SSRN*. https://papers.ssrn.com/sol3/papers.cfm?abstract_id=4560190

Khajeh, E. H. (2018). Impact of leadership styles on organizational performance. *Journal of Human Resources Management Research*. DOI: DOI: 10.5171/2018.687849

Koesters, S. C., Shea, T., & Satiani, B. (2017). *It's about the people, not being the boss*. https://typeset.io/papers/it-s-about-the-people-not-being-the-boss-1iirsb1aho

Korakis, G., & Poulaki, I. (2025). A systematic literature review on the relationship between emotional intelligence and transformational leadership—A critical approach. *Businesses*, *5*(1), 4. DOI: 10.3390/businesses5010004

Kumar, P. (2024). *Leadership styles and their influence on project team performance*. Nonhuman Journal., DOI: 10.70008/nhj.v1i06.29

Leadership – Advancing great leaders and leadership. (2023). In *IntechOpen Books*. https://www.intechopen.com/books/12141

Machynska, N., Blikhar, V., & Kuzhur, A. (2024). *Formação de competências de liderança no processo de preparação profissional de futuros especialistas no ensino superior* [Формування лідерських рис у процесі професійної підготовки майбутніх фахівців в умовах закладу вищої освіти]. Scientific Educational Review., DOI: 10.55643/ser.1.51.2024.556

Maxwell, J. C. (2011). *Os 5 níveis da liderança*. https://pt.scribd.com/document/568195267/OS-5-NIVEIS-DA-LIDERANCA

Nwagwu, U., & Henry, U. C. (2025). Emotional Intelligence and Leadership Effectiveness. Journal of Arts and Sociological Research.

Pizzolitto, E., Verna, I., & Venditti, M. (2022). Authoritarian leadership styles and performance: a systematic literature review and research agenda. Management Review Quarterly, 1-31.

Thompson, G., & Vecchio, R. P. (2009). Situational leadership theory: A test of three versions. *The Leadership Quarterly*, *20*(5), 837–848. DOI: 10.1016/j.leaqua.2009.06.014

Toor, S., & Ofori, G. (2008). Leadership versus management: How they are different, and why. *Leadership and Management in Engineering*, *8*(2), 61–71. DOI: 10.1061/(ASCE)1532-6748(2008)8:2(61)

Westoven, J. H. (2024). *Losing your best: How poor leadership can drive top talent away*. Innovative Human Capital. https://www.innovativehumancapital.com/article/losing-your-best-how-poor-leadership-can-drive-top-talent-away

Chapter 6
Absenteeism, Internal Marketing, and Productivity in a Hybrid Work Environment:
Preliminary Insights

Miguel Ângelo Fernandes Medeiros
Polytechnic Institute of Cávado and Ave, Portugal

Bruno Barbosa Sousa
http://orcid.org/0000-0002-8588-2422
Applied Management Research Unit (UNIAG), School of Hospitality and Tourism, Polytechnic University of Cávado and Ave (IPCA), Barcelos, Portugal

ABSTRACT

The transformation of work models in organizations has intensified over the last decade, being significantly accelerated by the COVID-19 pandemic. The forced adoption of remote work led many organizations to reassess traditional management practices, culminating in the consolidation of the hybrid model as a structural solution and not merely a temporary one. This chapter falls within the domain of human resource management and internal marketing, aiming to contribute to a deeper understanding of the role of internal marketing in responding to the emerging challenges of hybrid work, with a particular emphasis on the dynamics of absenteeism and organizational productivity.

DOI: 10.4018/979-8-2600-2178-1.ch006

INTRODUCTION

The world of work is undergoing one of the most profound transformations in its modern history. The widespread adoption of remote and hybrid work, accelerated by the COVID-19 pandemic, has permanently altered how organizations structure work, coordinate teams, and manage employee performance. What initially emerged as an emergency response has now evolved into a dominant organizational model across many sectors, particularly in knowledge-intensive and service-based industries. Hybrid work is defined as the combination of remote and on-site work, and is no longer a temporary arrangement, but a structural feature of contemporary organizational life (Allen, Golden, & Shockley, 2015; Contreras, Baykal, & Abid, 2020). While hybrid work offers substantial advantages, including flexibility, autonomy, and improved work-life balance, it also presents new managerial and ethical challenges. Physical distance, reduced informal interaction, and reliance on digital communication can weaken social bonds, dilute organizational culture, and make it harder to sustain employee engagement (Gibbs, Mengel, & Siemroth, 2021; Leonardi, 2021). In this environment, traditional approaches to supervision and control have become less effective, shifting the focus towards trust, communication, and employee experience as the foundations of organizational performance. Two phenomenoms have become particularly salient in hybrid organizations: absenteeism and productivity. Absenteeism is no longer limited to physical absence from the workplace; it increasingly takes the form of psychological withdrawal, disengagement, and reduced cognitive and emotional presence (Johns, 2010; Kahn, 1990). At the same time, productivity in hybrid contexts is no longer measured by time spent at the office, but by outcomes, collaboration quality, and sustained employee contribution (Bakker & Demerouti, 2017). These changes, force organizations to rethink how they motivate, connect, and support their people.

Within this shifting landscape, internal marketing (endomarketing) emerges as a powerful strategic framework. Originally developed within the marketing of services, internal marketing treats employees as internal customers whose needs, motivations, and experiences must be actively managed in order to deliver value to external stakeholders (Berry, 1981; Grönroos, 1990). Over time, this logic has become deeply tangled with human resource management, employer branding, and organizational culture, positioning internal marketing as a key driver of engagement, retention, and performance (Kotler & Keller, 2022; Armstrong, 2021).

In human-centered organizations, internal marketing goes beyond communication campaigns. It involves the systematic design of employee experiences through recognition, development, leadership, flexibility, and meaningful work. In hybrid environments, where physical presence no longer anchors organizational identity, internal marketing becomes even more critical for maintaining alignment, trust, and belonging.

This chapter explores the conceptual relationship between absenteeism, internal marketing, and productivity in hybrid work environments. It argues that internal marketing operates as a mediating system that connects human-centered talent management with organizational performance. By integrating insights from organizational behavior, marketing, and HRM, the chapter develops a framework that explains how internal marketing reduces absenteeism and sustains productivity by strengthening engagement, psychological safety, and organizational commitment.

2. CONCEPTUAL FOUNDATIONS

2.1 Internal Marketing as a Strategic Human-Centered Approach

Internal marketing was initially introduced by Berry (1981) as a response to quality problems in service organizations. His central idea was simple one but transformative: employees should be treated as internal customers, and their jobs as internal products. If employees are satisfied, motivated, and well supported, they will deliver better service to external customers. Grönroos (1990) expanded this view by framing internal marketing as a systematic managerial process aimed at aligning employees with the organization's service promise. In this perspective, employees are not merely performers of tasks; they are carriers of the brand, co-producers of value, and ambassadors of organizational identity. In contemporary organizations, internal marketing has become closely connected with human resource management and employer branding. Kotler and Keller (2022) define internal marketing as the set of practices designed to ensure that employees are motivated, skilled, and committed to delivering organizational value. Armstrong (2021) similarly emphasizes that internal marketing is not a collection of isolated initiatives but an integrated management philosophy that aligns communication, leadership, development, and reward systems.

From a human-centered perspective, internal marketing reflects an ethical commitment to employee dignity, voice, and well-being. It recognizes that sustainable organizational performance depends not only on technical competence but also on how people experience their work, their leaders, and their organization.

2.2 Employee Engagement, Psychological Contracts, and Motivation

The impact of internal marketing on performance operates largely through psychological mechanisms. One of the most important is employee engagement. In this line of thougt, Kahn (1990) conceptualized engagement as the degree to which individuals invest their physical, cognitive, and emotional energy into their work roles. Engaged employees are attentive, proactive, and emotionally connected to what they do.

Saks (2006) further demonstrated that organizational practices such as communication, recognition, and leadership support are key antecedents of engagement. Internal marketing directly targets these drivers by shaping how employees perceive their value, their future, and their relationship with the organization. Another important mechanism is the psychological contract, the set of implicit expectations between employees and employers (Rousseau, 1995). When organizations invest in communication, development, and well-being, employees interpret this as a signal of mutual respect and fairness. In return, they are more likely to reciprocate with commitment, effort, and loyalty. Self-Determination Theory (Deci & Ryan, 2000) also helps explain why internal marketing matters. According to this theory, people are most motivated when three basic needs are satisfied: autonomy, competence, and relatedness. Hybrid work arrangements can support autonomy, but without strong internal marketing they may undermine relatedness and competence. Internal marketing practices such as feedback, training, and recognition restore these psychological needs, sustaining intrinsic motivation and performance.

3. ABSENTEEISM IN THE HYBRID WORK ERA

Absenteeism has long been recognized as a critical organizational problem, associated with reduced productivity, increased costs, and deteriorating morale (Johns, 2010). Traditionally, absenteeism was measured as physical absence from the workplace. In hybrid work environments, however, absenteeism has become more complex and less visible. Hybrid work introduces new forms of withdrawal. Employees may be physically present online but psychologically disengaged, emotionally detached, or cognitively distracted. This phenomenon, sometimes referred to as "virtual absenteeism" or "presenteeism," reflects a decline in genuine work involvement rather than a simple absence from the office (Bakker & Demerouti, 2017).

Research suggests that remote and hybrid work can increase the risk of isolation, ambiguity, and emotional exhaustion if not properly managed (Gibbs et al., 2021; Kossek, Thompson, & Lautsch, 2015). When employees feel disconnected from their teams or undervalued by their organization, they are more likely to disengage, delay tasks, and psychologically withdraw, all of which resemble absenteeism in their effects. From a human-centered management perspective, absenteeism should therefore be understood not merely as a behavioral outcome but as a signal of deeper relational and motivational problems. It reflects how employees experience their work environment, their leadership, and their organizational culture.

4. PRODUCTIVITY BEYOND PHYSICAL PRESENCE

Productivity in hybrid organizations cannot be reduced to hours worked or physical visibility. It increasingly depends on knowledge sharing, creativity, collaboration, and sustained engagement. Bakker and Demerouti's (2017) Job Demands-Resources (JD-R) model is particularly relevant here. According to this model, employees perform the best version of themselves when they have access to sufficient psychological and organizational resources, such as support, feedback, and development opportunities. Hybrid work changes both demands and resources. While flexibility may reduce commuting stress and improves autonomy, it can also increase communication overload, role ambiguity, and emotional strain. Internal marketing plays a crucial role in ensuring that employees continue to receive the resources they need to perform effectively, even when working remotely.

Empirical research consistently shows that engaged employees are more productive, more innovative, and more resilient (Saks, 2022). Since internal marketing strengthens engagement, it indirectly sustains productivity by reinforcing the psychological and social conditions that enable high performance.

5. INTERNAL MARKETING IN HYBRID WORK ENVIRONMENTS

The hybridization of work has not merely changed where people work, it has fundamentally transformed how organizations relate to their employees. When daily physical co-presence disappears, organizations lose many of the informal mechanisms through which culture, commitment, and identity were traditionally reinforced. In this new reality, internal marketing becomes a central architecture through which organizations actively design and manage the employee experience. Hybrid work environments increase both employee autonomy and vulnerability. While employees gain flexibility and control over their schedules, they also face higher risks of isolation, blurred boundaries, and perceived invisibility. Internal marketing provides the managerial logic that allows organizations to address these risks in a systematic and ethical manner, by deliberately creating meaning, connection, and value for employees as internal customers. From a strategic perspective, internal marketing in hybrid contexts is not simply about keeping employees informed. It is about building a psychologically safe, motivating, and inclusive environment that sustains engagement and performance even when physical proximity is limited.

5.1 Internal Communication as Organizational Glue

In hybrid organizations, communication becomes the primary infrastructure of organizational life. Without the physical workplace to provide constant alignment and social reinforcement, employees rely almost entirely on formal and informal communication systems to understand priorities, expectations, and organizational identity. Welch and Jackson (2007) define internal communication as the strategic management of information, relationships, and dialogue within organizations. In hybrid environments, this definition takes on renewed importance. Communication is no longer simply a transmission of information; it becomes the main vehicle through which employees experience leadership, fairness, and belonging.

Men (2014) emphasizes that effective internal communication must be transparent, participative, and dialogical. Employees who feel heard and informed are more likely to trust management and invest effort in their work. Conversely, inconsistent or unclear communication in hybrid contexts can quickly generate anxiety, role ambiguity, and disengagement, all precursors of absenteeism. Digital communication platforms (e-mail, intranets, collaboration tools, enterprise social networks) play a crucial role in hybrid organizations (Leonardi, 2021). However, technology alone does not guarantee connection. Internal marketing ensures that these tools are used to reinforce shared meaning, recognize contributions, and maintain emotional proximity between employees and leaders.

5.2 Recognition, Visibility, and Psychological Presence

One of the hidden risks of hybrid work is the erosion of visibility. When employees are not physically present, their effort and contributions may go unnoticed, leading to feelings of neglect and unfairness. Over time, this reduces motivation and increases psychological withdrawal. Herzberg's (1966) two-factor theory highlights recognition as a key motivator of satisfaction and commitment. In hybrid environments, recognition must be intentionally designed rather than left to chance. Digital recognition systems, public acknowledgments in virtual meetings, and peer-to-peer appreciation platforms all become essential components of internal marketing. Saks (2022) shows that employees who receive regular feedback and recognition are more engaged and less likely to disengage or withdraw. Internal marketing thus functions as a visibility mechanism: it makes effort, competence, and contribution visible, even when work happens at a distance. Recognition is also an ethical issue. Fair acknowledgment of work protects employees from feeling exploited or forgotten, reinforcing dignity and organizational justice, both central to human-centered management.

5.3 Flexibility, Trust, and Work–Life Integration

Hybrid work has redefined the relationship between organizations and employees around the dimension of time and control. Kossek et al. (2015) argue that flexibility only produces positive outcomes when it is embedded in a culture of trust, clarity, and mutual responsibility.

From an internal marketing perspective, flexibility becomes part of the organization's value proposition to employees. It signals respect for individual needs, family life, and personal well-being. When employees perceive flexibility as genuine rather than symbolic, they reciprocate with loyalty and engagement (Allen et al., 2013). However, poorly managed flexibility can lead to overwork, digital overload, and burnout. Internal marketing plays a regulatory role by setting clear expectations, encouraging boundary management, and promoting healthy work rhythms. This prevents the hidden form of absenteeism that arises when employees are emotionally exhausted but still "logged in."

5.4 Learning, Development, and Future Employability

Hybrid organizations depend heavily on continuous learning. Digitalization, automation, and remote collaboration require new skills and adaptive capacities. Internal marketing integrates learning and development into the employee experience, signaling that the organization is invested in the employee's future, not just in their immediate output. Noe et al. (2021) show that perceived development opportunities are strongly associated with commitment and reduced turnover. In hybrid environments, digital training platforms, virtual mentoring, and career development conversations become powerful internal marketing tools. Development is also deeply ethical. By supporting employability and competence, organizations protect employees from technological obsolescence and uncertainty. This strengthens the psychological contract (Rousseau, 1995) and reduces the disengagement that often leads to absenteeism.

5.5 Culture, Belonging, and Organizational Identity

Perhaps the greatest challenge of hybrid work is cultural fragmentation. Without daily face-to-face interaction, employees may feel less connected to the organization's values, purpose, and community.

Schein (2010) defines organizational culture as shared assumptions that guide behavior. In hybrid contexts, these assumptions must be actively communicated and reinforced through symbols, rituals, leadership behavior, and storytelling. Internal marketing provides the narrative and symbolic infrastructure that keeps culture alive.

Engagement research (Saks, 2006; Bakker & Demerouti, 2017) consistently shows that belonging and identification are key drivers of effort and persistence. Internal marketing initiatives such as virtual onboarding, digital communities, and shared organizational rituals foster this sense of belonging, reducing the emotional distance that fuels absenteeism.

6. LINKING INTERNAL MARKETING, ABSENTEEISM, AND PRODUCTIVITY

Understanding the relationship between internal marketing, absenteeism, and productivity in hybrid work environments requires moving beyond simplistic cause–effect assumptions. In contemporary organizations, particularly those operating under hybrid arrangements, performance outcomes emerge from complex interactions between organizational practices, employee perceptions, and psychological processes. Internal marketing operates within this complexity not as a control mechanism, but as a relational and motivational system that shapes how employees choose to engage with their work. Absenteeism and productivity should therefore be interpreted as outcomes of employee experience, rather than isolated behavioral indicators. In hybrid contexts, where physical presence is intermittent and often decoupled from performance evaluation, employees' willingness to remain cognitively, emotionally, and behaviorally present becomes central. Internal marketing influences this willingness by shaping meaning, trust, and perceived organizational support. Internal marketing influences both outcomes by acting on three core mediators: employee engagement, psychological safety, and organizational commitment.

6.1 Reframing Absenteeism in Hybrid Organizations

Traditionally, absenteeism has been conceptualized as a physical absence from work, often linked to health issues, job dissatisfaction, or poor working conditions (Johns, 2010). However, hybrid work challenges this interpretation. Employees may be formally "present" logged into systems, attending virtual meetings, while simultaneously disengaged, unmotivated, or emotionally withdrawn. This phenomenon blurs the boundary between absenteeism and presenteeism, making disengagement harder to detect and manage. In this context, absenteeism should be reframed as a continuum of withdrawal behaviors, ranging from physical absence to psychological disengagement.

Research in organizational behavior suggests that withdrawal is often a response to perceived imbalance in the employment relationship, such as lack of recognition, weak communication, or perceived unfairness (Kahn, 1990; Rousseau, 1995). Internal marketing directly addresses these underlying drivers. By reinforcing clarity, recognition, and fairness, internal marketing reduces the likelihood that employees will disengage as a coping strategy. From this perspective, reduced absenteeism is not the result of stricter monitoring, but of improved relational quality between employees and the organization.

6.2 Internal Marketing as a Resource System

The Job Demands–Resources (JD-R) model provides a useful lens for understanding how internal marketing affects both absenteeism and productivity (Bakker & Demerouti, 2017). According to this model, job demands (e.g., workload, emotional strain, role ambiguity) lead to strain and disengagement when not balanced by adequate resources. Resources, foster motivation, resilience, and performance. Internal marketing can be conceptualized as an organizational resource system. Practices such as transparent communication, recognition, development opportunities, and supportive leadership increase employees' psychological and social resources. In hybrid work environments, where demands related to autonomy, self-regulation, and digital overload are often intensified, these resources become particularly critical. When employees have the perception of a strong internal marketing support, they are better equipped to cope with hybrid work demands. This reduces stress-related absenteeism and sustains productivity over time. Conversely, weak or inconsistent internal marketing amplifies job demands, increasing the likelihood of disengagement and withdrawal.

6.3 Engagement as a Central Mediating Mechanism

Employee engagement represents the most direct psychological mechanism linking internal marketing to both absenteeism and productivity. Engagement reflects a state of energetic, cognitive, and emotional connection to work (Kahn, 1990). Engaged employees are not only present, but fully invested in their roles. Saks (2006) empirically demonstrated that engagement mediates the relationship between organizational practices and performance outcomes. Internal marketing strengthens engagement by satisfying key psychological needs, clarifying expectations, and reinforcing a sense of purpose.

In hybrid environments, engagement becomes a stabilizing force that compensates for reduced physical interaction and informal socialization. From this perspective, absenteeism can be seen as the inverse of engagement. As engagement declines, withdrawal behaviors increase. Internal marketing interrupts this process by maintaining relational continuity, reinforcing identity, and sustaining motivation despite physical distance.

6.4 Psychological Safety, Trust, and Voluntary Presence

Psychological safety and trust play a critical role in determining whether employees remain present and productive in hybrid settings. Edmondson (1999) defines psychological safety as the belief that one can express ideas, concerns, or mistakes without fear of negative consequences. Hybrid work can undermine this safety by reducing informal feedback loops and increasing uncertainty. Internal marketing fosters psychological safety by promoting open communication, inclusive leadership, and fair recognition. When employees trust that their organization supports them and values their contributions, they are more likely to remain engaged and less likely to disengage or withdraw. Importantly, in hybrid environments, presence becomes largely voluntary. Employees have greater autonomy over how they allocate attention and effort. Internal marketing therefore shifts the logic of attendance and performance from compliance to commitment. Productivity is no longer enforced through surveillance, but earned through trust-based relationships.

6.5 Organizational Commitment and Self-Regulated Productivity

Organizational commitment reflects the emotional and moral bond between employees and the organization (Meyer & Allen, 1991). Internal marketing strengthens this bond by aligning individual values with organizational purpose and by reinforcing perceptions of mutual obligation. In hybrid work environments, commitment becomes a key driver of self-regulated behavior. Employees who feel committed are more likely to manage their time responsibly, collaborate proactively, and maintain performance standards without direct supervision. This form of productivity is more sustainable and less dependent on external control mechanisms. Internal marketing contributes to this process by transforming the employment relationship from transactional to relational. Absenteeism, within this framework, becomes a signal of weakened commitment rather than a disciplinary issue.

Addressing it therefore requires reinforcing meaning, fairness, and connection, being this ones, core elements of internal marketing.

6.6 Integrating Absenteeism and Productivity Through a Human-Centered Lens

The relationship between absenteeism and productivity is often treated as purely instrumental: reducing absence increases output. This chapter adopts a human-centered perspective, arguing that both outcomes are rooted in the quality of the employee–organization relationship. Internal marketing integrates absenteeism and productivity by addressing their shared psychological foundations. Practices that enhance or improve engagement, trust, and commitment simultaneously reduce withdrawal and enhance performance. In hybrid environments, this integration is essential, as traditional indicators of presence lose explanatory power. By positioning internal marketing as a relational and ethical system rather than a managerial technique, this chapter contributes to a more nuanced understanding of performance in human-centered organizations. Productivity is sustained not by monitoring attendance, but by cultivating meaningful, supportive, and trustworthy work environments.

7. A CONCEPTUAL FRAMEWORK FOR HYBRID ORGANIZATIONS

While existing literature has extensively examined internal marketing, absenteeism, and productivity as separate constructs, fewer studies have integrated these elements within a single conceptual framework tailored to hybrid work environments. The increasing prevalence of hybrid work arrangements calls for models that capture not only structural changes, but also the relational and psychological dynamics shaping employee behavior. This chapter proposes an integrative conceptual framework that positions internal marketing as a central organizational system linking human-centered management practices to absenteeism and productivity outcomes. The framework emphasizes that, in hybrid contexts, performance and attendance are not primarily driven by supervision or physical presence, but by engagement, trust, and perceived organizational support.

7.1 Rationale and Objectives of the Framework

The primary objective of the proposed framework is to explain how and why internal marketing influences absenteeism and productivity in hybrid organizations. Rather than treating absenteeism as an individual failure or productivity as a purely technical outcome, the framework adopts a relational and systemic perspective.

Specifically, the framework aims to:

- Conceptualize internal marketing as a multidimensional organizational system.
- Explain absenteeism as a form of withdrawal influenced by employee experience.
- Position productivity as a self-regulated and engagement-driven outcome.
- Integrate ethical and human-centered considerations into performance analysis.

By doing so, the framework aligns with contemporary shifts in organizational theory that emphasize meaning, well-being, and sustainability over short-term efficiency.

7.2 Structural Components of the Framework

The framework is organized into three interconnected levels: inputs, mediating processes, and outcomes. This structure reflects the dynamic and non-linear nature of employee behavior in hybrid work environments.

7.2.1 Internal Marketing Practices (Input Level)

At the input level, internal marketing is conceptualized as a set of coordinated organizational practices designed to create value for employees as internal customers. These practices include:

Strategic Internal Communication: Transparent, consistent, and dialogical communication that reduces ambiguity and fosters alignment.

Recognition and Feedback Systems: Formal and informal mechanisms that ensure visibility and fairness in acknowledging contributions.

Flexible Work Design: Policies that support autonomy while maintaining clarity and equity.

Learning and Development Opportunities: Continuous skill development that enhances employability and confidence.

Cultural and Identity-Building Practices: Rituals, narratives, and leadership behaviors that reinforce belonging and purpose.

These practices collectively shape how employees perceive their relationship with the organization.

7.2.2 Psychological and Relational Mediators (Process Level)

The second level of the framework captures the psychological and relational processes through which internal marketing practices exert their influence. Key mediators include:

Employee Engagement: The energetic and emotional investment in work roles.
Psychological Safety: The perception of being able to express oneself without fear.
Perceived Organizational Support: The belief that the organization values employee contributions and cares about well-being.
Trust and Organizational Commitment: The emotional and moral bonds that sustain long-term cooperation.

These mediators are particularly salient in hybrid contexts, where direct observation and informal social cues are reduced.

7.2.3 Organizational Outcomes (Output Level)

At the outcome level, the framework identifies both behavioral and performance-related consequences:

Reduced Absenteeism: Including both physical absence and psychological withdrawal.
Sustained Productivity: Defined as consistent, high-quality performance over time.
Enhanced Well-Being: As a complementary outcome that reinforces sustainability.

Importantly, the framework emphasizes that absenteeism and productivity are interconnected outcomes shaped by the same underlying processes.

7.3 Dynamic Relationships and Feedback Loops

Unlike static models, the proposed framework incorporates dynamic feedback loops. For example, sustained productivity can reinforce engagement and commitment, while high absenteeism may erode trust and psychological safety. These reciprocal relationships highlight the importance of continuous internal marketing efforts rather than isolated initiatives.

In hybrid organizations, feedback loops are especially critical, as delayed or distorted feedback can quickly undermine relational quality. Internal marketing serves as the mechanism through which organizations monitor, adjust, and realign employee experience over time.

7.4 Theoretical Integration and Contribution

The framework integrates multiple theoretical perspectives:

- Self-Determination Theory explains how internal marketing satisfies autonomy, competence, and relatedness needs.
- Psychological Contract Theory accounts for how internal marketing fulfills implicit expectations.
- JD-R Model clarifies how internal marketing acts as a resource system.
- Engagement Theory explains the motivational pathway to productivity and presence.

By synthesizing these theories, the framework offers a comprehensive explanation of employee behavior in hybrid work environments. It extends existing models by explicitly addressing absenteeism as a relational outcome and by situating productivity within a human-centered and ethical context.

7.5 Propositions for Future Research

Although this chapter is conceptual, the framework generates several propositions that can guide future empirical research:

Proposition 1: Internal marketing practices are negatively associated with absenteeism in hybrid work environments.

Proposition 2: Employee engagement mediates the relationship between internal marketing and productivity.

Proposition 3: Psychological safety moderates the relationship between internal marketing and absenteeism.

Proposition 4: Organizational commitment strengthens the link between engagement and sustained productivity.
Proposition 5: Alignment between internal and external employer branding amplifies the effectiveness of internal marketing.

These propositions provide a foundation for quantitative and qualitative studies that can test and refine the framework across different organizational contexts.

7.6 Positioning the Framework Within Human-Centered Organizations

The proposed framework aligns closely with the principles of human-centered organizations, which prioritize dignity, well-being, and meaningful work. By positioning internal marketing as a relational and ethical system, the framework challenges instrumental approaches that focus solely on control and efficiency.

In hybrid work environments, where autonomy and trust are unavoidable, organizations must rely on internal marketing to sustain engagement and performance. This framework provides both scholars and practitioners with a structured way to understand and manage these dynamics in a human-centered manner.

8. IMPLICATIONS FOR EMPLOYER BRANDING, ETHICS, AND TALENT MANAGEMENT

The rise of hybrid work has intensified the need for organizations to rethink how they attract, engage, and retain talent while maintaining ethical integrity and performance. Internal marketing surges in this context not merely as a managerial tool, but as a strategic and moral framework that connects employer branding, ethics, and talent management within human-centered organizations.

This section discusses how the conceptual framework proposed in this chapter informs each of these domains, highlighting their interdependence in hybrid work environments.

8.1 Internal Marketing as the Foundation of Employer Branding Credibility

Employer branding has traditionally focused on external communication aimed at attracting potential employees. However, a growing body of literature emphasizes that employer branding must be grounded in internal reality to remain credible and sustainable (Backhaus & Tikoo, 2004; Mosley, 2014).

Internal marketing provides the mechanism through which employer branding promises are translated into lived employee experiences. In hybrid organizations, where informal cultural cues are limited, internal marketing becomes the primary way employees interpret what the organization truly stands for. Flexibility policies, recognition practices, communication styles, and leadership behaviors all serve as signals of the organization's values.

When internal marketing is consistent and authentic, it reinforces employer brand credibility, reducing cynicism and disengagement. Conversely, misalignment between external employer branding messages and internal experiences can erode trust and increase withdrawal behaviors, including absenteeism. From this perspective, absenteeism can be interpreted as an early warning signal of employer brand incongruence.

8.2 Ethical Dimensions of Internal Marketing in Hybrid Work

Ethics occupies a central place in human-centered organizations, particularly in hybrid work contexts where power dynamics, visibility, and boundaries are reconfigured. Internal marketing carries ethical implications because it shapes how employees are treated, recognized, and supported.

Treating employees as internal customers implies acknowledging their autonomy, dignity, and legitimate needs. Ethical internal marketing practices include transparent communication, fair recognition, respect for work–life boundaries, and inclusive decision-making. These practices help prevent exploitation and digital overreach, common risks in hybrid environments.

Moreover, internal marketing contributes to procedural and interactional justice by ensuring that policies and decisions are communicated clearly and applied consistently. Ethical lapses, for example such as symbolic flexibility, unequal access to development, or performative well-being initiatives, undermine trust and contribute to disengagement and absenteeism.

In this sense, ethical internal marketing is not about compliance, but about relational integrity. It fosters a moral climate in which employees feel respected and valued, reinforcing their willingness to remain present and engaged.

8.3 Talent Management Beyond Control and Surveillance

Hybrid work challenges traditional talent management practices based on physical presence and direct supervision. In this new context, talent management must rely more heavily on trust, self-regulation, and relational commitment.

Internal marketing supports this transition by reframing talent management as a partnership rather than a control system. Practices such as continuous feedback, development-focused conversations, and personalized career pathways signal long-term investment in employees. These signals strengthen commitment and reduce the likelihood of disengagement-driven absenteeism.

Furthermore, internal marketing aligns talent management with sustainability. By emphasizing learning, employability, and well-being, organizations protect their human capital against burnout and turnover. Productivity, in this framework, is understood as a consequence of meaningful work and supportive relationships rather than constant monitoring.

8.4 Integrating Employer Branding, Ethics, and Talent Management

One of the key contributions of this chapter is the integration of employer branding, ethics, and talent management through the lens of internal marketing. Rather than treating these domains as separate functions, the proposed framework highlights their interdependence.

In hybrid organizations, internal marketing acts as the connective tissue that ensures coherence across these domains. Ethical principles guide internal marketing practices, which in turn shape employee experience and employer brand credibility. Talent management strategies operationalize these principles by translating them into daily practices.

This integration is particularly important in human-centered organizations, where performance outcomes are inseparable from ethical considerations and employee well-being. Absenteeism and productivity, within this integrated model, become indicators of organizational health rather than isolated metrics.

8.5 Strategic Implications for Human-Centered Organizations

For human-centered organizations, the implications of this analysis are both strategic and normative. Internal marketing should be elevated to a strategic function that informs leadership behavior, organizational design, and decision-making processes.

Leaders play a critical role in embodying internal marketing values, particularly in hybrid contexts where leadership visibility is mediated through communication.

Ethical leadership reinforces internal marketing credibility and strengthens trust, reducing disengagement and absenteeism.

Finally, organizations that integrate internal marketing into employer branding and talent management are better positioned to attract and retain talent in increasingly competitive and flexible labor markets. By aligning performance objectives with human-centered values, they create conditions for sustainable productivity and organizational resilience.

9. DISCUSSION

The purpose of this chapter was to develop a conceptual understanding of how internal marketing influences absenteeism and productivity in hybrid work environments, within the broader context of employer branding, ethics, and talent management. This discussion section reflects on the theoretical contributions of the chapter, situates the proposed framework within existing literature, and highlights key tensions and challenges inherent to hybrid work.

9.1 Advancing the Understanding of Absenteeism in Hybrid Contexts

One of the central contributions of this chapter is in its reconceptualization of absenteeism. While traditional literature has largely focused on physical absence as a measurable behavioral outcome, hybrid work arrangements complicate this distinction. Employees may remain technically present while disengaging cognitively or emotionally, rendering traditional absenteeism metrics insufficient.

By framing absenteeism as a continuum of withdrawal behaviors, this chapter aligns with contemporary perspectives in organizational psychology that emphasize psychological presence over physical attendance. This reframing has important implications for both research and practice. It suggests that absenteeism should be understood less as an individual failure and more as a relational outcome shaped by organizational practices and employee experience.

Internal marketing emerges as a critical lever in addressing this expanded notion of absenteeism. Rather than relying on monitoring or disciplinary mechanisms, organizations can reduce withdrawal by strengthening communication, recognition, and perceived organizational support. This approach aligns with human-centered management principles and challenges control-based paradigms that are increasingly misaligned with hybrid work realities.

9.2 Internal Marketing as a Relational Performance System

Another key contribution of this chapter is the positioning of internal marketing as a relational performance system rather than a functional HR or communication tool. Existing literature often treats internal marketing as a subset of internal communication or employee engagement initiatives. This chapter extends that view by conceptualizing internal marketing as an integrated system that shapes meaning, identity, and trust.

In hybrid environments, where informal interactions are reduced, internal marketing becomes one of the few mechanisms through which organizations can intentionally design the employee experience. The proposed framework highlights how internal marketing practices operate through psychological mediators such as engagement, psychological safety, and commitment, ultimately influencing productivity and absenteeism.

This relational perspective also helps reconcile tensions between flexibility and performance. Hybrid work increases autonomy but also demands higher levels of self-regulation. Internal marketing supports this self-regulation by fostering commitment and intrinsic motivation, thereby enabling sustainable productivity without excessive oversight.

9.3 Productivity Reconsidered Through a Human-Centered Lens

The chapter also contributes to ongoing debates about productivity in hybrid and remote work. Much of the existing discourse focuses on output measurement, digital surveillance, or efficiency gains. While these approaches may yield short-term results, they often neglect the psychological and ethical dimensions of work.

By linking productivity to engagement and commitment, this chapter reframes productivity as a human-centered outcome rather than a purely technical metric. Productivity, in this view, is sustained not through control, but through meaningful work, trust-based relationships, and perceived fairness. Internal marketing plays a crucial role in creating these conditions.

This perspective resonates with emerging critiques of surveillance-based management and supports calls for more ethical and sustainable approaches to performance management in hybrid organizations.

9.4 Implications for Employer Branding Consistency

The discussion also underscores the importance of internal–external alignment in employer branding. Hybrid work amplifies the visibility of organizational practices, as employees increasingly share their experiences through digital platforms and professional networks. Inconsistencies between employer branding promises and internal realities are therefore more likely to be exposed.

The proposed framework highlights how internal marketing serves as the internal expression of employer branding. When internal marketing practices align with external messaging, organizations strengthen brand credibility and reduce disengagement. Conversely, misalignment can lead to cynicism, psychological withdrawal, and absenteeism.

This insight contributes to employer branding literature by emphasizing the centrality of employee experience in sustaining brand equity, particularly in flexible and hybrid work contexts.

9.5 Ethical Tensions and Managerial Dilemmas in Hybrid Work

Hybrid work introduces several ethical tensions that deserve attention. Increased flexibility can coexist with intensified workloads, blurred boundaries, and digital exhaustion. Similarly, autonomy may be undermined by subtle forms of surveillance and performance pressure.

This chapter argues that internal marketing provides an ethical framework for navigating these tensions. Ethical internal marketing requires organizations to be transparent about expectations, respectful of boundaries, and consistent in their support. Symbolic or superficial initiatives risk undermining trust and exacerbating disengagement.

From this perspective, absenteeism and disengagement can be interpreted as ethical signals, indicators that employees perceive imbalance, unfairness, or misalignment in the employment relationship. Addressing these signals requires relational repair rather than punitive responses.

9.6 Contributions to Theory and Future Research Directions

From a theoretical standpoint, this chapter contributes by integrating internal marketing, absenteeism, and productivity into a single conceptual framework tailored to hybrid work environments. It bridges gaps between marketing, human resource management, organizational behavior, and ethics literatures.

The framework also generates several avenues for future research. Empirical studies could test the proposed relationships across sectors and cultural contexts, examine moderating variables such as leadership style or organizational size, and explore longitudinal dynamics of engagement and withdrawal in hybrid work.

Qualitative research could further investigate employee sensemaking processes and lived experiences of internal marketing in hybrid settings, providing deeper insights into relational dynamics.

9.7 Limitations and Reflexive Considerations

As a conceptual chapter, this work has inherent limitations. The absence of empirical data limits the ability to make causal claims. However, the purpose of this chapter is to provide a theoretically grounded framework that can guide future empirical investigation.

Additionally, hybrid work is not a homogeneous phenomenon. Variations in job type, organizational culture, and national context may influence how internal marketing practices are perceived and enacted. These contextual factors should be carefully considered in future research.

9.8 Toward Sustainable and Human-Centered Hybrid Organizations

Overall, this discussion reinforces the central argument of the chapter: that internal marketing plays a pivotal role in shaping absenteeism and productivity in hybrid work environments. By focusing on relationships, meaning, and ethical integrity, organizations can move beyond control-based approaches and toward more sustainable and human-centered models of work.

In an era where flexibility is increasingly non-negotiable, internal marketing provides a pathway for organizations to balance performance demands with human well-being. This balance is not only desirable but essential for long-term organizational resilience.

10. CONCLUSION

The transformation of work accelerated by hybrid models has reshaped not only where work takes place, but also how organizations relate to their employees. As physical co-presence becomes less central, traditional mechanisms of control, supervision, and cultural reinforcement lose effectiveness. In this evolving context, organizations are increasingly challenged to sustain engagement, manage absenteeism, and maintain productivity without compromising ethical standards or employee well-being.

This chapter set out to address this challenge by exploring the role of internal marketing as a strategic, relational, and human-centered approach to managing employee experience in hybrid work environments. Drawing on a comprehensive review of the literature, the chapter proposed a conceptual framework that integrates internal marketing, absenteeism, and productivity within the broader domains of employer branding, ethics, and talent management.

One of the core contributions of this chapter lies in its reconceptualization of absenteeism. Rather than viewing absenteeism solely as physical absence, the chapter highlighted the relevance of psychological withdrawal and disengagement in hybrid contexts. This broader understanding reflects the realities of contemporary work, where presence is increasingly mediated by digital systems and where disengagement can remain hidden behind formal attendance.

By positioning internal marketing as a system of organizational resources, the chapter demonstrated how practices such as transparent communication, recognition, flexibility, learning, and culture-building influence employee engagement, psychological safety, and organizational commitment. These mediating mechanisms help explain why internal marketing reduces absenteeism and supports sustained productivity, even in the absence of direct supervision. Importantly, the chapter emphasized that productivity in hybrid organizations should not be understood as a function of surveillance or control. Instead, productivity emerges from trust-based relationships, meaningful work, and ethical organizational practices. Internal marketing plays a central role in fostering these conditions, enabling employees to self-regulate, collaborate, and perform effectively over time.

From an employer branding perspective, the chapter reinforced the importance of internal–external alignment. Employer brand promises that are not supported by authentic internal marketing practices risk generating cynicism and disengagement. Conversely, organizations that invest in internal marketing enhance employer brand credibility and strengthen their ability to attract and retain talent in competitive labor markets. Ethically, the chapter argued that internal marketing reflects a commitment to human dignity and fairness. In hybrid work environments, where boundaries are more fluid and visibility is uneven, ethical internal marketing helps protect employees from exploitation, burnout, and invisibility. Absenteeism and disengagement, within this ethical lens, become signals of relational imbalance rather than issues to be addressed through punitive measures.

The implications for talent management are equally significant. Hybrid work requires a shift from transactional, presence-based management toward relational, trust-based approaches. Internal marketing supports this transition by emphasizing development, recognition, and long-term employability. By integrating these elements into talent management strategies, organizations can foster sustainable productivity and organizational resilience. While this chapter is conceptual in nature and does not provide empirical validation of the proposed framework, it offers a theoretically grounded foundation for future research. Scholars are encouraged to empirically test the framework across different organizational contexts, explore moderating factors, and examine longitudinal dynamics of engagement, absenteeism, and productivity in hybrid work settings. In conclusion, this chapter argues that internal marketing represents a critical bridge between human-centered values and organizational performance in the hybrid work era. Organizations that treat employees as internal customers, invest in meaningful work experiences, and uphold ethical integrity are better positioned to navigate the complexities of hybrid work. By doing so, they not only reduce absenteeism and sustain productivity, but also contribute to the creation of more humane, resilient, and sustainable organizations.

REFERENCES

Allen, T. D., Golden, T. D., & Shockley, K. M. (2015). How effective is telecommuting? Assessing the status of our scientific findings. *Psychological Science in the Public Interest : A Journal of the American Psychological Society, 16*(2), 40–68. DOI: 10.1177/1529100615593273 PMID: 26403188

Backhaus, K., & Tikoo, S. (2004). Conceptualizing and researching employer branding. *Career Development International, 9*(5), 501–517. DOI: 10.1108/13620430410550754

Bakker, A. B., & Demerouti, E. (2017). Job demands–resources theory: Taking stock and looking forward. *Journal of Occupational Health Psychology, 22*(3), 273–285. DOI: 10.1037/ocp0000056 PMID: 27732008

Contreras, F., Baykal, E., & Abid, G. (2020). E-leadership and teleworking in times of COVID-19 and beyond: What we know and where do we go. *Frontiers in Psychology, 11*, 590271. DOI: 10.3389/fpsyg.2020.590271 PMID: 33362656

Deci, E. L., & Ryan, R. M. (2000). The "what" and "why" of goal pursuits: Human needs and the self-determination of behavior. *Psychological Inquiry, 11*(4), 227–268. DOI: 10.1207/S15327965PLI1104_01

Edmondson, A. (1999). Psychological safety and learning behavior in work teams. *Administrative Science Quarterly, 44*(2), 350–383. DOI: 10.2307/2666999

Grönroos, C. (1990). *Service management and marketing: Managing the moments of truth in service competition*. Lexington Books.

Herzberg, F. (1966). *Work and the nature of man*. World Publishing.

Johns, G. (2010). Presenteeism in the workplace: A review and research agenda. *Journal of Organizational Behavior, 31*(4), 519–542. DOI: 10.1002/job.630

Kahn, W. A. (1990). Psychological conditions of personal engagement and disengagement at work. *Academy of Management Journal, 33*(4), 692–724. DOI: 10.2307/256287

Kossek, E. E., Thompson, R. J., & Lautsch, B. A. (2015). Balanced workplace flexibility: Avoiding the traps. *California Management Review, 57*(4), 5–25. DOI: 10.1525/cmr.2015.57.4.5

Leonardi, P. M. (2021). COVID-19 and the new technologies of organizing: Digital exhaust, digital footprints, and artificial intelligence in the wake of remote work. *Journal of Management Studies, 58*(1), 249–253. DOI: 10.1111/joms.12648

Men, L. R. (2014). Strategic internal communication: Transformational leadership, communication channels, and employee satisfaction. *Management Communication Quarterly*, *28*(2), 264–284. DOI: 10.1177/0893318914524536

Meyer, J. P., & Allen, N. J. (1991). A three-component conceptualization of organizational commitment. *Human Resource Management Review*, *1*(1), 61–89. DOI: 10.1016/1053-4822(91)90011-Z

Mosley, R. (2014). *Employer brand management: Practical lessons from the world's leading employers*. Wiley.

Noe, R. A., Clarke, A. D. M., & Klein, H. J. (2021). Learning in the twenty-first-century workplace. *Annual Review of Organizational Psychology and Organizational Behavior*, *8*, 245–275. DOI: 10.1146/annurev-orgpsych-012420-055226

Rousseau, D. M. (1995). *Psychological contracts in organizations: Understanding written and unwritten agreements*. Sage Publications. DOI: 10.4135/9781452231594

Saks, A. M. (2006). Antecedents and consequences of employee engagement. *Journal of Managerial Psychology*, *21*(7), 600–619. DOI: 10.1108/02683940610690169

Saks, A. M. (2022). Caring human resources management and employee engagement. *Human Resource Management Review*, *32*(3), 100835. DOI: 10.1016/j.hrmr.2021.100835

Schein, E. H. (2010). *Organizational culture and leadership* (4th ed.). Jossey-Bass.

Welch, M., & Jackson, P. R. (2007). Rethinking internal communication: A stakeholder approach. *Corporate Communications*, *12*(2), 177–198. DOI: 10.1108/13563280710744847

Chapter 7
Managing Generational Diversity:
Human Resourcens and Talent Management Strategies and Onboarding Effectiveness

Sara Leones Lima
Polytechnic University of Cávado and Ave, Portugal

Teresa Dieguez
Polytechnic University of Cávado and Ave, Portugal

Bruno Barbosa Sousa
http://orcid.org/0000-0002-8588-2422
Applied Management Research Unit (UNIAG), School of Hospitality and Tourism, Polytechnic University of Cávado and Ave (IPCA), Barcelos, Portugal

ABSTRACT

This chapter examines the strategic role of Human Resources (HR) in managing generational diversity and the effectiveness of onboarding in a municipal organization. Through a case study of "Faz Cultura", a public-sector cultural institution, the research explores challenges and opportunities emerging from the coexistence of different generations in the workplace. The study aims to assess how tailored onboarding strategies and intergenerational management policies influence employee retention, motivation, and overall organizational cohesion. A qualitative case study methodology was employed, utilizing semi-structured interviews, surveys, and document analysis to collect data from employees across different generational cohorts. The study also incorporated a comparative analysis of onboarding programs and

DOI: 10.4018/979-8-2600-2178-1.ch007

HR strategies, identifying patterns of adaptation and resistance among employees from different age groups. This study contributes to the growing body of literature on HR strategies in public-sector organizations by offering empirical insights.

1. INTRODUCTION

In an era of rapid digital transformation and evolving workplace dynamics, organizations face increasing challenges in managing generational diversity, workforce integration, and talent retention. Human Resource Management (HRM) plays a critical role in addressing these challenges by implementing strategies that align with the distinct expectations, work styles, and engagement preferences of different generational cohorts (Smith et al., 2020). A structured and strategic HRM approach is essential to ensure a harmonious and productive work environment, mitigating potential generational conflicts while maximizing employee potential and organizational performance (Bilan et al., 2020).

One of the most critical aspects of HRM in this context is onboarding, a process designed to facilitate the effective integration of new employees into an organization (Sharma & Stol, 2019). The long-term success of organizations largely depends on how quickly and efficiently employees adapt to the organizational culture, expectations, and work methodologies. Effective onboarding fosters engagement, reduces turnover, and ensures that employees align with the company's objectives and values. Moreover, HRM strategies should emphasize continuous training and leadership development, particularly in preparing managers to lead diverse teams and navigate an increasingly complex workforce landscape (Ismail et al., 2023).

In this constantly evolving environment, adaptability and technological innovation in HR processes are key to maintaining a competitive advantage. HR professionals must adopt a proactive and strategic approach, fostering an inclusive and motivating work environment that supports both individual employee growth and organizational success (Nicolás Agustín et al., 2021). A human-centered HR strategy not only enhances employee satisfaction and productivity but also strengthens long-term organizational resilience and competitiveness (Hines, 2021).

HR professionals are at the core of talent acquisition, retention, and engagement, playing a fundamental role in promoting a positive organizational culture and aligning HR practices with strategic objectives (Hongal et al., 2020). Organizations that cultivate a transparent, communicative, and development-focused environment tend to have higher levels of employee satisfaction, engagement, and innovation, leading to increased performance and sustainability (Ali & Anwar, 2021; Monteiro et al., 2020).

This research aims to examine the strategic role of HRM in an organizational setting, with a focus on onboarding and generational diversity management. Using a case study approach, this study analyzes the impact of HRM strategies on talent retention and organizational culture within Faz Cultura, a municipal institution. Additionally, the research explores the evolution of HRM practices, emphasizing the shift toward a people-centric approach that prioritizes employee well-being and organizational success.

The study is structured into four main sections. Chapter 1 presents a literature review, outlining key concepts such as strategic HRM, talent retention, onboarding, generational diversity, and the evolution of HR practices. Chapter 2 introduces the case study methodology, explaining the mixed-methods approach that combines qualitative and quantitative research techniques. It provides an overview of Faz Cultura, detailing its organizational structure, HR challenges, and employee engagement strategies. This chapter also includes data collection methods, such as surveys, interviews, and document analysis, followed by a discussion of findings. Chapter 3 presents the research results, focusing on the impact of HRM practices on employee satisfaction, onboarding effectiveness, and talent retention. The findings are compared with existing literature, highlighting both alignments and novel contributions. Finally, the last section outlines key conclusions and recommendations, emphasizing the role of HRM as a strategic pillar for organizational success. The study also discusses limitations and proposes future research directions to enhance HRM practices in public-sector organizations. This research offers practical recommendations for HR professionals, policymakers, and organizational leaders, contributing to the advancement of HRM practices in the contemporary workplace.

2. THEORETICAL BACKGROUND

2.1. The Evolution of Human Resource Management

Human Resource Management (HRM) has undergone a significant transformation, evolving from a purely administrative function to a strategic driver of organizational success (Dessler, 2022). Initially, HRM was limited to personnel administration, focusing on wage distribution, compliance with labor laws, and employee record management. During the Industrial Revolution, organizations viewed workers as mere economic inputs, prioritizing efficiency over employee well-being (Carvalheiro, 2011).

The early 20th century saw the emergence of scientific management, pioneered by Frederick Taylor, which introduced efficiency-based work models. While Taylor's approach enhanced productivity, it failed to consider human motivation and job satisfaction (Almeida, 2019). This gap was later addressed by Elton Mayo's Human Relations Movement, which demonstrated that psychological and social factors influence employee engagement and performance (Silva, 2019).

The mid-20th century introduced behavioral theories, such as Maslow's Hierarchy of Needs (1954) and McGregor's Theory X and Theory Y (1960), which emphasized intrinsic motivation, leadership engagement, and employee empowerment (Silva, 2019). By the 1980s, HRM had shifted towards a strategic function, with Ulrich (2012) positioning HR professionals as key contributors to business strategy and workforce planning.

With technological advancements and globalization, HRM transitioned into a data-driven discipline, integrating AI, analytics, and digital tools to streamline processes such as recruitment, performance management, and employee development (Marler & Boudreau, 2017). The COVID-19 pandemic accelerated hybrid work models, prompting HR professionals to prioritize workforce flexibility, remote management, and digital transformation (Maia, 2022). This shift underscores the increasing complexity of HRM, which now focuses on generational diversity, employee well-being, and digital adaptability (Souza et al., 2024).

2.2 Key Human Resource Management Practices

Modern HRM encompasses a range of strategic and operational activities aimed at optimizing employee engagement, organizational alignment, and workforce productivity (Carvalho & Rua, 2017). Among the most critical practices are recruitment and selection, training and development, performance management, compensation and benefits, and employee relations.

Recruitment and selection serve as the foundation of workforce planning, ensuring that organizations attract and retain high-potential employees (Ribeiro, 2005). AI-driven recruitment platforms, competency-based assessments, and structured interviews have enhanced the efficiency and accuracy of talent acquisition (Dessler, 2022). Effective recruitment strategies reduce turnover, enhance employer branding, and align talent acquisition with business needs (Armstrong & Taylor, 2020; Santos et al., 2023).

Training and development are equally vital, facilitating continuous learning and leadership growth (Beardwell & Thompson, 2017). Organizations increasingly employ personalized e-learning platforms, AI-powered learning pathways, and immersive training techniques to improve knowledge retention and professional growth (Prasad et al., 2024). A structured training framework typically follows four key phases: needs assessment, program design, implementation, and outcome evaluation (Rego et al., 2008).

Performance management has evolved beyond traditional annual appraisals, now incorporating continuous feedback systems, AI-driven performance tracking, and real-time goal setting (Torrington et al., 2020). By aligning individual performance with corporate objectives, organizations enhance accountability, motivation, and long-term workforce engagement (Carvalho & Rua, 2017).

Compensation and benefits are key drivers of employee retention and motivation (Bratton & Gold, 2017). Organizations are increasingly moving beyond fixed salary models, integrating performance-based incentives, flexible benefits, and employee well-being initiatives to attract and retain top talent (Sousa et al., 2006). The growing emphasis on work-life balance, mental health programs, and remote work incentives highlights the necessity of customized benefits packages that cater to diverse workforce needs (Ali & Anwar, 2021).

Employee relations play a pivotal role in workplace culture and engagement. Strong HR policies foster transparent communication, effective conflict resolution, and inclusive leadership practices (Armstrong & Taylor, 2020). Diversity and inclusion initiatives, in particular, are essential in promoting collaborative, innovative, and high-performance work environments (Dessler, 2022).

2.3 Talent Retention and Managing a Multigenerational Workforce

Talent retention has become a strategic imperative for organizations seeking to reduce turnover, enhance employee commitment, and sustain long-term workforce stability (Gandolfi et al., 2018). Traditional retention strategies focused on financial incentives and career growth opportunities, but today's workforce prioritizes flexibility, meaningful work, and value alignment (Younas & Bari, 2020). Organizations must therefore implement mentorship programs, leadership development initiatives, and hybrid work models to enhance job satisfaction (Collings et al., 2018).

The multigenerational workforce presents both opportunities and challenges for HRM. Baby Boomers (1946-1964) value job security and hierarchical structures, whereas Generation X (1965-1980) prioritizes work-life balance and professional autonomy (Santos et al., 2019). Millennials (1981-1996) seek career advancement, collaboration, and purpose-driven work, while Generation Z (1997 onwards) thrives in technology-driven, flexible, and socially responsible work environments (Dieguez et al., 2024).

To bridge generational gaps, HR professionals must implement customized engagement strategies, such as intergenerational mentorship programs, digital upskilling initiatives, and flexible work policies (Mihaela & Maria Cristina, 2016; Márquez et al., 2022). Encouraging knowledge transfer between senior and junior employees fosters cross-generational learning and collaboration (Faria, 2023).

2.4 The Role of Onboarding in HRM

Onboarding is a strategic HRM function that enhances employee integration, accelerates productivity, and strengthens workforce retention (Bauer, 2010). More than a procedural necessity, structured onboarding focuses on cultural immersion, job readiness, and long-term engagement (Carpenter, 2023).

An effective onboarding program follows a phased approach, beginning with pre-onboarding activities (e.g., welcome messages, document processing), followed by formal orientation sessions (company policies, values, and expectations), role-specific training, and long-term integration programs (Klein et al., 2015). Organizations employing AI-driven onboarding platforms, mentorship pairings, and employee engagement surveys enhance the onboarding experience and optimize new hire retention (Cable et al., 2013).

Despite its benefits, onboarding faces implementation challenges, including resource limitations, process standardization difficulties, and the need for personalized integration (Saks et al., 2011). Companies that prioritize structured onboarding strategies report higher employee engagement, lower turnover, and stronger cultural alignment (Wanberg, 2012).

3. CASE STUDY: METHODOLOGY AND DATA COLLECTION

This study adopts a mixed-methods approach, integrating both qualitative and quantitative methodologies to examine the strategic role of Human Resource Management (HRM) in onboarding effectiveness and generational diversity in the workplace. The research was conducted at Faz Cultura – Empresa Municipal de Braga, EM, focusing on the impact of HRM practices in fostering talent retention, organizational integration, and intergenerational collaboration.

3.1 Research Approach and Data Collection

A mixed-methods approach was chosen to ensure a comprehensive analysis of organizational processes, allowing for both quantitative evaluation of onboarding effectiveness and qualitative insights into employee perceptions and experiences. The integration of these methodologies enables the identification of nuanced behaviors and subjective perspectives, which are often overlooked in exclusively quantitative analyses (Hennink et al., 2020).

Qualitative methods allow for the chronological analysis of data, providing an in-depth understanding of the causal relationships between events and their outcomes (Lanka et al., 2021). This approach enables a focused examination of participant narratives, capturing the complexity of individual experiences and reducing the required sample size without compromising analytical depth. Empirical data collection techniques such as case studies, interviews, and personal narratives were employed, ensuring a robust foundation for analyzing HRM practices (Denzin & Lincoln, 2018).

In the onboarding context, qualitative analysis provided valuable insights into employee integration experiences, helping to identify key socialization factors that contribute to talent retention and engagement (O'Neil & Koekemoer, 2016). A successful onboarding process extends beyond technical training, incorporating peer interactions, managerial support, and cultural alignment to enhance the overall employee experience (Kuusisto, 2024).

For generational diversity, the mixed-methods approach allowed for a multifaceted evaluation of how different generations interact, communicate, and integrate into the organizational culture. Qualitative methods captured the subjective perceptions of intergenerational challenges, while quantitative data provided statistical evidence on patterns of collaboration and generational expectations (Ziede, 2020). The study thus benefited from a dual analytical lens, combining individual narratives with broad organizational trends.

However, the reliance on qualitative data may limit the study's generalizability. Given the subjective nature of qualitative analysis, response biases could have influenced participant answers, particularly in self-reported experiences. Additionally, the study's relatively small sample size (53 employees surveyed) may not be representative of broader municipal organizations, restricting the applicability of findings to other contexts. Future research could enhance the robustness of the findings by incorporating a larger sample and conducting comparative analyses across multiple municipal organizations to validate patterns observed in this case study

3.2 Survey Design and Data Validation

In this study, a questionnaire was employed as the primary data collection instrument. Its structure was carefully designed to systematically capture employees' perceptions and experiences in the workplace, ensuring clarity, relevance, and alignment with the research objectives. The questionnaire focused on both the onboarding process and intergenerational interactions within the organization. Each questionnaire began with a brief introduction outlining the study's purpose and the significance of the respondents' contributions. This contextualization reinforced the relevance of their responses. Before implementation, the questionnaire underwent a pre-validation and review process involving two Human Resources (HR) academics and three potential respondents. This step ensured clarity, consistency, and validity, enhancing the reliability of the collected data.

The onboarding questionnaire was divided into two versions: one for managers and another for new employees, each comprising ten questions. Both versions included sections on adaptation to organizational culture, functional performance, and behavioral integration. Responses were based on a five-point satisfaction scale (1 to 5), enabling participants to express their experiences in a structured and comparable manner. Additionally, an open-ended section allowed respondents to provide additional comments freely. The questionnaire on intergenerational diversity was applied to employees from different age groups within the organization, ranging from Baby Boomers to Generation Z. The objective was to understand how different generations interact, communicate, and collaborate in the professional context, identifying both challenges and opportunities in managing diverse teams. The questionnaire was structured into eight thematic groups, with a total of forty questions covering sociodemographic data, communication and feedback, commitment and motivation, work preferences, training and development, organizational culture and values, career expectations, and technology and workplace tools.

The questionnaire included closed-ended questions, primarily based on Likert scales, as well as open-ended questions to capture subjective perceptions regarding the impact of generational diversity in the workplace. Both multiple-choice questions and the Likert scale were used. The Likert scale is a widely adopted tool in research for measuring opinions, attitudes, perceptions, or agreement levels regarding a specific statement or issue. Developed by Rensis Likert in 1932, this scale allows responses to be measured along a continuum between two extremes, such as “strongly agree” and “strongly disagree.” By utilizing the Likert scale, the questionnaire enabled the collection of nuanced responses, allowing for a more detailed analysis of employee experiences and attitudes toward onboarding and intergenerational interactions.

Despite these methodological strengths, the study would benefit from stronger quantitative validation. Given the small sample size and potential response biases, statistical validation techniques such as correlation tests or regression models could have strengthened the reliability of the findings. Incorporating such statistical measures would allow for a more precise identification of trends and relationships among variables, reinforcing the credibility of the quantitative component.

The present study was developed as a case study focusing on the activities of the HR department at Faz Cultura, which was established in 2020 as an autonomous division separate from management, dedicated to People and Organizational Development. Its mission was redefined to emphasize the non-formal aspects of people management, addressing the challenges posed by the significant expansion of the workforce, the geographical dispersion of employees across two distinct buildings, and the impact of the COVID-19 pandemic on work organization models and employees' mental health. Consequently, the HR leadership identified four key areas of development: (i) Talent, Career, and Development, (ii) Communication and Engagement, (iii) Learning and Training, and (iv) Health, Balance, and Well-being. These focus areas facilitated the implementation of value-added initiatives within the organization.

3.3 Researched Institution: Faz Cultura

This case study focuses on Faz Cultura - Empresa Municipal de Cultura de Braga, EM, a municipal cultural company responsible for managing key cultural venues and projects in Braga, Portugal. Municipal companies in Portugal are legal entities created and controlled by municipalities to provide essential public services. These companies operate under municipal control while maintaining administrative and financial autonomy, ensuring efficient management tailored to local needs. Faz Cultura, established its Human Resources (HR) department in 2020 with an autonomous People and Organization unit. This shift aimed to prioritize non-formal aspects of HR management, focusing on fostering engagement and organizational cohesion amid workforce expansion, geographic dispersion across two office buildings, and the COVID-19 pandemic's impact on work models and employee well-being. The COVID-19 pandemic accelerated digital transformation, with 70% of employees working remotely. Internal recruitment processes were refined, and structured training programs were implemented, focusing on professional development and adaptation to new realities. A cultural climate assessment in late 2020 revealed a 71.3% employee satisfaction rate, highlighting strong engagement but concerns about career progression. In 2023, a performance management system was successfully introduced. Employee benefits include 25 vacation days, additional holidays, health insurance, and special leave policies. Faz Cultura is a pivotal institution in Braga's cultural landscape, fostering artistic development and international recognition. By ensuring efficient management and high-quality cultural offerings, it contributes significantly to the city's socio-economic and cultural advancement.

4. EMPIRICAL ANALYSIS

This case study focuses on Faz Cultura - Empresa Municipal de Cultura de Braga, EM, a municipal cultural company responsible for managing key cultural venues and projects in Braga, Portugal. The study analyzes a survey conducted among Faz Cultura employees to understand how different generations perceive aspects such as communication, feedback, work preferences, training, organizational culture, career expectations, technology, and inclusion. The analysis is based on theories of generational diversity/multiplicity, linking survey results with human resource management strategies described in the literature. The questionnaire was administered between October 24 and November 11, 2024.

4.1 Analysis of Generational Multiplicity at Faz Cultura

4.1.1 Sociodemographic data

The survey included 53 employees, achieving a 100% participation rate. Of the respondents, 11.3% belonged to the Baby Boomer generation, 22.6% to Generation X, 47.2% to Millennials (the majority group), and 15.1% to Generation Z (figure 1).

Figure 1. Generation of respondents

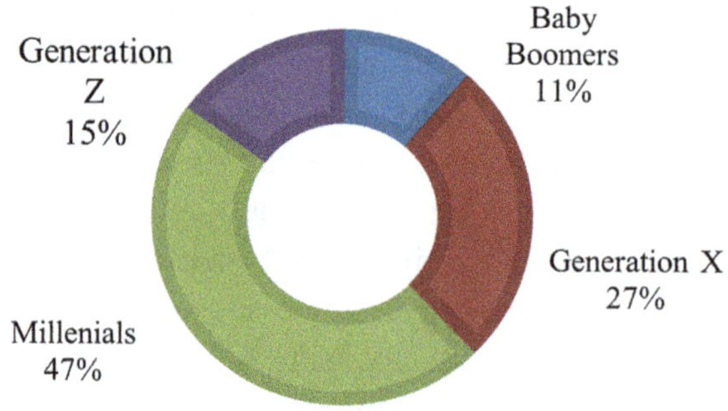

The gender distribution was balanced, with 50.9% women. Most employees hold higher education degrees, with 49% having a bachelor's degree, reflecting a highly qualified workforce. However, the presence of employees with secondary (22.6%) and basic education (9.5%) levels adds diversity in qualifications and perspectives.

In terms of work experience, 39.6% of employees have more than 20 years of experience, while 35.9% have up to 10 years, indicating a mix of seasoned professionals and those in the early or mid-career stages. One of the main challenges for the organization is integrating the experience of older employees with the innovation brought by younger generations while preventing conflicts arising from different work approaches. Implementing mentorship programs can help bridge these gaps, allowing experienced professionals to share their knowledge while learning new digital and innovative skills.

4.1.2 Communication and feedback preferences

Effective communication and feedback mechanisms are crucial for organizational cohesion at Faz Cultura, particularly in a multigenerational workforce. Employees from different generations- Baby Boomers, Generation X, Millennials, and Generation Z- demonstrate distinct preferences regarding communication styles and feedback expectations (Mihaela & Maria Cristina, 2016; Santos et al., 2019).

Older employees (Baby Boomers, Generation X) favor formal communication channels such as emails and scheduled meetings, valuing structured and hierarchical exchanges (Harris, 2020). In contrast, Millennials and Generation Z prioritize digital and real-time communication tools, such as Microsoft Teams and WhatsApp, emphasizing immediacy and collaboration (Dieguez et al., 2024).

Similarly, generational differences exist in feedback preferences. Baby Boomers and Generation X prefer structured, periodic feedback sessions, while Millennials and Generation Z seek continuous, informal, and real-time feedback integrated into digital platforms (Mihaela & Maria Cristina, 2016; Harris, 2020). This divergence often results in older employees perceiving frequent feedback as overwhelming, while younger employees may disengage in environments where feedback is infrequent (Santos et al., 2019).

To bridge these gaps, Faz Cultura should implement a hybrid communication model, balancing formal email structures with agile internal messaging tools. Furthermore, reverse mentoring programs, where younger employees enhance digital literacy among senior colleagues while gaining leadership skills, can foster intergenerational collaboration (Dieguez et al., 2024).

4.1.3 Employee Commitment and Motivation

Employee commitment and motivation are fundamental to workforce retention at Faz Cultura, yet generational differences influence their motivational drivers (Mihaela & Maria Cristina, 2016; Santos et al., 2019).

Older employees (Baby Boomers, Generation X) prioritize job stability, structured career paths, and long-term benefits such as pensions (Harris, 2020). Conversely, Millennials and Generation Z emphasize career progression, continuous learning, and professional development (Dieguez et al., 2024). Moreover, recognition expectations vary: Generation X and Millennials value both financial and non-financial rewards, whereas Generation Z is more inclined toward purpose-driven work and societal impact (Mihaela & Maria Cristina, 2016; Márquez et al., 2022).

To enhance motivation across different generations, Faz Cultura should implement structured career development programs tailored to diverse expectations, a transparent recognition system integrating financial and non-financial rewards, and leadership mentoring programs that promote intergenerational engagement (Santos et al., 2019).

4.1.4 Work Tools and Technology Adoption

Generational differences at Faz Cultura are evident in the adoption of digital tools and technology integration (Mihaela & Maria Cristina, 2016; Dieguez et al., 2024).

Baby Boomers prefer traditional methods such as printed documents and handwritten notes, demonstrating greater resistance to digital platforms (Harris, 2020). Generation X balances traditional and digital tools, displaying partial adaptation to new technologies (Márquez et al., 2022). In contrast, Millennials and Generation Z seamlessly integrate digital project management tools, such as Microsoft Outlook and Slack, favoring real-time collaboration (Dieguez et al., 2024).

To improve digital integration, Faz Cultura should provide customized digital training programs for older employees (Harris, 2020) and encourage intergenerational mentoring to facilitate knowledge exchange, allowing younger employees to support digital adoption while benefiting from the experience of senior colleagues (Mihaela & Maria Cristina, 2016).

4.1.5 Training and Development

Training and development are essential for fostering organizational growth and talent retention at Faz Cultura, yet generational differences shape learning preferences and expectations (Mihaela & Maria Cristina, 2016; Santos et al., 2019). Baby Boomers and Generation X favor structured, in-person training sessions that emphasize technical skill reinforcement and industry-specific expertise (Márquez et al., 2022). Millennials and Generation Z, in contrast, prefer flexible, blended learning approaches that integrate digital platforms with interactive, self-paced content (Dieguez et al., 2024). While online learning options are increasingly accepted, older employees demonstrate greater resistance to digital training, often citing a preference for hands-on, guided instruction (Mihaela & Maria Cristina, 2016). Millennials prioritize technical skill acquisition (hard skills) but also seek leadership training and professional development opportunities that prepare them for career advancement (Santos et al., 2019). Generation X values both technical expertise and soft skills, such as strategic communication and problem-solving.

Baby Boomers emphasize continuous learning within their existing roles, whereas Generation Z, still in the early stages of their careers, exhibits an openness to diverse training formats and interdisciplinary learning experiences (Dieguez et al., 2024). To address these generational preferences, Faz Cultura should implement a hybrid training model, combining in-person workshops with digital learning platforms to ensure accessibility for all employees (Márquez et al., 2022). Additionally, personalized training pathways should be developed to align development programs with generational needs and career progression goals (Santos et al., 2019). Another essential strategy involves intergenerational mentoring initiatives, where experienced employees guide younger colleagues in technical competencies while younger employees provide digital skill training to senior staff (Dieguez et al., 2024). By adopting these strategies, Faz Cultura can enhance workforce adaptability, promote lifelong learning, and strengthen employee engagement across generations.

4.1.6 Organizational Culture

Organizational culture plays a crucial role in employee engagement, collaboration, and workplace satisfaction at Faz Cultura. However, generational diversity shapes how employees perceive and interact with the company's mission, values, and work environment (Márquez et al., 2022; Santos et al., 2019). Survey results indicate that Millennials and Generation Z prioritize work-life balance, inclusivity, and social impact, seeking a culture that aligns with their personal values and fosters open communication (Harris, 2020). Generation X values transparent leadership, structured decision-making, and professional stability, while Baby Boomers emphasize organizational loyalty, hierarchical respect, and clear career pathways (Dieguez et al., 2024). Despite overall alignment with Faz Cultura's mission, generational differences can create gaps in engagement. Younger employees express a stronger demand for flexible work models, continuous feedback mechanisms, and employee recognition programs, whereas older employees prefer structured processes and traditional leadership approaches (Santos et al., 2019). These contrasting expectations highlight the need for adaptive cultural strategies that accommodate diverse work styles and values.

To foster an inclusive and engaging organizational culture, Faz Cultura should implement hybrid leadership models that balance hierarchical decision-making with participatory management, ensuring that all employees feel valued (Márquez et al., 2022). Establishing multigenerational mentorship programs can facilitate knowledge exchange between experienced professionals and younger employees, promoting mutual learning and collaboration (Dieguez et al., 2024). Strengthening internal communication strategies by integrating structured corporate updates with agile, interactive communication platforms can cater to diverse generational preferences (Santos et al., 2019). Expanding corporate social responsibility (CSR) initiatives is also essential, as Millennials and Generation Z highly value organizational impact beyond financial performance, reinforcing Faz Cultura's role as a socially responsible employer (Harris, 2020). Additionally, developing customized recognition and feedback systems ensures that both formal evaluations and real-time feedback align with employees' expectations and career aspirations (Mihaela & Maria Cristina, 2016). By adopting these strategies, Faz Cultura can create an adaptive and inclusive corporate culture that enhances employee satisfaction, strengthens intergenerational cohesion, and sustains long-term organizational growth.

4.1.7 Career expectations

Career progression expectations at Faz Cultura differ across generations due to varying levels of professional experience, ambition, and labor market conditions (Harris, 2020; Dieguez et al., 2024).

Millennials and Generation Z exhibit strong aspirations for rapid career advancement, emphasizing salary increases, continuous learning, and dynamic career paths (Mihaela & Maria Cristina, 2016; Santos et al., 2019). Generation X demonstrates a balanced approach, with some employees prioritizing stability while others seek growth opportunities. Baby Boomers, in contrast, prioritize job security and professional recognition over hierarchical ascension (Harris, 2020).

In the long term, Millennials and Generation X maintain career growth ambitions, albeit at different paces, while Generation Z begins to align with these expectations as they gain experience (Dieguez et al., 2024). To address these diverse needs, Faz Cultura should implement structured career progression pathways, mentorship programs for senior employees, and tailored professional development strategies that balance rapid career progression with long-term stability.

4.1.8 Work Tools and Technology Adoption

Generational differences are evident in the adoption of digital tools at Faz Cultura (Mihaela & Maria Cristina, 2016; Dieguez et al., 2024). Baby Boomers prefer traditional tools, such as notebooks and printed documents, and exhibit higher resistance to digital platforms (Harris, 2020). Generation X balances traditional and digital tools, demonstrating partial adaptation to new technologies but still relying on familiar methods (Márquez et al., 2022).

In contrast, Millennials and Generation Z fully integrate digital project management tools, such as Microsoft Outlook and Slack, favoring real-time collaboration and agile workflows (Dieguez et al., 2024). To enhance technological integration, Faz Cultura should implement customized digital training programs tailored to older employees' learning needs (Harris, 2020) and encourage intergenerational mentoring programs to facilitate digital adoption, fostering collaboration between experienced employees and digital-native generations (Mihaela & Maria Cristina, 2016).

4.1.9 Intergenerational collaboration

Intergenerational collaboration at Faz Cultura presents both opportunities and challenges, shaped by differing career expectations, work habits, and communication styles (Santos et al., 2019). Younger employees, particularly Millennials and Generation Z, prioritize continuous learning and digital collaboration, seeking real-time engagement and flexibility in teamwork. In contrast, older employees, including Baby Boomers and Generation X, prefer structured decision-making processes and mentorship-based knowledge transfer, emphasizing experience and stability (Dieguez et al., 2024). Differences in communication styles further complicate collaboration, as younger generations favor instant messaging and agile discussions, while older employees rely on formal meetings and hierarchical communication, often leading to misunderstandings (Márquez et al., 2022).

To enhance intergenerational collaboration, Faz Cultura should promote cross-generational teamwork by ensuring diverse project teams where knowledge exchange is encouraged (Santos et al., 2019). Implementing structured mentorship programs can facilitate knowledge transfer, allowing younger employees to contribute digital expertise while gaining leadership insights from senior colleagues (Mihaela & Maria Cristina, 2016). Additionally, leadership training programs should focus on inclusive communication strategies to bridge generational gaps and foster a more cohesive and productive workplace (Dieguez et al., 2024).

4.2 Onboarding in Human Resources Management

The establishment of the Human Resources (HR) department in 2020 marked a strategic turning point in recognizing people management as a critical pillar of organizational development. Faz Cultura, as a municipal company, operates across two distinct physical spaces—Theatro Circo and gnration—each with specialized teams managing key cultural projects in Braga, including Braga Media Arts and Braga 25. Given the geographical dispersion of its workforce, the growing number of employees, and the organizational challenges posed by the COVID-19 pandemic, the company faced an urgent need to structure a cohesive and strategic onboarding process.

Before the HR department's formalization, the onboarding process was largely informal and limited to bureaucratic procedures. New hires lacked structured orientation about the company's culture, mission, or values, leading to inconsistencies in how organizational knowledge was disseminated. This absence of a standardized onboarding framework resulted in low engagement, slower adaptation periods, and fragmented integration experiences, particularly among professionals transitioning from different sectors outside the cultural domain. In response, the HR department designed an onboarding process that aligned with the company's strategic vision. This structured approach aimed to reduce the time-to-productivity for new employees, foster engagement, and promote organizational cohesion, particularly in a multigenerational workforce. The model was developed to address generational differences, recognizing that Baby Boomers and Generation X prefer structured and hierarchical integration, whereas Millennials and Generation Z favor interactive, feedback-driven onboarding experiences.

The onboarding model consists of four key phases. The first phase, preboarding and recruitment alignment, ensures that candidates receive clear information about the organizational culture, expectations, and career progression opportunities. Since 2020, all recruitment and selection processes have been internally managed, strengthening HR's ability to align talent acquisition with organizational objectives. The second phase, the day-one experience and organizational induction, features a personalized onboarding session led by an HR representative, presenting the company's history, mission, structure, corporate benefits (referred to as "emotional salary"), workplace policies, and practical logistics such as parking and cafeteria access. To enhance engagement from day one, HR developed AI-powered introductory videos that provide an overview of key operational areas, offering visual, accessible insights into team functions and improving cross-departmental understanding and collaboration.

The third phase, continuous learning and cultural integration, recognizes that effective onboarding extends beyond the first day. HR implemented a structured 90-day follow-up program that includes guided workplace tours at Theatro Circo and gnration, allowing new hires to familiarize themselves with different teams and workspaces. A peer mentoring program leverages senior employees' expertise to support knowledge transfer, while an internal communication strategy ensures smoother integration by introducing new employees through company-wide announcements. The final phase, evaluation and adaptation, consists of a 90-day monitoring framework featuring a dual-feedback mechanism. Regular face-to-face meetings between new hires and direct supervisors assess progress, while structured surveys at 30 and 90 days post-hire gather insights from both employees and supervisors. These surveys measure adaptation to the company, functional integration, and behavioral engagement using a Likert scale from 1 (Very Dissatisfied) to 5 (Very Satisfied), allowing HR to identify integration challenges and intervene proactively.

Since its implementation in January 2022, the onboarding framework has been applied to 26 new employees, contributing to a significant reduction in turnover rates, which currently stand at 3.1%, and fostering a positive cultural assimilation across different generational cohorts. The HR department has played an active role in real-time monitoring, ensuring that discrepancies between employee and managerial perceptions are promptly addressed. Beyond retention, the onboarding strategy has reinforced Faz Cultura's attractiveness as an employer, supporting both internal mobility and the company's ability to retain specialized cultural talent. Job vacancies are strategically promoted via the company website and LinkedIn to engage professionals already aligned with Braga's cultural sector.

Despite its successes, the onboarding process requires ongoing refinements to align with emerging workforce trends. Future optimizations include customizing onboarding formats for different employee demographics, expanding digital resources through e-learning modules and AI-driven knowledge platforms, and strengthening feedback loops by incorporating real-time sentiment analysis tools to refine engagement strategies. A well-structured onboarding process is essential for sustaining organizational success, ensuring that employees are not only functionally integrated but also deeply engaged with the company's strategic mission and values. Faz Cultura's HR team remains committed to continuous improvement, reinforcing the philosophy that human capital is the organization's most valuable asset.

5. DISCUSSION OF FINDINGS

This research has highlighted the strategic importance of Human Resources (HR) at Faz Cultura, particularly in managing generational diversity and implementing effective integration practices such as onboarding. The study demonstrated that a structured onboarding and adaptation process has a significant impact on employee motivation, satisfaction, and retention, which is especially relevant in a multigenerational context.

The findings indicate that Generation Z and Millennials highly value close guidance during their initial months of employment, favoring continuous feedback and professional development opportunities. In contrast, Generation X and Baby Boomers, while less dependent on formal integration processes, benefit from initiatives that facilitate their adaptation to new technologies and work methodologies. In this regard, adopting differentiated intergenerational management strategies has proven essential in fostering a more inclusive, cohesive, and collaborative organizational environment.

The study also emphasized that generational diversity, beyond posing a challenge for HR management, represents a valuable opportunity for the organization. The coexistence of different generations in the same work environment necessitates personalized approaches that promote inclusion, cooperation, and organizational alignment. It became evident that Baby Boomers and Generation X tend to value stability and recognition of experience, whereas Millennials and Generation Z prioritize flexibility, technological innovation, and continuous development. Thus, policies that balance tradition and modernity are fundamental to optimizing the potential of each generation and preventing intergenerational conflicts.

Regarding talent retention and organizational commitment, the study found that different generations have distinct expectations regarding career progression and professional recognition. The personalization of incentives and the adoption of hybrid work models emerge as effective strategies to enhance employee satisfaction and retention. Additionally, the implementation of intergenerational mentoring programs has proven to be a promising solution for facilitating knowledge transfer between senior and junior employees, thereby strengthening organizational culture. By addressing this, the study can highlight the distinct challenges and advantages of HR management in municipal companies compared to corporate environments. Furthermore, while the study proposes HR strategies for Faz Cultura, the discussion should generalize these insights to broader municipal HRM practices. Including scalable recommendations that HR professionals in other public organizations can adopt would enhance the study's practical relevance.

Faz Cultura's organizational culture has demonstrated itself to be a key factor in employee integration and workplace well-being. The appreciation of generational diversity, the creation of spaces for dialogue, and the development of recognition mechanisms tailored to different age groups are essential practices for consolidating organizational identity and fostering a positive work environment.

6. STUDY LIMITATIONS

Despite its significant contributions, this research presents some limitations that should be considered.

Firstly, the study was conducted exclusively at Faz Cultura, a public-sector organization, which may limit the generalizability of the findings to other entities, particularly private companies or industries with distinct HR management dynamics. Future studies could benefit from a comparative analysis across different sectors, providing a broader perspective on intergenerational dynamics in the labor market.

Secondly, the methodology relied predominantly on qualitative approaches, with a lesser representation of quantitative data. While qualitative analysis allowed for an in-depth understanding of the subject matter, its interpretative nature introduces a degree of subjectivity in the findings. Participants' individual perceptions may have influenced responses, making it more challenging to extrapolate the results to other contexts. To address this limitation, future research should incorporate mixed-method approaches, combining qualitative insights with more robust quantitative analyses to measure indicators such as satisfaction levels, retention rates, and engagement patterns across generations.

Additionally, external factors, such as macroeconomic changes and social trends, may have influenced employee perceptions but were not examined in detail in this study. Events such as the COVID-19 pandemic and the rise of digitalization in the workplace may have had a significant impact on generational adaptation and HR management, highlighting the importance of considering these variables in future research.

Lastly, the interpretation of qualitative data is subject to researcher bias, as the categorization of themes and identification of patterns are inherently subjective processes. The selection of the most representative quotes and the organization of data may influence how the results are presented and understood, reinforcing the need for methodological transparency and triangulation of information sources.

7. RECOMMENDATIONS FOR FUTURE RESEARCH

Building on the identified limitations, several directions for future research are proposed, including sample expansion, longitudinal studies, leadership and organizational climate influence, integration of contextual variables, and refinement of onboarding practices.

Examining generational diversity across different organizational settings, including private, public, and diverse industry sectors, would provide a more comprehensive understanding of the challenges and opportunities associated with intergenerational management. Additionally, longitudinal studies tracking generational shifts within Faz Cultura and other organizations could help identify changing trends, anticipate workforce needs, and develop more effective management strategies.

Given the significant role of leadership in shaping employees' perceptions of the work environment, it would be valuable to explore how different management styles influence intergenerational discrepancies, employee retention, and motivation. Similarly, organizational climate—reflecting overall satisfaction and internal cooperation—may act as an integrating factor or, conversely, exacerbate generational tensions.

External factors such as economic crises, technological advancements, and labor law changes can also affect generational adaptation. Future research could examine how these variables impact age diversity management and talent retention strategies. Furthermore, a more detailed analysis of onboarding's impact across various organizational areas would help identify the most critical aspects for new employee adaptation. Conducting qualitative interviews and continuously monitoring employees' perceptions throughout the integration process could further refine onboarding practices. These could include a longitudinal study examining the long-term effects of onboarding on employee retention and job satisfaction, and comparative research between municipal HR strategies and private-sector onboarding models. Additionally, future research could focus on the role of AI-driven onboarding tools in facilitating generational integration, as well as policy implications for HR management in public-sector institutions..

8. FINAL CONSIDERATIONS

This study reinforces the need for a strategic and differentiated approach to managing generational diversity, recognizing age diversity as a driver of innovation and sustainable growth. Faz Cultura has the opportunity to strengthen its organizational culture through policies that balance the needs of different generations, fostering inclusion, collaboration, and talent retention.

Onboarding has emerged as a fundamental pillar for the effective integration of new employees, facilitating their adaptation to the organization's culture and internal processes. The findings indicate that, overall, employees feel integrated into the company and aligned with its culture. However, there is a discrepancy between managers' and employees' perceptions regarding the functional aspect of onboarding, with new hires reporting increased challenges in performing their duties. Thus, a well-structured onboarding program should not only ensure cultural integration but also provide adequate support for functional performance, ensuring a positive impact on productivity and professional satisfaction.

In a broader sense, this research contributes to a deeper understanding of HR's strategic role in building more resilient, innovative, and competitive organizations. Investing in human capital development and fostering an inclusive organizational culture not only enhances company performance but also prepares organizations to face emerging workforce challenges. It is hoped that the findings of this study will serve as a foundation for further reflections and best practices that position HR as a key driver of innovation and sustainable growth, particularly in the public sector.

REFERENCES

Ali, B. J., & Anwar, G. (2021). An Empirical Study of Employees' Motivation and Its Influence Job Satisfaction. *International Journal of Engineering Business Management, 5*(2), 21–30.

Almeida, D. L. (2019). As práticas de Gestão de Recursos Humanos: Estudo de caso numa empresa de metalomecânica da região de Aveiro. *Dissertação de Mestrado em Gestão.* Aveiro: Escola Superior de Gestão de Tomar – Instituto Politécnico de Tomar.

Armstrong, M., & Taylor, S. (2020). Armstrong's Handbook of Human Resource Management Practice - A Guide to the Theory and Practice of People Management (15th Edition ed.). United Kingdom: KoganPage, London.

Bauer, T. N. (2010). *Onboarding new employees: Maximizing success.* SHRM Foundation's Effective Practice Guideline Series.

Beardwell, J., & Thompson, A. (2017). *Human Resource Management: A Contemporary Approach.* Pearson.

Benítez Márquez, M. D., Sánchez Teba, E. M., Bermúdez González, G., & Núñez Rydman, E. S. (01 de Fevereiro de 2022). Generation Z Within the Workforce and in the Workplace: A Bibliometric Analysis. *Frontiers in Psychology, Volume 12.*

Bilan, Y., Mishchuk, H., Roshchyk, I., & Joshi, O. (Novembro de 2020). Hiring and retaining skilled employees in SMEs: problems in human resource practices and links with organizational success. *Business: Theory and Practice, 21*(2), pp. 780-791.

Bratton, J., & Gold, J. (2017). *Human Resource Management: Theory and Practice.* Palgrave Macmillan. DOI: 10.1057/978-1-137-58668-1

Cable, D. M., Gino, F., & Staats, B. R. (2013). Reinventing Employee Onboarding. *MIT Sloan Management Review, 54*(3), 23–28.

Carpenter, M. L. (2023). *Effective Onboar e Onboarding Str ding Strategies t ategies to Increase Talent Retention. Doctoral Study Submitted in Partial Fulfillment of the Requirements for the Degree of Doctor of Business Administration.* Walden University.

Carvalheiro, C. D. (2011). *A Evolução da Gestão de Recursos Humanos.* Relatório de Estágio Curricular, Universidade de Coimbra.

Carvalho, A., & Rua, O. L. (2017). *Gestão de Recursos Humanos - Abordagem das Boas Práticas.* Vida Economica Editorial.

Collings, D. G., Mellahi, K., & Cascio, W. F. (Junho de 2018). Global Talent Management and Performance in Multinational Enterprises: A Multilevel Perspective. *Journal of Management 45(2).*

Denzin, N. K., & Lincoln, Y. S. (2018). *The SAGE Handbook of Qualitative Research.* Sage Publications, Inc.

Dessler, G. (2022). *Human Resource Management.* Pearson.

Dieguez, T., Faria, A., & Loureiro, P. C. (2024). The Digital Frontier: Navigating the Challenges and Opportunities for Generation Z in the Labor Market. Em *Reskilling the Workforce for Technological Advancement* (pp. 82- 110). IGI Global.

Faria, A. F. (2023). *Tendências e Desafios da Geração Z no contexto da Transformação Digital. Tese de Mestrado em Gestão de Organizações.* IPCA.

Gandolfi, F., & Stone, S. (Outubro de 2018). Leadership, Leadership Styles, and Servant Leadership. *Journal of Management Research, 18(4)*, pp. 261-269.

Harris, K. (2020). *A New Gener A New Generation of W ation of Workers: Pr ers: Preparing for Gener eparing for Generation Z in the ation Z in the. Senior Theses.* University of South Carolina - Columbia.

Hennink, M., Hutter, I., & Bailey, A. (2020). Qualitative Research Methods. *Sage (Atlanta, Ga.).*

Hines, P. (Novembro de 2021). Human Centred Lean - An Introduction to the People Value Stream. *International Journal of Lean Six Sigma, 13 (5)*, 961-988.

Hongal, P., & Kinange, U. (Fevereiro de 2020). A Study on Talent Management and its Impact on Organization Performance - An Empirical Review. *International Journal of Engineering and Management Research, 10 (01)*, 64-71.

Ismail, A., Hidajat, T., Dora, Y. M., Prasatia, F. E., & Pranadani, A. (2023). *Leading the Digital Transformation: Evidence from Indonesia.* Asadel Publisher.

Klein, H. J., Polin, B., & Sutton, K. L. (2015). Specific Onboarding Practices for the Socialization of New Employees. *International Journal of Selection and Assessment, 23*(3), 263–283. DOI: 10.1111/ijsa.12113

Kuusisto, T. (2024). *Examining onboarding and employee engagement in field service teams: A case study of Europe and Africa area energy projects.* (UNIVERSITY OF VAASA, School of Technology and Innovation, Ed.) [Review of *Examining onboarding and employee engagement in field service teams: A case study of Europe and Africa area energy projects.*].

Lanka, E., Lanka, S. V., Rostron, A., & Singh, P. (2021). *Why We Need Qualitative Research in Management Studies*. Revista de Administração Contemporânea. DOI: 10.1590/1982-7849rac2021200297.en

Maia, G. (2022). Gestão de Pessoas e Recursos Humanos: Tendências Pós-Pandemia. *Revista Ibero-Americana de Humanidades. Ciência & Educação (Bauru)*, *8*(2), 705–728.

Marler, J. H., & Boudreau, J. W. (2017). An Evidence-Based Review of HR Analytics. *International Journal of Human Resource Management*, *28*(1), 1–24. DOI: 10.1080/09585192.2016.1244699

Mayo, E. (1933). *The Human Problems of an Industrial Civilization*. The Macmillan Co.

Mihaela, Ţ., & Maria Cristina, I. (2016). Generation Y's Work Values and Their Impact on thE HOSPITALIty Industry. *Cactus Tourism Journal*, *14*(2), 5–11.

Monteiro, B., Santos, V., Reis, I., Sampaio, M. C., Sousa, B., Martinho, F., José Sousa, M., & Au-Yong-Oliveira, M. (2020). Employer Branding Applied to SMEs: A Pioneering Model Proposal for Attracting and Retaining Talent. *Information (Basel)*, *11*(12), 574. DOI: 10.3390/info11120574

O'Neil, S., & Koekemoer, E. (2016). Two decades of qualitative research in Psychology, Industrial and Organisational Psychology and Human Resource Management within South Africa: A critical review. *SA Journal of Industrial Psychology*, *42*(1). Advance online publication. DOI: 10.4102/sajip.v42i1.1350

Prasad, D. B. V., Hamraaia, M. H. Y., & Sharma, D. A., B.c, S., & Pereira, M. C. S. (2024). The Impact of Technology on Human Resource Management: Trends and Challenges. *Educational Administration: Theory and Practice*, *30*(5), 9746–9752.

Rego, A., Cunha, M. P., Gomes, J. F., Cunha, R. C., Cabral-Cardoso, C., & Marques, C. A. (2008). *Manual de Gestão de Pessoas e do Capital Humano*. Edições Sílabo.

Ribeiro, A. L. (2005). *Gestão de Pessoas*. Saraiva.

Saks, A. M., & Gruman, J. (2011). Organizational Socialization and Positive Organizational Behaviour: Implications for Theory, Research, and Practice. *Canadian Journal of Administrative Sciences/Revue Canadienne des Sciences de l'Administration, 28(4)*, 14 - 26.

Santos, G. L., Gaspar, F. L., Rodrigues, M. B., & Baldissarelli, J. M. (2019). A Diversidade Geracional e as Políticas e Práticas de Recursos Humanos em Instituições de Ensino Superior. *Rev. Adm. UFSM, Santa Maria, v. 12, Edição Especial Ecoinovar*, pp. 1108-1126.

Santos, V., Simão, P., Reis, I., Sampaio, M. C., Martinho, F., & Sousa, B. (2023). Ethics and Sustainability in Hospitality Employer Branding. *Administrative Sciences, 13*(9), 202. DOI: 10.3390/admsci13090202

Sharma, G. G., & Stol, K.-J. (Outubro de 2019). Exploring Onboarding Success, Organizational Fit, and Turnover Intention of Software Professionals. *Journal of Systems and Software*, p. 159:110442.

Silva, S. M. (2019). *The Role of New Technologied for The Human Resources Management*. Universidade do Minho.

Smith, J., & Garriety, S. (2020). The art of flexibility: Bridging five generations in the workforce. Em J. Smith, & S. Garriety. *Strategic HR Review, 19*(3), 107–110. DOI: 10.1108/SHR-01-2020-0005

Sousa, M. J., Duarte, T., Sanches, P. G., & Gomes, J. (2006). *Gestão de Recursos Humanos*. Lidel.

Souza, M., Benati, N. A., & Pereira, A. (2024). A Evolução do Setor de RECURSOS Humanos: Análise Histórica e o Impacto das Tecnologias. *Deleted Journal, 5*(2), e116–e116. DOI: 10.54033/icmrv5n2-012

Torrington, D., Hall, L., Atkinson, C., & Taylor, S. (2020). *Human Resource Management* (11th Edition ed.). Pearson.

Ulrich, D., Younger, J., Brockbank, W., & Ulrich, M. (2012). *The New HR Competencies: Business Partnering from the Outside-In. The RBL Group*. New HR Competencies.

Wanberg, C. R. (2012). Facilitating Organizational Socialization: An Introduction. *In The Oxford Handbook of Organizational Socialization.*

Younas, M., & Bari, M. W. (2020). The relationship between talent management practices and retention of generation 'Y' employees: mediating role of competency development. *Economic Research-Ekonomska Istrazivanja, 33(1), Vol. 33, No. 1*, pp. 1330–1353.

Ziede, M. L. (2020). Human Resource Management and Sustainability Linkages: Building Theory From Functionalist and Interpretive Paradigms. Doctor Thesis, *Università degli Studi di Pisa*

KEY TERMS AND DEFINITIONS

Human resources: refers to the department responsible for managing people within organizations, encompassing activities such as selection, training, appraisal, and rewards, while also playing a strategic role in identifying and developing the skills necessary for organizational success.

Multigenerational workforce: refers to an organization that employs individuals from different generations—typically spanning up to five, from Baby Boomers to Gen Z—working together simultaneously. This diversity brings a wide range of perspectives, experiences, and technological skills, requiring management strategies that cater to varied communication styles, career goals, and work methods.

Talent management: is the strategic, ongoing process of attracting, identifying, developing, engaging, and retaining high-potential employees to meet current and future business goals. It ensures the right people with the right skills are in the right roles, covering the entire employee lifecycle from onboarding to succession planning.

Chapter 8
Doomscrolling, Digital Behavior, and Gen Z Workplace Dynamics:
Policy and Governance Implications for Human-Centered Human Resource Management

Janhavi Gupta
http://orcid.org/0009-0002-0142-721X
Christ University, India

Sharad Gupta
http://orcid.org/0000-0002-4994-3523
Christ University, India

ABSTRACT

The rapid integration of digital technologies into everyday organizational life has transformed how employees work, process information, and interact. Among the emerging digital habits, doomscrolling, defined as the compulsive consumption of negative online content, has gained attention for its disruptive psychological and behavioral consequences. Generation Z, being highly exposed to digital devices and content, is particularly susceptible to this phenomenon, now that they are entering the workforce. This book chapter examines the implications of digital behaviors such as doomscrolling on Generation Z workplace dynamics. It adopts a human-centred, ethical, and policy-oriented HRM perspective. Drawing on multidisciplinary literature from psychology, digital media, and HRM, the chapter identifies key challenges,

DOI: 10.4018/979-8-2600-2178-1.ch008

risks, and ethical concerns. Building on these nuances, the chapter proposes policy-oriented and governance-based HR interventions designed to promote employee mental health, digital well-being, and sustainable organizational development.

1. INTRODUCTION

The contemporary workplace has been transformed by digital platforms, mobile technologies, and social media, which are increasingly blurring the line between work and personal life (Cascio & Montealegre, 2016). While digital technologies have enabled flexible work environments, increased efficiency, and global connectivity, they have also intensified the amount of information that we consume daily and blurred work-life boundaries. One of the major emerging phenomena within this context is doomscrolling. Although doomscrolling has been widely discussed in the public discourse, its implications for human resource management remain underexplored.

From an organizational point of view, it extends beyond an individual habit. It represents the broader structural and governance challenges within the modern digital work systems. Employees are required to operate in increasingly digital work environments, fuelled by constant connectivity, performance monitoring, and algorithm-shaped information flows. These conditions heighten anxiety, emotional exhaustion, and stress, which directly affect job satisfaction, performance, and employee turnover. As a result, doomscrolling raises significant ethical and policy concerns regarding employee autonomy and employee safety, data governance, psychological health, and organizational performance.

This chapter examines doomscrolling through the lens of Human Resource Management (HRM) and organizational governance. It advocates that unmanaged and poorly governed digital behaviors can harm both employee well-being and the long-term sustainability of the organization. Rather than framing doomscrolling as a problem of individual self-control, the chapter conceptualizes it as a structurally reinforced behavior by social media algorithms and organizational norms, encouraging people to engage repeatedly with such content, and it becomes a habit. Aligning with the contemporary HRM scholarship, this chapter positions employee mental health and well-being as central, rather than peripheral, organizational priorities.

The chapter is structured in the following way. Section 2 presents the conceptual foundations and key definitions necessary for understanding the background of the chapter. It defines key concepts like digital work environments, workplace dynamics, doomscrolling, Generation Z and digital socialization. It also defines Digital Well-being and ethical human resource management. Section 3 outlines the various theoretical frameworks that are necessary for informing the study and

Human Resource Management policies that are required to manage doomscrolling. Section 4 examines the impact of Doomscrolling on the workplace dynamics in detail. Section 5 discusses the ethical and governance challenges that are associated with digital work environments, focusing on issues of employee surveillance data and digital inequality.

Section 6 proposes the HR policies and governance frameworks that organizations can adopt to manage techno stress and doomscrolling. It outlines the types of policies and guidelines that can help prevent cognitive overload and employee burnout, leadership accountability mechanisms, and digital literacy initiatives, evaluating their effects on employee behavior and psychological outcomes. Section 7 considers the broader organizational implications of digital well-being initiatives in relation to Employee branding, talent attraction and retention, organizational culture, and psychological safety. It advocates that proactive engagement and digital well-being can enhance the long-term sustainability of the organization.

Section 8 adopts a cross-cultural, sectoral, and forward-looking approach. It explores the differences in digital behavior and our reactions based on the cultural context, industries, the size of the organizations, and the work environment, which is enhanced with the help of AI. This discussion spotlights the necessity of dynamic and ethically informed HR strategies that help the organization to adapt to the changing digital environment. The last section, section 9, discusses what future directions this research could take, followed by concluding reflections in section 10.

In general, this chapter also brings up the emerging discussions on digital work and well-being. It emphasizes that doomscrolling is a serious HRM governance concern that impacts both employees and organizations, as well as the future of digital work, particularly in the technology-intensive, algorithm-driven, and highly connected workplace environments.

2. CONCEPTUAL FOUNDATIONS AND KEY DEFINITIONS

This section establishes the main concepts and foundational pillars that form the basis of analysis for doomscrolling, Generation Z workplace dynamics, and human-centred human resource management. By clearly defining the nature of the digital workplace, digital behaviors, generational digital socialization, and ethical HR governance, this section lays the conceptual foundation for understanding the emerging role of doomscrolling as a relevant workplace phenomenon and the need for proper policy and governance, special and psychological measures in contemporary HRM.

2.1 Digital Work Environments and Workplace Dynamics

Digital Work Environments refer to corporate environments that use virtual, technology-driven workspaces that encompass tools such as cloud computing, communication apps, and digital collaboration tools like Slack and Microsoft Teams, allowing their employees to work from any location and at any time ***(Merlo et al., 2025; Lane et al., 2023)***. These environments foster the "always-on" work culture that blurs the temporal, spatial, and psychological boundaries that people have in their work and non-work life. This reshapes how employees communicate, collaborate, and manage their roles in the workplace (Mazmanian, Orlikowski, & Yates, 2013; Derks, van Duin, Tims, & Bakker, 2015). Importantly, digital workplaces function as socio-technical environments that vigorously shape behavior, group norms, and organizational culture.

Workplace Dynamics within the context of Digital Environments is defined by the changing socialization patterns, communication, expectations of availability, and the power balance between employees, managers, and organizations (Orlikowski & Scott, 2008). Constant connectivity changes how people interact. It creates implicit norms of rapid responsiveness and 24/7 availability, generating cognitive and emotional strain that affects attention, trust, collaboration, and psychological safety (Barley, Meyerson & Grodal, 2011) (Edmondson, 2018).

From an HR perspective, workplace dynamics in the digital world are not shaped only by organizational culture and leadership styles, but also by the platform structure, algorithm, and digital infrastructure (Kellogg, Valentine & Christin, 2020). These factors directly influence employee well-being, engagement, and performance, making digital work environments an important concern for human-centred HR policy and governance frameworks.

2.2 Doomscrolling as a Digital Behavior Phenomenon

Doomscrolling refers to the compulsive, continuous, and prolonged consumption of negative digital content, particularly through social media and online news platforms, driven by algorithmic boosting, negativity bias, and information seeking due to uncertainty (Dhir et al., 2018; Kales, McCrae, & Grealish, 2020). Unlike normal digital media consumption, doomscrolling is characterized by repetitive exposure to upsetting online content, emotional dysregulation, and difficulty logging off, even with the adverse effects it has on mental health (Zhang et al., 2021).

Empirical research done by psychological experts links this behavior with anxiety, heightened stress, emotional exhaustion, and reduced grit (Garfin, Silver, & Holman, 2020). Algorithmic curation systems often intensify this pattern by prioritizing emotionally charged content that evokes and reinforces the cycles of negative engagement and compulsive consumption (Pariser, 2011; Sunstein, 2018). Doomscrolling is therefore not merely an individual habit but a structurally reinforced digital behavior deeply embedded within the digital social media ecosystems.

2.3 Generation Z and Digital Socialization

Generation Z is generally defined as the group of individuals born between the years 1997 to 2012 is the most digitally literate generation out of all generations to date. Smartphones, social media, online websites, apps, and real-time news feeds have become this generation's new normal. Many Gen Z individuals report spending significant time on their mobile devices and social media apps to socialize rather than to meet people in cafes or parks physically, which is also reflected in their professional lives. Digital socialization, in simple terms, is communicating or adopting social norms and cultural practices through online interactions in digital technologies.

Sharing reels and doomscrolling have become Gen Z's common digital behavior. Social media platforms are increasingly serving as spaces where people connect, share information, and collectively process crises. While these platforms can foster a sense of belonging and real-time connection, many people face negative criticism and fall into the habit of constant comparisons with others. Research suggests that heavy social media exposure led to poor mental health outcomes, spotlighting the double-edged nature of digital socialization ***(Gao et al., 2020)***..

2.4 Digital Well-Being and Mental Health at work

Digital well-being refers to the extent to which digital technologies support, rather than undermine, employees' psychological, emotional, and physical health. Employees are now required to constantly be in front of their screens from answering emails, calling and messaging platforms like Slack and Microsoft Teams, and Social Media apps. All this blurs the line between their personal and professional lives. Excessive screen time causes eye strain, stress, burnout, and cognitive overload. Apart from the physical strain that comes with sitting in one place and staring at a screen for long periods, there is also a huge toll on the mental health of an individual. Evidence shows that poor digital work environments and high ICT demands are associated with increased mental strain and declining mental health, underscoring the importance of a healthy digital lifestyle at work (Barber & Santuzzi, 2015).

2.5 Human-Centered Human Resource Management and Ethical Governance

All of the above prompt the organizations to come up with management and governance policies that cater to their human resources, taking care of their needs, well-being, and requirements. In this context, *Employee Experience* or EX becomes an important pillar for human-centered human resource management. It refers to all the experiences an employee has with their organization during their employment lifecycle. Research indicates that when organizations focus on improving the quality of EX at work, fostering a positive environment with the help of supportive HR practices and policies, employees become more loyal to the organization. The organization also sees a rise in its engagement levels, retention rates, productivity, and customer satisfaction (Shilpa Wadha et al., 2024). Looking from the Ethical Governance Perspective, prioritizing EX means commitment to dignity, fairness, and transparency, reinforcing trust in the organization in digitized workplaces (Beer et al., 2015).

3. THEORETICAL FRAMEWORKS INFORMING THE STUDY

This section of the book details the theoretical frameworks required to support the study of the effect of Doomscrolling on Human Resource Policy and Governance Policy formulation, setting the foundational base for analysis. The examples used to explain the theoretical concepts are illustrative secondary cases drawn from publicly available reports and prior studies.

3.1 Job Demands-Resources (JD-R) Model

According to Rehabeam (***Rehabeam & Unggul Kustiawan, 2025),*** the Job Demands-Resources Model explains how different work conditions affect employee well-being and performance with the help of two forces, job demands and job resources. Job demands are the factors that drain energy, like the workload, time pressure, and emotional strain, whereas job resources are the factors that motivate the employees to work, e.g., training, a supportive boss, and autonomy in work. These two factors have an inverse relationship, i.e., when there is a lack of resources, the demands increase, making the employees stressed, and vice versa.

To illustrate the model, the chapter draws from a real-life illustrative organizational example of Southwest Airlines. The company manages the higher-pressure aviation industry by strategically balancing stressors with support. The airlines' business model imposes intense job demands such as rapid 10-minute turnarounds", physical labor, and emotional exhaustion of managing travelers' grievances. According to the JD-R model, these demands typically trigger a "health impairment process" which leads to burnout. Southwest mitigates these stressors by providing an extensive amount of job resources, which include a high-trust culture that encourages peer support, significant decision-making autonomy for its frontline staff, and a playful environment that fosters resilience.

The balance shifts employees from the path of exhaustion to a motivational process. By equipping the staff with the necessary resources to manage their emotions and to meet the higher expectations, Southwest converts this professional stress into high work engagement and organizational loyalty. The result is that they gain a competitive advantage that helps employees to function despite the grueling pace, maintaining the lower turnover rates and meeting the high demands of the customers.

3.2 Technostress and Cognitive Load Theory

According to Sweller (1988), Cognitive Load Theory *(*Sweller, 1988*)* states that there is a certain amount of mental effort required by an individual to process information. In the context of the workplace, employees are constantly consuming large amounts of information daily. In addition to that, Gen Z employees are prone to doomscrolling, which makes them especially vulnerable to technostress. Technostress is when employees get overwhelmed while using technology excessively or one that is poorly designed, which leads to lower productivity and higher strain on the body and mind *(*Tarafdar et al., 2019*;* Mansuroğlu E. & Smith A.P, 2026*)*.

Microsoft will be the best example to illustrate the effect of these theories in the workplace. The employees often faced "techno-overload" and high "technostress" when Microsoft originally rolled out the Microsoft Teams application to the global workforce. The constant notifications they received during their working hours created a high extraneous cognitive load, which forced their brain to process numerous irrelevant interruptions instead of focusing on performing the main task they had.

To mitigate Microsoft designed focused modes and quiet hours for their employees to filter out distractions, thereby reducing the mental effort employees to perform their tasks and manage the tool they also focused on simplifying their user interface and automating the routine tasks to reduce the redundant work of the software allowing their employees to dedicate time for *germane load* or high-level problem-solving tasks that required human intervention. Strategic reduction of digital workload ensured that technology remained a helpful resource rather than a mental drain that led to burnout.

3.3 Self-Regulation and Emotional Regulation Theories

According to Zimmerman (Zimmerman, 1990), the Self-Regulation Theory stresses the importance of the learners' autonomy in goal setting, monitoring progress, and reflecting on the outcomes of their work. Workplaces need to provide employees with greater decision-making autonomy, and because of this, the organizations have adopted the ROWE framework. According to the Emotional Regulation Theory by Gross *(Gross, 1998),* individuals influence what emotions they have in a particular situation and how they experience and manage them. This determines how the employees and leaders manage their emotions, for example, stress in high-pressure situations in the office.

The company Zappos utilized the "Process model of Emotional Regulation" to manage the high emotional demands of customer service. They encouraged "Situation Selection" and "Cognitive Change" for difficult situations, which allowed their employees to personalize their workspaces and reframe the difficult customer calls as opportunities rather than personal attacks. This helped the staff to manage the gap between consumer emotions and service as expected by the brand, reducing the risk of emotional dissonance.

Zappos also supports the self-regulation theory through "Holacracy," an autonomous goal setting which prevents ego depletion, where one's willpower is exhausted due to constant control. By providing their employees with recovery resources like nap rooms and social spaces, the company allows the employees to replenish their energy and work towards organizational goals in one setting. This holistic approach ensures that the staff can maintain focus and emotional stability throughout the day, leading to higher productivity and more customer loyalty.

3.4 Ethical Human Resource Management and Stakeholder Theories

Ethical Human Resource Management integrates moral principles such as integrity and fairness in human resource management practices. It treats employees as stakeholders in the business and not merely as some resource to exploit. According to the Stakeholder Theory by Edward Freeman (Freeman, 1984), firms should balance the interests of their employees, stakeholders, communities, and customers to ensure long-term success. For employees, this means that their interests get taken care of and that they get included while making decisions. The employees get fair wages and better working conditions.

3.5 Digital Governance and Ethical AI Use

Organizations, due to the rise of tech and AI, are focusing more on creating policies around digital governance that provide the framework for managing technology in the workplace. It includes maintaining transparency, accountability, and inclusivity in its policies. For example, Doomscrolling has become so prominent in the workplace in the current times that organizations have created software that monitors the employees' browsing on company devices to ensure that they are being productive. However, this raises concerns about employee privacy in the workplace.

With the advent of Artificial Intelligence (AI) in 2020, the development of policies that govern the ethical use of AI in the workplace has become extremely critical. The majority of the Gen Z workforce excessively uses AI for their day-to-day tasks and office deliverables. All these behaviors raise concerns about the sensitive company data being fed into AI and leaked onto the internet. Thus, it mandates the companies to develop strict policies and laws that govern AI use within the organization.

4. DOOMSCROLLING AND GEN Z WORKPLACE DYNAMICS

This section of the chapter explains more about the factors that cause the phenomenon of doomscrolling in today's workforce, the psychological effects it has on employees, including their mental health, and how it affects their working styles. Next, we have the generational differences in the perceptions of how the different Gens work, from their work ethic to their working patterns. And finally, we have how Millennials and Generation Z work together in Team Dynamics.

4.1 Drivers of Doomscrolling in Digital Work Contexts

Doomscrolling is a phenomenon that becomes particularly common during times of crisis, where people continuously search for news, be it negative or positive, as a way to comfort themselves in uncertain times, and it eventually becomes a habit that is hard to break out of. This was especially the case for Gen Z during the COVID-19 Pandemic, when they were stuck in their homes with limited activities beyond consuming information. Another factor may be social media-related addiction and anxiety, where individuals with social media addiction spend hours on social media, often struggling to disengage from these platforms. Individuals experiencing anxiety also tend to engage in this behavior due to their tendency to seek similar feelings-inducing content.

Adolescents, including Gen Z, are more likely to develop a social media addiction. Several research studies also prove that there is a positive correlation between social media addiction and doomscrolling. Because of this, it becomes hard for employees to focus on tasks in the workplace, which can cause them to suffer from several mental health issues. With organizations becoming increasingly digital and online, it further isolates the employees and makes them prone to indulge in doomscrolling, which hampers overall productivity (Muhammed Akat & Erdal Hamarta, 2025).

4.2 Psychological and Behavioral Impacts on Gen Z Employees

Building on the conceptual foundations, doomscrolling is said to have severe mental health effects for people. According to research studies, doomscrolling may create a feedback loop, where the negative content consumed constantly increases emotional suffering, causing the individual to continue scrolling to numb the distress caused. This behavior heightens mental health issues like anxiety, insomnia, burnout, and trauma symptoms resembling Post-Traumatic Stress Disorder (PTSD) (Dr.A.Shaji George et al., 2024). Studies also revealed that doomscrolling led to emotional desensitization, negative self-concept, and cognitive overload (Ahmed Mohamed Fahmy Yousef, 2025).

According to a research study conducted on adolescents, screen time exceeded seven hours daily in 2020. Around 36% of the Adults stated that they constantly browsed pandemic-related content. This induces adrenaline and cortisol in their bodies, triggering the fight or flight response, leading to emotional exhaustion. The blue light that comes off mobile phones and laptops reduces melatonin production in the brain, which lowers the overall sleep quality for an individual (Dr.A.Shaji George et al., 2024).

4.3 Implications for Attention, Engagement, and Productivity

What are the implications of excessive social media usage and doomscrolling for Gen Z employees? Reduced overall attention span and focus, minimal engagement in the workplace, and declining productivity. Several studies report that without the use of phones and digital devices, people were able to be in the present moment and focus more on the task at hand. They also stated that doomscrolling impairs cognitive functioning, causing memory loss, making it difficult to plan and make proper decisions (Jacob Saindon, 2025; Ahmed Mohamed Fahmy Yousef, 2025). All of these factors hamper employee productivity and engagement in the organization, which in turn leads to a drop in profits.

Lack of focus in the workplace, the feeling of overwhelming information overload, and the guilt of wasted time, along with the "pressure to return to work," are some of the main reasons for low productivity. Doomscrolling causes employees and individuals to have the thought of "just one more reel won't hurt," resulting in significant unintentional loss of time. Another thing is that the constant consumption of short 30-second video-based content has left Gen Z with extremely short attention spans, which makes it harder for them to multitask, an essential skill for working in a corporation. People find joy in watching this short-form content on TikTok and YouTube Shorts, which also reduces intrinsic motivation to engage with other employees and connect in the office (Jacob Saindon, 2025).

4.4 Generational Perceptions and Managerial Misalignment

There is also a huge misconception between the Millennials and Generation Z regarding work ethics and work culture. There is a belief that generations differ in values, behavior, and attitude towards leadership, and these values are what cause the conflict between these two generations. Millennials have the thought that Gen Z employees are lazy and rude, and Gen Z thinks that Millennials are assertive, detail-oriented, and lacking authority. This is because Millennials, shaped by collaborative work environments and teamwork, prefer autonomy in the workplace; however, Generation Z, shaped by economic uncertainty and social media, prioritizes stability and clear boundaries between work and personal life.

Generation Z prefers to have more clarity in their work and prefers to understand the task at hand to map out the structured path to approach the task, rather than just eyeballing the work and beginning with it without a plan in place. Whereas Millennials prefer to plan while they work, what this means is that they begin the work they were assigned and then plan accordingly, taking into account the opinions and suggestions of their teammates to optimize their plans.

This difference in perspectives creates a misalignment where Millennial Managers interpret Gen Z's need for structure and order as resistance to change, autonomy, and a challenge to authority, while Gen Z may perceive Millennials' openness to ideas and tendency to micromanage as a lack of authority or clarity. This directly influences the leader-member exchange (LMX) quality, workplace collaboration, and organizational work effectiveness (Karina Gabrielova and Aaron A. Buchko, 2021).

4.5 Spillover Effects on Teams and Organization Culture

Given the complex and wide-scope effects of doomscrolling on Gen Z employees' productivity and engagement, together with the common misconception-based conflicts between Gen Z employees and their Millennial managers, effective collaboration on projects becomes highly challenging. These tensions often spill over into team dynamics, undermining the organization's effectiveness and ultimately ruining the company's performance.

Therefore, organizations must develop specific strategies and clear guidelines that address workplace dynamics, particularly those arising from doomscrolling and the use of AI at work. Implementing clearly defined and structured guidelines regarding digital device use and AI use policies can protect the company from accidentally exposing confidential company data, reducing unnecessary employee screen time, and promoting sensible technology use. The employees, through these policies, learn to leverage AI tools in a way that enhances organizational productivity rather than distracts from it.

5. ETHICAL, POLICY, AND GOVERNANCE CHALLENGES FOR HRM

Digitization has transformed labor by raising its connectivity, datafication, and algorithmic control. It has also increased ethical conflict with HRM. Doomscrolling is an occurrence that lies on the borderline when it comes to employee welfare, digital surveillance, and organizational accountability. It poses questions about autonomy, data ethics, and governance in modern workplaces. The examples used to support the chapter's arguments are merely illustrative secondary cases drawn from publicly available reports and prior studies.

5.1 Surveillance and Employee Autonomy

A lot of institutions are now implementing digital monitoring systems like keypad monitoring, tracking activity, and productivity tracking, particularly in remote and hybrid locations. Although these practices are justified by firms as being performance-enhancing, over-surveillance will destroy the autonomy and psychological security of the employees (Ball, 2010). Studies based on Self-Determination Theory indicate that less autonomy is associated with stress and disengagement as well as maladaptive coping mechanisms such as compulsive digital use (Deci and Ryan, 2000).

In reality, these tensions are pointed out by real examples. Intensive monitoring of employee activity in real-time was one of the aspects that came under attack during the COVID-19 pandemic by companies such as Amazon and Teleperformance (Moore, 2020). It was reported that employees in these kinds of environments had increased anxiety and vigilance of information. They grew to be more dependent on regular news coverage to predict threats to the organization/economy. Doomscrolling in this context became a way for employees to cope with the loss of control, in contrast to the belief that it was a distraction. Employees felt like their privacy was being compromised, which increased paranoia and reduced productivity as employees became increasingly conscious about being watched and perceptions of privacy invasion.

In ethical aspects, HRM needs to strike the right balance between acceptable performance management and autonomy. Adverse consequences can be reduced through open communication on monitoring practices and employee engagement in the policy formulation process (Bodie et al., 2017).

5.2 Data Ethics and Responsible use of HR Analytics

The emergence of people analytics has allowed HR departments to study the behavior of employees on a large scale. However, the moral application of such information is controversial. Stress, engagement, or risk inference algorithms on digital behavior can, unwittingly, support bias or cause intrusive interventions (Tambe et al., 2019).

IBM is a notable example. It expects analytics to determine the risk of employee turnover. Although the improved retention results are reported by the company, the scholars warn that this type of system should be regulated to prevent employee profiling in the absence of informed consent (Rasmussen & Ulrich, 2015). Using the same analytics to define the doomscrolling behaviour (e.g., monitoring news site visits) may be inappropriate as an ethical boundary that would be crossed by considering it to be surveillance instead of care.

Companies have started to monitor the employees' browsing data in order to monitor productivity issues, which is an unethical method of ensuring productivity and efficiency of employees. Accountable HR analytics must be based on transparency, proportionality, anonymity, and limit the purpose (Floridi et al., 2018). Well-being interventions should be supported by data and not used to punish people. Analytics should be done not only to ensure organizational growth but also the safety of employees in the company.

5.3 Right to Disconnect and Boundary Movement

The concept of doomscrolling is closely associated with the reduction in the distinction between work and non-work spheres. Staying connected by smartphones and collaboration tools is a challenge as being disconnected when faced with a crisis is challenging. Some governments and other organisations have responded by formalising the right to disconnect.

An example of this is Volkswagen, which introduced an email policy that shuts down email servers when some groups of employees are not working. This decreased considerably after-hours online intrusion (Derks et al., 2014). In France, AXA and Orange balanced corporate policy and national right-to-disconnect laws (Eurofound,

2020). Such programs assist in minimising the number of compulsive checking habits and exposure to unpleasant content on the internet.

HRM is central to the conversion of such rights into practice through establishing explicit expectations in the areas of availability, response times, and digital boundaries. In India, the government has proposed "The Right to Disconnect Bill" 2025, which is under discussion to curb the effects of the "always-on" culture on employees' mental health. It aims to grant employees the right to refuse calls/emails outside of work hours or on holidays (Shravan Anande and Hari Priya Murarikar, 2025).

5.4 Digital Inequality, Inclusion, and Fairness

In the era of Digitization and AI, there is a huge digital divide present. Digital well-being issues are disproportionately distributed among work groups. In the lower-skilled, customer-facing, or precarious jobs, employees tend to be more exposed to the digital realm, but they lack the knowledge base required to actually perform their jobs (van Dijk, 2020). Doomscrolling can then be attributed to previous inequalities. To cater to this, the Indian government brought a digital literacy campaign, Pradhan Mantri Gramin Digital Saksharta Abhiyan (PMGDISHA), to spread digital literacy in rural areas (PIB Delhi, 2025).

Even though the divide is less in urban settlements, it is still present. Gig employees on applications such as Uber and Deliveroo depend on mobile applications as the primary source of income, news, and evaluation algorithms. This constant connectedness that puts them under the pressure of work-related uncertainty as well as negative news cycles, thereby adding strains to their psychology (Wood et al., 2019). Gig workers can frequently access no official mental or online wellness assistance, unlike corporate employees.

The Government of India (CBWE, 2025) states that as of today, only 38% of Indian households are digitally literate, bifurcated between rural (25%) and urban (61%) areas. Inclusive HR governance should realise such inequalities and make well-being protections available to all employment set-ups, both contractors and platform workers, as well as the more traditional staff. They should also focus on continuously digitally upskilling their employees to bridge the gap between the existing skill sets and the rapidly evolving future demands.

5.5 Regulatory and Institutional Gaps in Digital Work Governance

Although technologies tend to revolve at a fast pace, i.e., every 2-3 years, especially with the onset of Generative AI, which evolved into Agentic AI, with people now developing specific task-oriented agents that assist them with their work. Companies and individuals are increasingly relying on these technologies in everyday operations and activities; however, there remains a lack of comprehensive rules and regulations that govern AI and the rapidly evolving digital landscape.

With AI-generated content so widely available, there are also shorts and reels that people watch to refresh and rejuvenate, particularly Gen Z employees, who are well-versed in AI usage. Most jurisdictions also do not regulate AI-based algorithmic management, online surveillance, and related psychological dangers, including doomscrolling (De Stefano, 2019).

Without strict regulations present to effectively govern AI involvement and usage, organizations such as Microsoft have resorted to self-governing strategies. The policies made by Microsoft to combat doomscrolling-based employee idle time and minimal engagement were based on internal research. The policies made, advised on reducing digital exhaustion by focusing on giving frequent device-free breaks to reduce eye strain, meeting-free days, and well-being analytics dashboards (Microsoft, 2021). These examples of suggestions show us how companies can help cover gaps in policy regulations, though self-regulation requires some degree of uniformity and responsibility.

6. HR POLICY INTERVENTIONS AND GOVERNANCE FRAMEWORKS

As digital behaviors such as doomscrolling increasingly become a part of our daily work routines, organizations must move beyond ad hoc well-being initiatives and adopt well-drafted, structured, ethical, policy-based HR interventions to control employee productivity. From a human-centred human resource management perspective, the objective of the policy should not be to eliminate digital work but to govern it in ways that employee well-being, autonomy, and mental health are protected while ensuring organizational effectiveness. This section outlines the key HR policy interventions that can help mitigate the negative impact of doomscrolling and promote healthier digital work habits.

6.1 Digital Well-Being Policies and Guidelines

Digital well-being policies are a foundational governance tool through which organizations articulate the expectations they have for their employees in relation to technology use, availability, AI usage, and professional boundaries. Such policies may include guidelines on after-hours communication, office conduct expectations, non-essential notifications, or digital engagement norms. Rather than forcefully enforcing the rules and regulations, human-centered HRM practices prioritize employee involvement in policy decisions and flexible work hours, ensuring that the digital well-being initiatives and other policies that are being made are supportive of the employees, rather than punitive. Clear organizational guidelines and suggestion policies normalize conversations between the Manager and the employee around any problems they face and legitimize their needs in a formal structure.

6.2 Preventive HR Strategies for Managing Doomscrolling

Preventive HR strategies focus on addressing doomscrolling before it escalates to a level where functioning becomes difficult or there is burnout. These strategies include spreading awareness about the different digital behaviour patterns, encouraging conscious tech use, and integrating digital well-being into onboarding and learning and development programs. HR can play a pivotal role by embedding micro-breaks or no-screen time periods into the schedule of their employees for digital detoxing. Humans are inherently social beings, and in this way, instead of looking at screens, employees get a chance to interact and connect with their colleagues, which is a very effective strategy in combating mental health problems in the workplace. HR can also recalibrate and redistribute the excess workload that employees have during high-stress times. By framing doomscrolling as a systematic risk in place of an individual failure, organizations can reinforce a positive and non-stigmatizing approach to employee health.

6.3 Leadership and Managerial Accountability

Leaders and Managers also play an important role in reshaping digital norms in their organization to promote healthy digital behaviors. Human-centred governance requires managerial support in order to make psychologically safe environments where employees feel comfortable sharing their feelings and disconnect when necessary, contrasting the "always-on" culture that is prevalent nowadays. Leadership development programs should therefore incorporate training on digital ethics, creating boundaries, and an emotionally intelligent management style. When managers demonstrate healthy work and digital habits, such as not messaging employees after work hours and promoting non-constant availability, they reinforce the organizational policies and help in fostering an environment that reduces doomscrolling and digital overload.

6.4 Training, Capability Building and Digital Literacy

Training and capacity-building initiatives are key for equipping employees with the skills to navigate digital workplaces efficiently and effectively. Training programs that focus on digital literacy, emotional regulation, digital-related upskilling, and self-management can help employees recognize and manage their compulsive digital behaviors. From an HR perspective, these programs should be inclusive and tailored to the diverse workforce present in the workplace. For instance, for Generation Z employees who face higher exposure to algorithm-driven content, there should be workshops that teach them attention span increasing techniques and focus management. Through these workshops and training sessions, managers ensure that there is lifelong learning and sustainable employee development.

6.5 Integrating Mental Health into HR Governance Systems

A human-centred HR policy framework integrates mental health and well-being into performance management, workforce planning, and workload distribution. This entails providing access to employee assistance programs, mental health resources, and support systems that are aligned with the global occupational health guidelines. Importantly, mental health governance emphasizes prevention and building resilience more than interventions. By including mental health within the HR systems, companies acknowledge the psychological impact of digital work environments and work towards improving employee well-being.

6.6 Types of HR Policies for Digital Well-Being and Their Effect on Employees

Instead of viewing digital well being programs as individual standalone programs, companies should have a more comprehensive governance framework that includes both the human centered values and the employee well-being, specific leadership practices develop accountability frameworks. Individual interventions which focus on reducing the effects of digital strain (like informal wellness programs) may be ineffective when the phenomena of digitally induced behaviors like doomscrolling depends on algorithmic systems.

A digital HR governance model that is human-oriented functions at more than one level. On the personal level, employees need to be digitally literate, have self-regulation skills, and have access to mental health services that would allow them to be conscious of their interaction with digital technologies. At the managerial level, leaders are able to critically model healthy digital behaviors, establish realistic availability expectations, and psychologically safe environments where employees can freely communicate about digital overload but in which they feel that they are not stigmatized.

At the organizational scale, the HR policies should officially introduce digital well-being into the performance management systems, leadership development programs, and the people analytics government frameworks. This contains clear rules on proper use of technology, ethical limit to monitoring and gathering of data, and employee voice and involvement in making digital governance decisions. Lastly, on the institutional level, organizations have to meet the developing labor regulations, professional standards and the expectations of the society on employee rights such as the right to disconnect and data protection with internal HR governance.

Through these layers becoming a unified system of governance, human-centered HRM will not only go beyond the reactive well-being programs but will also assume the active responsibility of managing the digital workplaces. This kind of strategy will also allow organizations to control digital practices in a morally responsible manner, ensure that employees remain healthy and well, and provide legitimacy and trust to an ever more technology-mediated workplace.

7. ORGANIZATIONAL IMPLICATIONS AND EMPLOYER BRANDING

The human-centered HRM and ethical governance approach to the problem of doomscrolling and digital well-being has additional organizational and strategic consequences. In addition to personal results, these practices affect the organizational culture, employer branding, and sustainability in the long run, while building employee trust, organizational legitimacy, and the firm's ability to attract and retain talent in digital work environments.

7.1 Digital Well-Being as an Employer Branding Asset

Employer branding in the digital well-being paradigm has become a relevant form of differentiation in an ever more competitive environment of labor markets, as corporate commitment to it. Human-focused and ethically-oriented HR practices indicate that the organizations are responsible, caring, and long-term people-oriented to external stakeholders. Instead of presenting digital well-being as a productivity instrument, its presentation as a fundamental organizational value makes it more believable and desirable to employers, especially in relation to digital generations of the workforce. This kind of signaling empowers the employer's reputation by making the identity of the organization more in line with modern demands of ethical and sustainable employment.

7.2 Talent Attraction, Engagement, and Retention

Digital cultures define the experiences of employees in their day-to-day activities and have a direct impact on talent-related performance. Employees will deposit themselves more to engage, demonstrate stronger commitment, and advocacy behavior when organizations proactively recognize digital strain and have established support systems in place. To Generation Z employees, whose job choices and decisions to stay are highly dependent on perceived organizational values and well-being provisions, digital well-being policies may turn into job choice and retention factors. Therefore, HR governance involving humans transforms ethical desire into quantifiable stability of the workforce.

7.3 Organizational Culture and Psychological Safety

HR governance strategies acknowledging the idea of digital overload have helped to create organizational cultures based on openness and psychological safety. Trust and cooperation are improved when employees are not afraid of being punished, and they feel safe to talk about the problems they face, such as digital stress, mental health issues, or boundary issues. The cultural environment promotes learning, flexibility, and innovation as it encourages openness and discussion. Humane HRM thus acts as a stabilizer in cultures where organizational conventions and requirements of the staff are synchronized in digital-intensive workplaces.

7.4 Long-Term Sustainability and Organizational Reputation

The key aspect of sustainable organizational development is the combination of technological productivity and the well-being of the employees. Moral regulation of digital practices decreases the risks of burnout, absenteeism, lack of engagement, and reputational damage in the long term. Companies that actively institutionalize digital well-being are socially responsible and visionary, with their actions creating trust within the staff, clients, and the wider stakeholders. Such practices eventually improve organizational resilience and legitimacy in a fast-changing, technology-driven environment.

8. CROSS-CULTURAL, SECTORAL, AND FUTURE ORIENTED PERSPECTIVES

Although doomscrolling and digitally induced strain are universal processes, they can take different forms and have different implications depending on the cultural, sectoral, and organizational contexts. HR governance needs, however, to be context sensitive as opposed to universal solutions.

8.1 Cultural Differences in Digital Behavior

Cultural expectations also shape the expectations of availability, authority, and work-life boundaries, thus determining digital behaviors in the workplace. Collectivist societies can be characterized by the implicit need to be always-on and monitoring digital overload, which may be increased in an adept digital environment; individualistic cultures might also have more concerns regarding personal space and freedom. HR policies regarding digital health should be culturally responsive so that the governance mechanisms do not interfere with the local norms, but also protect the autonomy and mental health of employees.

8.2 Sector-Specific Considerations

Digital strain is experienced in industries with varying intensity and nature. Information overload and sustained exposure to online content are especially endangered in knowledge-intensive and digitally mediated sectors, but might be otherwise in frontline and operational sectors due to various types of digital pressure that could emanate from monitoring or communication technology. The HR strategies in sectors need to be sensitive; therefore, to make sure that the digital well-being interventions are relevant, effective, and work-design-specific.

8.3 SMEs Vs. Large Organizations

The size of organizations has a great impact on the ability to govern. Large companies tend to have formal HR practices, analytics, and well-being programs, whereas small and medium-sized businesses have to use informal leadership and resource-effective measures. Nevertheless, irrespective of these variations, ethical leadership, openness, and sincere interest in the well-being of the employees can be applied to human-centered principles that can be can be operationalized across organizational levels, irrespective of the complexity of the structures.

8.4 Future of Work and AI-Augmented Environments

With the growing integration of algorithmic management, artificial intelligence, and data-driven decision-making processes into the work process, the digital interaction and information flows are bound to get more intense. These changes bring out new ethical challenges associated with surveillance, autonomy, accountability, and transparency. The models of HR governance will have to change so that the human-oriented and ethical principles will be integrated into future-of-work models, as the technological progress will make the employee welfare and dignity even better, not weaker.

8.5 Synthesis: A Multi-Level Governance Framework for Managing Doomscrolling

Based on the conceptual grounds, theoretical viewpoints, empirical observations, and policy deliberations found in the previous chapters, this chapter contributes to a multi-level governance rationality of explaining and dealing with doomscrolling in modern digital workplaces. Instead of viewing doomscrolling as a behavioral effect or single mental health problem, the chapter comprehensively brings together the evidence to reflect the idea that it is a systemically produced effect, as it occurs at the overlap of individual, organizational, and institutional and technological systems.

The impact of constant connection and crisis-induced information consumption and acceptance of short-form emotionally-driven content affect generation Z workers especially because they are highly susceptible to these factors. Nevertheless, according to what has been determined throughout the chapter the self-regulation of individuals individually is not enough to deal with such behaviors on a sustainable level.

At the organizational level HRM practices, leadership norms, digital work design and performance expectations are either critical in amplification or mitigation of doomscrolling tendencies. The policies of availability, surveillance, workload distribution, and AI utilization directly impact the perceptions of autonomy, psychological safety, and coping in employees. When integrated into recruitment, training, performance management, and well-being systems, human-centred HRM governance is a meso-level stabilizing pressure with the potential to break the technostress cycle and compulsive use of the digital world.

Regulatory systems, cultural standards, industrial peculiarities, and technological systems also influence digital behavior at the institutional and societal level. The existence of national labor laws, policies on right-to-disconnect, data protection regulations, and ethical AI guidelines introduces a set of conditions that the organization can be seen to be operating within. Cognitive load, emotive regulation skills, digital socialization pattern, and exposure to platforms having algorithms, impact the phenomenon of doomscrolling at the individual level.

The multi-level governance approach that is developed in this chapter emphasizes the fact that the interventions that are effective should be orchestrated vertically at these levels. And isolated programs like wellness programs that lack leadership responsibility, or surveillance programs that lack ethics, are prone to symbolic compliance and little behavioral change. Conversely, coordinated governance strategies that coordinate individual support systems, HR policies and institutional rules are more likely to have sustainable results.

The synthesis of these layers by the chapter establishes digital well-being governance as a system of dynamic, adaptive, and ethical governance, and not a set of rules. This way of operating allows organizations to react to the changing digital threats, such as doomscrolling, proactively, without compromising employee dignity, trust, and future resilience of organizations that are AI-enhanced and digitally intensive.

9. FUTURE RESEARCH DIRECTIONS

Additional studies in the future should explore the potential effects of doomscrolling on the workplace in regard to job satisfaction, employee engagement, turnover intention, absenteeism, and performance. The existing literature is close to the subject of digital overuse and well-being, yet it fails to specify how the recurrent exposure to negative online content alters attitudes, behaviors, and productivity of employees. A quantitative study that uses proven psychological and HR measurements might explain the cause and effect, whereas a qualitative one might be useful to understand the personal experience of the personnel and their coping strategies.

Longitudinal designs would be particularly effective to monitor the doomscrolling changes through time and career stages. As an example, doomscrolling may be more or less common between early-career employees and older ones, with organization changes, such as promotions, reorganization, or work insecurity, increasing or decreasing it. Carrying out research across various nations would allow the researchers to investigate how larger socio-economic influences, trends in the labor market, and cultural values influence digital practices and their professional implications. Inclusion of case studies of other companies would help in giving definite examples of how these obstacles are overcome and controlled within organizations.

There is also a need to incorporate cross-cultural and industry/sector-specific studies that would help in capturing varied digital behaviours and HR practices. Doomscrolling can be highly prevalent and affect different industries differently, as not all jobs have similar job demands and stress levels. Work, technology, and mental health attitudes within a culture determine the interaction between employees and the online content and the response of their employer. The comparative study may help identify the best practices and demonstrate what HR interventions are more effective within a specific cultural or industry environment.

The effectiveness of HRM-led digital well-being programs should be tested using experimental research. Digital detoxes, training on algorithms, mindfulness, or a policy that restricts after-hours screen time can be considered to assess how well they can decrease doomscrolling and improve employee health and productivity.

Randomized controlled trials would give solid evidence on the strategies that would be most effective and scaled up.

Lastly, interdisciplinary research involving the combination of HRM, psychology, and data science could provide a more comprehensive view of the mechanisms of doomscrolling. Individual vulnerability and emotional reactions could be explained with the help of psychological theory, HRM structures could facilitate responsible policy-making, and data analysis could be realized through examining digital behavior patterns at a large scale. By combining these viewpoints, we will get a better insight into the influence of algorithm-based platforms on employee behaviors and mental health, and create more ethical, effective, and sustainable workplace behaviors in the digital age.

10. CONCLUSION

This chapter examines doomscrolling, an emerging issue in modern workplaces, through the lens of Human Resource Management and organization governance. It has advocated that doomscrolling is not an individual issue of self-control, but it is being constructed and reinforced by digitally mediated work environments, algorithm-driven platforms, and organization practices. These digital practices are unregulated without any strict policies in place, which poses a danger to the well-being of employees and sustainable organizational development.

This chapter demonstrates that continuous connectivity surveillance in the workplace and the inability to separate our work and personal lives increase pressure, mental burnout, and cause anxiety. The obsessive use of social media to consume negative information on the Internet is one of the major reasons for the declining mental health of corporate employees. These circumstances result in making doomscrolling more probable, which in turn reduces job satisfaction, engagement, productivity, and turnover intent. In HRM terms, sabotaging this generates ethical and strategic issues, particularly in striking a balance between efficiency, control, and freedom of the employee in digital workplaces.

The chapter further explored HR policy interventions and governance frameworks that the organizations can adopt to manage the technostress and reduce doomscrolling. Policies related to digital well-being, the right to disconnect, leadership accountability, and prioritizing mental health and digital literacy were shown to have a positive effect on employee well-being engagement and trust when implemented with strong leadership support. This chapter also argued that isolated symbolic policies are not enough; digital well-being must go together with the mental health policies, and these policies must be embedded into the core HR governance system of the organization.

In considering the organizational influence, the chapters showed us that proactive approaches to digital well-being can strengthen employee branding, improve talent attraction and retention, and foster cultures that prioritize psychological safety. Moreover, a cross-cultural sectoral and future-oriented point of view highlighted that effective HR responses must be such that they are inclusive to all the people in the organization, being inclusive and context sensitive to all the types of human resources present in the organization. The policies also need to be adaptable to the different organizational environments, including the AI-inclusive workplaces.

Overall, this chapter contributes to HRM and digital work by positioning doom-scrolling as an organizational problem that can be solved with the help of policies rather than an individual one. It urges the HR executives and policy makers to be proactive, ethical, and strategic when managing digital behaviors within the work-place. A strong HR governance and policy framework is central to the protection of the mental health of employees and provides a sustainable and responsible performance of the organization in the digital era.

REFERENCES

Ahmed, M. F. Y. (2025). Doomscrolling behavior and cognitive overload: Implications for mental health and decision-making. *Journal of Behavioral Addictions, 14*(1), 45–61. DOI: 10.1556/2006.2024.00098

Ball, K. (2010). Workplace surveillance: An overview. *Labor History, 51*(1), 87–106. DOI: 10.1080/00236561003654776

Barber, L. K., & Santuzzi, A. M. (2015). Please respond ASAP: Workplace telepressure and employee recovery. *Journal of Occupational Health Psychology, 20*(2), 172–189. DOI: 10.1037/a0038278 PMID: 25365629

Barley, S. R., Meyerson, D. E., & Grodal, S. (2011). E-mail as a source and symbol of stress. *Organization Science, 22*(4), 887–906. DOI: 10.1287/orsc.1100.0573

Beer, M., Boselie, P., & Brewster, C. (2015). Back to the future: Implications for the field of HRM of the multistakeholder perspective proposed 30 years ago. *Human Resource Management, 54*(3), 427–438. DOI: 10.1002/hrm.21726

Bodie, M. T., Cherry, M. A., McCormick, M. L., & Tang, J. (2017). The law and policy of people analytics. *University of Colorado Law Review, 88*(4), 961–1042. https://lawreview.colorado.edu

Cascio, W. F., & Montealegre, R. (2016). How technology is changing work and organizations. *Annual Review of Organizational Psychology and Organizational Behavior, 3*(1), 349–375. DOI: 10.1146/annurev-orgpsych-041015-062352

Central Bureau of Workforce Economics. (2025). *Digital literacy and workforce readiness in India*. Government of India. https://dtnbwed.cbwe.gov.in/images/upload/Digital-Literacy_3ZNK.pdf

De Stefano, V. (2019). Negotiating the algorithm: Automation, artificial intelligence and labour protection. *Comparative Labor Law & Policy Journal, 41*(1), 15–46. ISSN 1999-2939.

Deci, E. L., & Ryan, R. M. (2000). The "what" and "why" of goal pursuits: Human needs and the self-determination of behavior. *Psychological Inquiry, 11*(4), 227–268. DOI: 10.1207/S15327965PLI1104_01

Derks, D., Bakker, A. B., Peters, P., & van Wingerden, P. (2014). Work-related smartphone use, work–family conflict and family role performance. *Human Relations; Studies Towards the Integration of the Social Sciences, 67*(9), 1045–1068. DOI: 10.1177/0018726714525234

Derks, D., van Duin, D., Tims, M., & Bakker, A. B. (2015). Smartphone use and work–home interference. *Journal of Occupational and Organizational Psychology*, *88*(1), 155–177. DOI: 10.1111/joop.12083

Dhir, A., Yossatorn, Y., Kaur, P., & Chen, S. (2018). Online social media fatigue and psychological wellbeing. *International Journal of Information Management*, *40*, 141–152. DOI: 10.1016/j.ijinfomgt.2018.01.012

Edmondson, A. C. (2018). *The Fearless Organization: Creating Psychological Safety in the Workplace for Learning, Innovation, and Growth*. John Wiley & Sons.

Eurofound. (2020). *Right to disconnect: Exploring company practices*. Publications Office of the European Union. https://www.eurofound.europa.eu/en/publications/all/right-disconnect-exploring-company-practices

Floridi, L., Cowls, J., Beltrametti, M., Chatila, R., Chazerand, P., Dignum, V., Luetge, C., Madelin, R., Pagallo, U., Rossi, F., Schafer, B., Valcke, P., & Vayena, E. (2018). AI4People—An ethical framework for a good AI society. *Minds and Machines*, *28*(4), 689–707. DOI: 10.1007/s11023-018-9482-5 PMID: 30930541

Freeman, R. E. (1984). *Strategic management: A stakeholder approach*. Pitman. DOI: 10.2139/ssrn.263511

Gabrielova, K., & Buchko, A. A. (2021). Here comes Generation Z. *Business Horizons*, *21*(1), 7–19. DOI: 10.1016/j.bushor.2021.02.013

Garfin, D. R., Silver, R. C., & Holman, E. A. (2020). Media exposure and public health consequences of COVID-19. *Health Psychology : Official Journal of the Division of Health Psychology, American Psychological Association*, *39*(5), 355–357. DOI: 10.1037/hea0000875 PMID: 32202824

Gross, J. J. (1998). The emerging field of emotion regulation. *Review of General Psychology*, *2*(3), 271–299. DOI: 10.1037/1089-2680.2.3.271

Keles, B., McCrae, N., & Grealish, A. (2020). A Systematic Review: The Influence of Social Media on Depression, Anxiety and Psychological Distress in Adolescents. *International Journal of Adolescence and Youth*, *25*, 79–93. DOI: 10.1080/02673843.2019.1590851

Kellogg, K. C., Valentine, M. A., & Christin, A. (2020). Algorithms at work. *The Academy of Management Annals*, *14*(1), 366–410. DOI: 10.5465/annals.2018.0174

Mansuroğlu, E., & Smith, A. P. (2026, March). Technostress and Employee Well-being: A Systematic Review of Empirical Evidence. *Computers in Human Behavior Reports*, *21*, 100941. Advance online publication. DOI: 10.1016/j.chbr.2026.100941

Li, Y., & Qiu, B. (2023). Relationship Between Doom-scrolling and Mental Health under the Influence of Recommendation Algorithms. *Lecture Notes in Education Psychology and Public Media, 15*, 148–157. DOI: 10.54254/2753-7048/15/20231048

Mazmanian, M., Orlikowski, W. J., & Yates, J. (2013). The autonomy paradox. *Organization Science, 24*(5), 1337–1357. DOI: 10.1287/orsc.1120.0806

Merlo, G., Rossi, A., & De Luca, F. (2025). Digital work environments and employee well-being. *Human Resource Management Review, 35*(1), 100934. DOI: 10.1016/j.hrmr.2024.100934

Moore, P. V. (2020). Surveillance, work and the pandemic. *The Political Quarterly, 91*(3), 542–552. DOI: 10.1111/1467-923X.12898 PMID: 32836412

Pariser, E. (2011). *The filter bubble*. Penguin Press. https://hci.stanford.edu/courses/cs047n/readings/The_Filter_Bubble.pdf

Rasmussen, T., & Ulrich, D. (2015). Learning from practice: How HR analytics avoids being a management fad. *Organizational Dynamics, 44*(3), 236–242. DOI: 10.1016/j.orgdyn.2015.05.008

Saindon, J. (2025). Attention fragmentation and cognitive decline associated with excessive smartphone use. *Journal of Cognitive Psychology, 37*(2), 134–149. DOI: 10.1080/20445911.2024.2389012

Shravan Anande, S., & Murarikar, H. P. (2025). India's proposed right to disconnect. *Indian Journal of Labour Law, 48*(2), 201–218. https://vidhilegalpolicy.in/blog/right-to-disconnect-in-india/

Sunstein, C. R. (2018). *Republic*. Princeton University Press., https://press.princeton.edu/books/hardcover/9780691175515/republic?srsltid=AfmBOoqdaUzf0Ow19ExzG8_MT4RTNv1uT7RNUM69vOEI8QUxxZw5yd86

Sweller, J. (1988). Cognitive load during problem solving. *Cognitive Science, 12*(2), 257–285. DOI: 10.1207/s15516709cog1202_4

Tambe, P., Cappelli, P., & Yakubovich, V. (2019). Artificial intelligence in human resources management. *California Management Review, 61*(4), 15–42. DOI: 10.1177/0008125619867910

Tarafdar, M., Cooper, C. L., & Stich, J. F. (2019). The technostress trifecta. *Journal of Management Information Systems, 36*(1), 1–34. DOI: 10.1080/07421222.2018.1556375

World Health Organization. (2022). *Guidelines on mental health at work*. https://www.who.int/publications/i/item/9789240053052

Zimmerman, B. J. (1990). Self-regulated learning and academic achievement. *Educational Psychologist*, *25*(1), 3–17. DOI: 10.1207/s15326985ep2501_2

Chapter 9
Human-Centered Recruitment and Selection:
Addressing Cultural Diversity in Indian Workplaces

Mohammed Umair
http://orcid.org/0009-0002-0476-5265
St. Joseph's University, India

ABSTRACT

This chapter outlines socio-cultural factors and impact of organizational diversity management strategies and bias-reducing mechanism on recruitment. By relying on case studies and literature, the chapter examines organizational practices like inclusive HR policies, structured recruitment systems, leadership commitment, and technology-enablement of hiring processes for equity in employment outcomes. According to the report, Indian organisations are ramping up their efforts to adopt diversity and inclusion initiatives globally, responding to workplace inequities. D&I initiatives contribute to fairer, more transparent, and more representative workforces. The chapter also shows how organizations adapt global staffing practices to local institutional realities, emphasizing the contextualization of diversity efforts. The finding recommends the integrated commitment by organization; standardized procedure of evaluation and monitoring facilitate recruitment diversity effective management for equitable and inclusive hiring outcome.

DOI: 10.4018/979-8-2600-2178-1.ch009

1.0: INTRODUCTION

Due to globalization, labour mobility and growth in international business, organizations are now more culturally diverse. In developing economies like India, there is demographic heterogeneity in individuals with different languages, religions, ethnicities, castes, genders, regions, etc. Thus, cultural diversity is an intrinsic characteristic of the labour market. Consequently, the management of cultural diversity in recruitment and selection become a crucial strategic issue of the organization, which enhances organization functionality, innovation, and competitiveness. The initial stage of human resource management (HRM) practices is the process of recruitment and selection. Furthermore, it plays a crucial role in the composition of workforce and organizational culture. Lastly, it has an impact on performance in the long term (Boxall & Purcell, 2016).

India is a unique context to examine culturally inclusive recruitment practices due to its social plurality and institutional complexity. According to Budhwar & Varma (2011) the nation is marked by considerable socio-cultural diversity like languages, religions, castes, regions significantly influencing the availability of employment, and behaviour at the job place. The varied nature on offer provides organizations with both opportunities and challenges. On the one hand, culturally diverse workforces open space for creativity and positive innovation while understanding broader markets (Cox, 1993; Stahl et al., 2010). On the flip side, biases, stereotypes, and institutional barriers can result in hindrances to equal access to employment opportunities, discrimination and ineffective talent acquisition processes (Roberson, 2006).

Recruitment practices and selection in India are affected not only by the strategies of the organizations but also by socio-cultural, institutional, and legal factors. The hiring choices and candidate selection procedures may be covertly shaped by issues like caste-based social stratification, gender norms, regional particularism and linguistic differences (Thorat & Newman, 2010). Moreover, recruitment processes in public enterprises get influenced by policies and provisions related to social justice, for instance, reservation policy for the socially and educationally backward castes. Besides, growing attention to diversity in the private sector too (Deshpande, 2011). India's structural and institutional contingencies set it apart from Western models of diversity management, calling for context-specific processes for inclusive recruitment and selection.

Theoretically, managing cultural diversity in recruitment and selection refers to several theories such as equal employment opportunity theory, social identity theory and diversity management perspectives. Social identity theory suggests that people often categorize themselves and others in social groups, which can categorise the way people make decisions such as a candidate evaluation and selection (Tajfel &

Turner, 1979). The recruitment processes might be affected by the implicit attitudes and stereotypes of hiring practitioners despite their formal commitment to fairness and meritocracy. Diversity management frameworks refer to process and practice systems that integrate diversity into the strategic processes of an organisation to enhance performance and wellbeing of employees (Thomas & Ely, 1996).

Indian organizations are becoming increasingly conscious regarding inclusive recruitment within the realms of diversity, equity, and inclusion (DEI) initiatives in the recent past.

Large multinational companies operating in India and big domestic firms are using a structured recruitment process, competency-based selection and bias reduction mechanisms to ensure diversity (Budhwar, Varma, Singh, & Dhar, 2017). Technological changes such as digital recruitment platforms and algorithm-based screening tools have further transformed recruitment processes. However, concerns remain about algorithmic bias and equitable access (Bogen & Rieke, 2018).

Even though diversity management is gaining increasing attention, much gap still remains in our understanding of managing cultural diversity for recruitment and selection in India. Much research points to persisting gender, caste and regional inequalities in employment outcomes, underscoring the need for more inclusive and transparent hiring processes (Deshpande, 2011; Thorat & Newman, 2010). Though limited, some empirical research focuses on how organizations implement diversity principles into recruitment processes, and how context shapes these processes.

Drawing on this backdrop, the chapter examines Human-Centered Recruitment and Selection, Addressing Cultural Diversity in Indian Workplaces with respect to the institutional influences, organizational practices, challenges and emerging strategies for inclusive hiring. Through a combination of theory and specific cases, this chapter aims to develop an understanding of the Indian context, thereby contributing to literature on strategic human resource management and diversity management in emerging economies.

1.0.a: Problem Statement

India's workers are culturally diverse and have institutional constraints and organizational practices that structure employment opportunities and social stratification. Though many studies show inequalities in labor market and structural discriminations, not much is researched on how Indian organizations manage cultural diversity in recruitment and selection at the organizational level.

Growing emphasis is being placed on diversity, equity and inclusion (DEI) initiatives but empirical evidence as to how organizations design inclusive recruitment strategies, reduce biases in hiring decisions and respond to socio-cultural diversity, in practice, it scant. Also, the extent to which organizational policies and leadership commitment and technology-mediated recruitment are culturally inclusive is under-researched.

Consequently, the key research problem of this study is to understand how Indian organizations manage cultural diversity in recruitment and selection and how organizational practices affect equitable hiring outcomes in India's socio-cultural environment.

1.0.b: Chapter Objectives

The study aims to achieve the following objectives:

1. To assess the effect of socio-cultural diversity factors on recruitment and selection practices in Indian organizations (caste, gender, religion, language, and regional identity).
2. To examine the organizational diversity management practices adopted to enhance recruitment and selection.
3. The objective of this study is to assess how HR policies, leadership commitment and structured recruitment systems can reduce bias in hiring.
4. To determine the success of diversity management practices in improving equity and diversity in recruitment outcomes.

Key Questions

1. How does cultural diversity shape recruitment and selection practices in Indian organizations?
2. What sources of bias and fairness concerns arise in selection processes?
3. How do Indian organizations adapt global staffing practices to local cultural contexts?
4. What lessons can inform culturally fair global recruitment and selection systems?

1.1: Literature Review

Indian Literature: Studies in an Indian context mostly focus on structural inequalities, institutional frameworks, and emerging diversity and inclusion practices impacting recruitment and selection.

Thorat and Newman (2010), in their work, provide significant empirical evidence of labour market discrimination in India, revealing limitations in hiring despite qualifications. Using field experiments based on job applications, the authors have found that equally qualified upper caste applicants offered an interview call more frequently than marginal caste counterparts. The researchers found that how society is organized strongly affects recruitment with people sometimes not getting jobs despite deserving it.

Deshpande's (2011) study in contemporary India relates to economic discrimination and inequalities in the labour market in India on the basis of caste, gender and social identity. According to the study, the recruitment process is likely influenced by historical inequalities, while also discusses institutional measures such as reservation policies for social justice and inclusivity in employment practices. Recruitment policies must take into account the wider socio-economic context in order to ensure equal opportunity.

In Budhwar and Varma (2011), the authors discuss new human resource management practices in India. They further show the significance of diversity management in recruitment systems. According to the writers, Indian organizations function in structurally complex socio-cultural galaxies characterized by regional identities, linguistic varieties and the social order. According to their studies, an increasing number of companies are using different formalized recruitment practices, competency-based selection systems and standardized HR procedures to eliminate bias but the use of informal networks and social connections still prevails.

Recent studies indicate that organizations in India are increasingly focusing on diversity, equity and inclusion (DEI). According to Sharma and Langford (2025), DEI strategies should be incorporated into productivity and recruitment processes in Indian organizations. The study conducted shows that a large number of organizations have started adopting diversity and inclusion initiatives as a central part of their HR strategies to streamline recruitment, engagement of employees as well as improvement in organizational performance. According to the study, commitment of leadership and structure of HR policies act as major facilitators for inclusive recruitment practices.

Indian literature collectively indicates that the recruitment and selection processes are shaped by structural inequality, institutional intervention and organizational practices.

International Literature: International scholarship provides theory and strategic perspectives on diversity management in recruitment and selection.

With proper management, diverse workforces can enhance organizational effectiveness (Cox, 1993). In other words, Cox (1993) creates a paradigm for managing cultural diversity. Cox's interactional model details the manner in which organizational culture, individual identity, and structural integration influence the individual outcomes of employees. To establish organizations that are culturally diversified, recruitment and selection systems are essential.

Thomas and Ely (1996) put forward a strategy for diversity which underscores the need for moving beyond the compliance-driven diversity toward diversity as a primary source for integration in diversity-driven practices of the organization. The model of diversity perspectives posits that when differences are valued and utilized strategically, recruitment practices that are inclusive foster organizational learning and innovation and enhance performance.

Roberson (2006) differentiates the meaning of both inclusion and diversity in organizations. An increase in diversity in the workforce through recruitment is no better than doing nothing, unless the organizations build inclusive systems to ensure equal participation and opportunity. The importance of fair selection procedures, objective evaluation criteria, and organizational commitment to inclusive practices is highlighted in the study.

The potential utilization of technology to expand the diversity of candidates in the recruitment process is an important issue. The paper by Bano et al. (2024) provides a mirror to diversity and inclusion in systems using artificial intelligence for recruitment. Digital hiring technologies can make the recruitment process much more efficient. However, if systemic diversity principles are not integrated in these systems, they pose the risk of reinforcing bias. The use of technology in recruitment will require context-sensitive diversity frameworks and inclusive design.

Various scholars have evaluated cultural diversity in recruitment and selection in different perspectives i.e. structural inequality; diversity management theory; organizational practices. International scholarship provides strong theoretical foundations to diversity as an organization resource, specifically emphasizing the role of recruitment systems, selection procedures and organizational culture (Cox 1993, Thomas and Ely 1996, Roberson 2006). Most of the studies focus on strategic diversity management frameworks, equal employment opportunity practices and organizational performance outcomes in a largely Western institutional context.

1.1.a: Conceptual Framework for the Study

The current research proposes an integrated conceptual framework to see how Indian organizations manage cultural diversity in recruitment and selection. The framework described in this study is derived from the diversity management theory (Cox, 1993), social identity theory (Tajfel &Turner, 1979) and strategic human resource management perspectives(Boxall and Purcell, 2016). Moreover, it explains the interaction of institutional context, organizational practices and recruitment outcomes.

According to the framework, the recruitment and selection results of Indian organizations are influenced by three major dimensions including socio-cultural context, organizational diversity management practices and recruitment outcomes.

1. External factors of social culture: India's labour market portrays itself through a complex socio-cultural environment characterized by caste, religion, gender,

language and region. Individual socio-political contexts influence access, recruiter perception, and organizational hiring (Thorat & Newman, 2010; Deshpande, 2011). Recruitment practices are also influenced by reservation policies, labour regulations and social norms.

2. Organizational Diversity Management Practices (Internal Factors): During recruitment and selection organizations tend to adopt formal and informal practices for cultural diversity management. These consist of.
   a. Diversity and inclusion policies
   b. Structured recruitment procedures
   c. Bias-free selection methods
   d. Competency-based evaluation systems
   e. Leadership commitment to diversity
   f. HR strategies promoting equal opportunity
   g. Use of technology in recruitment

Such approaches signal company commitment to reducing discrimination and increasing workforce diversity. Thomas and Ely (1996) and Roberson (2006).

3. Recruitment and Selection Outcomes

   The interaction between socio cultural context organizational practices influences recruitment outcomes such as.

   a. Workforce diversity and representation
   b. Fairness and transparency in hiring
   c. Equal employment opportunities
   d. Organizational effectiveness and inclusion.
4. Proposed Relationship

According to the framework, socio-cultural factors generate diversity-related challenges and organizational diversity management measures mediate their impact on recruitment outcomes. Human resource policies and recruitment systems have the potential to decrease bias in hiring.

1.1.b: Conceptual Model Structure

a. Caste, gender, culture, religion, language, region, institutional policy and law.
b. The influence of organizational diversity management practices that are DEI policies, HR systems, selection methods, leadership commitment and recruitment technology.

c. Recruitment outcomes should lead to workforce diversity, fairness, inclusion and equal opportunities.

This framework (a influences→ b Organizational Diversity and c leads to → Recruitment Outcomes). This helps in understanding the way Indian organizations engage in diversity management in recruitment and selection in a complex socio-cultural scenario.

1.2: Research Gap

Various scholars have evaluated cultural diversity in recruitment and selection in different perspectives i.e. structural inequality; diversity management theory; organizational practices. International scholarship provides strong theoretical foundations to diversity as an organization resource, specifically emphasizing the role of recruitment systems, selection procedures and organizational culture (Cox 1993, Thomas and Ely 1996, Roberson 2006). Most of the studies focus on strategic diversity management frameworks, equal employment opportunity practices and organizational performance outcomes in a largely Western institutional context.

Conversely, Indian scholarship has examined chiefly the structural and institutional determinants of employment outcomes, chiefly caste discrimination, gender discrimination, and other socio-economic barriers in labour markets (Thorat & Newman, 2010; Deshpande, 2011). The evidence of persistent discrimination in hiring is strong and underscores the need for institutional interventions such as reservation for social inclusion. Furthermore, in India, people practices are influenced by socio-cultural diversity, informal networks and changing organizational practices for recruitment and selection (Budhwar & Varma, 2011). More recent studies suggest that Indian organizations are increasingly implementing diversity, equity, and inclusion (DEI) programs as well as structured recruitment systems (Sharma & Langford, 2025).

Nonetheless, a number of important gaps remain in the literature. The existing literature in India largely on labour market discrimination and macro-level inequalities; not much focus has been placed on organizational-level practices and mechanisms through which cultural diversity is managed in recruitment and selection. There exists a paucity of evidence on how Indian organizations operationalize diversity policies, develop inclusive recruitment strategies and implement bias-reduction practices in real-life hiring decisions.

At second, there are no integrated frameworks linking India's socio-cultural context caste, religion, language, region, gender with organizational recruitment and human resource policies in the literature. Although structural inequalities are well documented, little is known about how organizations respond to these contextual challenges by deploying institutionalized diversity management practices.

In India, the management of cultural diversity in recruitment varies by sector and organization. However, sectoral and organization-specific research is limited. Research on the differences between public and private sector organizations, MNCs and domestic firms, and traditional and technology-driven recruitment system is still lacking. Recognizing these differences is crucial for effective diversity management.

Moreover, there is limited empirical evidence on the impact of the growing use of digital recruitment platforms, algorithm-based screening tools, a selection based on competency methods, and others on cultural diversity and inclusion in India. The relationship of technological recruitment practices and socio-cultural diversity is an emerging area requiring systematic study.

To conclude, there is a gap of context-specific empirical studies to connect the theory of diversity management with the Indian organizations' evidence. Organizational culture, the commitment of leadership, human resource policies and institutional pressures rarely see analysis as influencing a culturally inclusive recruitment outcome.

The current study entitled Managing Cultural Diversity in Recruitment and Selection: Evidence from Indian Organizations aims to fill these gaps by studying the organisational practices, institutional influences and diversity management strategies that shape recruitment and selection in Indian context. The research intends to offer empirical evidence on Indian organizations' management of cultural diversity in hiring which will add to the literature on strategic human resource management, diversity management and employment practices in emerging economies.

1.3: Methodology

Research design and approach

This study takes the qualitative research design route through case study analysis and review of previous studies to analyse the way Indian organizations manage cultural diversity in recruitment and selection. This allows for a deeper understanding of the organizational practices, institutional influences and context that inform diversity management in recruitment (Creswell, 2014).

An exploratory research design is employed to explore the diversity management practices, offering and organisational responses towards cultural diversity in India. The study adopts a multiple case study approach by examining documented instances of public sector organizations, private companies and multi-national corporations in India that are relevant to the diversity-related recruitment policies and practices in real-life settings (Yin, 2018).

The study further involves a systematic literature review including peer-reviewed journal articles, books and policy reports synthesizing previous findings on cultural diversity, employment disparities, and inclusive recruitment practices (Tranfield, Denyer, & Smart, 2003).

The organization is the unit of analysis. The data will be analysed using thematic analysis. This will help to find out the patterns, challenges and strategies for managing cultural diversity during recruitment and selection process.

1.4: Discussion

[A] Effect of Socio-Cultural Diversity Factors on Recruitment and Selection Practices in Indian Organizations

India's cultural environment influences organizational recruitment and selection practices. The assortment of caste, gender, religion, language, and regional identities in India shapes the nature of access to jobs, employer perceptions and hiring decisions. These socio-cultural factors work either through institutional arrangements that operate explicitly or through social norms and organizational practices that operate implicitly.

1. Caste and Recruitment Practices

In India, caste is still a major determinant of labour market outcomes. Research has found that recruitment decisions may still be influenced by the caste system. Medium-level difficulty: Thorat and Newman (2010) conducted field experiments and found that candidates from marginalized caste backgrounds received lesser calls for interviews compared to upper-caste candidates with similar qualifications. Inequities reflect implicit biases, social stereotypes, and informal hiring networks that favour those who are socially privileged.

Furthermore, caste affects access to social capital, which in turn influences education and professional networks and thus access to jobs (Deshpande 2011). Reservation policies in the public sector organizations aim to ensure representation of candidates from historically disadvantaged groups. However, private sector organizations largely follow merit-based recruitment systems which may inadvertently reproduce existing social inequalities in society.

Case-in-point

a. Tata Steel has implemented measures to improve employability of Scheduled Castes and Scheduled Tribes which includes recruitment, training, development activities, etc. (Tata Steel Sustainability Report, 2022).

b. The recruitment policies of the public sector, such as the State Bank of India, is in consonance with the reservation mandated under the Constitution to ensure representation of the marginalized caste groups (Government of India Reservation Policy; State Bank of India Annual Report, 2023).

Institutional efforts to reduce caste-based inequalities in recruitment seem evident in these initiatives.

2. Gender and Hiring Decisions

In India, gender gap exists in recruitment and selection practices in all sectors. Organizational hiring behavior is affected by traditional gender roles, occupational segregation, and employer perceptions about women's commitment to work, mobility and family responsibilities (Budhwar & Varma, 2011). It is harder for women to get leadership roles and jobs in certain male-dominated sectors.

Deshpande's (2011) findings suggest that women may experience gender bias when they are subjected to discriminatory screening, evaluation and career prospects. Yet, with organizations increasingly stressing on diversity, equity and inclusion (DEI) initiatives, several organizations have put in gender-inclusive recruitment policies, equal opportunity practices and women-only hiring programs to bolster female workforce.

Case-in-point

a. Infosys has made all efforts to ensure gender-inclusive staffing through diversity hiring, return-to-work programs designed for women professionals, and use of policies that support inclusive workplace conditions (Infosys ESG Report, 2023).
b. ICICI Bank Annual Report 2023 states that the company has taken initiatives like leadership programs, specific hiring to enhance women's presence in management.
c. As stated in Wipro's Sustainability Report, 2022, the company runs diversity hiring programmes and leadership development initiatives for gender-wise progression across levels.

These initiatives demonstrate growing organizational commitment to gender diversity in recruitment.

3. Religious Identity and Workplace Inclusion

Recruitment practices are shaped by religious heterogeneity, another significant socio-cultural factor in India. The hiring choice may depend on your religious identity due to cultural stereotypes and social perceptions. Minority religious groups may not find a job due to implicit bias or perceived differences in hiring managers' eyes. Research studies on discrimination on grounds of religion may not be as much as caste and gender. However, the available studies suggest that religious identity can impact workplace inclusion and hiring outcomes. This is especially the case when cultural norms and value of organizations intersect recruitment (Roberson, 2006). Organizations are increasingly prioritizing inclusive workplace policies for such issues.

Case-in-point

As per TCS Sustainability Report 2023, Tata Consultancy Services recruitment and selection policy offers equal opportunity employment regardless of religion, gender and social background. Multinational companies in India follow worldwide similar diversity and inclusion standards which promote religious inclusion and equal employment practices (Budhwar & Varma, 2011; TCS Sustainability Report, 2023). The aim of such practices is a more inclusive hiring environment.

4. Language and Recruitment Outcomes

India's linguistic diversity plays a major role in recruitment and selection processes as well Language proficiency is often considered an essential criterion for recruitment in service sectors, MNCs and customer-facing roles. Candidates fluent in the dominant language (e.g. English) or indigenous language of a region may hold an advantage. According to Budhwar and Varma (2011), preferences based on language may reveal their communication requirements. This aside, they could add to unequal access to employment which, in turn, favours specific education or regions. Language may function as a skill requirement or a source of exclusion in recruitment process.

Case-in-point

Global operations by design require that organizations have the necessary means of communication not only how they communicate amongst themselves but also their operations. The strong English communication skills – oral and written – required in global service delivery at Infosys and TCS (Infosys ESG Report, 2023; TCS Annual Report, 2023) reflect this need.

The banking and retail organizations often prefer to hire candidates who are proficient in local languages so they can serve local customers (Reserve Bank of India Reports on Banking Workforce Practices, 2022).

While language fulfills functional organizational purposes, it might create hurdles for applicants from diverse socio-educational and regional backgrounds.

5. Regional Identity and Employment Opportunities

Recruitment is influenced by regional identity in terms of preference for geographical candidates and others. Local applicants may be prioritized by organizations due to their knowledge of regional culture and language. But this may restrict diversity in the workforce and limit the opportunities of other candidates. Disparities in education, economic development, and employment infrastructure in the region further prevent states in India from having equal access to jobs (Deshpande, 2011). The differences in the structure affect the hiring pattern of organizations.

Case-in-point

Manufacturing locations prefer to recruit from local, surrounding communities. This helps strengthen local communities and stabilise the workforce (Tata Motors Sustainability Report, 2022).

Wipro Annual Report 2023; Infosys; ESG Report 2023: "IT companies such as Wipro and Infosys are recruiting nationally, though they are changing hiring strategies to fit the regional labour market and skill availability." Regional elements shape the labour pool and hiring strategies.

Implications for Recruitment and Selection

Given socio-cultural diversity factors, recruitment processes must take on greater transparency, uniformity and acceptability. The use of organizational strategies like standardized interviews, competency-based selection techniques, diversity training, and equal opportunities policies can reduce bias in hiring decisions (Thomas & Ely, 1996). The Indian recruitment scenario must address the socio-cultural influences on workforce diversity, organizational effectiveness, and social equity.

On the whole, it can be stated that the socio-cultural diversity factor shapes the recruitment and selection processes of the company in India. It duly impacts the employer's perception, general hiring decision and availability of candidates. Comprehending these impacts is crucial for formulating efficacious diversity management techniques and furthering inclusive employment standards.

[B] Organizational Diversity Management Practices Adopted to Enhance Recruitment and Selection

In India, organizations increasingly view diversity management as a human resource function of strategic importance, with a positive impact on recruitment effectiveness, workforce diversity, and organizational performance. Diversity management practices aim to address discrimination ensure equal opportunity and create an inclusive hiring system to socio-cultural inequalities. These practices include formal diversity policies, structured recruitment procedures, bias-reduction mechanisms, leadership commitment, and technology-enabled recruitment systems. Efforts of this nature allow organizations to attract different types of talent, improve quality of decision making, and enhance organizational legitimacy, (Roberson, 2006; Thomas & Ely, 1996).

1. Diversity and Inclusion Policies

A structured framework to ensure fairness and equity for recruitment and selection can be ensured with formal D&I polices. These policies show the organizations are dedicated to not being discriminated against gender, caste, religion, disability, etc. They also define the recruitment norms, representation targets and monitoring mechanisms to facilitate inclusive hiring.

Case-in-points

a. Tata Consultancy Services (TCS) strictly follows equal opportunity and non-discrimination policies that prohibit discrimination based on gender, caste, religion, disability, or cultural background. The organization incorporates diversity aspects into its recruitment system and promotes diversity in the workplace through global standards (TCS Sustainability Report, 2023).
b. Infosys has designed and implemented its diversity and equality framework that focuses on equitable hiring, accessibility, and representation of marginalized groups. According to the Infosys ESG Report, 2023, the company's recruitment policies emphasize equal opportunity employment and encourages people from different social and educational backgrounds to apply.
c. Wipro's policies promote gender diversity, inclusion of people with disabilities and hiring with equal opportunity. The company also measures diversity indi-

cators of the workforce to assess recruitment results and enhance representation (Wipro Sustainability Report, 2022).

The policies help in institutionalizing diversity management in the recruitment system and making the organization's practice legal and ethical.

2. Structured Recruitment and Selection Systems

Systematic selection of candidates reduces the subjectivity in hiring through the formal setting of evaluative criteria and selection procedures. Competency-based job descriptions, structured interviews, standardized testing (where appropriate) and objective assessments. Such systems improve transparency and limit the impact of personal bias or informal networks in recruitment (Boxall & Purcell, 2016).

Case-in-points

a. Infosys uses competency-based recruitment techniques which evaluate candidates on their technical skills, problem-solving capacity, and behavioural competencies. According to the Infosys Annual Report for 2023, the organization applies standardized evaluation processes and digital assessments to ensure an objective selection of candidates.
b. ICICI bank as part of the structured process has aptitude tests and structured interviews. These methods encourage recruiting on merit and reduce the subjectivity while assessing the candidate (ICICI Bank Annual Report, 2023).
c. Hindustan Unilever Limited (HUL) adopts structured leadership development and recruitment programs based on a standardized evaluation framework to scout talent from different educational and social backgrounds(HUL Annual Report, 2023).

Structured recruitment systems enhance the fairness and consistency of recruitment processes.

3. Bias-Reduction and Equal Opportunity Initiatives

To mitigate unconscious bias and facilitate inclusive hiring, organizations take several measures. Diversity awareness training and unconscious bias training, affirmative action programs and equal opportunity policies. The aim of this practice is to increase recruiter awareness and a fair evaluation of candidates (Thomas & Ely, 1996).

Case-in-points

a. Accenture India's recruitment teams undergo unconscious bias training so they are aware of bias and therefore make fair hiring decisions. The company furthermore creates inclusive hiring programs aimed at enhancing the diversity of its workforce (Accenture ESG Report (2023).

b. Tata steel has adopted affirmative action to increase employment opportunities for SC and ST. As per the Tata Steel Sustainability Report of 2022, the firm also backs skill development efforts and community outreach projects to enhance employment access.

c. Mahindra Group has established diversity training with a focus on inclusive hiring to promote equal opportunity employment while enhancing their inclusion (Mahindra Sustainability Report, 2023).

By these initiatives organization can offset structural inequalities for equal opportunity access to employment.

4. Leadership Commitment and Diversity Governance

It is critical that a strong commitment from leadership be there to implement diversity management practices effectively. Substantial involvement of senior leadership creates both accountability and allocation of resources towards the target goals. A number of organizations set up structures, diversity councils and monitoring to direct recruitment.

Case-in-points

a. Wipro has set up a Diversity and Inclusion Council that formulates diversity strategies, monitors workforce representation, and ensures inclusive hiring across the organizational units (Wipro Sustainability Report, 2022).

b. As part of its corporate strategy, Infosys incorporates diversity objectives and leadership performance indicators and therefore diversity management becomes a key organizational priority (Infosys ESG Report,2023).

c. According to the Tata Sustainability Reports (2022 – 2023), companies of Tata Group enforce diversity initiatives that are led by leadership and ethical employment practices to ensure that the organisation is committed to inclusive recruitment.

When leaders get involved, the organizational culture strengthens and policies are implemented.

5. Technology-Enabled Recruitment Practices

Thanks to modern technologies, recruitment has become efficient, transparent and accessible. Organizations are increasingly using platforms to Post Jobs, Manage Applications, Conduct Initial Assessments under Applicant tracking system to standardize evaluation and widen the pool to attract talent. Because technology removes human involvement in screening processes, it helps to minimize bias. However, corresponding fears of algorithmic bias continue to remain (Bogen & Rieke, 2018).

Case-in-points

a. TCS and Infosys use digital recruitment platforms, online assessments, and automated screening systems to standardize the hiring process and reach a wider range of diverse talent pools across regions (TCS Annual Report, 2023; Infosys ESG Report, 2023).
b. Reliance Industries Limited (RIL) utilizes technological recruitment systems and large-scale digital hiring procedures to attract candidates across regions and at different social and economic levels which is as per Reliance 2023 annual report.
c. Many big organizations in India use applicant tracking systems to evaluate candidates fairly and to attract more candidates.

The technology-driven recruitment approach provides more uniformity, curtails anomalies in recruitment processes, and boost access to job opportunities.

6. Inclusive Talent Development and Outreach Programs

Some organizations use targeted outreach and talent development programs to recruit from underrepresented groups. All such initiatives which include skill development, training partnerships and community initiatives would increase employability of diverse social groups.

Case-in-points

a. Infosys runs skill building programmes and education partnership initiatives to enhance the employability of various student groups 2023 ESG Report.
b. Tata Steel organizes various community development and vocational training initiatives for increasing the employability of disadvantaged communities (Tata Steel Sustainability Report, 2022).
c. The Mahindra Group also supports investments in social enterprises that diversify the workforce and enhance skills.

Programs like these help organizations build talent pipelines and inclusive hiring.

Implications for Recruitment and Selection

Diversity management practices in organizations help improve recruitment fairness, workforce representation, and inclusiveness in the workplace. Organizations can design structured policies, implement initiatives for bias reduction and commitment at leadership level owing to technological interventions for recruitment. Nonetheless, whether these practices will ever yield their desired benefits will depend on their consistent implementation, the cultures of the organization, and institutionalization.

Overall, Indian organizations are slowly adopting diversity management practices as a method to improve various recruitment and selection process. Inclusive employment systems are strengthened by these measures, which contribute significantly to responding to India's socio-cultural diversity.

[C] Role of HR Policies, Leadership Commitment, and Structured Recruitment Systems in Reducing Bias in Hiring

Many organizations now know that bias may creep into the recruitment and selection process, both conscious and unconscious, due to social and cultural factors like caste, gender, religion, language regionality, etc. To resolve this issue, organizations deploy structured human resource (HR) policies, leadership-led diversity programs, and standardized recruitment systems to ensure equitable, fair and transparent hiring decisions. These processes facilitate the reduction of subjective evaluations, ensure evaluation based on performance, and enhance diversity in the workforce (Roberson, 2006; Thomas & Ely, 1996).

1. HR Policies and Equal Employment Opportunity Practices

Human resource policies centre on creating uniform methodologies to recruit which minimises bias. It also provides detailed evaluation process to all candidates hence ensuring EEO. Policies may include safeguards against discrimination, diversity hiring, workplace inclusion or monitoring mechanisms to ensure adherence to ethical and legal standards.

HR policies assist companies in minimizing bias.

a. Set up transparent recruitment procedures.
b. Making sure of standardized evaluation criteria.
c. Ensuring everyone has equal access to jobs.
d. Monitoring diverse outcomes in recruitment choices.
e. Mechanisms for grievance redressal for discrimination.

Case-in-points

a. Infosys has extensive HR policies that help ensure employment opportunities are not denied to anyone on grounds of gender, caste, religion, disability, and culture. The company enacts inclusive hiring guidelines, implements measures to bolster accessibility and accessibility in IT and business, and maintains a monitoring system through the diversity dashboard. (Infosys ESG Report, 2023)
b. The Tata Consultancy Services (TCS) adopted a formal equal opportunity policy as part of its human resource framework. This policy prohibits various forms of discrimination and ensures that TCS's hiring practices are more or less the same across the globe (TCS Sustainability Report, 2023).
c. Hindustan Unilever Limited (HUL) implements a policy of non-discrimination based on gender, caste and creed. It aims at creating equal opportunity for all in hiring and performance evaluation (HUL Annual Report, 2023).
d. In India, many public sector organizations, including State Bank of India, adopt HR policies based on government reservation norms to ensure their recruitment is disadvantaged filling up. (State Bank of India Annual Report, 2023).

Fairness is institutionalized through such HR policies while a formal mechanism is provided to reduce APs discriminatory hiring.

2. Leadership Commitment to Diversity and Inclusion

The effectiveness of diversity management practices depends largely on leadership. Senior leadership matters in creating and shaping the cultural vision for organizations through recruitment, and resource-wide mechanisms. Diversity initiatives that are driven by leadership enforce accountability, promote inclusive behavior and help execute HR policies.

Commitment of Leadership Reduces Bias by:

a. Fostering diversity as a key tactical objective of the organization.
b. Constructing framework for diversity governance
c. Reviewing representation and inclusion results.
d. Endorsing a culture that is inclusive in nature.
e. Holding responsibility in recruitment operations.

Case-in-points

a. Wipro has a Diversity and Inclusion Council that helps in ensuring the diversity strategy, overseeing workforce diversity indicators and facilitating the recruitment across organizational units (Wipro Sustainability Report, 2022).
b. Infosys has established diversity objectives within their corporate strategy and the assessment of leadership performance indicators, which ensures that leadership is held accountable for the achieved diversity outcomes (2023 ESG Report Infosys).
c. Companies of the Tata Group have underscored the critical role of leaders in fostering ethical employment and an organizational culture that is inclusive. Diversity is reinforced as a core value of the organization (Tata Sustainability Reports, 2022–2023).
d. Leadership commitment at Accenture India manifests through global diversity targets, leadership diversity goals and inclusive hiring strategies (Accenture ESG Report, 2023).

When a leader is actively involved, diversity policies get implemented and an organizational environment which encourages equitable hiring is fostered.

3. Structured Recruitment and Selection Systems

The use of structured recruitment systems facilitates a reduction in bias. Objective evaluation methods, including competency-based assessments, structured interviews, standardized testing, and transparent selection criteria, are commonly used in these systems (Boxall & Purcell, 2016).

Utilizing ordered recruitment limits prejudice.

Unifying candidate performance appraisals by:

a. Restraining personal judgements.
b. Ensuring uniform assessment standards.
c. Improve transparency in selection decisions
d. Advocating for merit-based recruitment.

Case-in-points

a. According to the Infosys Annual Report 2023, competency-based recruitment models, standardized technical assessments and structured interviews ensure candidates' objective evaluation.
b. As part of its structured selection methods, the bank relies on aptitude examinations and standardized assessment frameworks to encourage merit-based recruitment (ICICI Bank Annual Report, 2023).
c. According to their 2023 Annual Report, the Tata Consultancy Services utilizes standardized online tests to help ensure uniformity in recruitment.
d. As stated in the annual report of 2023 of the Reliance Industries, Reliance Industries Limited employs large scale standardized recruitment processes backed up by technology-enabled screening processes to improve transparency and consistency.

Such approaches minimize human bias to achieve fairer recruitment results.

4. Training and Bias Awareness Programs

Recruiters also receive training in organizations to be familiar with unconscious bias and make inclusive decisions. Diversity training helps us understand social stereotypes and to evaluate candidates fairly.

Case-in-points

a. Accenture India has implemented unconscious bias training for hiring managers and recruitment teams to improve equitable decision making within recruitment processes (Accenture ESG Report, 2023).

b. The Mahindra Group conducts activities and programs to make workplaces inclusive and uses fair employment practices (Mahindra Sustainability Report, 2023).
c. Tata Steel has launched diversity sensitization programs to further enhance our inclusive workplace employees' behaviour and recruitment practices (Tata Steel Sustainability Report, 2022).

Training initiatives promote behavioural change while ensuring a fair selection process.

5. Technology-Enabled Recruitment Systems

Tools such as applicant tracking systems, digital assessments, and automated screening help address bias with candidate evaluation and access to jobs. According to Bogen and Rieke (2018), some early predictive policing systems reduce the need for human involvement in the first stages of screening and make them more transparent.

Case-in-points

a. TCS and Infosys employ digital recruitment platforms and online assessment tools to ensure the standardization of candidate evaluation and to expand their access to a diverse talent pool (TCS Annual Report, 2023; Infosys ESG Report, 2023).
b. As Reliance Industries Annual Report claims, technology-enabled processes for recruitment help outreach to candidates across geographical and sociological spectra.

Recruitment technology helps to improve efficiency and reduce subjective bias.

Implications for Bias Reduction in Hiring

The combination of HR policies, leadership commitment, and structured recruitment systems can help reduce bias in hiring decisions. The standards of fairness and lack of bias framed by the HR policies are to ensure commitment and organization accountability. Additionally, standard recruitment system's stipulations ensure that subjectivity in choosing the right candidate is cut down. When brought together they not only guaranteed transparency but also equality and diversity.

The adequacy of the various mechanisms would depend on their consistent implementation, organizational culture and regular monitoring of diversity outcomes.

In order to address socio-cultural bias, organizations should have policy frameworks, leadership support, and a standardized recruitment process.

The policies of HR, leadership commitments along with a structured recruitment system are the organizational mechanisms which possibly can reduce bias in recruitment and selection in Indian organizations.

[D] To determine the success of diversity management practices in improving equity and diversity in recruitment outcomes.

Diversity management is being adopted by Indian organizations at a rapid pace for fairness, transparency, and representation in hiring and selection. These practices are effective as seen in measurable improvements in diversity of the workforce, equitable hiring outcomes, less discrimination, inclusion in the organization culture and better organizational performance. Diversity management initiatives i.e., inclusive HR policies, systematised recruitment systems, leadership-driven diversity strategies, and targeted outreach programs can contribute to equitable employment opportunity and enhancing the legitimacy of the organization (Cox, 1993; Roberson, 2006; Thomas Ely, 1996).

1. Improved Workforce Representation and Diversity Outcomes

An important sign that Diversity Management was successful is that underrepresented social groups are represented in the workforces of organisations. Strategies of inclusive recruitment open up the scope of the talent pool, while also reducing structural barriers and bringing diverse candidates, including women, marginalised caste groups, persons with disabilities, and other candidates from varied socio-economic and regional backgrounds, into employment.

Organizations which monitor diversity metrics and target hiring such candidates make noticeable differences. Such actions improve social equity and help to achieve fair representation at all levels of the organization.

Case-in-points:

a. Through diversity hiring initiatives, women return-to-work programs and creating a gender-neutral workplace, Infosys has made substantial progress in gender representation. The organization further monitors diversity indicators to track hiring results and workforce composition. (Infosys ESG Report, 2023).
b. According to the Wipro Sustainability Report (2022), Wipro has improved the diversity of its employees through a focused recruitment strategy and the use

of diversity monitoring mechanisms. These mechanisms track diversity and monitor representation of gender, disability, and other social categories.

c. Tata Steel Sustainability Report 2022 states that Tata Steel has conscious representation of SCs and STs. Tata Steel has enhanced representation of SCs and STs through affirmative actions, inclusive recruitment practices, and community-based skill development initiatives. The interventions have the targeting operational areas.
d. Accenture India's inclusive hiring initiatives and accessible recruitment processes have increased representation of women and persons with disabilities (Accenture ESG Report, 2023).

The initiatives clearly show how structured diversity practices can lead to measurable diversity benefits.

2. Enhanced Fairness and Transparency in Recruitment Processes

Through the standardization of recruitment procedures and establishing common criteria of evaluation, diversity management practices contribute to fairness and transparency. Structured recruitment processes minimize discretionary decision-making and enable consistent assessment across candidates thus increasing the credibility of hiring. When an organization is transparent in recruitment the organization is more accountable and the candidates can trust the procedures of selection. The standardized evaluation methods will diminish the effect of socio-cultural biases like these due to caste, gender, or regional identity.

Case-in-points:

a. Tata Consultancy Services (TCS) follows standardized recruitment methods, digital hiring platforms, and competency-based assessments to ensure equal assessment of candidates and transparency of selection across various locations (TCS Annual Report, 2023).
b. ICICI Bank follows organized processes to recruit new employees. This entails the use of assessment tests, a clear evaluation criterion, transparent selection processes, and more.
c. Reliance Industries Limited employs large-scale digital recruitment systems that standardize screening and evaluation methods, bringing more transparency to hiring (Reliance Industries Annual Report, 2023).

d. Hindustan Unilever Limited (HUL) has structured programmes for leadership recruitment. Moreover, the selection processes are standardized which makes the selection fair (Annual Report 2023).

These practices strengthen the procedural justice that leads to fair recruitment results.

3. Reduction in Discrimination and Hiring Bias

Diversity management practices help to lower conscious and unconscious bias in recruitment decisions. Organizations utilize diversity training programs, equal opportunity policies and bias-awareness initiatives to improve sensitivity and appropriate judgment of recruiters. Bias-reduction initiatives help organizations use strategies for reducing structural inequalities. Such practices are vital in socio-cultural contexts where bias and social norms can come in the way of hiring.

Case-in-points:

a. Accenture ESG Report of 2023 tells us that India's Accenture is providing unconscious bias training programs to recruitment teams and hiring managers.
b. The Mahindra Group has implemented diversity awareness programs and inclusion at the workplace initiatives to encourage hiring fairness that reinforces equal opportunity employment Mahindra Sustainability Report 2023.
c. According to the Tata Steel Sustainability Report of 2022, these include programming designed to create awareness on diversity and sensitisation, affirmative action, etc., aimed at reducing structural inequalities and recruiting in an inclusive manner.
d. The Wipro Sustainability Report for 2022 states that Wipro adopts inclusive hiring and diversity training in order to diminish bias in recruitment decisions.

Through these efforts, candidates will be assessed with less discriminatory value judgments that foster more equitable evaluation and fairer hiring outcomes.

4. Enhanced Organizational Performance and Innovation

Inclusionary recruitment practices yield diversity in the workforce that enhances organizational effectiveness. Diverse teams have a variety of perspectives, knowledge and problem-solving approaches which makes the organization more adaptable and competitive (Cox, 1993). As diversity is increasingly recognized as a strategic resource by organizations, their employee engagement, creativity and service delivery improve in global markets.

Case-in-points:

- **Infosys** links diversity and inclusion initiatives to innovation capability, employee engagement, and organizational effectiveness, highlighting the strategic importance of inclusive recruitment (Infosys ESG Report, 2023).
- **TCS** emphasizes inclusive workplace practices as essential for global service delivery and knowledge-based operations, where diverse perspectives enhance innovation and performance (TCS Sustainability Report, 2023).
- **Wipro** recognizes workforce diversity as a driver of business performance, organizational learning, and sustainable growth (Wipro Sustainability Report, 2022).
- **Accenture India** reports that diversity initiatives contribute to organizational performance, talent retention, and improved decision-making quality (Accenture ESG Report, 2023).

These outcomes demonstrate the strategic benefits of diversity management beyond compliance objectives.

5. Strengthened Employer Branding and Talent Attraction

Successful diversity management practices improve organizational reputation and employer branding. Candidates from diverse backgrounds are more attracted to organizations that use and careful in demonstrating their commitment to equity and inclusion and so have greater access to wider talent pools. The organizations signify their commitment to fairness, social responsibility and ethical employment which increases the trust of stakeholders in them.

Case-in-points.

a. Tata Group companies focus on ethical employment, creating inclusive workplaces, and engaging with communities to enhance employer image and attract a diverse range of talent. (Tata Sustainability Reports, 2022–2023)
b. Accenture India's employer value proposition focuses on diversity and inclusion to drive talent attraction and retention (Accenture ESG Report, 2023).

c. According to the ESG report 2023 of Infosys, Diversity and inclusion by Infosys are one of the important aspects of their organizational culture leading to improvement in its global employer branding and recruitment efficacy.

These efforts enhance long-term sustainability for the organization.

6. Long-Term Social and Organizational Impact

Managing diversity effectively can have a great impact not only on organizational performance but also social equality by creating more job opportunities for disadvantaged groups and reducing inequalities in the labor market. Recruiting genuinely inclusive is an essential component for social mobility; it can help build economic participation and equitable workforce development in India.

7. Challenges and Limitations in Achieving Equity

Despite positive changes, recruitment outcomes are still not fair. Organizations may face challenges such as social norms, implicit bias, resistance to change, and divides between the emergence of policies and their implementation. Moreover, diversity efforts might aim for representation but not meaningful inclusion. As a result, organizations must take measures to continually monitor, manage and support effective diversity, with leadership commitment and alignment between policies and workplace culture (Roberson, 2006).

Implications for Recruitment Outcomes

Diversity management practices are successful when workforce representation is improved; recruitment processes are transparent; less discriminatory; effective organizational performance is created, and employer reputation is enhanced. Organizations that adopt inclusive HR policies, structured recruitment systems, and leadership-driven diversity strategies are more effective at achieving equality and diversity in recruitment outcomes.

To sum up, diversity management practices are crucial to enhancing the equity and diversity in recruitment and selection in India. By optimizing their human resources and promoting equal opportunities, organizations contribute to effective human resource management with the help of practices which aim at improving gender equality and enhancing women's leadership.

1.5: Key Findings

1. Cultural diversity shaping recruitment and selection practices

Cultural diversity plays a sizeable role in recruitment and selection practices of Indian organizations. It has a big influence on both access to employment for different candidates and the hiring decisions of organizations. India's social structure based on caste, gender, religion, language, and region determines recruitment perception and the labour force in the country.

Caste determines access to education, social connections, employment, etc. Reservation in public sector organization as an affirmation or compensatory discrimination policy. Preconceptions about gender roles are influencing the segregation of lines of work and employers' views regarding women's dedication to work and mobility. The way cultural beliefs and perceptions are shaped through religious identity can impact inclusion in the workplace, although formal discrimination is limited. The ability to communicate in English and regional languages has emerged as a skill requirement and barrier to access employment. The local hiring preference and economic development disparity influences recruitment through regional identity.

Organizations react to these socio-cultural movements by establishing diversity policies, formal recruitment systems, and inclusive hiring efforts. As a result, recruitment practices in Indian organizations are a reflection of the institutional environment.

2. Sources of bias and fairness concerns arise in selection processes

The chapter identifies various sources of bias and fairness issues in recruitment and selection in Indian organizations. Principal origins of bias are

1. Hiring bias refers to the stereotype and prejudices about caste, gender, religion, or regional identity.
2. Hiring that depends on personal contacts or social connections which could exclude marginalized populations.
3. Inconsistent assessment of candidates due to unstructured interviews and discretion in decision-making.
4. Preference for the dominant language may hurt candidates coming from diverse educational backgrounds.
5. A lack of access to education and skill development – creating differences in competitiveness.

6. The conventional knowledge of recruiters influences their perceptions and actions at the time of hiring.

These raise issues about fairness, transparency, and equal opportunity in recruitment. There is still a considerable gap between policy and practice although organizations are increasingly putting in place structured recruitment systems and diversity policies.

3. How do Indian organizations adapt global staffing practices to local cultural contexts?

Indian organizations, especially multinationals and big domestic companies, combine global human resource standards and local socio-cultural realities for global staffing practices. Global diversity frameworks promote equal opportunity, merit-based hiring, and inclusion; and are adapted to suit India's institutions and culture.

Key changes involve.

1. Policies to promote diversity and inclusion against caste, gender, and regional diversity.
2. Carrying out initiatives for affirmative action & community recruitment.
3. The structured recruitment systems and competency-based evaluation are as per global HR norms.
4. Public sector recruitment includes reservation policies and local regulations requirements.
5. Recruitment strategies to localize language requirements and regional hiring.
6. Use of online recruitment platforms to widen geographic access to talent pool diversity.

These adaptations mirror the necessity of harmonizing international organizational norms with national socio-cultural conditions and institutional frameworks.

4. What lessons can inform culturally fair global recruitment and selection systems?

The chapter has highlighted some key lessons for the construction of culturally fair recruitment and selection systems in global organisations.

To begin with, recruitment systems need to recognize the relevance of socio-cultural context for hiring outcomes and develop context-sensitive diversity strategies. Secondly, to avoid bias, structured recruitment processes such as standardized evaluation criteria, competency-based assessment and transparency in selection process should be in place. In the third place, strong HR policies and commitments from top leadership are required for consistent implementation. To enhance the sensitivity of recruiters and ensure inclusive hiring decisions, organizations must offer diversity training and bias-awareness programs.

Moreover, organizations must use technology-enabled recruitment systems carefully and promote transparency and reduce algorithmic bias. To promote equity in hiring, it is also very important to continuously monitor diversity outcomes and hold the organization accountable.

All in all, integrating institutional awareness and inclusive HR policies, leadership commitment and standardized evaluation practices is required for developing culturally fair recruitment systems. Through National and Global Level workforce diversity, these principles will guide organisations to manage diversity.

The results indicates that cultural diversity management requires systematic organizational interventions and contextual sensitivity. Likewise, study participants feel that diversity management can be effectively done with the systematic integration of organizational diversity management practices such as equitable opportunity creation, adjustment of graduates at workplace, and recruitment bias prevention.

1.6: Suggestions and Conclusions

Drawing from this chapter's findings, the chapter brings forth a few strategic and policy level suggestions for enhancing the cultural diversity management of the recruitment and selection processes in Indian organizations.

1. Revamping and Developing Inclusive HR Policies and Frameworks for Diversity.

Organizations must formulate and execute policies on diversity and inclusion, which includes socio-cultural factors like caste, gender, religion, language, and region. To ensure that the policies clearly define the equal opportunity clauses; anti discrimination principles and monitoring of recruitment processes. It is necessary for organisations to set up an accountability system to gauge impact.

2. Establishing a formal and standardized recruitment system

Organizations must have structured recruitment processes which are competency-based job descriptions, structured interviews, and objective evaluation criteria. Subjectivity in candidate assessment can be minimized through such measures and candidates will be less impacted by personal bias, informal networks, etc. It makes it fair, consistent and of credible hiring decisions.

3. Enhancing Director Commitment to Diversity Management

Top management and organizational leaders should actively promote diversity as a strategic priority. Leadership involvement is necessary for embedding diversity objectives into the organization's culture by ensuring adequate allocation of resources and executing inclusive recruitment practices. Diversity governance structures, such as diversity councils, can strengthen commitment.

4. Offering diversity training and bias awareness.

Recruitment teams and hiring managers should be regularly trained to understand unconscious bias and social stereotypes, and higher organizations should do it. Diversity training programs can enhance the objectivity of candidate assessment and inclusive decision-making.

5. Using technology for a more inclusive recruitment.

Recruiters must use technology-enabled recruitment platforms, digital assessments, and applicant tracking systems to standardize screening processes and broaden access to potential diverse candidates. Nonetheless, organizations need to make sure that technological tools are designed to prevent algorithmic bias.

6. Broadening outreach programs and developing talent.

To ensure better employability for the underprivileged sections of the society, organizations must invest in skills development, educational partnership and community outreach programs. Initiatives assist in building a diverse talent pipeline for equitable workforce participation.

7. Diversity outcomes should be continually monitored and evaluated.

It is important for organizations to regularly monitor their recruitment results. Organizations can close gaps in implementation and improve diversity management practices through continuous monitoring.

8. Policy and Institutional Support.

Government agencies and regulatory bodies need to promote diversity standards, strengthen equal employment policies and promote research on diversity management within organizations.

CONCLUSION

This chapter analyzed how Indian organizations manage diversified recruitment and selection processes in terms of their socio-cultural practice as an influence and their organizational diversity practices and strategies to eliminate bias in recruitment. Recruitment practices in India take place in a complex socio-cultural context consisting of factors such as caste, gender, religion, language, and region. These factors shape access to employment, organizational decision-making, and workforce composition.

The results reveal that businesses are progressively adopting practices, such as purpose-driven HR policies, a structured recruitment system, leadership-led diversity programmes and technology-enabled hiring processes, to address socio-cultural inequalities and to provide employment opportunities fairly. More inclusive workplace practices, hiring strategies and policies, and performance management contribute to fairness. Nevertheless, recruitment is still influenced by recommendations from existing employees, implicit bias, disconnection between policy and practice, social norms, etc.

The integration of global diversity standards with local socio-cultural contexts is essential for the effective development of recruitment systems. Indian organizations demonstrate adaptability by matching international human resource practices with institutional requirements and cultural realities.

To sum up, an effective management of cultural diversity in recruitment and selection process requires a holistic and contextual approach which involves commitment of organization, structured HR practices and monitoring diversity impacts continuously. Diversity management in organizations enhances effectiveness and social justice as well as develops an inclusive workforce and sustainable human resource management in the diverse socio-cultural context of India.

Diversity management practices may be empirically evaluated in the future along with comparative evaluation of the public-private organizations and the impact of new-age technologies on inclusive recruitment practices. These studies will help better understanding of culturally responsive recruitment systems in emerging economies.

REFERENCES.

Accenture. (2023). Environmental, Social and Governance (ESG) Report.

Bano, M., Zowghi, D., Mourao, F., Kaur, S., & Zhang, T. (2024). Diversity and inclusion in AI for recruitment: Lessons from industry workshop.

Bogen, M., & Rieke, A. (2018). *Help wanted: An examination of hiring algorithms, equity, and bias*. Upturn.

Boxall, P., & Purcell, J. (2016). *Strategy and human resource management* (4th ed.). Palgrave Macmillan. DOI: 10.1007/978-1-137-40765-8

Budhwar, P., & Varma, A. (2011). Emerging patterns of HRM in the new Indian economic environment. *Human Resource Management Review, 21*(3), 217–218.

Budhwar, P., Varma, A., Singh, V., & Dhar, R. (2017). HRM systems of Indian companies: Examining the role of HRM in organizational effectiveness. *Employee Relations, 39*(6), 996–1017.

Cox, T. (1993). *Cultural diversity in organizations: Theory, research and practice.* Berrett-Koehler.

Deshpande, A. (2011). *The grammar of caste: Economic discrimination in contemporary India.* Oxford University Press. DOI: 10.1093/acprof:oso/9780198072034.001.0001

Hindustan Unilever Limited. (2023). Annual Report.

ICICI Bank. (2023). Annual Report.

Infosys. (2023). Annual Report.

Infosys. (2023). Environmental, Social and Governance (ESG) Report.

Mahindra Group. (2023). *Sustainability Report.*

Motors, T. (2022). *Sustainability Report.*

Reliance Industries Limited. (2023). Annual Report.

Reserve Bank of India. (2022). Reports on Banking Workforce Practices.

Roberson, Q. M. (2006). Disentangling the meanings of diversity and inclusion. *Group & Organization Management, 31*(2), 212–236. DOI: 10.1177/1059601104273064

Sharma, V., & Langford, S. (2025). A study on diversity, equity, and inclusion for enhancing workplace productivity in India.

Stahl, G. K., Maznevski, M. L., Voigt, A., & Jonsen, K. (2010). Unraveling the effects of cultural diversity in teams. *Journal of International Business Studies, 41*(4), 690–709. DOI: 10.1057/jibs.2009.85 PMID: 33487775

State Bank of India. (2023). Annual Report.

Steel, T. (2022). *Sustainability Report.*

Tajfel, H., & Turner, J. C. (1979). An integrative theory of intergroup conflict. In The social psychology of intergroup relations.

Tata Consultancy Services. (2023). Annual Report.

Tata Consultancy Services. (2023).. . *Sustainability Report.*

Thomas, D. A., & Ely, R. J. (1996). Making differences matter: A new paradigm for managing diversity. *Harvard Business Review, 74*(5), 79–90.

Thorat, S., & Newman, K. S. (2010). *Blocked by caste: Economic discrimination in modern India.* Oxford University Press.

Wipro. (2022). Sustainability Report.

Wipro. (2023). Annual Report.

Chapter 10
Emotional Sustainability in Digitized Work Environments

Lidiane Rodrigues de Oliveira
http://orcid.org/0009-0000-6347-3268
ISLA Santarém, Portugal

Isabel Pinto dos Reis
ISLA Santarém, Portugal

Filipa Isabel Ferreira Martinho
ISLA Santarém, Portugal

ABSTRACT

The growing adoption of Artificial Intelligence (AI) in organizations creates strategic opportunities while intensifying psychosocial risks, particularly burnout. This chapter introduces the Convergent Emotional Intelligence–Artificial Intelligence–Burnout Model (MCIIB), which integrates Emotional Intelligence (EI), intelligent technologies, and professional exhaustion. Based on an integrative literature review, the model conceptualizes EI as a personal resource moderating the AI–burnout relationship. Organizational factors—AI governance, ethics, emotional culture, and digital maturity—further shape technology's psychosocial impact. Grounded in the Job Demands–Resources theory, Maslach's burnout model, and EI frameworks, the MCIIB advances eight testable hypotheses and provides evidence-based guidance for human-centered HRM. The chapter concludes that emotional sustainability in digital work environments depends on the balanced alignment of emotional competencies, ethical AI, and organizational support.

DOI: 10.4018/979-8-2600-2178-1.ch010

1. INTRODUCTION

1.1. The Imperative of Emotional Sustainability in the Digital Age

The 21st century has profoundly transformed the nature of work through the accelerated convergence of digital technologies and human activity. Although Artificial Intelligence (AI) systems promise substantial gains in productivity and efficiency (Brynjolfsson, 1993; Russell & Norvig, 2021), this transformation introduces significant psychosocial challenges.

Algorithm-mediated work environments are reshaping professional practices by intensifying work rhythms, expanding monitoring mechanisms, and reinforcing expectations of continuous connectivity (Barley et al., 2011; Leonardi & Treem, 2020; Zuboff, 2019). In this context, emotional sustainability becomes a strategic imperative for preserving well-being and performance amid rapid and disruptive change.

1.2. The Burnout Landscape and New Technological Demands

Burnout, recognized by the World Health Organization (WHO, 2019) as an occupational phenomenon resulting from chronic, inadequately managed workplace stress, has reached critical proportions across sectors (Amanullah & Shankar, 2020; Gallup, 2022). Global data reveal an increasing prevalence, making it a central concern for health and productivity (American Institute of Stress, 2023; OECD, 2022).

Traditionally characterized by exhaustion, emotional detachment, and reduced professional effectiveness (Maslach et al., 2001; Maslach & Jackson, 1981), burnout acquires new dimensions in digitized environments where technostress emerges (Tarafdar et al., 2019). The incorporation of AI-based technologies introduces additional demands, including algorithmic dependence, continuous adaptation requirements, and fears of professional replacement (Brougham & Haar, 2018; Kellogg et al., 2020; Nam, 2019).

This raises a central question: which personal and organizational resources can mitigate burnout and sustain well-being in increasingly technologized work ecosystems?

1.3. The Strategic Role of Emotional Intelligence

Emotional Intelligence (EI), initially proposed by Salovey and Mayer (1990), refers to the ability to recognize emotional signals, integrate them into cognitive processing, and regulate affective responses in personal and professional interactions

(Goleman, 1995; Mayer & Salovey, 1997). In organizational contexts, EI functions as a personal resource that promotes adaptability and well-being (Bakker & Demerouti, 2007). Meta-analyses demonstrate consistent negative correlations between EI and burnout ($r = -.44$, $p < .001$) and positive correlations with work engagement ($r = .48$, $p < .001$) (Miao et al., 2018; Sánchez-Gómez & Breso, 2020). However, much of this literature predates the widespread adoption of AI technologies, raising a critical question: to what extent does EI maintain its protective function in algorithm-mediated work ecosystems?

1.4. Research Gap and Model Proposal

Despite extensive but fragmented research on AI, burnout, and EI, an integrative model explaining how AI functions as a demand and/or resource, how EI moderates its effects, and how organizational factors shape burnout risk remains lacking. This chapter addresses this gap by proposing the Convergent EI–AI–Burnout Model (MCIIB).

1.5. Chapter Structure

This theoretical-conceptual essay (Meneghetti, 2011) is organized as follows: Section 2 presents the theoretical foundations of burnout, EI, and AI at work. Section 3 describes the methodological design. Section 4 analyzes AI applications and psychosocial risks in Human Resource Management. Section 5 details the MCIIB, its assumptions, architecture, and eight hypotheses. Section 6 discusses the model and outlines a research agenda. Section 7 addresses practical implications, and Section 8 presents conclusions.

2. THEORETICAL FRAMEWORK

2.1. Emotional Intelligence: Concepts, Models, and Evidence

2.1.1. Conceptual Evolution of EI

Emotional Intelligence (EI), as defined in Section 1.3, was initially proposed by Salovey and Mayer (1990) as a set of skills related to emotional information processing. In their expanded formulation, EI is described as the ability to identify emotional signals, integrate them into reasoning, interpret affective meanings across contexts, and regulate emotional responses effectively (Mayer & Salovey, 1997).

Goleman (1995) contributed to the dissemination of the construct by proposing a broader model encompassing personal and social competencies. In organizational settings, this approach highlights intrapersonal dimensions, such as self-awareness and self-regulation, alongside interpersonal skills that facilitate emotional understanding and coordination at work (Goleman, 2012).

Bar-On (1997) conceptualizes EI as a set of emotional and social dispositions that influence how individuals cope with environmental demands, forming the basis of the Emotional Quotient Inventory (EQ-i). Despite conceptual differences, these models converge in viewing EI as a set of developable competencies rather than a fixed trait, underscoring its relevance for performance and well-being at work.

2.1.2. Dimensions and Mechanisms of EI

Despite theoretical differences among models—ranging from ability-based to trait and mixed perspectives—there is broad consensus regarding a common functional core of Emotional Intelligence (EI). This core comprises four capacities: emotional perception (identifying relevant emotional signals); emotional understanding (interpreting their meaning); emotional regulation (deliberately adjusting affective responses); and strategic use of emotions (integrating emotions into reasoning and decision-making).

Among these capacities, emotional regulation is central. It involves modulating the intensity and duration of emotions, expressing them appropriately, and influencing others' emotional states in ethical and adaptive ways. Strategies such as cognitive reappraisal, interpretive reframing of adverse situations, and seeking social support are widely documented regulatory mechanisms. Within the Job Demands–Resources (JD-R) framework (Bakker & Demerouti, 2007), emotional regulation represents the primary mechanism through which EI operates as a personal resource buffering work demands.

2.1.3. EI in the Organizational Context

Sánchez-Gómez and Breso (2020) identify three key mechanisms through which EI reduces burnout: the use of adaptive emotional regulation strategies; the strengthening of psychological resources (e.g., self-efficacy and resilience); and the enhancement of interpersonal relationships that function as social support within work contexts.

Context-specific studies further support these international findings. In Portugal, Claro (2024) found that workers with higher EI report lower burnout and stronger organizational commitment. Similarly, Gaspar (2021) observed that employees with high EI exhibit greater engagement and lower emotional exhaustion, describing this profile as "emotional prospectors." In increasingly digitalized work environments, the relevance of EI becomes even more pronounced, as technology-mediated interactions reduce natural emotional cues and require more sophisticated emotional regulation capacities.

Overall, the literature positions Emotional Intelligence as a robust personal resource within the Job Demands–Resources framework (Bakker & Demerouti, 2007), underpinning both its protective role against burnout and its relevance for engagement in technologically mediated organizational contexts.

2.1.4. Measuring EI

EI is predominantly measured using two approaches:

- Performance-based measures: such as the Mayer-Salovey-Caruso Emotional Intelligence Test (MSCEIT), which assesses emotional processing ability.
- Self-report measures: such as the EQ-i 2.0, based on Bar-On's model, assessing individual perceptions of emotional competencies.

Both approaches have advantages and limitations and are widely used in organizational research.

2.2. Burnout as an Organizational Phenomenon

2.2.1. Conceptualization and Dimensions of Burnout

Burnout, initially described by Freudenberger (1974) and later systematized by Maslach and Jackson (1981), refers to an occupational syndrome characterized by emotional exhaustion, detachment (or cynicism) toward work, and reduced professional effectiveness. As discussed in Section 1.2, it is a phenomenon associated with adverse and chronic working conditions. Maslach et al. (2001) point out that burnout emerges mainly from dysfunctional organizational configurations, shifting the explanatory focus from the individual to work systems.

2.2.2. Burnout Assessment Instruments

Among the most widely used instruments for assessing burnout is the Oldenburg Burnout Inventory (OLBI), which operationalizes the construct through two dimensions, exhaustion and disengagement. In a Portuguese-speaking context, the cross-cultural adaptation of the OLBI presented robust evidence of construct validity and internal consistency, reinforcing its suitability for Portuguese samples of workers (Sinval et al., 2019). Within the MCIIB framework, however, the Maslach Burnout Inventory–General Survey (MBI-GS) is adopted as the primary reference instrument, ensuring consistency with international JD-R-based research.

2.2.3. Prevalence and Impacts of Burnout

Epidemiological evidence shows a growing prevalence of burnout on a global scale (Gallup, 2022; Eurofound, 2022; OECD, 2022). The associated costs are significant: it is estimated that US companies lose between US$ 125 and 190 billion annually due to burnout (American Institute of Stress, 2023).

Although specific to one market, these figures reflect the massive economic impact of burnout internationally. In addition to economic impacts, burnout affects mental health, performance, absenteeism, and turnover (Maslach et al., 2001).

2.2.4. Job Demands–Resources (JD-R) Model

The JD-R (Bakker & Demerouti, 2007) is one of the most influential theoretical frameworks for understanding burnout. It describes two central pathways:

1. Exhaustion pathway: high and chronic demands → reduced energy → burnout.
2. Motivational pathway: work resources and personal resources (such as EI) → engagement → well-being.

The premise that personal resources moderate the negative effects of demands is a central element of the model and underpins hypothesis H2 of the MCIIB. Figure 1 presents the structural diagram of the JD-R, highlighting the position of personal resources as moderators—a role that fits Emotional Intelligence.

Figure 1. Job Demands–Resources (JD-R) Model Diagram

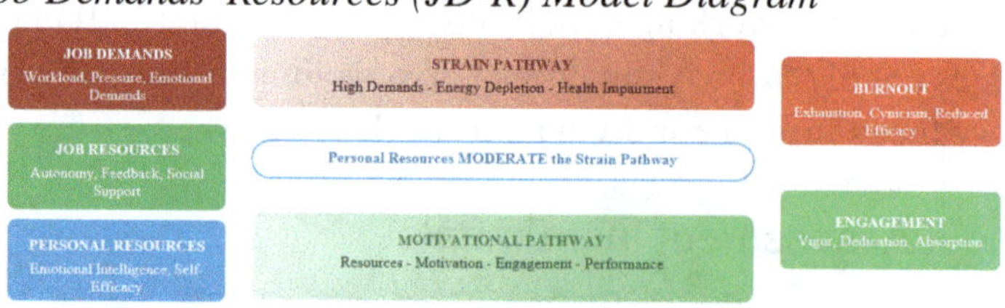

Note. *The JD-R model presents two main pathways: exhaustion (demands burnout) and motivation (resources engagement), with personal resources acting as moderators. Adapted from Bakker and Demerouti (2007).*

2.3. Work Engagement: Counterpoint to Burnout

2.3.1. Conceptualization

Engagement is defined as a positive psychological state characterized by vigor, dedication, and absorption (Schaufeli et al., 2002). Kahn (1990) describes it, in turn, as the integrated mobilization of physical, cognitive, and affective resources in the performance of a professional role.

2.3.2. Relationship with Burnout

Burnout and engagement at work are not merely correlated constructs; they are theoretically conceived as opposite poles of the same continuum of occupational well-being (Schaufeli & Bakker, 2004). While burnout manifests itself through exhaustion and cynicism, engagement is characterized by vigor and dedication.

This antithetical relationship is at the heart of the Job Demands–Resources (JD-R) Model, which posits two distinct psychophysiological processes:

1. The Path of Wear and Tear: High Job Demands (e.g., workload, emotional pressure) deplete energy resources and lead to burnout.
2. The Motivational Path: An abundance of Job Resources (e.g., autonomy, feedback) and Personal Resources (such as EI) leads to engagement and well-being.

Thus, in JD-R, engagement emerges directly from the availability and mobilization of resources, acting as a protective mechanism against exhaustion.

2.3.3. EI as a Predictor of Engagement

Emotional Intelligence (EI) acts not only as a protective factor against burnout but also as a catalyst for work engagement, reinforcing the motivational pathway of the JD-R model.

Applied studies (Lee & Chelladurai, 2018) identify mechanisms through which EI enhances engagement, including increased work meaning and alignment with organizational goals; strengthened interpersonal relationships that amplify social resources; adaptive coping strategies for daily challenges; and effective emotional regulation, preserving energy for dedication and vigor. Overall, EI plays a doubly strategic role in engagement by fostering positive psychological states while building resilience to meet work demands, including those associated with Artificial Intelligence, thereby supporting its central role in the Convergent Model (MCIIB).

2.4. Artificial Intelligence and Work Transformation

2.4.1. Definition and Taxonomy

Artificial Intelligence can be understood as computer systems that perform functions that, under natural conditions, would require human cognitive processes, such as inference, learning, pattern recognition, and content generation (Russell & Norvig, 2021). These systems range from rule-based deterministic models to deep learning architectures and generative systems.

2.4.2. Adoption of AI in Organizations

The use of AI has grown exponentially in recent years (Deloitte, 2023). In the HRM field, it is estimated that 72% of organizations use AI in at least one function (Gartner, 2023). However, highlighting adoption alone is not enough; it is necessary to assess the technology's effective capacity to generate value (Mikalef & Gupta, 2021).

2.4.3. Technology Acceptance Models

Traditional models such as the Technology Acceptance Model (TAM; Davis, 1989) and the Unified Theory of Acceptance and Use of Technology (UTAUT; Venkatesh et al., 2003) explain technology acceptance based on perceptions of usefulness, ease of use, and social influence. However, these eminently cognitive models neglect emotional factors, which constitutes a critical theoretical gap in the study of the adoption of pervasive and psychosocially impactful technologies, such as Artificial Intelligence in the workplace.

2.4.4. The Technological Productivity Paradox

Brynjolfsson (1993) proposes the "productivity paradox": technological investments do not always translate into proportional gains. In the emotional realm, a "well-being paradox" emerges: AI, despite automating tasks, can increase stress by intensifying the pace, surveillance, and reducing autonomy.

2.5. Theoretical Convergences: Integrating Emotional Intelligence (EI), Artificial Intelligence (AI), and Burnout

Although frequently examined as distinct domains, the bodies of literature on emotional intelligence (EI), artificial intelligence (AI), and burnout converge on several core dimensions that collectively underpin the EI–AI–Burnout Convergent Model (MCIIB):

- Emotional demands: AI-driven systems may intensify emotional demands through increased surveillance, performance monitoring, and accelerated work pace;

- Personal resources: EI functions as a key personal resource that buffers individuals against the adverse psychological effects associated with AI-mediated work environments;
- Emotional regulation: Emotional regulation represents a central mechanism underlying both burnout prevention and successful adaptation to digitally intensified workplaces;
- Autonomy and meaning: AI may erode job autonomy and threaten the perceived meaning of work, whereas EI supports the preservation of agency, purpose, and psychological ownership.

These theoretical convergences are supported by a robust body of empirical evidence accumulated over the past two decades. Meta-analytic findings consistently indicate that EI is associated with lower levels of burnout ($\rho = -.45$) and higher job performance (Miao et al., 2018), while also moderating the relationship between job demands and burnout (Sánchez-Gómez & Breso, 2020; $\beta = -.28$). Research conducted in technology-mediated organizational contexts further demonstrates that organizational support and transparency mitigate burnout risks (Chen et al., 2024), and that emotional climate moderates the impact of digitalization on employee well-being. Experimental studies additionally confirm that EI-focused interventions, such as mindfulness-based programs, produce significant improvements in emotional competencies ($d = .64$) and meaningful reductions in burnout symptoms (Ghossoub et al., 2020). Collectively, this body of evidence provides a solid empirical foundation for the eight hypotheses advanced within the MCIIB framework.

3. METHODOLOGY

3.1. Nature and design of the study

This chapter is a theoretical-conceptual essay whose objective is to propose the Convergent EI–AI–Burnout Model (MCIIB), articulating the central constructs of Emotional Intelligence (EI), Artificial Intelligence applied to work (AI), and burnout. Theoretical essays serve to problematize established knowledge, synthesize different lines of research, and generate hypotheses and agendas for subsequent empirical studies (Meneghetti, 2011). The central focus of this work is the development of the MCIIB; no primary data were collected or analyzed.

A deductive–inductive approach was adopted: we started from consolidated theoretical framework (e.g., the Job Demands–Resources Model—JD-R) to derive theoretical propositions (deductive reasoning) and, in parallel, we analyzed recent empirical evidence to inductively refine and validate the proposed relationships between the constructs.

3.2. Literature review strategy

The theoretical construction of the MCIIB was based on an integrative literature review, an approach suitable for synthesizing diverse forms of evidence—quantitative, qualitative, review-based, and conceptual—and for developing theoretical frameworks (Rother, 2007). Unlike systematic reviews with meta-analysis, integrative reviews emphasize interpretive synthesis and transdisciplinary integration.

The bibliographic search was conducted in Scopus, Web of Science, PubMed, and SciELO, with Google Scholar used to identify gray literature and verify citations. Technical reports from organizations such as WHO, Gallup, Gartner, McKinsey, Deloitte, and PwC were also included. The review covered the period 2014–2024, with the strategic inclusion of seminal pre-2014 works (e.g., Goleman, 1995; Maslach & Jackson, 1981; Salovey & Mayer, 1990). Search strings combined terms across the three study axes (e.g., "emotional intelligence" AND burnout; "artificial intelligence" AND workplace; "technostress" AND burnout) and were limited to publications in English, Portuguese, and Spanish.

Inclusion criteria comprised empirical studies, reviews, meta-analyses, and theoretical essays published in peer-reviewed journals, as well as technical reports focused on organizational contexts. Exclusion criteria eliminated exclusively clinical studies, student-only samples, and inaccessible texts. The screening process followed standardized steps—identification, duplicate removal, title and abstract screening, full-text assessment, and final inclusion—with systematic data extraction.

Although integrative rather than meta-analytic, the review applied qualitative quality assessment criteria, including methodological rigor, sample adequacy, and risk of bias. Lower-quality studies were retained but weighted cautiously. The synthesis followed a thematic approach adapted from Braun and Clarke (2006), with theoretical triangulation integrating the JD-R framework, meta-analytic evidence, and recent empirical findings to validate propositions and identify gaps.

4. ARTIFICIAL INTELLIGENCE IN HUMAN RESOURCE MANAGEMENT: APPLICATIONS AND PSYCHOSOCIAL RISKS

Artificial Intelligence (AI) has become a central element in the contemporary landscape of Human Resource Management (HRM). Its applications range from administrative automation to sophisticated predictive analytics and emotional monitoring systems. Although the operational benefits are widely recognized, the incorporation of AI also introduces significant psychosocial risks, capable of intensifying work demands and contributing to burnout.

4.1 Overview of AI Adoption in HRM

Artificial Intelligence (AI) has been rapidly incorporated into Human Resource Management (HRM) on a global scale. According to the Society for Human Resource Management (SHRM, 2023), around one in four organizations use AI to support HR-related activities. The top three areas are recruitment, interviewing, and hiring (64%), learning and development, and performance management. This trend is corroborated by European and global reports (e.g., Gartner, 2023), which point to AI as the main driver of transformation in HRM practices in the coming years.

These figures demonstrate a rapid and massive technological expansion that is reconfiguring management practices and intensifying the need to understand its psychosocial implications.

4.2. Taxonomy of AI Applied to HRM

In the context of HRM, Artificial Intelligence is multifaceted, and its impact depends on the functionality it performs. Table 1 summarizes the AI types most relevant to HRM (Predictive, Generative, Affective, and Prescriptive), highlighting the duality of their psychosocial impact. Within the Job Demands–Resources (JD-R) Model, AI has a dual role:

- Job demands: AI may act as a stressor by increasing algorithmic surveillance, intensifying work pace, generating technical complexity, or pressuring data-driven decisions.
- Work resources: AI may also function as a resource by automating routine tasks, reducing uncertainty, and supporting organizational decisions.

This duality is shaped by organizational factors—such as ethical governance, transparency, and supportive climate—and by personal resources, particularly

Emotional Intelligence (EI), which influences how workers interpret and respond to AI-related demands (Chen et al., 2024).

Table 1. Taxonomy of Organizational Artificial Intelligence in Human Resource Management and Associated Psychosocial Impacts

Type of AI	Description	Examples in HRM	Job Demands (Stressors)	Job Resources (Facilitators)
Predictive AI	Analysis of historical data to forecast future trends, behaviors, or risks	HR analytics; turnover prediction; performance forecasting; fraud detection	Algorithmic complexity; pressure for data-driven decisions; continuous skill updating	Reduced uncertainty; decision support; early risk identification
Generative AI	Creation of new content (text, images, code) based on learned patterns	ChatGPT; automated job descriptions; personalized onboarding materials; training content generation	Fear of job displacement; need for output validation; technological dependence; authorship and ethical concerns	Automation of repetitive tasks; enhanced creativity; reduced cognitive load; content personalization
Affective / Emotional AI	Detection, interpretation, and response to human emotions via facial expressions, voice, or text	Sentiment analysis; facial emotion recognition; empathetic chatbots; well-being monitoring systems	Emotional privacy invasion; affective surveillance; monitoring discomfort; threat to human uniqueness	Personalized emotional feedback; early burnout detection; adaptive support; improved employee experience
Prescriptive AI	Recommendation of actions based on data analysis and scenario simulation	Recommendation systems; resource allocation; personalized training paths; decision-support systems	Reduced decision autonomy; overreliance on recommendations; questioning of human judgment; error-related anxiety	Process optimization; reduced cognitive bias; improved efficiency; structured decision support

Note. AI systems may combine multiple functional capabilities. Psychosocial impacts vary according to ethical governance, transparency, and organizational context.

Figure 2, which presents the Psychosocial Risk Matrix, illustrates the risk gradient associated with different types of organizational AI. This matrix considers both the nature of the technology and the level of governance implemented, allowing HR managers to visually identify which contexts require priority Emotional Intelligence interventions to mitigate burnout.

Figure 2. Psychosocial Risk Matrix by Type of Organizational AI and Governance Level

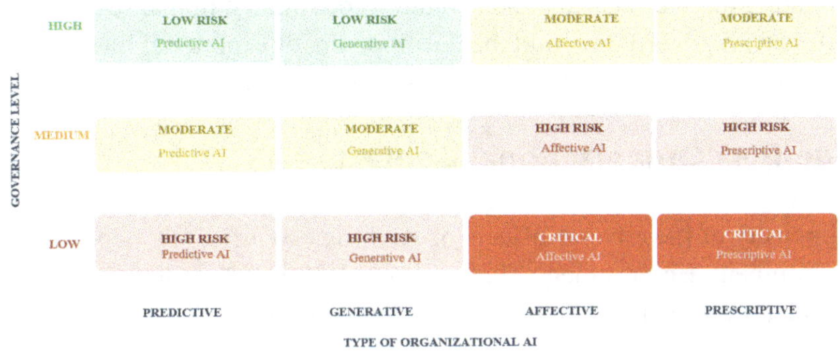

Note. *The classification represents relative risks considering technological demands and ethical governance.*

4.3. Demonstrated Benefits of AI for HR

When implemented with robust governance, AI offers multiple benefits: operational efficiency (Tambe et al., 2019), early identification of occupational risks, personalized learning, and strategic decision-making support. In addition, AI can promote the reduction of human biases (although algorithmic biases may arise; Raghavan et al., 2020). Ethical frameworks, such as the European Commission's (2019) guidelines for trustworthy AI, emphasize transparency, human oversight, and accountability as essential governance principles. Continuous monitoring systems can also assist in the early detection of signs of burnout and the promotion of preventive actions.

4.4. AI Paradox: Efficiency vs. Well-being

Despite tangible benefits, the literature highlights a well-being paradox: technologies designed to reduce workload may instead increase stress and burnout. This paradox manifests across three main dimensions:

- **Time Paradox:** AI saves time but raises expectations of speed and constant availability, intensifying work (Barley et al., 2011).
- **Autonomy Paradox:** Automated decision-making can reduce perceived human agency, generating insecurity and technological dependence.
- **Relational Paradox:** While expanding communication, AI reduces emotional depth and social cues, fostering isolation (Leonardi & Treem, 2020).

Within the Job Demands–Resources framework, these paradoxes reflect the strain pathway, in which intensified demands erode energy and increase burnout risk. Mitigating these effects depends on three core pillars: human-centered system design, ethical AI governance, and the development of Emotional Intelligence (EI), particularly in algorithm-mediated decision-making contexts.

4.5. High-Risk Organizational Contexts

The intensity of the adverse effects of AI varies significantly depending on the work environment. Environments that are more susceptible to technology-induced burnout and more vulnerable require targeted interventions. These contexts include:

- Highly Emotionally Demanding Professions: Sectors such as healthcare, education, and social work, where emotional labor is intense, making workers more vulnerable to exhaustion exacerbated by Affective and monitoring AI.
- High-Pressure Sectors: Environments such as finance, consulting, and technology, characterized by fast-paced rhythms and high performance demands.
- Organizations with Low Digital Maturity: Where AI is poorly implemented, increasing technostress and technical complexity for employees.
- Low Trust Cultures: Where AI amplifies perceptions of surveillance and lack of autonomy, contributing to cynicism and disengagement (components of burnout).

4.6. Sectoral Evidence of AI Impacts

Recent studies show that the influence of EI on mitigating burnout under digitization and automation varies significantly across sectors, with findings that reinforce the role of EI in different contexts:

- Health: Residency directors with high EI show less exhaustion ($r = -.42$) even under heavy digitization (Khesroh et al., 2022).
- Education: EI sustains motivation and well-being in technologized environments.
- Services: EI is associated with lower emotional exhaustion in contexts of pressure and automation (Lee & Chelladurai, 2018).
- Asia: meta-analysis shows that EI significantly reduces burnout under technological mediation (Chen et al., 2024).

5. CONVERGENT EI–AI–BURNOUT MODEL (MCIIB)

5.1. Presentation of the Model

The Convergent Emotional Intelligence–Artificial Intelligence–Burnout Model (MCIIB) integrates three fundamental dimensions of contemporary work: human emotional competencies, intelligent technologies, and the risk of occupational burnout. The model is based on the principle that emotional sustainability in digitized environments depends on how individuals process technological demands, mobilize personal resources, and interact with organizational factors.

Emotional Intelligence (EI) is positioned as an essential personal resource, capable of modulating how workers interpret and respond to the psychosocial effects of Artificial Intelligence (AI). Extending the Job Demands–Resources framework, the MCIIB proposes that EI exerts a protective effect that reduces burnout risk in highly technological contexts.

Figure 3 presents the general architecture of the model, composed of four hierarchical levels and multiple relational pathways through which AI influences burnout, directly or indirectly, depending on organizational conditions and individuals' level of EI.

Figure 3 Architectural Structure of the Convergent EI–AI–Burnout Model (MCIIB)

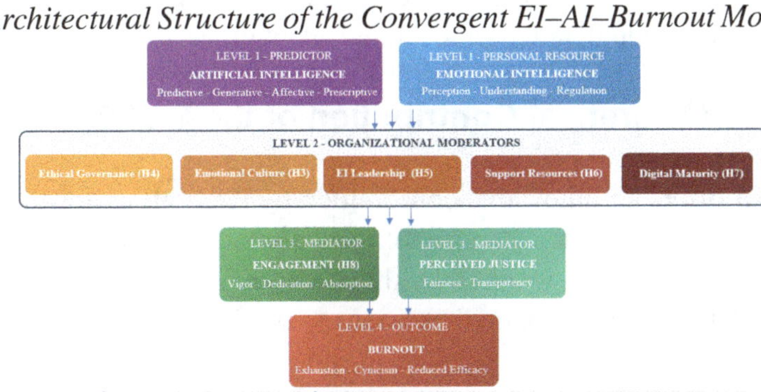

Note. *The model presents four levels: (1) predictor variables, (2) organizational moderators, (3) emotional and motivational mediators, and (4) occupational outcomes. Solid arrows indicate direct relationships; dashed arrows represent moderation effects. EI = Emotional Intelligence; AI = Artificial Intelligence.*

5.2. Fundamental Assumptions of the Model

The MCIIB is based on the principles of Bakker and Demerouti's (2007) Job Demands–Resources (JD-R) Model, one of the most widely used frameworks for understanding burnout and engagement. The JD-R is particularly well suited to the context of digitalization because:

- it clearly differentiates between demands and resources.
- it explains how high demands can lead to burnout.
- it predicts that personal resources, such as EI, moderate adverse effects.
- it allows for the integration of organizational and technological factors.

On this basis, the MCIIB assumes five central theoretical assumptions:

- Relative technological neutrality: the effects of AI are not intrinsic to the technology, but depend on design, implementation, and organizational governance.
- EI as a personal resource: EI reduces the impact of technological demands, aligning with the JD-R principle that personal resources cushion stress.
- Dual nature of AI: AI can function simultaneously as a demand (e.g., surveillance, intensification) and as a resource (e.g., automation, informational support).
- Moderating organizational context: Emotional culture, governance, leadership, and digital maturity modulate the intensity of AI effects on burnout.
- Dynamic process: The effects of AI and the use of EI evolve over time, according to individual and organizational adaptations.

5.3. Original Theoretical Contribution of the MCIIB

The MCIIB offers an innovative contribution by integrating, for the first time, human emotional competencies and intelligent technologies into an explanatory model of burnout. Although inspired by the JD-R, the model advances beyond its original formulation in three main dimensions:

- Reconceptualization of AI as a hybrid source of demands and resources: MCIIB proposes that AI should not be treated only as a technical tool, but as an ecosystemic element that alters work dynamics, social relationships, decision-making flows, and perceptions of autonomy. As a result, the model now captures contemporary phenomena such as algorithmic surveillance, cognitive intensification, and technological dependence, aspects that go beyond the traditional categories of JD-R.
- Expanded role of Emotional Intelligence: unlike traditional literature that treats EI as one of many personal resources, the MCIIB positions EI as a cross-cutting moderator, simultaneously influencing multiple technological

demands. EI is understood as a strategic competence for emotional navigation in digitized environments.
- Inclusion of contemporary psychosocial mechanisms: MCIIB adds processes not covered in JD-R, such as: meaning-making in automated environments; technology-mediated preservation of emotional bonds; emotional regulation strategies for coping with digital stressors.

Thus, the MCIIB updates the JD-R to the reality of advanced digitization, offering a robust framework to explain how AI, EI, and burnout interrelate.

5.4. Relational Hypotheses of the Model

Based on the theoretical review and the proposed integration, the MCIIB presents eight relational hypotheses that structure its functioning.

5.4.1. Relationships between AI, Governance, and Burnout

H1 – Exposure to AI increases burnout when AI governance is insufficient. When implemented in a non-transparent or invasive manner, AI acts as a chronic demand, increasing insecurity, surveillance, and pressure to perform. The literature has identified a positive correlation between AI usage intensity and burnout in contexts without governance (Chen et al., 2024).

H4 – Ethical AI governance reduces the negative impact of AI exposure on burnout. Transparency, participation, and accountability decrease perceptions of injustice and technological anxiety (Lee, 2018).

5.4.2. The Moderating Role of Emotional Intelligence

H2 – Emotional Intelligence (EI) is proposed to mitigate the positive relationship between AI exposure and burnout. Individuals with high EI use emotional regulation, reframing, and social strategies that reduce the impact of demands introduced by AI. Prior studies have demonstrated that EI significantly moderates the relationship between job demands and burnout (Sánchez-Gómez & Breso, 2020), supporting the theoretical plausibility of a similar buffering role in AI-intensive environments.

Figure 4 illustrates this interaction, visually representing how high EI mitigates the increase in burnout as AI exposure intensifies.

Figure 4. Moderating Effect of Emotional Intelligence on the Relationship Between AI Exposure and Burnout

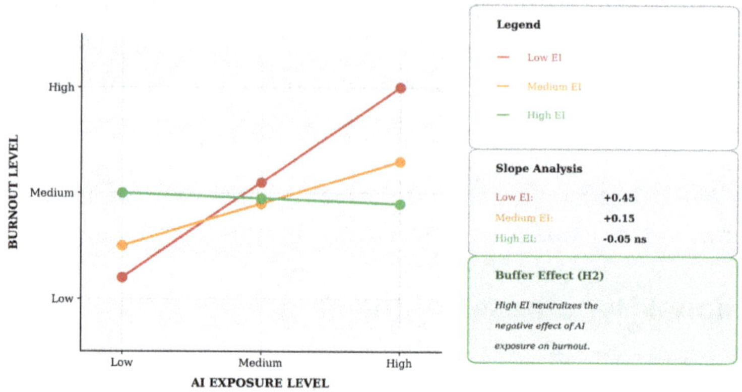

Note. *EI = Emotional Intelligence; AI = Artificial Intelligence. The graph illustrates the buffer effect of EI. The slopes represent the rate of change in burnout per unit of exposure to AI: Low EI (+0.45), Medium EI (+0.15), and High EI (−0.05, not significant). Positive correlations indicate increased risk; negative correlations indicate a protective effect.*

5.4.3. Organizational and Leadership Factors

Hypothesis 3 (H3) A positive organizational emotional culture strengthens the protective effect of Emotional Intelligence (EI) on the relationship between AI exposure and burnout. A culture that values empathy, support, and authenticity creates an environment in which AI is perceived and used to empower, rather than control, workers. Empirical evidence indicates that a positive emotional climate significantly moderates the relationship between digitalization and well-being.

Hypothesis 5 (H5) states that emotionally intelligent leadership minimizes the negative impacts of AI. Leaders with high EI are able to recognize early signs of distress, adapt work demands, provide support, and model healthy use of technology. This relationship is theoretically supported by meta-analytic evidence showing that Emotional Intelligence is strongly associated with lower burnout and higher well-being (Miao et al., 2018), providing a foundation for the role of emotionally intelligent leadership proposed in H5.

5.4.4. Resources, Maturity, and Mediation

Hypothesis 6 (H6) The availability of organizational resources (psychological support, well-being, training) reduces the effect of AI exposure on burnout. Well-being programs, psychological support, and adequate training function as resources that compensate for the demands of digitization. This is a fundamental principle of the JD-R Model (Bakker & Demerouti, 2007).

Hypothesis 7 (H7) Digital maturity negatively moderates the relationship between AI implementation and technostress, reducing psychosocial risks. Organizations with robust infrastructure, adequate training, and established processes implement AI more smoothly and effectively, functioning as a contextual organizational resource. *Industry-based evidence* suggests that digital maturity predicts satisfaction with technology and reduces resistance to change (Kane et al., 2019), providing practical and contextual support for H7.

Finally, Hypothesis 8 (H8) proposes that engagement (vigor, dedication, absorption) partially mediates the relationship between EI and burnout in high AI contexts. The mechanism is that EI promotes engagement, which in turn acts as a protective buffer against burnout. The mediation is supported by the literature, which indicates that engagement is strongly related to burnout (Schaufeli & Bakker, 2004, share 10–25% of their variance) and mediates personal resource effects.

Taken together, Hypotheses 6 to 8 capture the resource-based and processual mechanisms through which organizations and individuals regulate the psychosocial impact of AI. While H6 and H7 model organizational resources and digital maturity as contextual buffers that attenuate technological strain, H8 introduces a motivational pathway by positioning work engagement as a mediating mechanism between Emotional Intelligence and burnout in high-AI environments. These relationships, embedded in the Job Demands–Resources framework, complete the explanatory architecture of the MCIIB by integrating structural, technological, and psychological resource dynamics. Table 2 summarizes the full set of eight hypotheses and their expected directional effects.

Table 2. Summary of the Eight Hypotheses of the MCIIB Model (Convergent EI–AI–Burnout Model)

H	Predictor(s)	Moderator/Mediator	Outcome	Expected Direction (Summary)
H1	AI Exposure	Governance Quality ↓	Burnout	AI exposure without adequate governance increases burnout
H2	AI Exposure	Emotional Intelligence (EI)	Burnout	Higher EI exerts a protective effect, attenuating the AI–burnout relationship
H3	Emotional Intelligence (EI)	Emotional Culture (Moderator)	Burnout	Strong emotional culture enhances the protective effect of EI
H4	AI Exposure	Ethical AI Governance	Burnout	Ethical AI governance reduces burnout risk
H5	AI Exposure	Emotionally Intelligent Leadership	Burnout	EI-based leadership reduces the negative impact of AI exposure
H6	AI Exposure	Organizational Resources	Burnout	Organizational resources mitigate technological demands

continued on following page

Table 2. Continued

H	Predictor(s)	Moderator/Mediator	Outcome	Expected Direction (Summary)
H7	AI Implementation	Digital Maturity	Technostress	Higher digital maturity reduces technostress
H8	Emotional Intelligence	Engagement (Mediation)	Burnout	EI increases engagement, which in turn reduces burnout

Note. H = hypothesis; EI = Emotional Intelligence; AI = Artificial Intelligence. Negative interaction: the effect of AI on burnout decreases when EI is high.

After a detailed presentation of the eight relational hypotheses, the following section describes the hierarchical organization of the model's components.

5.5. Hierarchical Organization of MCIIB Components

The architecture of the Convergent Model (MCIIB) is organized into four hierarchical levels, reflecting the causal complexity of JD-R: Level 1 (Central Predictive Variables: Artificial Intelligence and Emotional Intelligence); Level 2 (Contextual Moderating Variables: Ethical Governance, EI Leadership, Emotional Culture, Support Resources, and Digital Maturity); Level 3 (Mediating Variables: Engagement and Perceptions of Justice); and Level 4 (Outcome Variable: Burnout). This structure aims to test the direct and indirect pathways of EI on occupational outcomes.

5.6. Underlying Psychological Mechanisms

The MCIIB is supported by three central psychological mechanisms, operating at the process level, that explain how high Emotional Intelligence (EI) moderates the impacts of Artificial Intelligence (AI) by reinforcing protection against burnout:

- Adaptive Emotional Regulation (Focus on Stressor): Workers with high EI use sophisticated emotional regulation strategies (e.g., cognitive reappraisal, support seeking) to cope with specific technological stressors, such as algorithmic surveillance and information overload.
- Meaning Construction (Focus on Mastery): EI facilitates meaning and purpose in AI-mediated work by redefining mastery as the ability to use technology as a tool, rather than compete with it.
- Preservation of Human Connections (Focus on Social Resource): Emotionally intelligent workers intentionally cultivate quality relationships, prioritizing emotionally rich communication to preserve social support, a vital buffer against burnout.

5.7. Integrated Understanding of MCIIB Model Relationships

As visually represented in Figure 3, the Convergent EI-AI-Burnout Model demonstrates the complexity of the proposed hypothetical relationships. Artificial Intelligence (AI) is positioned as a predictor variable with a bidirectional effect on burnout, which can either increase or reduce exhaustion depending on the conditions of implementation. Emotional Intelligence (EI) is positioned as a key personal resource, hypothesized to exert both a direct protective effect on burnout and an indirect effect mediated by engagement (H8).

The five Organizational Moderating Variables (emotional culture, ethical governance, EI leadership, support resources, and digital maturity) modulate the strength and direction of the relationships between AI and burnout. Their role is decisive in determining whether technology will function predominantly as a facilitating resource or as an additional stressor. The visual representation of the MCIIB is therefore essential for understanding emotional sustainability in digitized environments.

6. DISCUSSION

6.1. Convergences with the Existing Literature

The Convergent Emotional Intelligence–Artificial Intelligence–Burnout Model (MCIIB) demonstrates strong alignment with multiple theoretical traditions, reinforcing its conceptual and empirical plausibility.

Convergence with the Job Demands–Resources (JD-R) Model

The proposition that Emotional Intelligence (EI) operates as a personal resource buffering technological demands derives directly from the core assumptions of the Job Demands–Resources model (Bakker & Demerouti, 2007). The MCIIB extends this framework by specifying how this mechanism unfolds within accelerated digital work environments characterized by the pervasive adoption of AI-based systems.

Convergence with the Emotional Intelligence and Burnout Literature

Hypothesis H2 is consistent with extensive empirical evidence documenting stable and negative associations between Emotional Intelligence and burnout (Miao et al., 2018; Sánchez-Gómez & Breso, 2020; Chen et al., 2024; Claro, 2024). The MCIIB advances this literature by situating the protective function of EI within highly technologized work contexts, in which digital stressors amplify the relevance of emotional competencies as psychological resources.

Convergence with Recent Empirical Evidence on Technostress

Recent empirical findings further support the core propositions of the MCIIB. Shaban et al. (2025), in a study of 180 critical care nurses, demonstrated that Emotional Intelligence significantly mediates the relationship between technostress and burnout (indirect effect = 0.23, $p = .002$). EI was negatively associated with both technostress ($r = -.45$, $p < .01$) and burnout ($r = -.49$, $p < .01$), reinforcing its protective role in technology-intensive work environments. Although EI was modeled as a mediator rather than a moderator, these findings provide indirect support for Hypothesis H2 by showing that EI reduces burnout under technology-related stress, conceptually analogous to AI-intensive contexts.

Convergence with Technostress Research

The stressors specified in the MCIIB—such as algorithmic surveillance, work intensification, and technological insecurity—are fully consistent with the technostress literature (Tarafdar et al., 2019) and research on digital work intensification (Barley et al., 2011).

Convergence with Critical Perspectives on Artificial Intelligence

Concerns regarding surveillance, control, and loss of autonomy resonate with critical perspectives on Artificial Intelligence (Zuboff, 2019; Kellogg et al., 2020). However, the MCIIB avoids a deterministic or exclusively critical stance by recognizing that AI may also function as an organizational resource when embedded within robust ethical governance and emotionally intelligent organizational systems. Together, these convergences highlight the incremental explanatory value of the MCIIB in contemporary digital work environments.

6.2. Disagreements and Controversies

Although it presents important convergences, the MCIIB also addresses areas of debate highlighted in the literature.

Tension regarding technological optimism

Part of the management literature tends to emphasize efficiency and productivity gains associated with AI. The MCIIB takes a more balanced position by proposing that such benefits can coexist with significant psychosocial risks.

Debate on causality between EI and burnout.

Although some authors suggest that burnout can deteriorate emotional capacities (i.e., burnout → EI), the MCIIB maintains—based on the conceptualization of EI as a relatively stable competence—the opposite direction: EI → burnout. EI is thus presented as an antecedent resource and not a consequence of exhaustion.

Divergence from technological determinism.

The model rejects the idea that AI has inherent impacts. By emphasizing organizational moderators (governance, culture, leadership), the MCIIB aligns itself with socio-technical perspectives that treat technology as constructed and interpreted in a social context.

6.3. Limitations of the Model

Despite its conceptual value, the model presents both theoretical and empirical limitations that must be acknowledged.

- Lack of empirical validation: The MCIIB is a theoretical-conceptual model and lacks rigorous empirical testing, particularly through Structural Equation Modeling (SEM).
- Structural complexity: The inclusion of multiple moderators and mediators increases explanatory richness but reduces parsimony, posing challenges for empirical operationalization.
- Additional variables not considered: Individual factors such as personality, resilience, or coping strategies were not incorporated, although they may significantly influence burnout.
- Contextual specificity: The formulation is predominantly based on corporate contexts in developed economies, which may limit generalization to informal or digitally immature settings.
- Rapid technological evolution: The pace of AI innovation suggests that the model should be understood as a framework anchored in the current historical moment, subject to continuous revision as new evidence emerges.

6.4. Distinctive Strengths and Contributions

Despite its limitations, the MCIIB makes significant contributions to HR literature and practice.

Theoretical originality

It is the first framework to systematically integrate EI, AI, and burnout in a JD-R-based manner, filling a clear gap in the field.

Conceptual sophistication

The model avoids binary readings of AI (benefit vs. risk) and proposes a nuanced approach that recognizes the coexistence of simultaneous and contradictory effects.

Practical relevance

The MCIIB identifies actionable organizational variables (governance, culture, leadership, digital maturity), offering a clear roadmap for mitigating psychosocial risks.

Interdisciplinarity

It integrates knowledge from Organizational Psychology, Technology Studies, Organizational Behavior, and Algorithmic Ethics.

6.5. Future Research Agenda

Several priority areas for future research emerge from the MCIIB.

Multimethodological empirical validation

Quantitative (SEM, HLM) and qualitative (interviews, digital ethnographies) studies should test the hypotheses and mechanisms formulated.

Differentiation of EI dimensions

Identify whether perception, understanding, use, or emotional regulation are the most decisive dimensions in moderating the effects of AI.

Effects of algorithmic governance.

Empirically examine which practices of transparency, fairness, and participation reduce algorithmic stressors.

Sectoral and cultural comparisons

Analyze how the model behaves in specific sectors (health, education, finance, technology) and in different cultural contexts.

Longitudinal studies

Necessary to investigate the direction of causality and temporal dynamics between EI, AI, and burnout.

Applied interventions

Evaluate EI development programs, training for the ethical use of AI, and emotional governance policies as preventive strategies.

Conclusion of the Discussion

The discussion presented shows that the MCIIB dialogues with existing literature, introduces original contributions, recognizes limitations, and opens a solid path for future research. This combination strengthens its usefulness as a framework for understanding and guiding emotional sustainability in digitized environments.

7. IMPLICATIONS FOR HUMAN RESOURCE MANAGEMENT

The main practical contribution of the Convergent EI–AI–Burnout Model (MCIIB) is to offer a strategic and operational roadmap for Human Resource Management (HR), aiming to promote emotional sustainability, mitigate psychosocial risks, and prevent burnout in digitalized work environments. The proposed actions articulate two central axes:

(a) development of Emotional Intelligence (EI) as a fundamental personal resource and
(b) ethical governance of Artificial Intelligence (AI) as a structuring organizational resource.

7.1. Development of Emotionally Intelligent Leadership

The literature shows that leaders with high EI promote psychological safety, well-being, and resilience in their teams (Goleman, 1995; Miao et al., 2018). Thus, investing in the development of EI in leadership is a critical mechanism for preventing systemic burnout.

7.1.1. Empathetic Leadership Training

Workshops on active listening, constructive feedback, and conscious emotional communication enable managers to recognize and intervene early when signs of stress appear. Essential components include:

- identifying nonverbal emotional signs
- feedback techniques that preserve autonomy and psychological safety
- modeling adaptive emotional regulation strategies

7.1.2. Individual Mentoring for Managers

Mentoring programs strengthen leaders' self-awareness and self-regulation. Emotionally intelligent managers reduce the transfer of pressure to teams and promote emotionally supportive environments (Kahn, 1990). Studies show that the conscious use of emotional skills reduces exhaustion ($r = -.42$) and increases overall well-being (Khesroh et al., 2022).

7.2. EI Development for All Employees

According to Assumption 2 of the MCIIB, EI is a cross-cutting personal resource, not restricted to leadership.

7.2.1. Emotional Intelligence Workshops

Practical programs developing the pillars of EI (Goleman, 1995)—emotional awareness, self-management, empathy, and social skills—make employees more resilient to digital demands.

Strategies include:

- mindfulness practices for self-awareness
- cognitive reappraisal exercises
- stress management techniques

7.2.2. Resilience and Well-Being Programs

Robust empirical evidence supports the effectiveness of emotional intelligence–focused interventions. Ghossoub et al. (2020) reported significant increases in emotional intelligence (d = .64) following guided meditation programs, while documented meaningful reductions in burnout (d = –.48) alongside improvements in work engagement (d = .52) after EI-based training initiatives.

To ensure that the EI–AI–Burnout Convergent Model (MCIIB) can be effectively operationalized and continuously refined within organizational contexts, its core constructs must be translated into measurable and actionable indicators. Key metrics should include emotional intelligence levels (assessed via the MSCEIT or EQ-i), burnout symptoms (MBI-GS), work engagement (UWES), emotional climate indices, and perceptions of AI governance. Assessment frequencies may range from quarterly to annual, depending on the nature and stability of each indicator. Collectively, these metrics enable human resource functions to systematically monitor the effectiveness of EI development initiatives, AI governance practices, and burnout prevention strategies through a data-driven approach.

7.3. Strategic Implementation Roadmap (5 Phases)

To operationalize the EI–AI–Burnout Convergent Model (MCIIB), a five-phase implementation cycle is proposed, aligning diagnostic, developmental, governance, and sustainability processes over a 12-month period. This roadmap is illustrative rather than prescriptive, ensuring that emotional intelligence development and ethical AI governance evolve in an integrated, cumulative manner rather than as fragmented or isolated initiatives.

The implementation framework comprises five sequential phases: (1) Diagnostic Assessment (Months 1–2), aimed at establishing baseline levels of psychosocial risk, emotional competencies, and digital readiness; (2) Design and Structuring (Months 2–4), focused on the development of EI-based interventions and AI governance frameworks; (3) Implementation and Capacity Building (Months 4–8), involving the delivery of training programs and organizational capability enhancement initiatives; (4) Monitoring and Evaluation (continuous), dedicated to tracking key performance indicators (KPIs), psychosocial outcomes, and emerging risks; and (5) Sustainability and Institutionalization (Months 9–12), which consolidates validated practices into formal human resource policies and organizational routines. Figure 5 illustrates this phased framework, highlighting critical milestones, key deliverables, and success indicators associated with each stage.

Figure 5. Five-Phase Implementation Framework for the MCIIB Model (12 Months)

Note. *The framework consists of five sequential phases: Diagnosis (Months 1-2), Planning (Months 2-4), Implementation (Months 4-8), Monitoring (Continuous), and Refinement/Sustainment (Months 9-12). Each phase includes key activities and specific deliverables. EI = Emotional Intelligence; AI = Artificial Intelligence; KPIs = Key Performance Indicators.*

7.4 MCIIB Mini-Case Studies

The following mini-case studies (fictitious but theoretically grounded) are illustrative and theory-driven, demonstrating how the core hypotheses of the Convergent Emotional Intelligence–Artificial Intelligence–Burnout Model (MCIIB) can be operationalized across different organizational contexts.

7.4.1. Case 1 — Technology Industry: EI as a Personal Resource (H2)

AlphaTech, a technology-driven organization, was experiencing elevated burnout and voluntary turnover among software developers due to high AI-related cognitive and emotional demands. A six-month Emotional Intelligence development program focused on emotional regulation, stress management, and adaptive coping was implemented. Following the intervention, burnout and turnover were substantially reduced, and organizational performance indicators improved, illustrating the practical relevance of Hypothesis H2.

This case exemplifies how Emotional Intelligence functions as a personal resource that buffers the psychosocial strain associated with AI-intensive work.

7.4.2. Case 2 — Contact Center: Ethical Governance of AI (H1/H4)

BetaCall introduced affective AI technologies for performance monitoring without sufficient transparency or employee involvement, leading to heightened perceptions of surveillance and technostress. After the introduction of ethical governance mechanisms—including an AI ethics committee, transparent communication policies, and non-punitive data use guidelines—perceived injustice declined and employee trust increased.

This case illustrates how ethical AI governance can transform AI from a psychosocial stressor into a supportive organizational resource.

7.4.3. Case 3 — Healthcare Sector: Emotional Leadership (H3/H5)

Gamma Hospital implemented electronic medical records, initially generating emotional overload, resistance, and workflow disruption. After targeted Emotional Intelligence training for clinical and administrative leaders, both employee satisfaction and system adoption improved. This case demonstrates how emotionally intelligent leadership and a supportive emotional culture moderate the adverse psychosocial effects of digital transformation.

7.5. Ethical governance of Artificial Intelligence (AI)

Ethical governance of Artificial Intelligence constitutes a central pillar of the Convergent Emotional Intelligence–Artificial Intelligence–Burnout Model (MCIIB) (H4). Without adequate governance structures, AI systems risk being perceived as instruments of surveillance, control, and unfair evaluation, which amplifies technostress, emotional exhaustion, and organizational distrust. Conversely, when embedded within transparent, participatory, and ethically grounded frameworks, AI can function as a supportive organizational resource rather than a psychosocial risk factor.

7.6. Burnout Monitoring and Prevention

Effective burnout prevention within the MCIIB framework requires continuous monitoring of psychosocial and organizational indicators. Strategic metrics include standardized burnout measures (e.g., MBI-GS), absenteeism, voluntary turnover, work engagement, and sentiment analysis derived from employee feedback systems. Together, these indicators enable organizations to track psychosocial risk trajectories and identify emerging patterns of distress.

Preventive interventions should be guided by ethical and transparent data use. AI systems can potentially be used to detect early warning signals of psychosocial risk and to inform supportive interventions, rather than punitive control, in alignment with principles of ethical governance and employee trust.

7.7. Digital Well-being Policies

Digital well-being policies constitute a critical organizational resource for mitigating technostress and protecting employees from chronic digital overload. A key mechanism is the institutionalization of the right to disconnect, which helps preserve work–life boundaries, reduces after-hours digital intrusion, and prevents emotional exhaustion.

In addition, digital ergonomics and workflow design play a central role in managing cognitive load. Practices such as no-meeting days, structured management of digital notifications, and the simplification of digital workflows reduce unnecessary interruptions and enhance employees' capacity for sustained attention and recovery.

7.8. EI as a Pillar of Organizational Sustainability

Within the MCIIB framework, Emotional Intelligence constitutes a core driver of the "People" dimension of organizational sustainability, as conceptualized in the triple bottom line (Elkington, 1997). By strengthening emotional awareness, self-regulation, empathy, and relational competence, EI contributes to lower burnout, higher work engagement, a healthier emotional culture, and the long-term sustainability of human capital.

8. CONCLUSION

8.1. Summary of Theoretical and Practical Contributions

This chapter presented the Convergent Emotional Intelligence–Artificial Intelligence–Burnout Model (MCIIB), which integrates human emotional competencies, intelligent technologies, and professional burnout processes into a unified theoretical framework. Developed through an integrative literature review, the model synthesizes evidence from organizational psychology, human resource management, and digital work research, offering both conceptual advancement and practical relevance.

The main theoretical contributions include:

- A novel conceptual integration of Emotional Intelligence, Artificial Intelligence, and burnout, grounded in the Job Demands–Resources (JD-R) model and tailored to digitally mediated work environments.
- The specification of three key psychological mechanisms—emotional regulation, meaning-making, and the preservation of human connection—through which EI is theorized to exert its protective role.

- The identification of five organizational moderators (ethical AI governance, emotional culture, emotionally intelligent leadership, organizational support resources, and digital maturity) that shape whether technology functions as a demand or a resource.
- The formulation of eight testable hypotheses, providing a coherent agenda for future empirical research.

From a practical Human Resource Management perspective, the chapter contributes by:

- Offering a structured diagnostic framework for identifying psychosocial risks associated with AI implementation.
- Providing concrete intervention pathways for developing Emotional Intelligence among leaders and employees (Section 7).
- Proposing an ethical AI governance architecture capable of transforming technology into a supportive organizational resource rather than an additional stressor.

8.2. Emotional Sustainability as an Imperative

The central thesis of the MCIIB is that emotional sustainability in digitized work environments constitutes a strategic organizational imperative rather than an optional concern. Organizations that fail to integrate Emotional Intelligence with ethical AI governance are likely to experience elevated burnout, increased turnover, and cultural erosion. By contrast, organizations that implement AI in emotionally intelligent and ethically responsible ways are better positioned to foster engagement, retain talent, and sustain long-term performance.

Within this framework, Emotional Intelligence is theorized to function both as a protective buffer against burnout (H2) and as a driver of work engagement (H8), thereby reinforcing the social and psychological foundations of organizational resilience.

8.3. Call for Empirical Validation

The MCIIB is explicitly proposed as a theoretical and propositional model that requires rigorous empirical testing. To advance this research agenda, three complementary lines of inquiry are recommended:

- Quantitative validation, using structural equation modeling, longitudinal designs, and multilevel analyses to test the proposed moderation and mediation mechanisms (H2–H8).
- Qualitative inquiry, including case studies, interviews, and phenomenological approaches, to deepen understanding of the psychological processes underlying EI–AI–burnout dynamics.
- Ecological validation, through applications across sectors, organizational sizes, and cultural contexts, to assess the robustness and generalizability of the model.

8.4. Final Reflection: Humanizing Technology

The convergence of Emotional Intelligence and Artificial Intelligence represents one of the defining challenges of work in the twenty-first century. Rather than choosing between human or artificial intelligence, organizations are increasingly required to harmonize both forms so that technology amplifies, rather than undermines, what is most human in work.

Humanizing technology means designing, implementing, and governing AI in ways that preserve autonomy, dignity, and human connection.

Technologizing humanization means using AI deliberately to reduce unnecessary burdens, personalize support, and free cognitive and emotional capacity for creativity, care, and collaboration.

Ultimately, the future of work will be shaped not by the sophistication of the AI systems organizations deploy, but by the emotional maturity with which those systems are integrated into organizational life.

REFERENCES

Amanullah, S., & Ramesh Shankar, R. (2020). The impact of COVID-19 on physician burnout globally: A review. *Health Care*, *8*(4), 421.

American Institute of Stress. (2023). Workplace stress survey 2023. https://www.stress.org/workplace-stress

Bakker, A. B., & Demerouti, E. (2007). The job demands–resources model: State of the art. *Journal of Managerial Psychology*, *22*(3), 309–328. DOI: 10.1108/02683940710733115

Bar-On, R. (1997). *The Emotional Quotient Inventory (EQ-i): A measure of emotional intelligence*. Multi-Health Systems.

Barley, S. R., Meyerson, D., & Grodal, S. (2011). E-mail as a source and symbol of stress. *Organization Science*, *22*(4), 887–906. DOI: 10.1287/orsc.1100.0573

Braun, V., & Clarke, V. (2006). Using thematic analysis in psychology. *Qualitative Research in Psychology*, *3*(2), 77–101. DOI: 10.1191/1478088706qp063oa

Brougham, D., & Haar, J. (2018). Smart technology, artificial intelligence, robotics, and algorithms (STARA): Implications for work and human resource management. *Journal of Management & Organization*, *24*(5), 407–421. DOI: 10.1017/jmo.2016.55

Brynjolfsson, E. (1993). The productivity paradox of information technology. *Communications of the ACM*, *36*(12), 66–77. DOI: 10.1145/163298.163309

Chen, Y.-C., Huang, Z.-L., & Chu, H.-C. (2024). Relationships between emotional labor, job burnout, and emotional intelligence. *BMC Psychology*, *12*(1), 672. Advance online publication. DOI: 10.1186/s40359-024-02167-w PMID: 39558444

Claro, F. A. (2024). *Inteligência emocional no ambiente de trabalho* [Unpublished master's thesis]. Universidade de Lisboa.

Davis, F. D. (1989). Perceived usefulness, perceived ease of use, and user acceptance of information technology. *Management Information Systems Quarterly*, *13*(3), 319–340. DOI: 10.2307/249008

Deloitte. (2023). *Global human capital trends 2023: New expectations for AI in HR*. https://www2.deloitte.com/us/en/insights/focus/human-capital-trends.html

Elkington, J. (1997). *Cannibals with forks: The triple bottom line of 21st century business*. Capstone.

European Commission. (2019). *Ethics guidelines for trustworthy AI.* https://digital-strategy.ec.europa.eu/en/library/ethics-guidelines-trustworthy-ai

Freudenberger, H. J. (1974). Staff burnout. *The Journal of Social Issues, 30*(1), 159–165. DOI: 10.1111/j.1540-4560.1974.tb00706.x

Gallup. (2022). *State of the global workplace: 2022 report.* https://www.gallup.com/workplace/349484/state-of-the-global-workplace.aspx

Gartner. (2023). *Hype cycle for human resource management, 2023.* https://www.gartner.com/en/human-resources

Gaspar, R. M. (2021). *Inteligência emocional, engagement e burnout em trabalhadores portugueses* [Unpublished doctoral dissertation]. Universidade do Porto.

Ghossoub, Z., Nadler, R., & El-Aswad, N. B. (2020). Emotional intelligence, resilience, self-care, and self-leadership in healthcare workers burnout. *Universal Journal of Public Health, 8*(5), 155–162. DOI: 10.13189/ujph.2020.080501

Goleman, D. (1995). *Emotional intelligence: Why it can matter more than IQ.* Bantam Books.

Goleman, D. (2012). *Working with emotional intelligence.* Bloomsbury Publishing.

Kahn, W. A. (1990). Psychological conditions of personal engagement and disengagement at work. *Academy of Management Journal, 33*(4), 692–724. DOI: 10.2307/256287

Kane, G. C., Palmer, D., Phillips, A. N., Kiron, D., & Buckley, N. (2019). Accelerating digital innovation inside and out: Agile teams, ecosystems, and ethics. MIT Sloan Management Review and Deloitte Insights. https://www2.deloitte.com/us/en/insights/focus/digital-maturity/digital-innovation-ecosystems-organizational-agility.html

Kellogg, K. C., Valentine, M. A., & Christin, A. (2020). Algorithms at work. *Annual Review of Sociology, 46*, 29–51. DOI: 10.1146/annurev-soc-121919-054857

Khesroh, E., Butt, M., Kalantari, A., Leslie, D. L., Bronson, S., Rigby, A., & Aumiller, B. (2022). The use of emotional intelligence skills in combating burnout among residency and fellowship program directors. *BMC Medical Education, 22*, 127. DOI: 10.1186/s12909-022-03187-z

Lee, M. K. (2018). Understanding perception of algorithmic decisions: Fairness, trust, and emotion in response to algorithmic management. *Big Data & Society, 5*(1), 2053951718756684. Advance online publication. DOI: 10.1177/2053951718756684

Lee, Y., & Chelladurai, P. (2018). Emotional intelligence, emotional labor, coach burnout, job satisfaction, and turnover intention in sport leadership. *European Sport Management Quarterly, 18*(4), 393–412. DOI: 10.1080/16184742.2017.1406971

Leonardi, P. M., & Treem, J. W. (2020). Behavioral visibility: A new paradigm for organization studies in the age of digitization, digitalization, and datafication. *Organization Studies*. Advance online publication. DOI: 10.1177/0170840620970728

Maslach, C., & Jackson, S. E. (1981). The measurement of experienced burnout. *Journal of Organizational Behavior, 2*(2), 99–113. DOI: 10.1002/job.4030020205

Maslach, C., Schaufeli, W. B., & Leiter, M. P. (2001). Job burnout. *Annual Review of Psychology, 52*(1), 397–422. DOI: 10.1146/annurev.psych.52.1.397 PMID: 11148311

Mayer, J. D., & Salovey, P. (1997). What is emotional intelligence? In Salovey, P., & Sluyter, D. J. (Eds.), *Emotional development and emotional intelligence* (pp. 3–34). Basic Books.

Meneghetti, F. K. (2011). O que é um ensaio teórico? *Revista de Administração Contemporânea, 15*(2), 320–332. https://doi.org/DOI: 10.1590/S1415-65552011000200010

Miao, C., Humphrey, R. H., & Qian, S. (2018). A cross-cultural meta-analysis of how leader emotional intelligence influences subordinate task performance and organizational citizenship behavior. *Journal of World Business, 53*(4), 463–474. DOI: 10.1016/j.jwb.2018.01.003

Mikalef, P., & Gupta, M. (2021). Artificial intelligence capability: Conceptualization, measurement calibration, and empirical study on its impact on organizational creativity and firm performance. *Information & Management, 58*(3), 103434. Advance online publication. DOI: 10.1016/j.im.2021.103434

Nam, T. (2019). Technology usage, expected job sustainability, and perceived job insecurity. *Technological Forecasting and Social Change, 138*, 155–165. DOI: 10.1016/j.techfore.2018.08.017

Organisation for Economic Co-operation and Development. (2022). *Promoting health and well-being at work: Policy and practices* (Policy brief). OECD Publishing. https://www.oecd.org/health/promoting-health-and-well-being-at-work-policy-and-practices.pdf

PwC. (2023). 2023 AI business predictions. https://www.pwc.com/us/en/tech-effect/ai-analytics/ai-predictions.html

Raghavan, V., Barocas, S., Kleinberg, J., & Levy, K. (2020). Algorithmic fairness. In *Proceedings of the 2020 Conference on Fairness, Accountability, and Transparency* (pp. 101–112). ACM. https://doi.org/DOI: 10.1145/3351095.3372878

Rother, E. T. (2007). Revisão sistemática versus revisão integrativa. *Acta Paulista de Enfermagem*, *20*(2), v–vi. DOI: 10.1590/S0103-21002007000200001

Russell, S., & Norvig, P. (2021). *Artificial intelligence: A modern approach* (4th ed.). Pearson.

Salovey, P., & Mayer, J. D. (1990). Emotional intelligence. *Imagination, Cognition and Personality*, *9*(3), 185–211. DOI: 10.2190/DUGG-P24E-52WK-6CDG

Sánchez-Gómez, M., & Breso, E. (2020). Emotional intelligence as a moderator. *Psicothema*, *32*(4), 604–611. DOI: 10.7334/psicothema2020.219

Schaufeli, W. B., & Bakker, A. B. (2004). Job demands, job resources, and burnout interventions. *Journal of Organizational Behavior*, *25*(3), 293–315. DOI: 10.1002/job.248

Schaufeli, W. B., Salanova, M., González-Romá, V., & Bakker, A. B. (2002). Engagement and burnout. *Journal of Happiness Studies*, *3*(1), 71–92. DOI: 10.1023/A:1015630930326

Shaban, M., Ezzelregal Abdelgawad, M., Elsayed, S. M., & Abdallah, H. M. M. (2025). The mediating role of emotional intelligence in the relationship between technostress and burnout prevention among critical care nurses: A structural equation modelling approach. *BMC Nursing*, *24*(1), 255. Advance online publication. DOI: 10.1186/s12912-025-02852-0 PMID: 40050866

SHRM. (2023). *AI in HR: The adoption and application of artificial intelligence*. https://www.shrm.org/

Sinval, J., Queirós, C., Pasian, S. R., & Marôco, J. (2019). Transcultural adaptation of the Oldenburg Burnout Inventory. *Frontiers in Psychology*, *10*, 338. Advance online publication. DOI: 10.3389/fpsyg.2019.00338 PMID: 30914985

Tambe, P., Cappelli, P., & Yakubovich, V. (2019). Artificial intelligence in human resources management: Challenges and a path forward. *California Management Review*, *61*(4), 15–42. DOI: 10.1177/0008125619867910

Tarafdar, M., Cooper, C. L., & Stich, J.-F. (2019). The technostress trifecta — techno eustress, techno distress and design: Theoretical directions and an agenda for research. *Information Systems Journal*, *29*(1), 6–42. DOI: 10.1111/isj.12169

Venkatesh, V., Morris, M. G., Davis, G. B., & Davis, F. D. (2003). User acceptance of information technology. *Management Information Systems Quarterly*, *27*(3), 425–478. DOI: 10.2307/30036540

World Health Organization. (2019). ICD-11: International statistical classification of diseases and related health problems. https://icd.who.int/

Zuboff, S. (2019). *The age of surveillance capitalism*. PublicAffairs.

KEY TERMS AND DEFINITIONS

Emotional Intelligence (EI): The capacity to perceive, understand, use, and regulate one's own and others' emotions, functioning as a personal resource that enhances adaptation and well-being in organizational contexts.

Burnout: An occupational syndrome characterized by emotional exhaustion, cynicism toward work, and reduced professional efficacy, resulting from chronic workplace stress inadequately managed.

Artificial Intelligence (AI): Computer systems capable of performing cognitive functions—such as learning, pattern recognition, and decision-making—that would naturally require human intelligence.

Job Demands-Resources Model (JD-R): A theoretical framework explaining how job demands lead to exhaustion (strain pathway) while job and personal resources promote engagement (motivational pathway).

Technostress: Psychological strain resulting from the inability to cope with or adapt to technological demands in the workplace, including information overload, algorithmic surveillance, and continuous connectivity expectations.

Emotional Regulation: The deliberate capacity to modulate the intensity, duration, and expression of emotional responses in adaptive ways, representing a core mechanism through which EI protects against burnout.

Work Engagement: A positive psychological state characterized by vigor, dedication, and absorption, theoretically positioned as the antithesis of burnout on the occupational well-being continuum.

Ethical AI Governance: Organizational practices ensuring transparency, fairness, accountability, and human oversight in the implementation and operation of AI systems, moderating the psychosocial impacts of technology.

Digital Maturity: An organization's capacity to effectively implement, integrate, and leverage digital technologies, including adequate infrastructure, training, and established processes that reduce technostress during AI adoption.

Chapter 11
Fostering Well Being and Mental Health in Human-Centered Organisations:
Employee Well Being, Burnout, Mindful Organising

R. Aadira
http://orcid.org/0009-0009-2979-803X
Saveetha School of Management, Saveetha University, India

G. S. Gigi
http://orcid.org/0009-0000-0552-256X
Saveetha School of Management, Saveetha University, India

ABSTRACT

Employee well-being has emerged as a major concern to contemporary organizations since it influences individual and organizational performance. Studies have revealed that employees feel motivated, committed and more productive when they feel supported and engaged. Organizations integrated between hedonic and eudaimonic strategies to well-being, i.e. emphasize positive emotions and life satisfaction, personal development, meaningful work, and autonomy can enable employees to prosper. HR practices that are human-centered such as flexible work, high-involvement systems, ethical leadership, and wellness programs decrease stress, burnout, and mental health stigma.Companies can achieve sustainable talent management, organizational success and mental health of employees by integrating well-being in organizational culture to form inclusive, ethical and high-performing workplaces that aligns employee mental health with organizational success.

DOI: 10.4018/979-8-2600-2178-1.ch011

INTRODUCTION

The question of employee well being has become one of the key issues in the context of the modern organizational research, as it is a sign of the increasing importance of the employee health and involvement in the context of sustainable organizational performance. The initial research has found out that employee's well being has been associated with positive personal and corporate results. As an example, a study by (Bakker & Demerouti, 2008) has proved that workers with elevated well-being levels are more engaged and also tend to be proactive in achieving organizational objectives. In addition, meta-level studies undertaken by (Judge & Bono, 2001) also support the high positivity of the connection of employee's well-being and results of organisation and emphasize the need to invest strategically in employee wellness programs. The existing literature has confirmed that the practices in human resource management are very important tools that can enable organizations to shape the welfare of employees. (Harter et al., 2002) .In particular, it is indicated that a set of HR's activities can influence the well-being of employees, and the high-performance HR systems have an association with better psychological climates and increased work engagement (Kataria, 2014). Moreover, it has been found that such practices can positively improve the performance of employees due to the impact they have on their physical, social and psychological well-being (Khoreva, 2018). However, more detailed and systematic well-being programs are still necessary because most organizations still underestimate the significance of proactive well-being promotion at the workplace (Synytsia, 2020). The issue is especially acute within the healthcare industry, with the pandemic causing the further worsening of the mental health of the staff members, making the previously effective organizational strategies that have been rooted in shareholder value (Synytsia, 2020) pretty ineffective in an intricate and unpredictable global setting ridden with intersecting societal crises (Fyke & Buzzanell, 2013; Fyke & Buzzanell, 2013).

It is also becoming understood that the purely economic aspect of the topic is not enough to explain the in-depth human aspects of organizational life, and certain challenges like employee burnout rates remain constant (Gogia et al., 2024; Homer-Dixon, 2020). This awareness requires a change of paradigm in favor of humanistic organising, where human dignity and well-being are considered indispensable conditions to organizational success (Cooren et al., 2011; Lee & So, 2007; Nielsen & Einarsen, 2018). Humanistic organizing has a wider understanding of value creation, which takes into account both financial and social results, in contrast to profit maximization that is the focus of humanistic organizing (Glavas & Kelley, 2014; Dutton et al., 2006). The point of view is similar to conscious capitalism (Kabat-Zinn, 2003) and economy of the common good (Dunne, 2015). At the center of this change process is conscious organizational communication, which is a thoughtful and reflective process of interaction inside and outside of the organization. Although traditionally mindfulness has been linked with an individual psychological well-being (Weick et al., 1999; Sharf, 2014; Ghoshal, 2005), the concept of mindfulness applied in an organizational setting (so-called mindful organizing) (Schoeneborn et al., 2014) offers a crucial approach to integrating the humanistic values and establishing ethical, resilient, and sustainable modes of organizing into modern workplaces

1 WELL BEING

1.1 Hedonic VS Eudamonic Well Being

Much of the existing research suggests that academics and practitioners attach significant importance to promoting optimal employee welfare, which goes beyond the efforts of only curing mental issues. Less focus is being devoted to the mental health of the employees compared to the psychological distress, there are studies that have investigated the benefits of increased psychological health, and its relevance to increased individual performance (Carver & Scheier, 2000). The human resources (HR) role in organizations is critical in mitigating such aspects of employee well-being. Several theoretical and empirical models in the literature have confirmed the role of activities of HR in the overall performance of the company (Gupta & Govindarajan, 2000). At the center of hedonic view of well-being is the existence of motivational feelings as opposed to demotivates feelings and includes a cognitive aspect of well-being as it relates to life satisfaction and an affective aspect that deals with emotional well-being (Keyes et al., 2002). Contrary to this, the eudaimonic approach to psychological well-being (PWB), formulated in the 1980s, is based on adult development theory(Ryff et al., 2004). Such a view gives more importance on self-realization, personal development, and independent operation. In line with the conceptualization by Ryff, other studies have identified PWB using those dimensions including, accepting oneself, good social relationship, independence, competency, and continuing development of self (Ryan & Deci, 2000; Fisher, 2014). Structurally and managerially, the organization practices, such as routines of the organisations, restructurable working facilities have been found to promote the psychological well-being of employees (Parameswaran, 2021).

1.2 Mental Health

Economically, vast research has shown that the cost of having workforce with mental issues to the organizations go upto crores each year. (Moitra et al., 2022). The empirical evidence also shows that mentally ill employees have a high tendency to be less productive and have cognitive impairments (Hennekam et al., 2020). The stigmatization by unparalleled assumption that mentally ill employees are naturally less productive than their colleagues continues to reinforce the continued stigmatization in that managers report not wanting to hire mentally ill individuals (Richards, 2012). The previous studies support the idea that mentally ill employees are usually viewed as irrational, unable to compete, and threat to the workforce (Corrigan et al., 2005). In addition to strengthening negative stereotypes, stigma reduces the discriminatory aspects of people with mental illness (Follmer & Jones, 2017), thus determining and limiting the career patterns of such people. On the other hand, consistent employment makes people more functional and recovering as it provides routine and the sense of security towards their well-being and economic independence (van Niekerk, 2009). Most mentally ill people claim that they would like to work (Owens & Wagner, 2015), employed people claim that work is something meaningful and valued in their lives (Eklund et al., 2012).

2 . THEORETICAL FOUNDATIONS LINKING WELL- BEING AND EMPLOYER BRANDING

2.1 Perceived Organisational Support

Rhoades and Eisenberger expounded that POS is organizational support that guarantees the employees that the organization they work in values and takes care of their input and listens to their grievances, is sensitive to their issues in life and that they are treated justly by the organization (Rhoades & Eisenberger, 2002).In this respect, Rhoades and Eisenberger elaborated that POS is organizational support that determines the level of contribution, takes care of the welfare of the employees, hears their complaints, listens to their issues in life and ensures that the employees On the same note, (Ali, 2014) says that POS refers to how much employees are convinced that organizations appreciate their role and care about them. In line with this, according to Rhoades and Eisenberger in (Arshadi & Hayavi, 2013), POS is an organizational perception of the employees.

2.2 Social - Exchange Theory

Social - exchange theory is a general framework that has cut across various fields in social science such as business and social studies. Though the term is a theory, it is not a singular one; rather it is more of many concepts(Rusli et al., 2024). In line, all the social- exchange theories explain social life is the relationship between individuals (Cropanzano & Mitchell, 2005).

2.3 Job - Demand Resource Theory

The concept of job demand is associated with work factors that demand continual investment and thus are associated with physiological and mental expenditures (Mitchell et al., 2012; Demerouti et al., 2001). To address such demands, people deliberately work on the crafting of their job by actively adjusting to demands of the job and available resources (Bakker & Demerouti, 2017; Wrzesniewski & Dutton, 2001). As an illustration, a junior scholar is able to increase the resources available in the job by asking a supervisor to provide regular feedback. These increased job resources then lead to an increased motivation, and thus a new positive self-reinforcing loop, what is sometimes referred to as a gain spiral (Tims et al., 2012). On the other hand, researchers too have highlighted another circumstance, a negative self-reinforcing process that is self-undermining and is also called a loss spiral. Self-undermining refers to the action that leads to creating barriers that can hamper performance (Van Wingerden et al., 2017).

2.4 Psychological Contract Theory

When one of the two involved in the exchange relationship, or, more specifically, the employer, satisfies his or her side of the bargain, or, in other words, the psychological contract (PC) is fulfilled, the other party, i.e., the employee, will most probably pay back by fulfilling his or her part of the deal, thus, fulfilling his or her obligations themselves (Cropanzano et al., 2017). Nevertheless, current research has emphasised largely on the reacts of employees to employer in a negative manner with few exceptions (Tekleab & Taylor, 2003). These reactions are not usually positive, as meta-analytic data prove that employee affect, attitude, and behavior affect by employer PC breach are negative (Bal et al., 2008; Zhao et al., 2007). In addition, the PC of an employee is never fixed but evolves in different stages with time. (Rousseau et al., 2018) developed the Dynamic - Phase Model of that describes the way PC is developed, maintained and changed by an employee during the period of organizational service. According to this model, four major stages are distinguished, which are Creation, Maintenance, Repair, and Renegotiation.

3. IMPORTANCE OF HUMAN- CENTERED WORK PLACE

Human-centered AI (HCAI) paradigm focuses on the development of artificial intelligence systems that are focused on human interests, defending the agency of their users, and promoting their general well-being online. This view is very much related to ethical thinking in the context of user experience when the usability issues and the moral acceptability overlap. Nevertheless, critical researchers like (Ryan, 2024) caution that the anthropocentric approach can be very narrow and it can promote anthropocentrism that might overvalue the power of individual human to the neglect of the ecological, cultural, and shared aspects. The importance of the organizational culture's role is being flexible and connected with the aspects of traditional HR theories is very important (Lepeley et al., 2020). Human based approach to HRM considers employees law using technological advancements to increase productivity. As an illustration, digital space reaches more and more in using algorithms in the process of choosing workers (Köchling & Wehner, 2020). It has been stated that employees must be allowed in the creation and implementation of algorithm-based systems that make some of the basic decisions about their work, such as hiring and compensation choices (Wood et al., 2019). Human-focused HRM lies on the basis of equality where employee enrichment are main. This is the same view as the United Nations in its promise of leaving no one behind is the main principle of the Sustainable Development Goals (McArthur et al., 2018).

4. WORKPLACE STRESSORS AND PSYCHOLOGICAL RISK

Despite the possibility of high workload levels to trigger behaviors, such as self initiative and ability to guide others approaches (58. Job demands can be considered as all that necessitates people to devote more energy and effort to their activities in order to reach some goals and fulfill some needs and even have a chance to grow and develop personally (Bakker & Costa, 2014). Technology in work place may help people do their jobs more easily and reduce their workload, but when it is used in a way that creates stress, it can negatively affect employee's health and well being .(Van den Broeck et al., 2010). The technological shifts have also come with new ills to people at work and in their everyday living (Sandoval-Reyes et al., 2019). Consequently employees may develop insecurities when the exiting technologies get improved day by day eg when software is introduced and employees worry about losing their job because younger colleagues learn it quickly.(Ghislieri et al., 2018; Tims et al., 2015). (Gemmano et al., 2020) and(Tims et al., 2012) According to JD-R theory job crafting is a good strategy where employees can make changes to work according to their wish like tasks, relationship etc to match in a better way in job. Job crafting helps employees adapt to changes in work.People who involve highly in job crafting are more equipped to handle new, challenging situations eg An employee can ask for support or guidance from colleagues when a new technology is tough or A worker reorganising their works so that they can focus more on activities they are good at and less on those that are weak.(Zito et al., 2019). This way, they can manage change by using the resources and decreasing stressors in the workplace (Petrou et al., 2018).

5. OUTCOMES OF WELL BEING ORIENTED ORGANISATIONS

The opportunities of career advancement is critical as it helps in promoting employee wellness and mental health. Previous studies point to the fact that operational fairness is an important interdependent variable that affects the career growth of staff and their psychological well-being (Vakola et al., 2020). There is a further evidence indicating that the realization of professional objectives adds up to the cognitive wellness. In this respect, the COVID-19 pandemic, among others, can be reimagined as the possibility to improve the well-being of the employees by introducing a series of organized career development programs (Tang et al., 2021). Also, quality of work indicates a positive mediating relationship between wellness and quality of work, whereas career outlooks play the role of mediating the connection between work experiences and psychological health (Autin et al., 2020). It has also been defined that operational fairness is a highly important predictor of employees wellness and mental health (Wan & Duffy, 2022). Empirical inquiries show that when operational fairness is positively perceived several positive results, such as enhanced role satisfaction, greater loyalty, better physical health, and overall professional functioning, are observed, which makes career-related activities predictors of health and wellness (Sharma & Kumra, 2020). Research also goes ahead to prove that operational fairness does not only affect the well-being of an individual but also role satisfaction and performance outcomes (Eib et al., 2018). Fair treatment at work place is closely associated with better performance, healthier, happier employees. (Prilleltensky, 2011)Adaptability in the workplace helps people manage stress, feel good and work more effectively.(Alonso & Elovainio, 2022). Specifically, mental adaptability was thus found to be a major determinant that had significant influence on psychological well-being and the performance of work-related behaviors (Kim et al., 2019).

In addition, the flexibility of working hours and places, such as time and space freedom, has turned out to be potentially beneficial to the psychological well-being and health in general (Bond et al., 2013). In line with this, flexible work arrangements have been linked to positive health and wellness outcomes by giving the employees more autonomy and control in their workplace (Kirwin & Ettinger, 2022). Also, the research evidence suggests that career readiness is positively linked to psychological health of new employees when they have positive relationships with both their managers and colleagues (Graham, 2014). Research also indicates that peer support can be effective than the managerial support in protecting the psychological health.

Additionally, the level of peer support and autonomy in performing tasks have been reported to impact the cognitive wellness of the employees in a positive way (Kawai & Yamazaki, 2006). One can also notice that the improvement of the relations with the managers and colleagues, as well as the decrease in the mental stress can greatly decrease the chance of illness-related absenteeism (Di Marco et al., 2018).

6 .ETHICAL ORGANISATIONAL CLIMATE AND ITS EFFECT EMPLOYEE'S MENTAL HEALTH

A postulation forwarded by (Bala & Pandve, 2021) was that the organizational climate would directly affect the outcome of the work, in a positive or a negative way. In particular, positive work incentives like appealing work environment, sound personnel policies, benefits package, good job designs and competitive remunerations make the work interesting and provide an enabling environment which motivates employees. (Stokes et al., 2013) on the contrary pointed out that negative work incentives, which make work uninterested, unchallenging, or disappointing, may increase absenteeism, turnover, and workplace accidents. The Conservation of Resources (COR) theory suggests that people make effort to obtain, sustain, and safeguard resources that are necessary in coping with stress and sustaining a mental state. In an ethical work climate, emotional support, fair practices, and ethical leadership are the resources that are important in minimizing stresses at work and enhancing positive mental states (Dineen & Allen, 2016). Besides, ethical leadership plays a core role in building a supportive environment among the staff, which subsequently decreases burnout and improves mental health outcomes (Hobfoll et al., 2018). Organizational climates that are supportive are typified by a sense of pride in the employees, reasonable remunerations, and consideration of staff needs, in these situations the employees feel that their time and efforts are safe thus leading to greater levels of commitment and performance (Borelli et al., 2025). The education sector is one of the most important areas where the ethical climate should be critically established in academic integrity, fair assessment, and inclusiveness, which is also supported by equality, diversity, and governance policies. The ethical cultures within educational establishments are upheld with the help of clear grading, fair treatment of students and employees, and compliance with the existing academic ethical rules (Stokes et al., 2013). Also, corporate social responsibility (CSR) programs contribute to better ethical climates as managing environmental, social, and governance (ESG) issues leads to enhanced perceptions of fairness and lessens work-related stress among employees (Kong, 2024).Although adherence to the law will keep everything within the framework, ethical leadership and employee involvement is also vital in terms of maintaining ethical climates. In turn, the companies that have high ethical climates are always characterized by a greater level of employee satisfaction, lower turnover, and better mental health (Crane et al., 2020).

6.1 Real Life Implications of Organisational Climates on Mental Health

The Unilever, Patagonia, Google, and Wells Fargo case studies help to demonstrate the actual, concrete implications of ethical working environments on the mental well being of employees. As an example, the Project Aristotle that Google conducted showed that enhancing psychological safety by maintaining ethical leadership was an efficient way to decrease anxiety and burnout in workforce members (Mayer et al., 2012; Newman et al., 2017). In addition, Satya Nadella made empathy as a core value stating employees choice must be taken into account while decision making. This intentional change of ethics and inclusive environment has subsequently facilitated greater employee engagement and innovation which consequently has led to massive changes in product development and company's results (Kim et al., 2020). On the same note, Patagonia has given rights fpr their employees to voice out for ethical concerns like safety violations that could harm people or the environment, Unfair treatment of employees or supplier, environmental harm which is caused by company which has resulted in positive ways such as employees feel valued and involved employees contribute more ideas and improvements (Smith et al., 2013).

7. WELL BEING THROUGH DIVERSITY AND ETHICAL HRM

The diversity-centered corporate- social responsibility (CSR) activities incline towars greatly to human resource management (HRM) through the fair treatment and granting of equal opportunities to every employee. As an example, a recent study by. (Guerreiro et al., 2023) shows that diversity-oriented CSR initiatives enhance contentment at work and decrease resigning ideas of employees, especially minority groups. Likewise, the study by (Makhbul et al., 2024) has revealed that in those cases where CSR efforts go hand in hand with the diversity effort, the employees demonstrate greater organizational commitment and loyalty since they feel valued and honored. Also, in addition to facilitating engagement, HRM practices that value diversity and inclusion generate good leadership and transparency in organizational leadership. In line with this, (Appolloni et al., 2025) found out that companies that are highly dedicated to diversity and CSR will make ethical decisions and their work environment focuses on the satisfaction of employees. Moreover, diversity and inclusion programs serve as an intermediary between CSR activities and how the employees perceive their work, making the workplace more supportive and fair in general. In turn, (Abuzaid et al., 2024) believe that the inclusion of diversity in the context of CSR enhances the levels of employee satisfaction and psychological health. Moreover, the encouragement of inclusive practices also enhances the sense of belonging in employees, which helps to reinforce the impression of CSR on well-being. It has been shown that diversity-based CSR initiatives including gender equality initiatives, inclusive recruitment and employee resource groups contribute to job satisfaction and organizational trust. Moreover, (Cavicchioli & Kocollari, 2024) underlines the fact that employees at diverse workplaces feel increased psychological safety, which lowers stress and serves as a contributor to mental health. Lastly, (Han et al., 2024) demonstrate that underrepresented employees who work in an inclusive organization having a strong CSR policy can experience a higher work-life balance and emotional well-being. To sum up, (Li et al., 2024) believe that CSR initiatives should be the most efficient when companies build the culture of inclusiveness that acknowledges the needs of diverse workers.

8. PRACTICAL RECOMMENDATIONS FOR MANAGERS AND HR PROFESSIONALS

According to the explanation by (Tang et al., 2023), the paradigmatic evolution of the traditional compartmentalization shift implies that the organizational priorities and practices have to be reconsidered. Following this, Luthans et al. (Rugulies, 2012) highlight that environment that encompasses the principles of well-being in the organizational culture is critical to ensuring the flourishing of employees. This point of view is developed by recent studies, suggest training and development programs as the way to improve the well-being of employees and their resilience. In particular, the article by (Luthans et al., 2007) shows that the use of specific interventions aimed at helping employees manage stress, emotional intelligence, and mindfulness will help them improve the quality of coping strategies, which, in addition to personal well-being, will contribute to improving the overall organizational performance. The same results are supported by (Smith & Williams, 2023) that demonstrate that these interventions are effective in the stress reduction and positive mental health results among the employees. Organisations can enhance the employees ability o bounce back from negative emotions and capacity to handle work related stress by developing skills mainly through psychological flexibility interventions like ACT (Aikens et al., 2014). Development of emotional intelligence and the culture of psychological safety, which complements these strategies, have been found to help employees feel better and lead to improved performance at the organizational level. Employee assistance programs and peer support networks are some of the initiatives in this context that offer the social and structural support required by the employees to deal with stressors at work and become resilient (Zarvijani et al., 2021).The practical effect of such programs also takes place, as (Park & Lee, 2023) inform about the fact that the implementation of the wellness programs in the organization leads to a decrease in absenteeism, increase of productivity, and a decrease in the cost of healthcare. (Campbell et al., 2016)Mental health week being programs like emotional intelligence training, mindfulness improves employee's content-fullness at work, enthusiasm at work and low turnover. Despite knowing that mental health initiatives are beneficial, organizations may struggle to implement them because of cultural barriers especially the social stigma of mental health in the workplace.(Rich et al., 2017). In order to overcome these challenges, organizations ought to carry out detailed needs assessment in order to discover workforce-specific well being problems and opportunities. The inclusion of employees into the designing and the execution of these initiatives can also contribute to their relevance, acceptance, and success (Rugulies, 2012). Organizations must promote work-life balance, mental health, policies to align with values, strengthen reputation, attract and retain talent. (Nielsen et al., 2017; Marsh et al., 2018). Taken together, these initiatives support the fact that the well-being needs to be integrated into organizational culture as a strategic issue, but not an incidental one.

9. FUTURE RESEARCH DIMENSIONS

Companies that embrace these principles improve the engagements and productivity of employees as well as reputation. Evidence-based insights into how well-being initiatives affect loyalty, motivation, and organizational commitment should be investigated in further studies as evidence-based recommendations on how ethical talents management practices should be. Digital technologies, such as AI, algorithmic management, and surveillance systems, have their opportunities and risks. Studies are required to investigate the morality of practices based on technology especially their consequences on mental health and work-life limits. Internationally affecting crises, including pandemics, financial unpredictability, and climate-related disruptions, also support the necessity of the workforce resilience. Exploring the possibility of the organizational way of supporting employees during uncertain moments in an ethical way could improve the confidence, involvement, and the value of the employer brand. Some of the gaps that exist are lack of cross-cultural research, paucity of longitudinal studies on prolonged effects of well-being programs on both workers outcome and reputation of the organization. Further studies integrating quantitative and qualitative design can provide practical results to human-focused strategies that support employee welfare and ethically-based employer branding, which can ensure long-term talent management in high-performing work conditions.

10. CONCLUSION

Well being of the employees has become a strategic need whose benefits go beyond reducing the occurrence of mental illness to the overall performance of the company. By incorporating hedonic and eudaimonic views, organizations are able to nurture good emotions, life satisfaction, personal development, autonomy and meaningful work relationships and hence promote a well-rounded psychological wellbeing. Human-centered HR activities such as flexible working, high-involvement systems and ethical leaders help to establish conducive working conditions that minimize stress, burnout, and stigma related to mental health issues. Theoretical models, all highlight the mutual dependence of organizational support, the well-being of employees, and the results of their performance. Empirical interventions, such as resilience training, mindfulness programs, career development programs, peer support networks, and wellness programs, have been proven to have demonstrable effects on engagement and satisfaction, retention, and productivity. The organizational plans of the future need to focus on the evaluation of the needs related to the workforce, engagement of employees in the process of intervention design and management of the emerging ethical issues of the digital technologies, AI, and algorithmic management. The longitudinal and cross-cultural study analyzes the prolonged effect of goodness programs on being loyal, motivated, committed to the organization, and branded by the employer. Incorporating well-being within the organizational culture allows organizations to create ethical, inclusive and high-performing working environments which alligns mental health, sustainable talent management, and improved employee and organizational performance.

REFERENCES

Abuzaid, A. N., Al-Faouri, E. H., Alateeq, M. M., Madadha, S.-M., Ghadi, M. Y., Al-Qatawenh, A. S., Abdelkarim Almajali, D., & Almajali, H. A. K. (2024). The relationship between perceptions of high-performance work systems and corporate social responsibility (CSR) considering the moderating effect of a positive diversity climate. *Sustainability (Basel)*, *16*(10), 4267. DOI: 10.3390/su16104267

Aikens, K. A., Astin, J., Pelletier, K. R., Levanovich, K., Baase, C. M., Park, Y. Y., & Bodnar, C. M. (2014). Mindfulness goes to work: Impact of an online workplace intervention. *Journal of Occupational and Environmental Medicine*, *56*(7), 721–731. DOI: 10.1097/JOM.0000000000000209

Ali, H. (2014). Perceived organizational support and organizational citizenship behavior: The case of Kuwait. *International Journal of Business Administration*, *5*(3), 59–59. DOI: 10.5430/ijba.v5n3p59

Alonso, L., & Elovainio, M. (2022). Organizational justice and health: Reviewing two decades of studies. *Journal of Theoretical Social Psychology*, *2022*, 1–13. DOI: 10.1155/2022/3218883

Appolloni, A., Liu, J., Zhang, Y., & Li, Y. (2025). Linking top management commitment and circular practice through human resource perspective: Do diversity, equity, and inclusion (DEI) make a difference in corporate responsibility? *Corporate Social Responsibility and Environmental Management*, *32*(2), 2746–2768. Advance online publication. DOI: 10.1002/csr.3099

Arshadi, N., & Hayavi, G. (2013). The effect of perceived organizational support on affective commitment and job performance: Mediating role of OBSE. *Procedia: Social and Behavioral Sciences*, *84*, 739–743. DOI: 10.1016/j.sbspro.2013.06.637

Autin, K., Blustein, D., Ali, S., & Garriott, P. (2020). Career development impacts of COVID-19: Practice and policy recommendations. *Journal of Career Development*, *47*(5), 487–494. DOI: 10.1177/0894845320944486

Bakker, A. B., & Costa, P. L. (2014). Chronic job burnout and daily functioning: A theoretical analysis. *Burnout Research*, *1*(3), 112–119. DOI: 10.1016/j.burn.2014.04.003

Bakker, A. B., & Demerouti, E. (2008). Towards a model of work engagement. *Career Development International*, *13*(3), 209–223. DOI: 10.1108/13620430810870476

Bakker, A. B., & Demerouti, E. (2017). Job demands-resources theory: Taking stock and looking forward. *Journal of Occupational Health Psychology, 22*(3), 273–285. DOI: 10.1037/ocp0000056

Bal, P. M., De Lange, A. H., Jansen, P. G., & Van Der Velde, M. E. (2008). Psychological contract breach and job attitudes: A meta-analysis of age as a moderator. *Journal of Vocational Behavior, 72*(1), 143–158. DOI: 10.1016/j.jvb.2007.10.005

Bala, S. B. N., & Pandve, H. (2021). Prevalence and factors associated with sickness absenteeism among pharmaceutical industrial workers of Hyderabad, India. *Asian Journal of Medical Sciences, 12*(1), 81–86. DOI: 10.3126/ajms.v12i2.31211

Bond, F., Lloyd, J., & Guenole, N. (2013). The work-related acceptance and action questionnaire: Initial psychometric findings. *Journal of Occupational and Organizational Psychology, 86*(3), 331–347. DOI: 10.1111/joop.12001

Borelli, J. L., Wang, Y., Li, F. H., Russo, L. N., Tironi, M., Yamashita, K., Zhou, E., Lai, J., Nguyen, B., Azimi, I., Marcotullio, C., Labbaf, S., Jafarlou, S., Dutt, N., & Rahmani, A. (2025). Detection of depressive symptoms in college students using multimodal passive sensing data and light gradient boosting machine: Longitudinal pilot study. *JMIR Formative Research, 9*, e67964. DOI: 10.2196/67964

Campbell, M., Thomson, H., Fenton, C., & Gibson, M. (2016). Lone parents, health, wellbeing and welfare to work: A systematic review of qualitative studies. *BMC Public Health, 16*(1), 188. Advance online publication. DOI: 10.1186/s12889-016-2880-9

Carver, C. S., & Scheier, M. F. (2000). Control processes and self-organization as complementary principles underlying behaviour. *Personality and Social Psychology Review : An Official Journal of the Society for Personality and Social Psychology, Inc., 6*(4), 304–315. DOI: 10.1207/S15327957PSPR0604_05

Cavicchioli, M., & Kocollari, U. (2024). The 5 E(lements) of employee-centric corporate social responsibility and their stimulus on happiness at work. *Corporate Social Responsibility and Environmental Management, 31*(3), 1959–1976. DOI: 10.1002/csr.2667

Cooren, F., Kuhn, T., Cornelissen, J. P., & Clark, T. (2011). Communication, organizing and organization: An overview and introduction to the special issue. *Organization Studies, 32*(9), 1149–1170. DOI: 10.1177/0170840611410836

Corrigan, P. W., Kerr, A., & Knudsen, L. (2005). The stigma of mental illness: Explanatory models and methods for change. *Applied & Preventive Psychology, 11*(3), 179–190. DOI: 10.1016/j.appsy.2005.07.001

Crane, M. F., Kangas, M., Karin, E., Searle, B., & Chen, D. (2020). Leveraging the experience of stressors: The role of adaptive systematic self-reflection. *Anxiety, Stress, and Coping*, *33*(3), 231–247. DOI: 10.1080/10615806.2020.1732359

Cropanzano, R., Anthony, E. L., Daniels, S. R., & Hall, A. V. (2017). Social exchange theory: A critical review with theoretical remedies. *The Academy of Management Annals*, *11*(1), 479–516. DOI: 10.5465/annals.2015.0099

Cropanzano, R., & Mitchell, M. S. (2005). Social exchange theory: An interdisciplinary review. *Journal of Management*, *31*(6), 874–900. DOI: 10.1177/0149206305279602

Demerouti, E., Bakker, A. B., Nachreiner, F., & Schaufeli, W. B. (2001). The job demands-resources model of burnout. *The Journal of Applied Psychology*, *86*(3), 499–512. DOI: 10.1037/0021-9010.86.3.499

Di Marco, M., Venter, O., Possingham, H. P., & Watson, J. E. M. (2018). Changes in human footprint drive changes in species extinction risk. *Nature Communications*, *9*(1), 4621. DOI: 10.1038/s41467-018-07049-5

Dineen, B. R., & Allen, D. G. (2016). Third party employment branding: Human capital inflows and outflows following "Best Places to Work" certifications. *Academy of Management Journal*, *59*(1), 90–112. DOI: 10.5465/amj.2013.1091

Dunne, J. D. (2015). Buddhist styles of mindfulness: A heuristic approach. In Ostafin, B. D., Robinson, M. D., & Meier, B. P. (Eds.), *Handbook of Mindfulness and Self-Regulation* (pp. 251–270). Springer., DOI: 10.1007/978-1-4939-2263-5_18

Dutton, J. E., Worline, M. C., Frost, P. J., & Lilius, J. (2006). Explaining compassion organizing. *Administrative Science Quarterly*, *51*(1), 59–96. DOI: 10.2189/asqu.51.1.59

Eib, C., Bernhard-Oettel, C., Hanson, L., & Leineweber, C. (2018). Organizational justice and health: Studying mediators and lagged relationships. *Journal of Occupational Health Psychology*, *23*(4), 553–567. DOI: 10.1037/ocp0000115

Eklund, M., Hermansson, A., & Håkansson, C. (2012). Meaning in life for people with schizophrenia: Does it include occupation? *Journal of Occupational Science*, *19*(2), 93–105. DOI: 10.1080/14427591.2011.605833

Fisher, C. D. (2014). Conceptualizing and measuring wellbeing at work. In Chen, P. Y., & Cooper, C. L. (Eds.), *Work and wellbeing* (pp. 9–33). Wiley Blackwell., DOI: 10.1002/9781118539415.wbwell018

Follmer, K. B., & Jones, K. S. (2017). Stereotype content and social distancing from employees with mental illness: The moderating roles of gender and social dominance orientation. *Journal of Applied Social Psychology*, *47*(9), 492–504. DOI: 10.1111/jasp.12455

Fyke, J. P., & Buzzanell, P. M. (2013). The ethics of conscious capitalism: Wicked problems in leading change and changing leaders. *Human Relations; Studies Towards the Integration of the Social Sciences*, *66*(12), 1545–1569. DOI: 10.1177/0018726713485306

Fyke, J. P., & Buzzanell, P. M. (2013). The ethics of conscious capitalism: Wicked problems in leading change and changing leaders. *Human Relations; Studies Towards the Integration of the Social Sciences*, *66*(12), 1545–1569. DOI: 10.1177/0018726713485306

Gemmano, G., Signore, F., Caffò, A. O., Palmisano, G. L., Bosco, A., & Manuti, A. (2020). Work engagement and job crafting as conditions of ambivalent employees' adaptation to organizational change. *The Journal of Applied Behavioral Science*, *57*, 57–79. DOI: 10.5465/AMBPP.2019.14266

Ghislieri, C., Molino, M., & Cortese, C. G. (2018). Work and organizational psychology looks at the fourth industrial revolution: How to support workers and organizations? *Frontiers in Psychology*, *9*, 2365. DOI: 10.3389/fpsyg.2018.02365

Ghoshal, S. (2005). Bad management theories are destroying good management practices. *Academy of Management Learning & Education*, *4*(1), 75–91. DOI: 10.5465/amle.2005.16132558

Glavas, A., & Kelley, K. (2014). The effects of perceived corporate social responsibility on employee attitudes. *Business Ethics Quarterly*, *24*(2), 165–202. DOI: 10.5840/beq20143206

Gogia, E. H., Shao, Z., Khan, K., Rehman, M. Z., Haddad, H., & Al-Ramahi, N. M. (2024). Exploring the relationship of organizational virtuousness, citizenship behavior, job performance, and combatting ostracism through structural equation modeling. *BMC Psychology*, *12*(1), 384. DOI: 10.1186/s40359-024-01873-9

Graham, C. (2014). Late-life work and well-being. *IZA World of Labor: Evidence-Based Policy Making*. Advance online publication. DOI: 10.15185/izawol.107

Guerreiro, M., Muhs, C., Carvalho Neves, M., Engel, L., & Fernandes Cardoso, L. (2023). Green marketing: A case study of the outdoor apparel brand Patagonia. *Responsibility and Sustainability*, *8*(2), 49–57. DOI: 10.5281/zenodo.8078762

Gupta, A. K., & Govindarajan, V. (2000). Knowledge flows within multinational corporations. *Strategic Management Journal*, *21*(4), 473–496. DOI: 10.1002/(SICI)1097-0266(200004)21:4<473::AID-SMJ84>3.0.CO;2-I

Han, X., Li, Q., & Wang, X. (2024). Investigating how corporate social responsibility affects employees' thriving at work: A social exchange perspective. *Sustainability (Basel)*, *16*(3), 1095. DOI: 10.3390/su16031095

Harter, J. K., Schmidt, F. L., & Hayes, T. L. (2002). Business-unit-level relationship between employee satisfaction, employee engagement, and business outcomes: A meta-analysis. *The Journal of Applied Psychology*, *87*(2), 268–279. DOI: 10.1037/0021-9010.87.2.268

Hennekam, S., Richard, S., & Grima, F. (2020). Coping with mental health conditions at work and its impact on self-perceived job performance. *Employee Relations*, *42*(3), 626–645. DOI: 10.1108/ER-05-2019-0211

Hobfoll, S. E., Halbesleben, J., Neveu, J.-P., & Westman, M. (2018). Conservation of resources in the organizational context: The reality of resources and their consequences. *Annual Review of Organizational Psychology and Organizational Behavior*, *5*(1), 103–128. DOI: 10.1146/annurev-orgpsych-032117-104640

Homer-Dixon, T. (2020). The age of global risk: Three responses. *Global Policy*, *11*(5), 547–556. DOI: 10.1111/1758-5899.12849

Judge, T. A., & Bono, J. E. (2001). Relationship of core self-evaluations traits—self-esteem, generalized self-efficacy, locus of control, and emotional stability—with job satisfaction and job performance: A meta-analysis. *The Journal of Applied Psychology*, *86*(1), 80–92. DOI: 10.1037/0021-9010.86.1.80

Kabat-Zinn, J. (2003). Mindfulness-based interventions in context: Past, present, and future. *Clinical Psychology : a Publication of the Division of Clinical Psychology of the American Psychological Association*, *10*(2), 144–156. DOI: 10.1093/clipsy.bpg016

Kataria, A. (2014). High performance HR practices and employee well-being: A mediation model. *Human Resource Management*, *53*(3), 407–426. DOI: 10.1002/hrm.21608

Kawai, K., & Yamazaki, Y. (2006). The effects of pre-entry career maturity and support networks on newcomers' mental health. *Journal of Occupational Health*, *48*(6), 451–461. DOI: 10.1539/joh.48.451

Keyes, C. L., Schmotkin, D., & Ryff, C. D. (2002). Optimizing well-being: The empirical encounter of two traditions. *Journal of Personality and Social Psychology*, *82*(6), 1007–1022. DOI: 10.1037/0022-3514.82.6.1007

Khoreva, V. (2018). High performance work systems and employee well-being: An investigation of the mediating role of job crafting. *International Journal of Human Resource Management*, *29*(17), 2579–2600. DOI: 10.1080/09585192.2016.1277822

Kim, J., Henly, J. R., Golden, L. M., & Lambert, S. J. (2019). Workplace flexibility and worker well-being by gender. *Journal of Marriage and the Family*, *82*(3), 892–910. DOI: 10.1111/jomf.12633

Kim, S., Lee, H., & Connerton, T. P. (2020). How psychological safety affects team performance: Mediating role of efficacy and learning behavior. *Frontiers in Psychology*, *11*, 1581. DOI: 10.3389/fpsyg.2020.01581

Kirwin, M., & Ettinger, A. (2022). Working mothers during COVID-19: A cross-sectional study. *BMC Public Health*, *22*(1), 435. Advance online publication. DOI: 10.1186/s12889-021-12468-z

Köchling, A., & Wehner, M. C. (2020). Discriminated by an algorithm: A systematic review of discrimination and fairness by algorithmic decision-making in the context of HR recruitment and HR development. *Business Research*, *13*(3), 795–848. DOI: 10.1007/s40685-020-00134-w

Kong, K. G. (2024). Prevailing moral standards in higher education institutions. International Journal on Culture, History, &. *Religion*, *6*(2), 32–42. DOI: 10.63931/ijchr.v6i2.4

Lee, M. Y. P., & So, D. W. C. (2007). Corporate slogans of corporations operating in Greater China. *Corporate Communications*, *12*(1), 58–74. DOI: 10.1108/13563280710723750

Lepeley, M. T., Kuschel, K., Beutell, N., Pouw, N., & Eijdenberg, E. L. (Eds.). (2020). *The wellbeing of women in entrepreneurship: A global perspective*. Routledge., DOI: 10.4324/9780429279836

Li, R. Y. M., Alzuman, A., & Manta, O. (2024). Balancing wellbeing and responsibility: CSR's role in mitigating burnout in hospitality under UN-SDGs. *Sustainability (Basel)*, *16*(8), 3374. DOI: 10.3390/su16083374

Luthans, F., Youssef, C. M., & Avolio, B. J. (2007). *Psychological capital: Developing the human competitive edge*. Oxford University Press., DOI: 10.1093/acprof:oso/9780195187526.001.0001

Makhbul, Z. K. M., Alam, S. S., & Zihan, W. (2024). Green human resource management in practice: Assessing the impact of readiness and corporate social responsibility on organizational change. *Sustainability (Basel)*, *16*(3), 1153. DOI: 10.3390/su16031153

Marsh, G., Lewis, V., Macmillan, J., & Gruszin, S. (2018). Workplace wellness: Industry associations are well placed and some are ready to take a more active role in workplace health. *BMC Health Services Research*, *18*(1), 565. DOI: 10.1186/s12913-018-3364-7

Mayer, D. M., Kuenzi, M., Greenbaum, R., Bardes, M., & Salvador, R. (2012). How low is ethical leadership flow? Test of a trickle-down model. *Organizational Behavior and Human Decision Processes*, *108*(1), 1–13. DOI: 10.1016/j.obhdp.2008.04.002

McArthur, J. W., Rasmussen, K., & Rozema, J. G. (2018). Who and what gets left behind? Assessing Canada's domestic status on the Sustainable Development Goals. *Canadian Public Policy*, *44*(supplement 1), S26–S42. DOI: 10.3138/cpp.2017-061

Mitchell, M. S., Cropanzano, R., & Quisenberry, D. M. (2012). Social exchange theory, exchange resources, and interpersonal relationships: A modest resolution of theoretical difficulties. In Törnblom, K., & Kazemi, A. (Eds.), *Handbook of social resource theory: Theoretical extensions, empirical insights, and social applications* (pp. 99–118). Springer., DOI: 10.1007/978-1-4614-4175-5_6

Moitra, P., Santomauro, D. F., Collins, P. Y., Vos, T., & Whiteford, H. (2022). The global gap in treatment coverage for major depressive disorder: A systematic review and Bayesian meta-regression analysis. *PLoS Medicine*, *19*(2), e1003901. DOI: 10.1371/journal.pmed.1003901

Newman, A., Donohue, R., & Eva, N. (2017). Psychological safety: A systematic review of the literature. *Human Resource Management Review*, *27*(3), 521–535. DOI: 10.1016/j.hrmr.2017.01.001

Nielsen, K., & Einarsen, S. (2018). Outcomes of exposure to workplace bullying: A meta-analytic review. *Work and Stress*, *32*(1), 1–23. DOI: 10.1080/02678373.2022.2080775

Nielsen, K., Nielsen, M. B., Ogbonnaya, C., Känsälä, M., Saari, E., & Isaksson, K. (2017). Workplace resources to improve both employee well-being and performance: A systematic review and meta-analysis. *Work and Stress*, *31*(2), 101–120. DOI: 10.1080/02678373.2017.1304463

Owens, E. G., & Wagner, S. L. (2015). Barriers to employment for people with severe mental illness: A review, and implications for supported employment approaches. *Work : A Journal of Prevention, Assessment, and Rehabilitation*, *50*(2), 309–320. DOI: 10.3233/WOR-152085

Parameswaran, H. (2021). Flexible work designs, as a strategic tool for twenty-first-century intricacies: A descriptive analysis amongst healthcare employees in the United Arab Emirates. *Acta Polytechnica Hungarica*, *18*(11), 135–150. DOI: 10.12700/APH.18.11.2021.11.8

Park, H., & Lee, K. S. (2023). The association of adolescents' mental health with economic impact during the COVID-19 pandemic: A nationally representative survey. *BMC Public Health*, *23*, 853. DOI: 10.1186/s12889-023-15808-3

Petrou, P., Demerouti, E., & Schaufeli, W. B. (2018). Crafting the change: The role of employee job crafting behaviors for successful organizational change. *Journal of Management*, *44*(5), 1766–1792. DOI: 10.1177/0149206315624961

Prilleltensky, I. (2011). Wellness as fairness. *American Journal of Community Psychology*, *49*(1–2), 1–21. DOI: 10.1007/s10464-011-9448-8

Rhoades, L., & Eisenberger, R. (2002). Perceived organizational support: A review of the literature. *The Journal of Applied Psychology*, *87*(4), 698–714. DOI: 10.1037/0021-9010.87.4.698

Rich, S. A., Hanna, S., Wright, B. J., & Bennett, P. C. (2017). Fact or fable: Increased wellbeing in voluntary simplicity. *International Journal of Wellbeing*, *7*(2), 64–77. DOI: 10.5502/ijw.v7i2.589

Richards, J. (2012). Examining the exclusion of employees with Asperger syndrome from the workplace. *Personnel Review*, *41*(5), 630–646. DOI: 10.1108/00483481211249148

Rousseau, D. M., Hansen, S. D., & Tomprou, M. (2018). A dynamic phase model of psychological contract processes. *Journal of Organizational Behavior*, *39*(9), 1081–1098. DOI: 10.1002/job.2284

Rugulies, R. (2012). Studying the effect of the psychosocial work environment on risk of ill-health: Towards a more comprehensive assessment of working conditions. *Scandinavian Journal of Work, Environment & Health*, *38*(3), 187–191. DOI: 10.5271/sjweh.3296

Rugulies, R. (2012). Studying the effect of the psychosocial work environment on risk of ill-health: Towards a more comprehensive assessment of working conditions. *Scandinavian Journal of Work, Environment & Health, 38*(3), 187–191. DOI: 10.5271/sjweh.3296

Rusli, U., Masnia, M., Usman, A., & Mediaty, M. (2024). The role of supply chain management in enhancing corporate operational performance: A systematic literature review. *Indonesian Interdisciplinary Journal of Sharia Economics, 8*(1), 1076–1090. DOI: 10.31538/iijse.v8i1.5981

Ryan, M. (2024). We're only human after all: A critique of human-centered AI. *AI & Society*. Advance online publication. DOI: 10.1007/s00146-024-01976-2

Ryan, R. M., & Deci, E. L. (2000). Self-determination theory and the facilitation of intrinsic motivation, social development, and well-being. *The American Psychologist, 55*(1), 68–78. DOI: 10.1037/0003-066X.55.1.68

Ryff, C. D., Singer, B. H., & Love, G. D. (2004). Positive health: Connecting well-being with biology. *Philosophical Transactions of the Royal Society of London. Series B, Biological Sciences, 359*(1449), 1383–1394. DOI: 10.1098/rstb.2004.1521

Sandoval-Reyes, J., Acosta-Prado, J. C., & Sanchís-Pedregosa, C. (2019). Relationship amongst technology use, work overload, and psychological detachment from work. *International Journal of Environmental Research and Public Health, 16*(23), 4602. DOI: 10.3390/ijerph16234602

Schoeneborn, D., Blaschke, S., & Cooren, F. (2014). Communication theory and its use in organization studies. *Organization Studies, 35*(2), 173–202. DOI: 10.1177/0170840613509966

Sharf, R. (2014). Mindfulness and meditation: Traditional Buddhist sources and modern interpretations. *Journal of the American Academy of Religion, 83*(3), 461–487. DOI: 10.1093/jaarel/lfu045

Sharma, P. K., & Kumra, R. (2020). Relationship between workplace spirituality, organizational justice and mental health: Mediation role of employee engagement. *Journal of Advances in Management Research, 17*(5), 627–650. DOI: 10.1108/JAMR-01-2020-0007

Smith, K. A., & Williams, R. S. (2023). Targeted training interventions for employee well-being: A meta-analysis. *The Journal of Applied Psychology, 109*(2), 210–224. DOI: 10.1037/apl0000910

Smith, W. K., Gonin, M., & Besharov, M. L. (2013). Managing social-business tensions: A review and research agenda for social enterprise. *Business Ethics Quarterly, 23*(3), 407–442. DOI: 10.5840/beq201323327

Stokes, P., Larson, M., Balasubrahmanyam, S., Singh, S. K., Jain, A. K., Giga, S. I., & Cooper, C. L. (2013). Perceived organizational support as a moderator in the relationship between organisational stressors and organizational citizenship behaviors. *The International Journal of Organizational Analysis, 21*(3), 313–334. DOI: 10.1108/IJOA-Mar-2012-0574

Stokes, P., Larson, M., Balasubrahmanyam, S., Singh, S. K., Jain, A. K., Giga, S. I., & Cooper, C. L. (2013). Perceived organizational support as a moderator in the relationship between organisational stressors and organizational citizenship behaviors. *The International Journal of Organizational Analysis, 21*(3), 313–334. DOI: 10.1108/IJOA-Mar-2012-0574

Synytsia, A. (2020). Education as a Means of Affirming Democracy Values in John Dewey's Pragmatism: Modern Perspective. *Journal of Education Culture and Society, 11*(1), 30–41. DOI: 10.15503/jecs2020.1.30.41

Tang, A. D., Luu, T. T., & Chen, W. K. (2023). Internal corporate social responsibility and customer-oriented organizational citizenship behavior: The mediating roles of job satisfaction, work-family facilitation, life satisfaction, and affective commitment. *Journal of Sustainable Tourism, 32*(5), 986–1007. DOI: 10.1080/09669582.2023.2195134

Tang, M., Montgomery, M., Collins, B., & Jenkins, K. (2021). Integrating career and mental health counseling: Necessity and strategies. *Journal of Employment Counseling, 58*(1), 23–35. DOI: 10.1002/joec.12155

Tekleab, A. G., & Taylor, M. S. (2003). Aren't there two parties in an employment relationship? Antecedents and consequences of organization-employee agreement on contract obligations & violations. *Journal of Organizational Behavior, 24*(5), 585–608. DOI: 10.1002/job.204

Tims, M., Bakker, A. B., & Derks, D. (2012). Development and validation of the job crafting scale. *Journal of Vocational Behavior, 80*(1), 173–186. DOI: 10.1016/j.jvb.2011.05.009

Tims, M., Bakker, A. B., & Derks, D. (2012). Development and validation of the job crafting scale. *Journal of Vocational Behavior, 80*(1), 173–186. DOI: 10.1016/j.jvb.2011.05.009

Tims, M., Bakker, A. B., & Derks, D. (2015). Job crafting and its relationships with person-job fit and meaningfulness: A three-wave study. *Journal of Vocational Behavior, 91*, 87–96. DOI: 10.1016/j.jvb.2015.11.007

Vakola, M., Petrou, P., & Katsaros, K. (2020). Work engagement and job crafting as conditions of ambivalent employees' adaptation to organizational change. *The Journal of Applied Behavioral Science, 57*(1), 57–79. DOI: 10.1177/0021886320967173

Van den Broeck, A., Vansteenkiste, M., De Witte, H., Soenens, B., & Lens, W. (2010). Capturing autonomy, competence, and relatedness at work: Construction and initial validation of the work-related basic need satisfaction scale. *Journal of Occupational and Organizational Psychology, 83*(4), 981–1002. DOI: 10.1348/096317909X481382

van Niekerk, L. (2009). Participation in work: A source of wellness for people with psychiatric disability. *Work : A Journal of Prevention, Assessment, and Rehabilitation, 32*(4), 455–465. DOI: 10.3233/WOR-2009-0856

Van Wingerden, J., Bakker, A. B., & Derks, D. (2017). The longitudinal impact of a job crafting intervention. *European Journal of Work and Organizational Psychology, 26*(1), 107–119. DOI: 10.1080/1359432X.2016.1224233

Wan, W., & Duffy, R. D. (2022). Decent work and turnover intention among new generation employees: The mediating role of job satisfaction and the moderating role of job autonomy. *SAGE Open, 12*(2), 21582440221094591. DOI: 10.1177/21582440221094591

Weick, K. E., Sutcliffe, K. M., & Obstfeld, D. (1999). Organizing for high reliability: Processes of collective mindfulness. *Research in Organizational Behavior, 21*, 81–123. DOI: 10.1016/S0191-3085(99)21003-X

Wood, A. J., Lehdonvirta, V., Graham, M., & Hjorth, I. (2019). Good gig, bad gig: Autonomy and algorithmic control in the global gig economy. *Work, Employment and Society, 33*(1), 56–75. DOI: 10.1177/0950017018785616

Wrzesniewski, A., & Dutton, J. E. (2001). Crafting a job: Revisioning employees as active crafters of their work. *Academy of Management Review, 26*(2), 179–201. DOI: 10.2307/259118

Zarvijani, S. A. H., Moghaddam, L. F., & Parchebafieh, S. (2021). Acceptance and commitment therapy on perceived stress and psychological flexibility of psychiatric nurses: A randomized control trial. *BMC Nursing, 20*(1), 239. DOI: 10.1186/s12912-021-00763-4

Zhao, H. A. O., Wayne, S. J., Glibkowski, B. C., & Bravo, J. (2007). The impact of psychological contract breach on work-related outcomes: A meta-analysis. *Personnel Psychology*, *60*(3), 647–680. DOI: 10.1111/j.1744-6570.2007.00087.x

Zito, M., Cortese, C. G., & Colombo, L. (2019). The role of resources and flow at work in well-being. *SAGE Open*, *9*(2), 1–12. DOI: 10.1177/2158244019849732

KEY TERMS AND DEFINITIONS

Burnout: A condition of chronic physical and emotional fatigue as a result of being exposed to chronic stressors at the workplace. The burnout rates remain high enough to point to the shortcomings of the models that focus only on economic management and the necessity of active well-being programs.

Employee Well-Being: A multidimensional construct that incorporates physical, psychological, and social health of employees at the workplace. Employee well-being levels are always associated with the increased engagement, resilience, and the long-term organizational performance.

High-Performance Work Systems (HPWS): A consistent set of HR practices that aim at increasing employee skills, motivation, and engagement. A HPWS is linked to better psychological climates and enhanced work engagement due to their beneficial effects on the well-being of the employees.

Human Resource Management Practices: It has structured organizational policies and practices that would focus on managing people effectively such as recruitment, development, and employee support systems. Strategic HRM practices are important in determining the well-being of employees through the provision of supportive psychological and social work environments.

Humanistic Organizing: An organizational strategy that ensures that humans are given first consideration in terms of dignity, well-being, and ethical responsibility in addition to the economic performance. When such a sentence is added, Humanistic organizing is a paradigm shift that is not focused on shareholder primacy but more inclusive and sustainable value creation.

Mindful Organizing: This is the aggregate use of mindfulness concepts in organizational process to improve awareness, adaptability and ethical decision-making. Mindful organizing helps organizations to become more responsive to complexity and uncertainty and also promote the psychological well-being of employees.

Organizational Communication: The processes of information, meaning and values creation and sharing within and outside the organization. Conscious organizational communication is an important mechanism that entails integration of humanistic values and overall well-being of employees.

Sustainable Organization Performance:. An organization that has achieved long-term success: balancing both financial and social performance and employee welfare.Sustainability performance is becoming more and more hinged on how well organizations are able to incorporate employee well being in their overall strategic goals.

Compilation of References

Abasilim, D. U. (2024). *Exploring the concept of leadership*. Humanities and Social Sciences., DOI: 10.7862/rz.2024.hss.01

Abbas, M., & Ali, R. (2023). Transformational versus transactional leadership styles and project success: A meta-analytic review. *European Management Journal*, *41*(1), 125–142. DOI: 10.1016/j.emj.2021.10.011

Abualfalayeh, G. (2025). Strategic HR management: Bridging organizational goals and employee performance. *Journal of Cultural Analysis and Social Change*, *10*(2), 4065–4069. DOI: 10.64753/jcasc.v10i2.2232

Abuzaid, A. N., Al-Faouri, E. H., Alateeq, M. M., Madadha, S.-M., Ghadi, M. Y., Al-Qatawenh, A. S., Abdelkarim Almajali, D., & Almajali, H. A. K. (2024). The relationship between perceptions of high-performance work systems and corporate social responsibility (CSR) considering the moderating effect of a positive diversity climate. *Sustainability (Basel)*, *16*(10), 4267. DOI: 10.3390/su16104267

Accenture. (2023). Environmental, Social and Governance (ESG) Report.

Ahmed, M. F. Y. (2025). Doomscrolling behavior and cognitive overload: Implications for mental health and decision-making. *Journal of Behavioral Addictions*, *14*(1), 45–61. DOI: 10.1556/2006.2024.00098

Aikens, K. A., Astin, J., Pelletier, K. R., Levanovich, K., Baase, C. M., Park, Y. Y., & Bodnar, C. M. (2014). Mindfulness goes to work: Impact of an online workplace intervention. *Journal of Occupational and Environmental Medicine*, *56*(7), 721–731. DOI: 10.1097/JOM.0000000000000209

Albert, S., & Whetten, D. A. (1985). Organizational identity. *Research in Organizational Behavior*, *7*, 263–295.

Albrecht, S. L. (2012). The influence of job, team and organizational level resources on employee well-being, engagement, commitment and extra-role performance: Test of a model. *International Journal of Manpower, 33*(7), 840–853. DOI: 10.1108/01437721211268357

Al-Hussaini, S. H., Turi, J. A., Altamimi, A. N., Khan, M. A., & Ahmad, M. (2019, March 26). Impact of talent management strategies on employee performance behaviour with the mediating role of talent management outputs. *Archives of Business Research, 7*(3).

Ali, B. J., & Anwar, G. (2021). An Empirical Study of Employees' Motivation and Its Influence Job Satisfaction. *International Journal of Engineering Business Management, 5*(2), 21–30.

Ali, H. (2014). Perceived organizational support and organizational citizenship behavior: The case of Kuwait. *International Journal of Business Administration, 5*(3), 59–59. DOI: 10.5430/ijba.v5n3p59

Al-Jaber, A., Alzghoul, A., Alghizzawi, M., AlFraihat, S. F., Elhawi, R., & Banihani, T. (2025). Integrating HRM strategies to achieve Sustainable Development Goals: The mediating roles of employee well-being and corporate governance. *Administrative Sciences, 15*(12), 474. DOI: 10.3390/admsci15120474

Allen, T. D., Golden, T. D., & Shockley, K. M. (2015). How effective is telecommuting? Assessing the status of our scientific findings. *Psychological Science in the Public Interest : A Journal of the American Psychological Society, 16*(2), 40–68. DOI: 10.1177/1529100615593273 PMID: 26403188

Almeida, D. L. (2019). As práticas de Gestão de Recursos Humanos: Estudo de caso numa empresa de metalomecânica da região de Aveiro. *Dissertação de Mestrado em Gestão.* Aveiro: Escola Superior de Gestão de Tomar – Instituto Politécnico de Tomar.

Alonso, L., & Elovainio, M. (2022). Organizational justice and health: Reviewing two decades of studies. *Journal of Theoretical Social Psychology, 2022*, 1–13. DOI: 10.1155/2022/3218883

Aman, A. (2024). A review on e-learning and employability skills. *International Research Journal of Multidisciplinary Scope., 5*(3), 682–698. DOI: 10.47857/irjms.2024.v05i03.0782

Amanullah, S., & Ramesh Shankar, R. (2020). The impact of COVID-19 on physician burnout globally: A review. *Health Care, 8*(4), 421.

Ambler, T., & Barrow, S. (1996). The employer brand. *Journal of Brand Management*, *4*(3), 185–206. DOI: 10.1057/bm.1996.42

American Institute of Stress. (2023). Workplace stress survey 2023. https://www.stress.org/workplace-stress

Angrave, D., Charlwood, A., Kirkpatrick, I., Lawrence, M., & Stuart, M. (2016). HR and analytics: Why HR is set to fail the big data challenge. *Human Resource Management Journal*, *26*(1), 1–11. DOI: 10.1111/1748-8583.12090

Anyanugo, M. O., Ololube, N. P., & Okuru, C. L. (2024). Establishing the basis for organizational success through effective leadership. *SAR Journal of Humanities and Social Science*, *6*(4), 156–169. DOI: 10.36346/sarjhss.2024.v06i04.003

Appolloni, A., Liu, J., Zhang, Y., & Li, Y. (2025). Linking top management commitment and circular practice through human resource perspective: Do diversity, equity, and inclusion (DEI) make a difference in corporate responsibility? *Corporate Social Responsibility and Environmental Management*, *32*(2), 2746–2768. Advance online publication. DOI: 10.1002/csr.3099

Armstrong, M., & Taylor, S. (2020). Armstrong's Handbook of Human Resource Management Practice - A Guide to the Theory and Practice of People Management (15th Edition ed.). United Kingdom: KoganPage, London.

Arora, S., Malhotra, L., & Ruhil, M. (2024). Aligning Strategic HR Management with Business Objectives: Examining the Effect on Organizational Effectiveness and Performance. *ShodhKosh: Journal of Visual and Performing Arts*, *5*(3), 31–42. DOI: 10.29121/shodhkosh.v5.i3.2024.1657

Arshadi, N., & Hayavi, G. (2013). The effect of perceived organizational support on affective commitment and job performance: Mediating role of OBSE. *Procedia: Social and Behavioral Sciences*, *84*, 739–743. DOI: 10.1016/j.sbspro.2013.06.637

Ashforth, B. E., & Mael, F. (1989). Social identity theory and the organization. *Academy of Management Review*, *14*(1), 20–39. DOI: 10.2307/258189

Autin, K., Blustein, D., Ali, S., & Garriott, P. (2020). Career development impacts of COVID-19: Practice and policy recommendations. *Journal of Career Development*, *47*(5), 487–494. DOI: 10.1177/0894845320944486

Babashahi, L., Barbosa, C. E., Lima, Y., Lyra, A., Salazar, H., Argôlo, M., Almeida, M. A., & Souza, J. M. (2024, June 16). AI in the workplace: A systematic review of skill transformation in the industry. *Administrative Sciences*, *14*(6), 127. DOI: 10.3390/admsci14060127

Backhaus, K., & Tikoo, S. (2004). Conceptualizing and researching employer branding. *Career Development International*, *9*(5), 501–517. DOI: 10.1108/13620430410550754

Bakker, A. B., & Costa, P. L. (2014). Chronic job burnout and daily functioning: A theoretical analysis. *Burnout Research*, *1*(3), 112–119. DOI: 10.1016/j.burn.2014.04.003

Bakker, A. B., & Demerouti, E. (2007). The job demands–resources model: State of the art. *Journal of Managerial Psychology*, *22*(3), 309–328. DOI: 10.1108/02683940710733115

Bakker, A. B., & Demerouti, E. (2008). Towards a model of work engagement. *Career Development International*, *13*(3), 209–223. DOI: 10.1108/13620430810870476

Bakker, A. B., & Demerouti, E. (2017). Job demands–resources theory: Taking stock and looking forward. *Journal of Occupational Health Psychology*, *22*(3), 273–285. DOI: 10.1037/ocp0000056 PMID: 27732008

Bala, S. B. N., & Pandve, H. (2021). Prevalence and factors associated with sickness absenteeism among pharmaceutical industrial workers of Hyderabad, India. *Asian Journal of Medical Sciences*, *12*(1), 81–86. DOI: 10.3126/ajms.v12i2.31211

Ball, K. (2010). Workplace surveillance: An overview. *Labor History*, *51*(1), 87–106. DOI: 10.1080/00236561003654776

Bal, P. M., De Lange, A. H., Jansen, P. G., & Van Der Velde, M. E. (2008). Psychological contract breach and job attitudes: A meta-analysis of age as a moderator. *Journal of Vocational Behavior*, *72*(1), 143–158. DOI: 10.1016/j.jvb.2007.10.005

Bano, M., Zowghi, D., Mourao, F., Kaur, S., & Zhang, T. (2024). Diversity and inclusion in AI for recruitment: Lessons from industry workshop.

Barber, L. K., & Santuzzi, A. M. (2015). Please respond ASAP: Workplace telepressure and employee recovery. *Journal of Occupational Health Psychology*, *20*(2), 172–189. DOI: 10.1037/a0038278 PMID: 25365629

Barley, S. R., Meyerson, D. E., & Grodal, S. (2011). E-mail as a source and symbol of stress. *Organization Science*, *22*(4), 887–906. DOI: 10.1287/orsc.1100.0573

Barocas, S., & Selbst, A. D. (2016). Big data's disparate impact. *California Law Review*, *104*(3), 671–732. DOI: 10.15779/Z38BG31

Bar-On, R. (1997). *The Emotional Quotient Inventory (EQ-i): A measure of emotional intelligence*. Multi-Health Systems.

Barroso, D. C. P. (2012). *O perfil de um líder – O futuro da Delta Cafés* (Dissertação de mestrado, ISCTE – Instituto Universitário de Lisboa). Repositório ISCTE. https://repositorio.iscte-iul.pt/bitstream/10071/5428/1/Tese_Daniela%20Barroso.pdf

Bauer, T. N. (2010). *Onboarding new employees: Maximizing success*. SHRM Foundation's Effective Practice Guideline Series.

Beardwell, J., & Thompson, A. (2017). *Human Resource Management: A Contemporary Approach*. Pearson.

Beer, M., Boselie, P., & Brewster, C. (2015). Back to the future: Implications for the field of HRM of the multistakeholder perspective proposed 30 years ago. *Human Resource Management, 54*(3), 427–438. DOI: 10.1002/hrm.21726

Bekin, S. F. (2004). *Endomarketing: Como praticá-lo com sucesso* (3rd ed.). Prentice Hall.

Benítez Márquez, M. D., Sánchez Teba, E. M., Bermúdez González, G., & Núñez Rydman, E. S. (01 de Fevereiro de 2022). Generation Z Within the Workforce and in the Workplace: A Bibliometric Analysis. *Frontiers in Psychology, Volume 12*.

Berry, L. L. (1981). The employee as customer. In Donnelly, J. H., & George, W. R. (Eds.), *Marketing of services* (pp. 271–278). American Marketing Association.

Bilan, Y., Mishchuk, H., Roshchyk, I., & Joshi, O. (Novembro de 2020). Hiring and retaining skilled employees in SMEs: problems in human resource practices and links with organizational success. *Business: Theory and Practice, 21*(2), pp. 780-791.

Blau, P. M. (1964). *Exchange and power in social life*. Wiley.

Blyznyuk, T., & Bliznyuk, O. (2024). Contemporary theories of leadership: Cross-cultural analysis. *Economy and Society*, (66). Advance online publication. DOI: 10.32782/2524-0072/2024-66-42

Bodie, M. T., Cherry, M. A., McCormick, M. L., & Tang, J. (2017). The law and policy of people analytics. *University of Colorado Law Review, 88*(4), 961–1042. https://lawreview.colorado.edu

Bogen, M., & Rieke, A. (2018). *Help wanted: An examination of hiring algorithms, equity, and bias*. Upturn.

Bond, F., Lloyd, J., & Guenole, N. (2013). The work-related acceptance and action questionnaire: Initial psychometric findings. *Journal of Occupational and Organizational Psychology, 86*(3), 331–347. DOI: 10.1111/joop.12001

Borelli, J. L., Wang, Y., Li, F. H., Russo, L. N., Tironi, M., Yamashita, K., Zhou, E., Lai, J., Nguyen, B., Azimi, I., Marcotullio, C., Labbaf, S., Jafarlou, S., Dutt, N., & Rahmani, A. (2025). Detection of depressive symptoms in college students using multimodal passive sensing data and light gradient boosting machine: Longitudinal pilot study. *JMIR Formative Research, 9*, e67964. DOI: 10.2196/67964

Boudreau, D. W., Ulrich, J. S., & Buhler, E. P. (2023). The interplay between Human Resource strategies and strategic alignment: A comprehensive review of conceptual and empirical literature in the United States. *Journal of Strategy and Management, 7*(5), 1–10. DOI: 10.53819/81018102t4170

Boxall, P., & Purcell, J. (2016). *Strategy and human resource management* (4th ed.). Palgrave Macmillan. DOI: 10.1007/978-1-137-40765-8

Bratton, J., & Gold, J. (2017). *Human Resource Management: Theory and Practice*. Palgrave Macmillan. DOI: 10.1057/978-1-137-58668-1

Braun, V., & Clarke, V. (2006). Using thematic analysis in psychology. *Qualitative Research in Psychology, 3*(2), 77–101. DOI: 10.1191/1478088706qp063oa

Breaz, T.-R.-O., & Jaradat, M. (2023). Strategic Human Resource Management: Aligning HR practices with organizational goals. In *Proceedings of the 17th International Management Conference "Management beyond Crisis: Rethinking Business Performance"* (pp. 552–559). Bucharest, Romania.

Brougham, D., & Haar, J. (2018). Smart technology, artificial intelligence, robotics, and algorithms (STARA): Implications for work and human resource management. *Journal of Management & Organization, 24*(5), 407–421. DOI: 10.1017/jmo.2016.55

Brunsson, N. (1989). *The organization of hypocrisy: Talk, decisions and actions in organizations*. Wiley.

Brynjolfsson, E. (1993). The productivity paradox of information technology. *Communications of the ACM, 36*(12), 66–77. DOI: 10.1145/163298.163309

Budhwar, P., & Varma, A. (2011). Emerging patterns of HRM in the new Indian economic environment. *Human Resource Management Review, 21*(3), 217–218.

Budhwar, P., Varma, A., Singh, V., & Dhar, R. (2017). HRM systems of Indian companies: Examining the role of HRM in organizational effectiveness. *Employee Relations, 39*(6), 996–1017.

Bwalya, A. (2023). Leadership styles. *Global Scientific Journal, 11*(8).

Cable, D. M., Gino, F., & Staats, B. R. (2013). Reinventing Employee Onboarding. *MIT Sloan Management Review, 54*(3), 23–28.

Cable, D. M., & Turban, D. B. (2003). The value of organizational reputation in the recruitment context: A brand-equity perspective. *Journal of Applied Social Psychology, 33*(11), 2244–2266. DOI: 10.1111/j.1559-1816.2003.tb01883.x

Cahyono, N. D. (2024). The role of emotional intelligence in HR leadership: Building strong teams in a multigenerational context. *The Journal of Applied Organizational Studies*. http://thejoas.com/index.php/thejoas/article/view/114/152

Campbell, M., Thomson, H., Fenton, C., & Gibson, M. (2016). Lone parents, health, wellbeing and welfare to work: A systematic review of qualitative studies. *BMC Public Health, 16*(1), 188. Advance online publication. DOI: 10.1186/s12889-016-2880-9

Cappelli, P., & Tavis, A. (2018). HR goes agile. *Harvard Business Review, 96*(2), 46–52.

Carpenter, M. L. (2023). *Effective Onboar e Onboarding Str ding Strategies t ategies to Increase Talent Retention. Doctoral Study Submitted in Partial Fulfillment of the Requirements for the Degree of Doctor of Business Administration*. Walden University.

Carroll, A. B. (1979). A three-dimensional conceptual model of corporate performance. *Academy of Management Review, 4*(4), 497–505. DOI: 10.2307/257850

Carvalheiro, C. D. (2011). *A Evolução da Gestão de Recursos Humanos*. Relatório de Estágio Curricular, Universidade de Coimbra.

Carvalho, A., & Rua, O. L. (2017). *Gestão de Recursos Humanos - Abordagem das Boas Práticas*. Vida Economica Editorial.

Carver, C. S., & Scheier, M. F. (2000). Control processes and self-organization as complementary principles underlying behaviour. *Personality and Social Psychology Review : An Official Journal of the Society for Personality and Social Psychology, Inc., 6*(4), 304–315. DOI: 10.1207/S15327957PSPR0604_05

Cascio, W. F., & Montealegre, R. (2016). How technology is changing work and organizations. *Annual Review of Organizational Psychology and Organizational Behavior, 3*(1), 349–375. DOI: 10.1146/annurev-orgpsych-041015-062352

Castro, M. V. de M., de Araújo, M. L., Ribeiro, A. M., Demo, G., & Meneses, P. P. M. (2020). Implementation of strategic human resource management practices: A review of the national scientific production and new research paths. *Revista de Gestão, 27*(3), 229–246. DOI: 10.1108/REGE-10-2018-0102

Căvescu, A. M., & Popescu, N. (2025, August 5). Predictive analytics in human resources management: Evaluating AIHR's role in talent retention. *AppliedMath.*, *5*(3), 99. DOI: 10.3390/appliedmath5030099

Cavicchioli, M., & Kocollari, U. (2024). The 5 E(lements) of employee-centric corporate social responsibility and their stimulus on happiness at work. *Corporate Social Responsibility and Environmental Management, 31*(3), 1959–1976. DOI: 10.1002/csr.2667

Central Bureau of Workforce Economics. (2025). *Digital literacy and workforce readiness in India*. Government of India. https://dtnbwed.cbwe.gov.in/images/upload/Digital-Literacy_3ZNK.pdf

Chen, Y.-C., Huang, Z.-L., & Chu, H.-C. (2024). Relationships between emotional labor, job burnout, and emotional intelligence. *BMC Psychology*, *12*(1), 672. Advance online publication. DOI: 10.1186/s40359-024-02167-w PMID: 39558444

Chhabra, N. L., & Sharma, S. (2014). Employer branding: Strategy for improving employer attractiveness. *The International Journal of Organizational Analysis*, *22*(1), 48–60. DOI: 10.1108/IJOA-09-2011-0513

Chiew, T. K., Ahmed, U., & Taha, A. (2013). Internal marketing and its implications for HRM and organizational performance. *International Journal of Business and Society*, *14*(3), 469–488.

Chiew, T. K., Ahmed, U., & Taha, A. (2025). Internal marketing and organizational performance: A systematic review. *Journal of Business Research*, *170*, 114320. DOI: 10.1016/j.jbusres.2025.114320

Chouldechova, A. (2017). Fair prediction with disparate impact: A study of bias in recidivism prediction instruments. *Big Data*, *5*(2), 153–163. DOI: 10.1089/big.2016.0047

Chowdhury, T. I., Saeedi, A. S., Karim, A. M., Ahmed, A. R., & Karim, A. M. (2024). Effective contemporary leadership in tertiary education: Global stakeholders' viewpoint. *International Journal of Academic Research in Business and Social Sciences*. https://hrmars.com/index.php/IJARBSS/article/view/20466

Christina, J. L., Alamelu, R., & Nigama, K. (2025). Synthesizing the impact of sustainable human resource management on corporate sustainability through multi method evidence. *Discover Sustainability*, *6*(1), 666. DOI: 10.1007/s43621-025-01557-3

Claro, F. A. (2024). *Inteligência emocional no ambiente de trabalho* [Unpublished master's thesis]. Universidade de Lisboa.

Collings, D. G., Mellahi, K., & Cascio, W. F. (Junho de 2018). Global Talent Management and Performance in Multinational Enterprises: A Multilevel Perspective. *Journal of Management 45(2).*

Colquitt, J. A. (2001). On the dimensionality of organizational justice: A construct validation of a measure. *The Journal of Applied Psychology*, *86*(3), 386–400. DOI: 10.1037/0021-9010.86.3.386

Contreras, F., Baykal, E., & Abid, G. (2020). E-leadership and teleworking in times of COVID-19 and beyond: What we know and where do we go. *Frontiers in Psychology*, *11*, 590271. DOI: 10.3389/fpsyg.2020.590271 PMID: 33362656

Conway, N., & Briner, R. B. (2005). *Understanding psychological contracts at work: A critical evaluation of theory and research.* Oxford University Press., DOI: 10.1093/acprof:oso/9780199280643.001.0001

Cooren, F., Kuhn, T., Cornelissen, J. P., & Clark, T. (2011). Communication, organizing and organization: An overview and introduction to the special issue. *Organization Studies*, *32*(9), 1149–1170. DOI: 10.1177/0170840611410836

Core Values. (2023). *Putting people first: The power of the human-centered approach.* https://corevalues.com

Corrigan, P. W., Kerr, A., & Knudsen, L. (2005). The stigma of mental illness: Explanatory models and methods for change. *Applied & Preventive Psychology*, *11*(3), 179–190. DOI: 10.1016/j.appsy.2005.07.001

Cox, T. (1993). *Cultural diversity in organizations: Theory, research and practice.* Berrett-Koehler.

Coyle-Shapiro, J. A.-M., & Kessler, I. (2003). The employment relationship in the UK public sector: A psychological contract perspective. *Journal of Public Administration: Research and Theory*, *13*(2), 213–230. DOI: 10.1093/jopart/mug018

Crane, M. F., Kangas, M., Karin, E., Searle, B., & Chen, D. (2020). Leveraging the experience of stressors: The role of adaptive systematic self-reflection. *Anxiety, Stress, and Coping*, *33*(3), 231–247. DOI: 10.1080/10615806.2020.1732359

Crenshaw, K. (1989). Demarginalizing the intersection of race and sex: A Black feminist critique of antidiscrimination doctrine, feminist theory and antiracist politics. *University of Chicago Legal Forum*, *1989*(1), 139–167.

Cropanzano, R., Anthony, E. L., Daniels, S. R., & Hall, A. V. (2017). Social exchange theory: A critical review with theoretical remedies. *The Academy of Management Annals*, *11*(1), 479–516. DOI: 10.5465/annals.2015.0099

Cropanzano, R., & Mitchell, M. S. (2005). Social exchange theory: An interdisciplinary review. *Journal of Management, 31*(6), 874–900. DOI: 10.1177/0149206305279602

CultureMonkey. (2025). *What is employee brand advocacy: Definition and top examples*. https://www.culturemonkey.io

da Silva, L. M. T., de Albuquerque, L. G., & Costa, B. K. (2021). O alinhamento estratégico entre cultura organizacional e estratégias de gestão de pessoas. *Revista Eletrônica de Ciência Administrativa, 20*(1), 120–149. DOI: 10.21529/RECADM.2021005

Dastin, J. (2018, October 10). Amazon scraps secret AI recruiting tool that showed bias against women. Reuters.

Davis, F. D. (1989). Perceived usefulness, perceived ease of use, and user acceptance of information technology. *Management Information Systems Quarterly, 13*(3), 319–340. DOI: 10.2307/249008

de S. Soomro, A. A. (2024). Perceived organizational support and employer branding: The mediating role of employee engagement and retention. *Journal of Management Insights, 5*(1), 23–39.

De Stefano, V. (2019). Negotiating the algorithm: Automation, artificial intelligence and labour protection. *Comparative Labor Law & Policy Journal, 41*(1), 15–46. ISSN 1999-2939.

Deci, E. L., & Ryan, R. M. (2000). The 'what' and 'why' of goal pursuits: Human needs and the self-determination of behavior. *Psychological Inquiry, 11*(4), 227–268. DOI: 10.1207/S15327965PLI1104_01

Deloitte. (2023). *Global human capital trends 2023: New expectations for AI in HR*. https://www2.deloitte.com/us/en/insights/focus/human-capital-trends.html

Demerouti, E., Bakker, A. B., Nachreiner, F., & Schaufeli, W. B. (2001). The job demands-resources model of burnout. *The Journal of Applied Psychology, 86*(3), 499–512. DOI: 10.1037/0021-9010.86.3.499

Denzin, N. K., & Lincoln, Y. S. (2018). *The SAGE Handbook of Qualitative Research*. Sage Publications, Inc.

Derks, D., Bakker, A. B., Peters, P., & van Wingerden, P. (2014). Work-related smartphone use, work–family conflict and family role performance. *Human Relations; Studies Towards the Integration of the Social Sciences, 67*(9), 1045–1068. DOI: 10.1177/0018726714525234

Derks, D., van Duin, D., Tims, M., & Bakker, A. B. (2015). Smartphone use and work–home interference. *Journal of Occupational and Organizational Psychology, 88*(1), 155–177. DOI: 10.1111/joop.12083

Deshpande, A. (2011). *The grammar of caste: Economic discrimination in contemporary India.* Oxford University Press. DOI: 10.1093/acprof:oso/9780198072034.001.0001

Dessler, G. (2022). *Human Resource Management.* Pearson.

Dhir, A., Yossatorn, Y., Kaur, P., & Chen, S. (2018). Online social media fatigue and psychological wellbeing. *International Journal of Information Management, 40*, 141–152. DOI: 10.1016/j.ijinfomgt.2018.01.012

Di Marco, M., Venter, O., Possingham, H. P., & Watson, J. E. M. (2018). Changes in human footprint drive changes in species extinction risk. *Nature Communications, 9*(1), 4621. DOI: 10.1038/s41467-018-07049-5

Dieguez, T., Faria, A., & Loureiro, P. C. (2024). The Digital Frontier: Navigating the Challenges and Opportunities for Generation Z in the Labor Market. Em *Reskilling the Workforce for Technological Advancement* (pp. 82- 110). IGI Global.

DiMaggio, P. J., & Powell, W. W. (1983). The iron cage revisited: Institutional isomorphism and collective rationality in organizational fields. *American Sociological Review, 48*(2), 147–160. DOI: 10.2307/2095101

Dineen, B. R., & Allen, D. G. (2016). Third party employment branding: Human capital inflows and outflows following "Best Places to Work" certifications. *Academy of Management Journal, 59*(1), 90–112. DOI: 10.5465/amj.2013.1091

Dirks, K. T., & Ferrin, D. L. (2002). Trust in leadership: Meta-analytic findings and implications for research and practice. *The Journal of Applied Psychology, 87*(4), 611–628. DOI: 10.1037/0021-9010.87.4.611

Donaldson, T., & Preston, L. E. (1995). The stakeholder theory of the corporation: Concepts, evidence, and implications. *Academy of Management Review, 20*(1), 65–91. DOI: 10.2307/258887

Dunne, J. D. (2015). Buddhist styles of mindfulness: A heuristic approach. In Ostafin, B. D., Robinson, M. D., & Meier, B. P. (Eds.), *Handbook of Mindfulness and Self-Regulation* (pp. 251–270). Springer., DOI: 10.1007/978-1-4939-2263-5_18

Dutton, J. E., & Dukerich, J. M. (1991). Keeping an eye on the mirror: Image and identity in organizational adaptation. *Academy of Management Journal, 34*(3), 517–554. DOI: 10.2307/256405

Dutton, J. E., Worline, M. C., Frost, P. J., & Lilius, J. (2006). Explaining compassion organizing. *Administrative Science Quarterly*, *51*(1), 59–96. DOI: 10.2189/asqu.51.1.59

Edmondson, A. (1999). Psychological safety and learning behavior in work teams. *Administrative Science Quarterly*, *44*(2), 350–383. DOI: 10.2307/2666999

Edmondson, A. C. (2018). *The Fearless Organization: Creating Psychological Safety in the Workplace for Learning, Innovation, and Growth*. John Wiley & Sons.

Edwards, M. R. (2010). An integrative review of employer branding and OB theory. *Personnel Review*, *39*(1), 5–23. DOI: 10.1108/00483481011012809

Eib, C., Bernhard-Oettel, C., Hanson, L., & Leineweber, C. (2018). Organizational justice and health: Studying mediators and lagged relationships. *Journal of Occupational Health Psychology*, *23*(4), 553–567. DOI: 10.1037/ocp0000115

Eisenberger, R., Huntington, R., Hutchison, S., & Sowa, D. (1986). Perceived organizational support. *The Journal of Applied Psychology*, *71*(3), 500–507. DOI: 10.1037/0021-9010.71.3.500

Eisenhardt, K. M. (1989). Building theories from case study research. *Academy of Management Review*, *14*(4), 532–550. DOI: 10.2307/258557

Eisenhardt, K. M., & Graebner, M. E. (2007). Theory building from cases: Opportunities and challenges. *Academy of Management Journal*, *50*(1), 25–32. DOI: 10.5465/amj.2007.24160888

Eklund, M., Hermansson, A., & Håkansson, C. (2012). Meaning in life for people with schizophrenia: Does it include occupation? *Journal of Occupational Science*, *19*(2), 93–105. DOI: 10.1080/14427591.2011.605833

Elkington, J. (1997). *Cannibals with forks: The triple bottom line of 21st century business*. Capstone.

Ermetova, Z., & Abajanova, G. (2024). Leadership in modern organizations. https://journalsnuu.uz/index.php/1/article/view/1215/464

Eurofound. (2020). *Right to disconnect: Exploring company practices*. Publications Office of the European Union. https://www.eurofound.europa.eu/en/publications/all/right-disconnect-exploring-company-practices

European Commission. (2019). *Ethics guidelines for trustworthy AI*. High-Level Expert Group on Artificial Intelligence.

European Commission. (2019). *Ethics guidelines for trustworthy AI.* https://digital-strategy.ec.europa.eu/en/library/ethics-guidelines-trustworthy-ai

European Parliament and Council. (2024). *Regulation (EU) 2024/1689 laying down harmonised rules on artificial intelligence (Artificial Intelligence Act).* Official Journal of the European Union.

Faria, A. F. (2023). *Tendências e Desafios da Geração Z no contexto da Transformação Digital. Tese de Mestrado em Gestão de Organizações.* IPCA.

Farinha, J. (2019). *O impacto da comunicação dos líderes na responsabilidade e autonomia dos colaboradores* (Tese de doutoramento). Repositório Científico de Acesso Aberto de Portugal. https://comum.rcaap.pt/bitstream/10400.26/31064/1/Dissertação%20de%20Doutoramento%20em%20Gestão%20-%20Joao%20Farinha.pdf

Farinha, J., & de Fátima Pina, M. (2025). Leadership's role in driving sustainable AI: A conceptual model for ESG-conscious AI governance. In K. Arai (Ed.), *Intelligent systems and applications* (Lecture Notes in Networks and Systems). Springer. https://doi.org/DOI: 10.1007/978-3-031-86079-9_2

Farinha, J., & Santos, J. (2025). Leading organizational resilience: A framework for sustainable performance in turbulent environments. In K. Arai (Ed.), *Intelligent systems and applications* (Lecture Notes in Networks and Systems). Springer. https://doi.org/DOI: 10.1007/978-3-031-86079-9_3

Farinha, J. (2022). A liderança e os desafios da era digital. *Revista Portuguesa de Gestão, 15*(2), 45–60.

Farinha, J. (2024). Leading from a distance: The key characteristics of an e-leader. In Sousa, M. J. (Ed.), *New research on leadership styles and performance* (pp. 219–250). Nova Science Publishers, Inc., DOI: 10.52305/ZKQP3465

Farinha, J., & Sousa, M. J. (2015). How leadership fosters communication and impacts employees' responsibility and autonomy. In *ECMLG 2015* (pp. xx–xx). Academic Conferences International.

Fisher, C. D. (2014). Conceptualizing and measuring wellbeing at work. In Chen, P. Y., & Cooper, C. L. (Eds.), *Work and wellbeing* (pp. 9–33). Wiley Blackwell., DOI: 10.1002/9781118539415.wbwell018

Fleshman, J. W. (2020). How to develop a leadership training program. *Clinics in Colon and Rectal Surgery, 33*(5), 305–310. DOI: 10.1055/s-0040-1712975 PMID: 32624715

Floridi, L. (2023). The ethics of artificial intelligence: Principles, challenges, and opportunities.

Floridi, L., Cowls, J., Beltrametti, M., Chatila, R., Chazerand, P., Dignum, V., Luetge, C., Madelin, R., Pagallo, U., Rossi, F., Schafer, B., Valcke, P., & Vayena, E. (2018). AI4People—An ethical framework for a good AI society. *Minds and Machines*, *28*(4), 689–707. DOI: 10.1007/s11023-018-9482-5 PMID: 30930541

Folger, R., & Konovsky, M. A. (1989). Effects of procedural and distributive justice on reactions to pay raise decisions. *Academy of Management Journal*, *32*(1), 115–130. DOI: 10.2307/256422

Follmer, K. B., & Jones, K. S. (2017). Stereotype content and social distancing from employees with mental illness: The moderating roles of gender and social dominance orientation. *Journal of Applied Social Psychology*, *47*(9), 492–504. DOI: 10.1111/jasp.12455

Fombrun, C. J. (1996). *Reputation: Realizing value from the corporate image.* Harvard Business School Press.

França, T. J., São Mamede, H., Barroso, J. M., & Dos Santos, V. M. (2023, April 1). Artificial intelligence applied to potential assessment and talent identification in an organisational context. *Heliyon*, *9*(4). PMID: 37035361

Freeman, R. E. (1984). *Strategic management: A stakeholder approach.* Pitman.

Freeman, R. E. (1984). *Strategic management: A stakeholder approach.* Pitman. DOI: 10.2139/ssrn.263511

Freudenberger, H. J. (1974). Staff burnout. *The Journal of Social Issues*, *30*(1), 159–165. DOI: 10.1111/j.1540-4560.1974.tb00706.x

Fyke, J. P., & Buzzanell, P. M. (2013). The ethics of conscious capitalism: Wicked problems in leading change and changing leaders. *Human Relations; Studies Towards the Integration of the Social Sciences*, *66*(12), 1545–1569. DOI: 10.1177/0018726713485306

Gabrielova, K., & Buchko, A. A. (2021). Here comes Generation Z. *Business Horizons*, *21*(1), 7–19. DOI: 10.1016/j.bushor.2021.02.013

Galiakberova, A. A., Mukhametshin, A. G., Dyrin, S. P., Asratyan, N. M., Kornilova, I. V., & Galiev, R. M. (2024). Tipologia dos estilos de liderança em função do processo de tomada de decisão e da orientação para a tarefa/pessoa [Типология стилей руководства в зависимости от характера принятия решений и ориентации на дело/человека]. *Management Science.* Advance online publication. DOI: 10.26794/2304-022X-2024-14-3-135-146

Gallup. (2022). *State of the global workplace: 2022 report.* https://www.gallup.com/workplace/349484/state-of-the-global-workplace.aspx

Gandolfi, F., & Stone, S. (Outubro de 2018). Leadership, Leadership Styles, and Servant Leadership. *Journal of Management Research, 18(4)*, pp. 261-269.

Garfin, D. R., Silver, R. C., & Holman, E. A. (2020). Media exposure and public health consequences of COVID-19. *Health Psychology : Official Journal of the Division of Health Psychology, American Psychological Association*, *39*(5), 355–357. DOI: 10.1037/hea0000875 PMID: 32202824

Gartner. (2023). *Hype cycle for human resource management, 2023.* https://www.gartner.com/en/human-resources

Gaspar, R. M. (2021). *Inteligência emocional, engagement e burnout em trabalhadores portugueses* [Unpublished doctoral dissertation]. Universidade do Porto.

Gebreheat, G., Teame, H., & Costa, E. I. (2023). The impact of transformational leadership style on nurses' job satisfaction: An integrative review. *SAGE Open Nursing*, *9*, 23779608231197428. DOI: 10.1177/23779608231197428 PMID: 37691720

Gemmano, G., Signore, F., Caffò, A. O., Palmisano, G. L., Bosco, A., & Manuti, A. (2020). Work engagement and job crafting as conditions of ambivalent employees' adaptation to organizational change. *The Journal of Applied Behavioral Science*, *57*, 57–79. DOI: 10.5465/AMBPP.2019.14266

Ghislieri, C., Molino, M., & Cortese, C. G. (2018). Work and organizational psychology looks at the fourth industrial revolution: How to support workers and organizations? *Frontiers in Psychology*, *9*, 2365. DOI: 10.3389/fpsyg.2018.02365

Ghoneim, M. (2024). Strategic integration of Explainable AI in Recruitment: Towards a framework for Ethical decision-making and Stakeholder confidence.

Ghoshal, S. (2005). Bad management theories are destroying good management practices. *Academy of Management Learning & Education*, *4*(1), 75–91. DOI: 10.5465/amle.2005.16132558

Ghossoub, Z., Nadler, R., & El-Aswad, N. B. (2020). Emotional intelligence, resilience, self-care, and self-leadership in healthcare workers burnout. *Universal Journal of Public Health*, *8*(5), 155–162. DOI: 10.13189/ujph.2020.080501

Gilmore, J. H., & Pine, B. J. (2007). *Authenticity: What consumers really want*. Harvard Business Review Press.

Gioia, D. A., Schultz, M., & Corley, K. G. (2000). Organizational identity, image, and adaptive instability. *Academy of Management Review*, *25*(1), 63–81. DOI: 10.2307/259263

Glavas, A., & Kelley, K. (2014). The effects of perceived corporate social responsibility on employee attitudes. *Business Ethics Quarterly*, *24*(2), 165–202. DOI: 10.5840/beq20143206

Gogia, E. H., Shao, Z., Khan, K., Rehman, M. Z., Haddad, H., & Al-Ramahi, N. M. (2024). Exploring the relationship of organizational virtuousness, citizenship behavior, job performance, and combatting ostracism through structural equation modeling. *BMC Psychology*, *12*(1), 384. DOI: 10.1186/s40359-024-01873-9

Goleman, D. (1995). *Emotional intelligence: Why it can matter more than IQ*. Bantam Books.

Goleman, D. (2012). *Working with emotional intelligence*. Bloomsbury Publishing.

Goodman, B., & Flaxman, S. (2017). European Union regulations on algorithmic decision-making and a 'right to explanation.'. *AI Magazine*, *38*(3), 50–57. DOI: 10.1609/aimag.v38i3.2741

Gradinarova, N. (2021). *Leadership vs. management: Understanding the key differences and similarities*. https://typeset.io/papers/leadership-vs-management-understanding-the-key-differences-gfslxdyfvx

Graham, C. (2014). Late-life work and well-being. *IZA World of Labor: Evidence-Based Policy Making*. Advance online publication. DOI: 10.15185/izawol.107

Green, B. (2019). The false promise of risk assessments: Epistemic racism and the limits of fairness. *Proceedings of the 2019 ACM Conference on Fairness, Accountability, and Transparency*, 337–344. DOI: 10.1145/3287560.3287591

Grönroos, C. (1990). Relationship approach to marketing in service contexts: The marketing and organizational behavior interface. *Journal of Business Research*, *20*(1), 3–11. DOI: 10.1016/0148-2963(90)90037-E

Grönroos, C. (1990). *Service management and marketing: Managing the moments of truth in service competition*. Lexington Books.

Gross, J. J. (1998). The emerging field of emotion regulation. *Review of General Psychology, 2*(3), 271–299. DOI: 10.1037/1089-2680.2.3.271

Guenole, N., Ferrar, J., & Feinzig, S. (2017). *The power of people: How successful organizations use workforce analytics to improve business performance*. Pearson FT Press.

Guerreiro, M., Muhs, C., Carvalho Neves, M., Engel, L., & Fernandes Cardoso, L. (2023). Green marketing: A case study of the outdoor apparel brand Patagonia. *Responsibility and Sustainability, 8*(2), 49–57. DOI: 10.5281/zenodo.8078762

Gunda, V. N., & Muzira, J. (2025). *Leveraging Predictive Analytics for Workforce Planning*. Succession Planning, And Organizational Development.

Gupta, A. K., & Govindarajan, V. (2000). Knowledge flows within multinational corporations. *Strategic Management Journal, 21*(4), 473–496. DOI: 10.1002/(SICI)1097-0266(200004)21:4<473::AID-SMJ84>3.0.CO;2-I

Gutterman, A. S. (2023). *Leadership traits and attributes. SSRN*. https://papers.ssrn.com/sol3/papers.cfm?abstract_id=4560190

Han, X., Li, Q., & Wang, X. (2024). Investigating how corporate social responsibility affects employees' thriving at work: A social exchange perspective. *Sustainability (Basel), 16*(3), 1095. DOI: 10.3390/su16031095

Harris, K. (2020). *A New Gener A New Generation of W ation of Workers: Pr ers: Preparing for Gener eparing for Generation Z in the ation Z in the. Senior Theses*. University of South Carolina - Columbia.

Harter, J. K., Schmidt, F. L., & Hayes, T. L. (2002). Business-unit-level relationship between employee satisfaction, employee engagement, and business outcomes: A meta-analysis. *The Journal of Applied Psychology, 87*(2), 268–279. DOI: 10.1037/0021-9010.87.2.268 PMID: 12002955

Heger, B. (2024). Enabling Strategic Workforce Planning Through Skills, Artificial Intelligence, and Internal Talent Marketplace. Strategic Workforce Planning: Best Practices and Emerging Directions, 164.

Hennekam, S., Richard, S., & Grima, F. (2020). Coping with mental health conditions at work and its impact on self-perceived job performance. *Employee Relations, 42*(3), 626–645. DOI: 10.1108/ER-05-2019-0211

Hennink, M., Hutter, I., & Bailey, A. (2020). Qualitative Research Methods. *Sage (Atlanta, Ga.)*.

Hermansyah, Tukiran, M., Herlina, E., & Andrianto, M. T. (2022). A review of Strategic Human Resources Management in organization. *Budapest International Research and Critics Institute-Journal (BIRCI-Journal), 5*(2), 14422–14431. https://doi.org/DOI: 10.33258/birci.v5i2.5309

Hernández-Herrera, J. R., Ortiz-Bejar, J., & Ortiz-Bejar, J. (2026). Adaptive and Personalized Learning in Higher Education: An Artificial Intelligence-Based Approach. *Education Sciences, 16*(1), 109.

Herzberg, F. (1966). *Work and the nature of man.* World Publishing.

Highhouse, S. (2008). Stubborn reliance on intuition and subjectivity in employee selection. *Industrial and Organizational Psychology: Perspectives on Science and Practice, 1*(3), 333–342. DOI: 10.1111/j.1754-9434.2008.00058.x

Hindustan Unilever Limited. (2023). Annual Report.

Hines, P. (Novembro de 2021). Human Centred Lean - An Introduction to the People Value Stream. *International Journal of Lean Six Sigma, 13 (5)*, 961-988.

Hobfoll, S. E., Halbesleben, J., Neveu, J.-P., & Westman, M. (2018). Conservation of resources in the organizational context: The reality of resources and their consequences. *Annual Review of Organizational Psychology and Organizational Behavior, 5*(1), 103–128. DOI: 10.1146/annurev-orgpsych-032117-104640

Homer-Dixon, T. (2020). The age of global risk: Three responses. *Global Policy, 11*(5), 547–556. DOI: 10.1111/1758-5899.12849

Hongal, P., & Kinange, U. (Fevereiro de 2020). A Study on Talent Management and its Impact on Organization Performance - An Empirical Review. *International Journal of Engineering and Management Research, 10 (01)*, 64-71.

Hossain, M. Z., Arefin, T., & Urme, U. N. (2025). The financial impact of Strategic HRM practices: Linking employee investments to organizational performance. *European Journal of Management. Economics and Business, 2*(2), 25–39. DOI: 10.59324/ejmeb.2025.2(2).02

HR.com. (2025). *HR.com's state of employer branding 2025.* HR.com.

ICICI Bank. (2023). Annual Report.

Infosys. (2023). Annual Report.

Infosys. (2023). Environmental, Social and Governance (ESG) Report.

Ismail, A., Hidajat, T., Dora, Y. M., Prasatia, F. E., & Pranadani, A. (2023). *Leading the Digital Transformation: Evidence from Indonesia.* Asadel Publisher.

Jobin, A., Ienca, M., & Vayena, E. (2019). The global landscape of AI ethics guidelines. *Nature Machine Intelligence*, *1*(9), 389–399. DOI: 10.1038/s42256-019-0088-2

John, A. S., & Hajam, A. A. (2024). Leveraging Predictive Analytics for Enhancing Employee Engagement and Optimizing Workforce Planning: A Data-Driven HR Management Approach. *International Journal of Innovation in Management. Economics and Social Sciences*, *4*(4), 33–41.

Johns, G. (2010). Presenteeism in the workplace: A review and research agenda. *Journal of Organizational Behavior*, *31*(4), 519–542. DOI: 10.1002/job.630

Judge, T. A., & Bono, J. E. (2001). Relationship of core self-evaluations traits—self-esteem, generalized self-efficacy, locus of control, and emotional stability—with job satisfaction and job performance: A meta-analysis. *The Journal of Applied Psychology*, *86*(1), 80–92. DOI: 10.1037/0021-9010.86.1.80

Just, J. (2024). Natural language processing for innovation search–Reviewing an emerging non-human innovation intermediary. *Technovation*, *129*, 102883. DOI: 10.1016/j.technovation.2023.102883

Kabat-Zinn, J. (2003). Mindfulness-based interventions in context: Past, present, and future. *Clinical Psychology : a Publication of the Division of Clinical Psychology of the American Psychological Association*, *10*(2), 144–156. DOI: 10.1093/clipsy.bpg016

Kahn, W. A. (1990). Psychological conditions of personal engagement and disengagement at work. *Academy of Management Journal*, *33*(4), 692–724. DOI: 10.2307/256287

Kaliannan, M., Darmalinggam, D., Dorasamy, M., & Abraham, M. (2023, March 1). Inclusive talent development as a key talent management approach: A systematic literature review. *Human Resource Management Review*, *33*(1), 100926. DOI: 10.1016/j.hrmr.2022.100926

Kane, G. C., Palmer, D., Phillips, A. N., Kiron, D., & Buckley, N. (2019). Accelerating digital innovation inside and out: Agile teams, ecosystems, and ethics. MIT Sloan Management Review and Deloitte Insights. https://www2.deloitte.com/us/en/insights/focus/digital-maturity/digital-innovation-ecosystems-organizational-agility.html

Karanges, E., Johnston, K., Beatson, A., & Lings, I. (2015). The influence of internal communication on employee engagement: A pilot study. *Public Relations Review*, *41*(1), 129–131. DOI: 10.1016/j.pubrev.2014.12.003

Kashoob, B.. (2025). Strategic Human Resources Management. *Journal of Posthumanism, 5*(4), 643–650.

Kataria, A. (2014). High performance HR practices and employee well-being: A mediation model. *Human Resource Management, 53*(3), 407–426. DOI: 10.1002/hrm.21608

Kawai, K., & Yamazaki, Y. (2006). The effects of pre-entry career maturity and support networks on newcomers' mental health. *Journal of Occupational Health, 48*(6), 451–461. DOI: 10.1539/joh.48.451

Keles, B., McCrae, N., & Grealish, A. (2020). A Systematic Review: The Influence of Social Media on Depression, Anxiety and Psychological Distress in Adolescents. *International Journal of Adolescence and Youth, 25*, 79–93. DOI: 10.1080/02673843.2019.1590851

Kellogg, K. C., Valentine, M. A., & Christin, A. (2020). Algorithms at work. *Annual Review of Sociology, 46*, 29–51. DOI: 10.1146/annurev-soc-121919-054857

Kellogg, K. C., Valentine, M. A., & Christin, A. (2020). Algorithms at work: The new contested terrain of control. *The Academy of Management Annals, 14*(1), 366–410. DOI: 10.5465/annals.2018.0174

Kess-Momoh, A. J., Tula, S. T., Bello, B. G., Omotoye, G. B., & Daraojimba, A. I. (2024). Strategic human resource management in the 21st century: A review of trends and innovations. *World Journal of Advanced Research and Reviews, 21*(1), 746–757. DOI: 10.30574/wjarr.2024.21.1.0105

Keyes, C. L., Schmotkin, D., & Ryff, C. D. (2002). Optimizing well-being: The empirical encounter of two traditions. *Journal of Personality and Social Psychology, 82*(6), 1007–1022. DOI: 10.1037/0022-3514.82.6.1007

Khajeh, E. H. (2018). Impact of leadership styles on organizational performance. *Journal of Human Resources Management Research*. DOI: DOI: 10.5171/2018.687849

Khesroh, E., Butt, M., Kalantari, A., Leslie, D. L., Bronson, S., Rigby, A., & Aumiller, B. (2022). The use of emotional intelligence skills in combating burnout among residency and fellowship program directors. *BMC Medical Education, 22*, 127. DOI: 10.1186/s12909-022-03187-z

Khoreva, V. (2018). High performance work systems and employee well-being: An investigation of the mediating role of job crafting. *International Journal of Human Resource Management, 29*(17), 2579–2600. DOI: 10.1080/09585192.2016.1277822

Khuntia, R. (2025, April 1). From Job Security to Skill Security: Embracing Adaptability in India's Evolving Job Market. *Splint International Journal of Professionals.*, *12*(2), 261–266. DOI: 10.5958/2583-3561.2025.00022.0

Kim, J., Henly, J. R., Golden, L. M., & Lambert, S. J. (2019). Workplace flexibility and worker well-being by gender. *Journal of Marriage and the Family*, *82*(3), 892–910. DOI: 10.1111/jomf.12633

Kim, S., Lee, H., & Connerton, T. P. (2020). How psychological safety affects team performance: Mediating role of efficacy and learning behavior. *Frontiers in Psychology*, *11*, 1581. DOI: 10.3389/fpsyg.2020.01581

King, C., & Grace, D. (2008). Internal branding: Exploring the employee's perspective. *Journal of Brand Management*, *15*(5), 358–372. DOI: 10.1057/palgrave.bm.2550136

Kirwin, M., & Ettinger, A. (2022). Working mothers during COVID-19: A cross-sectional study. *BMC Public Health*, *22*(1), 435. Advance online publication. DOI: 10.1186/s12889-021-12468-z

Kleinberg, J., Mullainathan, S., & Raghavan, M. (2016). Inherent trade-offs in the fair determination of risk scores. *Proceedings of the 8th Innovations in Theoretical Computer Science Conference*. DOI: 10.4230/LIPIcs.ITCS.2017.43

Klein, H. J., Polin, B., & Sutton, K. L. (2015). Specific Onboarding Practices for the Socialization of New Employees. *International Journal of Selection and Assessment*, *23*(3), 263–283. DOI: 10.1111/ijsa.12113

Kochling, A., & Wehner, M. C. (2020). Discriminated by an algorithm: A systematic review of discrimination and fairness by algorithmic decision-making in the context of HR recruitment and HR development. *Business Research*, *13*(3), 795–848. 1. DOI: 10.1007/s40685-020-00134-w

Koesters, S. C., Shea, T., & Satiani, B. (2017). *It's about the people, not being the boss*. https://typeset.io/papers/it-s-about-the-people-not-being-the-boss-1iirsb1aho

Kong, K. G. (2024). Prevailing moral standards in higher education institutions. International Journal on Culture, History, &. *Religion*, *6*(2), 32–42. DOI: 10.63931/ijchr.v6i2.4

Korakis, G., & Poulaki, I. (2025). A systematic literature review on the relationship between emotional intelligence and transformational leadership—A critical approach. *Businesses*, *5*(1), 4. DOI: 10.3390/businesses5010004

Kossek, E. E., Thompson, R. J., & Lautsch, B. A. (2015). Balanced workplace flexibility: Avoiding the traps. *California Management Review*, *57*(4), 5–25. DOI: 10.1525/cmr.2015.57.4.5

Kumar, P. (2024). *Leadership styles and their influence on project team performance.* Nonhuman Journal., DOI: 10.70008/nhj.v1i06.29

Kuusisto, T. (2024). *Examining onboarding and employee engagement in field service teams: A case study of Europe and Africa area energy projects.* (UNIVERSITY OF VAASA, School of Technology and Innovation, Ed.) [Review of *Examining onboarding and employee engagement in field service teams: A case study of Europe and Africa area energy projects.*].

Langer, M., Konig, C. J., & Papathanasiou, M. (2019). Highly automated job interviews: Acceptance under the influence of stakes. *International Journal of Selection and Assessment*, *27*(3), 217–234. DOI: 10.1111/ijsa.12246

Lanka, E., Lanka, S. V., Rostron, A., & Singh, P. (2021). *Why We Need Qualitative Research in Management Studies.* Revista de Administração Contemporânea. DOI: 10.1590/1982-7849rac2021200297.en

Leadership – Advancing great leaders and leadership. (2023). In *IntechOpen Books*. https://www.intechopen.com/books/12141

Lee, M. K. (2018). Understanding perception of algorithmic decisions: Fairness, trust, and emotion in response to algorithmic management. *Big Data & Society*, *5*(1), 2053951718756684. Advance online publication. DOI: 10.1177/2053951718756684

Lee, M. Y. P., & So, D. W. C. (2007). Corporate slogans of corporations operating in Greater China. *Corporate Communications*, *12*(1), 58–74. DOI: 10.1108/13563280710723750

Lee, Y., & Chelladurai, P. (2018). Emotional intelligence, emotional labor, coach burnout, job satisfaction, and turnover intention in sport leadership. *European Sport Management Quarterly*, *18*(4), 393–412. DOI: 10.1080/16184742.2017.1406971

Lee, Y., & Kim, K. H. (2021). Enhancing employee advocacy on social media: The value of an internal relationship management approach. *Corporate Communications*, *26*(5), 869–884. DOI: 10.1108/CCIJ-05-2020-0088

Leonardi, P. M. (2021). COVID-19 and the new technologies of organizing: Digital exhaust, digital footprints, and artificial intelligence in the wake of remote work. *Journal of Management Studies*, *58*(1), 249–253. DOI: 10.1111/joms.12648

Leonardi, P. M., & Treem, J. W. (2020). Behavioral visibility: A new paradigm for organization studies in the age of digitization, digitalization, and datafication. *Organization Studies*. Advance online publication. DOI: 10.1177/0170840620970728

Lepeley, M. T., Kuschel, K., Beutell, N., Pouw, N., & Eijdenberg, E. L. (Eds.). (2020). *The wellbeing of women in entrepreneurship: A global perspective*. Routledge., DOI: 10.4324/9780429279836

Leventhal, G. S. (1980). What should be done with equity theory? In Gergen, K. J., Greenberg, M. S., & Willis, R. H. (Eds.), *Social exchange: Advances in theory and research* (pp. 27–55). Plenum Press. DOI: 10.1007/978-1-4613-3087-5_2

Lind, E. A., & Tyler, T. R. (1988). *The social psychology of procedural justice*. Plenum Press. DOI: 10.1007/978-1-4899-2115-4

Li, R. Y. M., Alzuman, A., & Manta, O. (2024). Balancing wellbeing and responsibility: CSR's role in mitigating burnout in hospitality under UN-SDGs. *Sustainability (Basel), 16*(8), 3374. DOI: 10.3390/su16083374

Li, Y., & Qiu, B. (2023). Relationship Between Doom-scrolling and Mental Health under the Influence of Recommendation Algorithms. *Lecture Notes in Education Psychology and Public Media, 15*, 148–157. DOI: 10.54254/2753-7048/15/20231048

Luthans, F., Youssef, C. M., & Avolio, B. J. (2007). *Psychological capital: Developing the human competitive edge*. Oxford University Press., DOI: 10.1093/acprof:oso/9780195187526.001.0001

Machynska, N., Blikhar, V., & Kuzhur, A. (2024). *Formação de competências de liderança no processo de preparação profissional de futuros especialistas no ensino superior* [Формування лідерських рис у процесі професійної підготовки майбутніх фахівців в умовах закладу вищої освіти]. Scientific Educational Review., DOI: 10.55643/ser.1.51.2024.556

Mael, F., & Ashforth, B. E. (1992). Alumni and their alma mater: A partial test of the reformulated model of organizational identification. *Journal of Organizational Behavior, 13*(2), 103–123. DOI: 10.1002/job.4030130202

Mahindra Group. (2023). *Sustainability Report.*

Maia, G. (2022). Gestão de Pessoas e Recursos Humanos: Tendências Pós-Pandemia. *Revista Ibero-Americana de Humanidades. Ciência & Educação (Bauru), 8*(2), 705–728.

Makhbul, Z. K. M., Alam, S. S., & Zihan, W. (2024). Green human resource management in practice: Assessing the impact of readiness and corporate social responsibility on organizational change. *Sustainability (Basel)*, *16*(3), 1153. DOI: 10.3390/su16031153

Mancuso, I., Petruzzelli, A. M., Panniello, U., & Vaia, G. (2025, May 1). The bright and dark sides of AI innovation for sustainable development: Understanding the paradoxical tension between value creation and value destruction. *Technovation*, *143*, 103232. DOI: 10.1016/j.technovation.2025.103232

Mansuroğlu, E., & Smith, A. P. (2026, March). Technostress and Employee Well-being: A Systematic Review of Empirical Evidence. *Computers in Human Behavior Reports*, *21*, 100941. Advance online publication. DOI: 10.1016/j.chbr.2026.100941

Marler, J. H., & Boudreau, J. W. (2017). An evidence-based review of HR analytics. *International Journal of Human Resource Management*, *28*(1), 3–26. DOI: 10.1080/09585192.2016.1244699

Marsh, G., Lewis, V., Macmillan, J., & Gruszin, S. (2018). Workplace wellness: Industry associations are well placed and some are ready to take a more active role in workplace health. *BMC Health Services Research*, *18*(1), 565. DOI: 10.1186/s12913-018-3364-7

Maslach, C., & Jackson, S. E. (1981). The measurement of experienced burnout. *Journal of Organizational Behavior*, *2*(2), 99–113. DOI: 10.1002/job.4030020205

Maslach, C., Schaufeli, W. B., & Leiter, M. P. (2001). Job burnout. *Annual Review of Psychology*, *52*(1), 397–422. DOI: 10.1146/annurev.psych.52.1.397 PMID: 11148311

Matten, D., & Crane, A. (2005). Corporate citizenship: Toward an extended theoretical conceptualization. *Academy of Management Review*, *30*(1), 166–179. DOI: 10.5465/amr.2005.15281448

Maxwell, J. C. (2011). *Os 5 níveis da liderança*. https://pt.scribd.com/document/568195267/OS-5-NIVEIS-DA-LIDERANCA

Mayer, D. M., Kuenzi, M., Greenbaum, R., Bardes, M., & Salvador, R. (2012). How low is ethical leadership flow? Test of a trickle-down model. *Organizational Behavior and Human Decision Processes*, *108*(1), 1–13. DOI: 10.1016/j.obhdp.2008.04.002

Mayer, J. D., & Salovey, P. (1997). What is emotional intelligence? In Salovey, P., & Sluyter, D. J. (Eds.), *Emotional development and emotional intelligence* (pp. 3–34). Basic Books.

Mayer, R. C., Davis, J. H., & Schoorman, F. D. (1995). An integrative model of organizational trust. *Academy of Management Review, 20*(3), 709–734. DOI: 10.2307/258792

Mayo, E. (1933). *The Human Problems of an Industrial Civilization.* The Macmillan Co.

Mazmanian, M., Orlikowski, W. J., & Yates, J. (2013). The autonomy paradox. *Organization Science, 24*(5), 1337–1357. DOI: 10.1287/orsc.1120.0806

McAllister, D. J. (1995). Affect- and cognition-based trust as foundations for interpersonal cooperation in organizations. *Academy of Management Journal, 38*(1), 24–59. DOI: 10.2307/256727

McArthur, J. W., Rasmussen, K., & Rozema, J. G. (2018). Who and what gets left behind? Assessing Canada's domestic status on the Sustainable Development Goals. *Canadian Public Policy, 44*(supplement 1), S26–S42. DOI: 10.3138/cpp.2017-061

Meneghetti, F. K. (2011). O que é um ensaio teórico? *Revista de Administração Contemporânea, 15*(2), 320–332. https://doi.org/DOI: 10.1590/S1415-65552011000200010

Men, L. R. (2014). Strategic internal communication: Transformational leadership, communication channels, and employee satisfaction. *Management Communication Quarterly, 28*(2), 264–284. DOI: 10.1177/0893318914524536

Men, L. R., & Yue, C. A. (2019). Creating a positive emotional culture: Effect of internal communication and impact on employee supportive behaviors. *Public Relations Review, 45*(3), 101764. DOI: 10.1016/j.pubrev.2019.03.001

Merlo, G., Rossi, A., & De Luca, F. (2025). Digital work environments and employee well-being. *Human Resource Management Review, 35*(1), 100934. DOI: 10.1016/j.hrmr.2024.100934

Meyer, J. P., & Allen, N. J. (1991). A three-component conceptualization of organizational commitment. *Human Resource Management Review, 1*(1), 61–89. DOI: 10.1016/1053-4822(91)90011-Z

Miao, C., Humphrey, R. H., & Qian, S. (2018). A cross-cultural meta-analysis of how leader emotional intelligence influences subordinate task performance and organizational citizenship behavior. *Journal of World Business, 53*(4), 463–474. DOI: 10.1016/j.jwb.2018.01.003

Mihaela, Ţ., & Maria Cristina, I. (2016). Generation Y's Work Values and Their Impact on thE HOSPITALIty Industry. *Cactus Tourism Journal, 14*(2), 5–11.

Mikalef, P., & Gupta, M. (2021). Artificial intelligence capability: Conceptualization, measurement calibration, and empirical study on its impact on organizational creativity and firm performance. *Information & Management, 58*(3), 103434. Advance online publication. DOI: 10.1016/j.im.2021.103434

Mir, A. I. (2024, November 30). Application of AI in talent management: A systematic review of benefits, challenges, and prospects. *Academy of Education and Social Sciences Review., 4*(4), 612–630. DOI: 10.48112/aessr.v4i4.941

Mitchell, M. S., Cropanzano, R., & Quisenberry, D. M. (2012). Social exchange theory, exchange resources, and interpersonal relationships: A modest resolution of theoretical difficulties. In Törnblom, K., & Kazemi, A. (Eds.), *Handbook of social resource theory: Theoretical extensions, empirical insights, and social applications* (pp. 99–118). Springer., DOI: 10.1007/978-1-4614-4175-5_6

Mitchell, R. K., Agle, B. R., & Wood, D. J. (1997). Toward a theory of stakeholder identification and salience: Defining the principle of who and what really counts. *Academy of Management Review, 22*(4), 853–886. DOI: 10.2307/259247

Mittelstadt, B. D., Allo, P., Taddeo, M., Wachter, S., & Floridi, L. (2016). The ethics of algorithms: Mapping the debate. *Big Data & Society, 3*(2), 1–21. DOI: 10.1177/2053951716679679

Moitra, P., Santomauro, D. F., Collins, P. Y., Vos, T., & Whiteford, H. (2022). The global gap in treatment coverage for major depressive disorder: A systematic review and Bayesian meta-regression analysis. *PLoS Medicine, 19*(2), e1003901. DOI: 10.1371/journal.pmed.1003901

Monteiro, B., Santos, V., Reis, I., Sampaio, M. C., Sousa, B., Martinho, F., José Sousa, M., & Au-Yong-Oliveira, M. (2020). Employer Branding Applied to SMEs: A Pioneering Model Proposal for Attracting and Retaining Talent. *Information (Basel), 11*(12), 574. DOI: 10.3390/info11120574

Moore, P. V. (2020). Surveillance, work and the pandemic. *The Political Quarterly, 91*(3), 542–552. DOI: 10.1111/1467-923X.12898 PMID: 32836412

Morgan, D. L. (1997). *Focus groups as qualitative research* (2nd ed.). Sage. DOI: 10.4135/9781412984287

Morhart, F., Malär, L., Guèvremont, A., Girardin, F., & Grohmann, B. (2015). Brand authenticity: An integrative framework and measurement scale. *Journal of Consumer Psychology, 25*(2), 200–218. DOI: 10.1016/j.jcps.2014.11.006

Morrison, E. W., & Robinson, S. L. (1997). When employees feel betrayed: A model of how psychological contract violation develops. *Academy of Management Review, 22*(1), 226–256. DOI: 10.2307/259230

Mosley, R. (2014). *Employer brand management: Practical lessons from the world's leading employers*. Wiley.

Mosley, R. (2015). Employer brand management: Practical lessons from the world's leading employers. *Strategic HR Review, 14*(1/2), 1–7. DOI: 10.1108/SHR-01-2015-0001

Murugesan, U., Subramanian, P., Srivastava, S., & Dwivedi, A. (2023, June 1). A study of artificial intelligence impacts on human resource digitalization in industry 4.0. *Decision Analytics Journal., 7*, 100249. DOI: 10.1016/j.dajour.2023.100249

Mwambela, A. (2024). Strategic human resource management integration and organizational performance: Evidence from profit-oriented companies in Zambia. *Journal of Innovative Business and Management, 16*(1), 2–18. DOI: 10.32015/JIBM.2024.16.1.2

Nam, T. (2019). Technology usage, expected job sustainability, and perceived job insecurity. *Technological Forecasting and Social Change, 138*, 155–165. DOI: 10.1016/j.techfore.2018.08.017

Nastase, C., Adomnitei, A., & Apetri, A. (2025). Strategic Human Resource Management in the digital era: Technology, transformation, and sustainable advantage. *Merits, 5*(4), 23. DOI: 10.3390/merits5040023

Newman, A., Donohue, R., & Eva, N. (2017). Psychological safety: A systematic review of the literature. *Human Resource Management Review, 27*(3), 521–535. DOI: 10.1016/j.hrmr.2017.01.001

Nielsen, K., & Einarsen, S. (2018). Outcomes of exposure to workplace bullying: A meta-analytic review. *Work and Stress, 32*(1), 1–23. DOI: 10.1080/02678373.2022.2080775

Nielsen, K., Nielsen, M. B., Ogbonnaya, C., Känsälä, M., Saari, E., & Isaksson, K. (2017). Workplace resources to improve both employee well-being and performance: A systematic review and meta-analysis. *Work and Stress, 31*(2), 101–120. DOI: 10.1080/02678373.2017.1304463

Nkomo, S. M., & Hoobler, J. M. (2014). A historical perspective on diversity ideologies in the United States: Reflections on human resource management research and practice. *Human Resource Management Review, 24*(3), 245–257. DOI: 10.1016/j.hrmr.2014.03.006

Noe, R. A., Clarke, A. D. M., & Klein, H. J. (2021). Learning in the twenty-first-century workplace. *Annual Review of Organizational Psychology and Organizational Behavior, 8*, 245–275. DOI: 10.1146/annurev-orgpsych-012420-055226

Nwagwu, U., & Henry, U. C. (2025). Emotional Intelligence and Leadership Effectiveness. Journal of Arts and Sociological Research.

O'Neil, S., & Koekemoer, E. (2016). Two decades of qualitative research in Psychology, Industrial and Organisational Psychology and Human Resource Management within South Africa: A critical review. *SA Journal of Industrial Psychology, 42*(1). Advance online publication. DOI: 10.4102/sajip.v42i1.1350

OECD. (2019). *Recommendation of the Council on Artificial Intelligence (OECD/LEGAL/0449)*. OECD.

Onyekachi, A., Okoro, U., & Iqbal, Z. (2025). Predictive Analytics in Talent Management: Enhancing Recruitment and Retention through AI.

Organisation for Economic Co-operation and Development. (2022). *Promoting health and well-being at work: Policy and practices* (Policy brief). OECD Publishing. https://www.oecd.org/health/promoting-health-and-well-being-at-work-policy-and-practices.pdf

Oswald, F. L., & Putka, D. J. (Eds.). (2016). *Statistical methods for personnel research.* Society for Industrial and Organizational Psychology.

Owens, E. G., & Wagner, S. L. (2015). Barriers to employment for people with severe mental illness: A review, and implications for supported employment approaches. *Work : A Journal of Prevention, Assessment, and Rehabilitation, 50*(2), 309–320. DOI: 10.3233/WOR-152085

Parameswaran, H. (2021). Flexible work designs, as a strategic tool for twenty-first-century intricacies: A descriptive analysis amongst healthcare employees in the United Arab Emirates. *Acta Polytechnica Hungarica, 18*(11), 135–150. DOI: 10.12700/APH.18.11.2021.11.8

Pariser, E. (2011). *The filter bubble*. Penguin Press. https://hci.stanford.edu/courses/cs047n/readings/The_Filter_Bubble.pdf

Park, H., & Lee, K. S. (2023). The association of adolescents' mental health with economic impact during the COVID-19 pandemic: A nationally representative survey. *BMC Public Health, 23*, 853. DOI: 10.1186/s12889-023-15808-3

Pasquale, F. (2015). *The black box society: The secret algorithms that control money and information*. Harvard University Press. DOI: 10.4159/harvard.9780674736061

Pavlakou, E., Katsarou, M., Misiou, M., Nakou, M., Papakosta, M. A., & Papavasilopoulos, V. (2025). The Impact of Artificial Intelligence on Learning and Development-Case Studies in Companies of Different Sectors. *Current Res. J. Soc. Sci. & Human.*, *8*(1), 49–66. DOI: 10.12944/CRJSSH.8.1.05

Petrou, P., Demerouti, E., & Schaufeli, W. B. (2018). Crafting the change: The role of employee job crafting behaviors for successful organizational change. *Journal of Management*, *44*(5), 1766–1792. DOI: 10.1177/0149206315624961

Pizzolitto, E., Verna, I., & Venditti, M. (2022). Authoritarian leadership styles and performance: a systematic literature review and research agenda. Management Review Quarterly, 1-31.

Prasad, D. B. V., Hamraaia, M. H. Y., & Sharma, D. A., B.c, S., & Pereira, M. C. S. (2024). The Impact of Technology on Human Resource Management: Trends and Challenges. *Educational Administration: Theory and Practice*, *30*(5), 9746–9752.

Prifti, K., Vrusho, B., Toci, Ç., Prendi, L., & Gjuzi, J. B. (2025). Strategic Human Resource Management and its impact on organizational performance: Empirical insights. *International Journal of Innovative Technology and Interdisciplinary Sciences*, *8*(3), 550–594. DOI: 10.15157/IJITIS.2025.8.3.550-594

Prilleltensky, I. (2011). Wellness as fairness. *American Journal of Community Psychology*, *49*(1–2), 1–21. DOI: 10.1007/s10464-011-9448-8

PwC. (2023). 2023 AI business predictions. https://www.pwc.com/us/en/tech-effect/ai-analytics/ai-predictions.html

Raghavan, V., Barocas, S., Kleinberg, J., & Levy, K. (2020). Algorithmic fairness. In *Proceedings of the 2020 Conference on Fairness, Accountability, and Transparency* (pp. 101–112). ACM. https://doi.org/DOI: 10.1145/3351095.3372878

Rahman, M. S., & Ahmad, F. (2022). Internal employer brand, employee engagement and perceived organizational support: A review of literature. *The Economics and Business Review*, *8*(2), 45–59. DOI: 10.18559/ebr.2022.2.3

Raji, I. D., Smart, A., White, R. N., Mitchell, M., Gebru, T., Hutchinson, B., Smith-Loud, J., Theron, D., & Barnes, P. (2020). Closing the AI accountability gap: Defining an end-to-end framework for internal algorithmic auditing. *Proceedings of the ACM Co* DOI: 10.1145/3351095.3372873

Rasmussen, T., & Ulrich, D. (2015). Learning from practice: How HR analytics avoids being a management fad. *Organizational Dynamics*, *44*(3), 236–242. DOI: 10.1016/j.orgdyn.2015.05.008

Redondo, J. A., Inocêncio, F., & Silva, R. (2019). O endomarketing como estratégia na gestão de pessoas: Clima organizacional e compromisso. *Revista Gestão e Desenvolvimento, 16*(2), 67–86. DOI: 10.26458/1728

Rego, A., Cunha, M. P., Gomes, J. F., Cunha, R. C., Cabral-Cardoso, C., & Marques, C. A. (2008). *Manual de Gestão de Pessoas e do Capital Humano*. Edições Sílabo.

Reliance Industries Limited. (2023). Annual Report.

Reserve Bank of India. (2022). Reports on Banking Workforce Practices.

Rhoades, L., & Eisenberger, R. (2002). Perceived organizational support: A review of the literature. *The Journal of Applied Psychology, 87*(4), 698–714. DOI: 10.1037/0021-9010.87.4.698

Ribeiro, A. L. (2005). *Gestão de Pessoas*. Saraiva.

Richards, J. (2012). Examining the exclusion of employees with Asperger syndrome from the workplace. *Personnel Review, 41*(5), 630–646. DOI: 10.1108/00483481211249148

Rich, S. A., Hanna, S., Wright, B. J., & Bennett, P. C. (2017). Fact or fable: Increased wellbeing in voluntary simplicity. *International Journal of Wellbeing, 7*(2), 64–77. DOI: 10.5502/ijw.v7i2.589

Roberson, Q. M. (2006). Disentangling the meanings of diversity and inclusion. *Group & Organization Management, 31*(2), 212–236. DOI: 10.1177/1059601104273064

Rodgers, W., Murray, J. M., Stefanidis, A., Degbey, W. Y., & Tarba, S. Y. (2023, March 1). An artificial intelligence algorithmic approach to ethical decision-making in human resource management processes. *Human Resource Management Review, 33*(1), 100925. DOI: 10.1016/j.hrmr.2022.100925

Rother, E. T. (2007). Revisão sistemática versus revisão integrativa. *Acta Paulista de Enfermagem, 20*(2), v–vi. DOI: 10.1590/S0103-21002007000200001

Rousseau, D. M. (1989). Psychological and implied contracts in organizations. *Employee Responsibilities and Rights Journal, 2*(2), 121–139. DOI: 10.1007/BF01384942

Rousseau, D. M. (1995). Psychological contracts in organizations: Understanding written and unwritten agreements. *Sage (Atlanta, Ga.)*. Advance online publication. DOI: 10.4135/9781452231594

Rousseau, D. M., Hansen, S. D., & Tomprou, M. (2018). A dynamic phase model of psychological contract processes. *Journal of Organizational Behavior, 39*(9), 1081–1098. DOI: 10.1002/job.2284

Rožman, M., Oreški, D., & Tominc, P. (2022). Integrating artificial intelligence into a talent management model to increase the work engagement and performance of enterprises. *Frontiers in Psychology, 13*, 1014434. DOI: 10.3389/fpsyg.2022.1014434 PMID: 36506984

Ruck, K., Welch, M., & Menara, B. (2017). Employee voice: An antecedent to organizational engagement? *Public Relations Review, 43*(5), 904–914. DOI: 10.1016/j.pubrev.2017.04.008

Rugulies, R. (2012). Studying the effect of the psychosocial work environment on risk of ill-health: Towards a more comprehensive assessment of working conditions. *Scandinavian Journal of Work, Environment & Health, 38*(3), 187–191. DOI: 10.5271/sjweh.3296

Rusli, U., Masnia, M., Usman, A., & Mediaty, M. (2024). The role of supply chain management in enhancing corporate operational performance: A systematic literature review. *Indonesian Interdisciplinary Journal of Sharia Economics, 8*(1), 1076–1090. DOI: 10.31538/iijse.v8i1.5981

Russell, S., & Norvig, P. (2021). *Artificial intelligence: A modern approach* (4th ed.). Pearson.

Ryan, M. (2024). We're only human after all: A critique of human-centered AI. *AI & Society*. Advance online publication. DOI: 10.1007/s00146-024-01976-2

Ryan, R. M., & Deci, E. L. (2000). Self-determination theory and the facilitation of intrinsic motivation, social development, and well-being. *The American Psychologist, 55*(1), 68–78. DOI: 10.1037/0003-066X.55.1.68

Ryff, C. D., Singer, B. H., & Love, G. D. (2004). Positive health: Connecting well-being with biology. *Philosophical Transactions of the Royal Society of London. Series B, Biological Sciences, 359*(1449), 1383–1394. DOI: 10.1098/rstb.2004.1521

Saindon, J. (2025). Attention fragmentation and cognitive decline associated with excessive smartphone use. *Journal of Cognitive Psychology, 37*(2), 134–149. DOI: 10.1080/20445911.2024.2389012

Saks, A. M., & Gruman, J. (2011). Organizational Socialization and Positive Organizational Behaviour: Implications for Theory, Research, and Practice. *Canadian Journal of Administrative Sciences/Revue Canadienne des Sciences de l'Administration, 28(4)*, 14 - 26.

Saks, A. M. (2006). Antecedents and consequences of employee engagement. *Journal of Managerial Psychology, 21*(7), 600–619. DOI: 10.1108/02683940610690169

Saks, A. M. (2022). Caring human resources management and employee engagement. *Human Resource Management Review, 32*(3), 100835. DOI: 10.1016/j.hrmr.2021.100835

Saleem, F., & Iglesias, O. (2016). Mapping the domain of internal branding research: A bibliometric and content analysis. *Journal of Brand Management, 23*(6), 1–20. DOI: 10.1057/s41262-016-0005-5

Salovey, P., & Mayer, J. D. (1990). Emotional intelligence. *Imagination, Cognition and Personality, 9*(3), 185–211. DOI: 10.2190/DUGG-P24E-52WK-6CDG

Salvadorinho, J., Ferreira, C., & Teixeira, L. (2024, June 1). A technology-based framework to foster the lean human resource 4.0 and prevent the great resignation: The talent management lift. *Technology in Society, 77*, 102510. DOI: 10.1016/j.techsoc.2024.102510

Sánchez-Gómez, M., & Breso, E. (2020). Emotional intelligence as a moderator. *Psicothema, 32*(4), 604–611. DOI: 10.7334/psicothema2020.219

Sandoval-Reyes, J., Acosta-Prado, J. C., & Sanchís-Pedregosa, C. (2019). Relationship amongst technology use, work overload, and psychological detachment from work. *International Journal of Environmental Research and Public Health, 16*(23), 4602. DOI: 10.3390/ijerph16234602

Santos Filha, A. L., dos, , Lima, F. V. R., & Oliveira, J. F. (2021). Gestão de recursos humanos, comunicação organizacional e alinhamento estratégico: Proposição de um modelo teórico. *Research. Social Development, 10*(8), e22710817224. DOI: 10.33448/rsd-v10i8.17224

Santos, G. L., Gaspar, F. L., Rodrigues, M. B., & Baldissarelli, J. M. (2019). A Diversidade Geracional e as Políticas e Práticas de Recursos Humanos em Instituições de Ensino Superior. *Rev. Adm. UFSM, Santa Maria, v. 12, Edição Especial Ecoinovar*, pp. 1108-1126.

Santos, V., Simão, P., Reis, I., Sampaio, M. C., Martinho, F., & Sousa, B. (2023). Ethics and Sustainability in Hospitality Employer Branding. *Administrative Sciences, 13*(9), 202. DOI: 10.3390/admsci13090202

Schaufeli, W. B., & Bakker, A. B. (2004). Job demands, job resources, and burnout interventions. *Journal of Organizational Behavior, 25*(3), 293–315. DOI: 10.1002/job.248

Schaufeli, W. B., Salanova, M., González-Romá, V., & Bakker, A. B. (2002). Engagement and burnout. *Journal of Happiness Studies*, *3*(1), 71–92. DOI: 10.1023/A:1015630930326

Schein, E. H. (2010). *Organizational culture and leadership* (4th ed.). Jossey-Bass.

Schmidt, F. L., & Hunter, J. E. (1998). The validity and utility of selection methods in personnel psychology: Practical and theoretical implications of 85 years of research findings. *Psychological Bulletin*, *124*(2), 262–274. DOI: 10.1037/0033-2909.124.2.262

Schoeneborn, D., Blaschke, S., & Cooren, F. (2014). Communication theory and its use in organization studies. *Organization Studies*, *35*(2), 173–202. DOI: 10.1177/0170840613509966

Shaban, M., Ezzelregal Abdelgawad, M., Elsayed, S. M., & Abdallah, H. M. M. (2025). The mediating role of emotional intelligence in the relationship between technostress and burnout prevention among critical care nurses: A structural equation modelling approach. *BMC Nursing*, *24*(1), 255. Advance online publication. DOI: 10.1186/s12912-025-02852-0 PMID: 40050866

Sharf, R. (2014). Mindfulness and meditation: Traditional Buddhist sources and modern interpretations. *Journal of the American Academy of Religion*, *83*(3), 461–487. DOI: 10.1093/jaarel/lfu045

Sharma, G. G., & Stol, K.-J. (Outubro de 2019). Exploring Onboarding Success, Organizational Fit, and Turnover Intention of Software Professionals. *Journal of Systems and Software*, p. 159:110442.

Sharma, V., & Langford, S. (2025). A study on diversity, equity, and inclusion for enhancing workplace productivity in India.

Sharma, P. K., & Kumra, R. (2020). Relationship between workplace spirituality, organizational justice and mental health: Mediation role of employee engagement. *Journal of Advances in Management Research*, *17*(5), 627–650. DOI: 10.1108/JAMR-01-2020-0007

Shneiderman, B. (2020). Human-centered artificial intelligence: Reliable, safe & trustworthy. *International Journal of Human-Computer Interaction*, *36*(6), 495–504. DOI: 10.1080/10447318.2020.1741118

Shore, L. M., Randel, A. E., Chung, B. G., Dean, M. A., Holcombe Ehrhart, K., & Singh, G. (2011). Inclusion and diversity in work groups: A review and model for future research. *Journal of Management*, *37*(4), 1262–1289. DOI: 10.1177/0149206310385943

Shravan Anande, S., & Murarikar, H. P. (2025). India's proposed right to disconnect. *Indian Journal of Labour Law, 48*(2), 201–218. https://vidhilegalpolicy.in/blog/right-to-disconnect-in-india/

SHRM. (2023). *AI in HR: The adoption and application of artificial intelligence.* https://www.shrm.org/

Silva, S. M. (2019). *The Role of New Technologied for The Human Resources Management.* Universidade do Minho.

Sinval, J., Queirós, C., Pasian, S. R., & Marôco, J. (2019). Transcultural adaptation of the Oldenburg Burnout Inventory. *Frontiers in Psychology, 10*, 338. Advance online publication. DOI: 10.3389/fpsyg.2019.00338 PMID: 30914985

Smith, J., & Garriety, S. (2020). The art of flexibility: Bridging five generations in the workforce. Em J. Smith, & S. Garriety. *Strategic HR Review, 19*(3), 107–110. DOI: 10.1108/SHR-01-2020-0005

Smith, K. A., & Williams, R. S. (2023). Targeted training interventions for employee well-being: A meta-analysis. *The Journal of Applied Psychology, 109*(2), 210–224. DOI: 10.1037/apl0000910

Smith, W. K., Gonin, M., & Besharov, M. L. (2013). Managing social-business tensions: A review and research agenda for social enterprise. *Business Ethics Quarterly, 23*(3), 407–442. DOI: 10.5840/beq201323327

Sousa, M. J., Duarte, T., Sanches, P. G., & Gomes, J. (2006). *Gestão de Recursos Humanos.* Lidel.

Souza, M., Benati, N. A., & Pereira, A. (2024). A Evolução do Setor de RECURSOS Humanos: Análise Histórica e o Impacto das Tecnologias. *Deleted Journal, 5*(2), e116–e116. DOI: 10.54033/icmrv5n2-012

Spence, M. (1973). Job market signaling. *The Quarterly Journal of Economics, 87*(3), 355–374. DOI: 10.2307/1882010

Stahl, G. K., Maznevski, M. L., Voigt, A., & Jonsen, K. (2010). Unraveling the effects of cultural diversity in teams. *Journal of International Business Studies, 41*(4), 690–709. DOI: 10.1057/jibs.2009.85 PMID: 33487775

Staniec, I., & Kalińska-Kula, M. (2021). Internal employer branding as a way to improve employee engagement. *Problems and Perspectives in Management, 19*(3), 139–151. DOI: 10.21511/ppm.19(3).2021.04

State Bank of India. (2023). Annual Report.

Stokes, P., Larson, M., Balasubrahmanyam, S., Singh, S. K., Jain, A. K., Giga, S. I., & Cooper, C. L. (2013). Perceived organizational support as a moderator in the relationship between organisational stressors and organizational citizenship behaviors. *The International Journal of Organizational Analysis*, *21*(3), 313–334. DOI: 10.1108/IJOA-Mar-2012-0574

Storey, J., & Wright, P. M. (2023). *Strategic Human Resource Management: A Research Overview* (2.ª ed.). Routledge. DOI: 10.4324/9781003364276

Strauss, A., & Corbin, J. (1998). *Basics of qualitative research: Techniques and procedures for developing grounded theory* (2nd ed.). Sage.

Sunstein, C. R. (2018). *Republic*. Princeton University Press., https://press.princeton.edu/books/hardcover/9780691175515/republic?srsltid=AfmBOoqdaUzf0Ow19ExzG8_MT4RTNv1uT7RNUM69vOEI8QUxxZw5yd86

Sweller, J. (1988). Cognitive load during problem solving. *Cognitive Science*, *12*(2), 257–285. DOI: 10.1207/s15516709cog1202_4

Synytsia, A. (2020). Education as a Means of Affirming Democracy Values in John Dewey's Pragmatism: Modern Perspective. *Journal of Education Culture and Society*, *11*(1), 30–41. DOI: 10.15503/jecs2020.1.30.41

Tajfel, H., & Turner, J. C. (1979). An integrative theory of intergroup conflict. In The social psychology of intergroup relations.

Tajfel, H., & Turner, J. C. (1979). An integrative theory of intergroup conflict. In Austin, W. G., & Worchel, S. (Eds.), *The social psychology of intergroup relations* (pp. 33–47). Brooks/Cole.

Tambe, P., Cappelli, P., & Yakubovich, V. (2019). Artificial intelligence in human resources management. *California Management Review*, *61*(4), 15–42. DOI: 10.1177/0008125619867910

Tang, A. D., Luu, T. T., & Chen, W. K. (2023). Internal corporate social responsibility and customer-oriented organizational citizenship behavior: The mediating roles of job satisfaction, work-family facilitation, life satisfaction, and affective commitment. *Journal of Sustainable Tourism*, *32*(5), 986–1007. DOI: 10.1080/09669582.2023.2195134

Tang, M., Montgomery, M., Collins, B., & Jenkins, K. (2021). Integrating career and mental health counseling: Necessity and strategies. *Journal of Employment Counseling*, *58*(1), 23–35. DOI: 10.1002/joec.12155

Tarafdar, M., Cooper, C. L., & Stich, J. F. (2019). The technostress trifecta. *Journal of Management Information Systems*, *36*(1), 1–34. DOI: 10.1080/07421222.2018.1556375

Tarafdar, M., Cooper, C. L., & Stich, J.-F. (2019). The technostress trifecta — techno eustress, techno distress and design: Theoretical directions and an agenda for research. *Information Systems Journal*, *29*(1), 6–42. DOI: 10.1111/isj.12169

Tata Consultancy Services. (2023). Annual Report.

Tavares, M. C., & Vaz, M. (2025). Rethinking performance evaluation: Strategic alignment in the service sector through a case-based framework. *Administrative Sciences*, *15*(10), 390. DOI: 10.3390/admsci15100390

Tekleab, A. G., & Taylor, M. S. (2003). Aren't there two parties in an employment relationship? Antecedents and consequences of organization-employee agreement on contract obligations & violations. *Journal of Organizational Behavior*, *24*(5), 585–608. DOI: 10.1002/job.204

Tessarini, G.Junior, & Saltorato, P. (2021, September). Workforce agility: A systematic literature review and a research agenda proposal. *Innovar (Universidad Nacional de Colombia)*, *31*(81), 155–167. DOI: 10.15446/innovar.v31n81.95582

Thelen, P. D., & Men, L. R. (2023). The role of internal communication in fostering employee advocacy: A social exchange perspective. *International Journal of Business Communication*, *60*(4), 929–956. DOI: 10.1177/2329488420975832

Theurer, C. P., Lievens, F., & Slaughter, J. E. (2018). Employer branding: A brand equity-based literature review and research agenda. *International Journal of Management Reviews*, *20*(1), 155–179. DOI: 10.1111/ijmr.12121

Thomas, D. A., & Ely, R. J. (1996). Making differences matter: A new paradigm for managing diversity. *Harvard Business Review*, *74*(5), 79–90.

Thompson, G., & Vecchio, R. P. (2009). Situational leadership theory: A test of three versions. *The Leadership Quarterly*, *20*(5), 837–848. DOI: 10.1016/j.leaqua.2009.06.014

Thorat, S., & Newman, K. S. (2010). *Blocked by caste: Economic discrimination in modern India*. Oxford University Press.

Tims, M., Bakker, A. B., & Derks, D. (2012). Development and validation of the job crafting scale. *Journal of Vocational Behavior*, *80*(1), 173–186. DOI: 10.1016/j.jvb.2011.05.009

Tims, M., Bakker, A. B., & Derks, D. (2015). Job crafting and its relationships with person-job fit and meaningfulness: A three-wave study. *Journal of Vocational Behavior*, *91*, 87–96. DOI: 10.1016/j.jvb.2015.11.007

Tippins, N. T., Oswald, F. L., & McPhail, S. M. (2021). Scientific, legal, and ethical concerns about AI-based personnel selection tools: A call to action. *Personnel Assessment and Decisions*, *7*(2), 1–22. DOI: 10.25035/pad.2021.02.001

Toor, S., & Ofori, G. (2008). Leadership versus management: How they are different, and why. *Leadership and Management in Engineering*, *8*(2), 61–71. DOI: 10.1061/(ASCE)1532-6748(2008)8:2(61)

Top Employers Institute. (2024). *Engaging employees from a human-centric perspective*. https://www.top-employers.com

Torrington, D., Hall, L., Atkinson, C., & Taylor, S. (2020). *Human Resource Management* (11th Edition ed.). Pearson.

Tusquellas, N., Palau, R., & Santiago, R. (2024, November 1). Analysis of the potential of artificial intelligence for professional development and talent management: A systematic literature review. *International Journal of Information Management Data Insights*, *4*(2), 100288. DOI: 10.1016/j.jjimei.2024.100288

Tyskbo, D., & Firtin, C. E. (2025, August 8). Contextualizing talent management: A practice-based study of Turkish SMEs and large organizations. *Journal of Small Business Management*, , 1–41.

Ulrich, D., Younger, J., Brockbank, W., & Ulrich, M. (2012). *The New HR Competencies: Business Partnering from the Outside-In. The RBL Group*. New HR Competencies.

Ulrich, M. D., Way, S. A., & Wright, P. M. (2024). Building strategic human capabilities that drive performance. *International Journal of Human Resource Management*, *35*(20), 3341–3373. DOI: 10.1080/09585192.2024.2408026

Universum. (2024). *Measure employer branding ROI: KPIs & proven examples*. https://universumglobal.com

van de Poel, I., Royakkers, L., & Zwart, S. D. (2012). *Moral responsibility and the problem of many hands*. Routledge.

Van den Broeck, A., Ferris, D. L., Chang, C.-H., & Rosen, C. C. (2016). A review of self-determination theory's basic psychological needs at work. *Journal of Management*, *42*(5), 1195–1229. DOI: 10.1177/0149206316632058

Van den Broeck, A., Vansteenkiste, M., De Witte, H., Soenens, B., & Lens, W. (2010). Capturing autonomy, competence, and relatedness at work: Construction and initial validation of the work-related basic need satisfaction scale. *Journal of Occupational and Organizational Psychology, 83*(4), 981–1002. DOI: 10.1348/096317909X481382

Van Hoye, G., & Lievens, F. (2009). Tapping the grapevine: A closer look at word-of-mouth as a recruitment source. *The Journal of Applied Psychology, 94*(2), 341–352. DOI: 10.1037/a0014066

van Niekerk, L. (2009). Participation in work: A source of wellness for people with psychiatric disability. *Work : A Journal of Prevention, Assessment, and Rehabilitation, 32*(4), 455–465. DOI: 10.3233/WOR-2009-0856

Van Wingerden, J., Bakker, A. B., & Derks, D. (2017). The longitudinal impact of a job crafting intervention. *European Journal of Work and Organizational Psychology, 26*(1), 107–119. DOI: 10.1080/1359432X.2016.1224233

Varsha, P. S. (2023, April 1). How can we manage biases in artificial intelligence systems–A systematic literature review. *International Journal of Information Management Data Insights, 3*(1), 100165. DOI: 10.1016/j.jjimei.2023.100165

Venkatesh, V., Morris, M. G., Davis, G. B., & Davis, F. D. (2003). User acceptance of information technology. *Management Information Systems Quarterly, 27*(3), 425–478. DOI: 10.2307/30036540

Vrontis, D., Christofi, M., Pereira, V., Tarba, S., Makrides, A., & Trichina, E. (2022). Artificial intelligence, robotics, advanced technologies and human resource management: A systematic review. *International Journal of Human Resource Management, 33*(6).

Wachter, S., Mittelstadt, B., & Russell, C. (2017). Counterfactual explanations without opening the black box: Automated decisions and the GDPR. *Harvard Journal of Law & Technology, 31*(2), 841–887.

Wanberg, C. R. (2012). Facilitating Organizational Socialization: An Introduction. *In The Oxford Handbook of Organizational Socialization.*

Wan, W., & Duffy, R. D. (2022). Decent work and turnover intention among new generation employees: The mediating role of job satisfaction and the moderating role of job autonomy. *SAGE Open, 12*(2), 21582440221094591. DOI: 10.1177/21582440221094591

Wash, G. L. (2023). Strategy and competencies for future-ready business. *International Journal of Research in Human Resource Management, 5*(1), 11–20. https://www.humanresourcejournal.com. DOI: 10.33545/26633213.2023.v5.i1a.123

Weick, K. E., Sutcliffe, K. M., & Obstfeld, D. (1999). Organizing for high reliability: Processes of collective mindfulness. *Research in Organizational Behavior, 21*, 81–123. DOI: 10.1016/S0191-3085(99)21003-X

Welch, M., & Jackson, P. R. (2007). Rethinking internal communication: A stakeholder approach. *Corporate Communications, 12*(2), 177–198. DOI: 10.1108/13563280710744847

Westoven, J. H. (2024). *Losing your best: How poor leadership can drive top talent away*. Innovative Human Capital. https://www.innovativehumancapital.com/article/losing-your-best-how-poor-leadership-can-drive-top-talent-away

Whittlestone, J., Nyrup, R., Alexandrova, A., & Cave, S. (2019). The role and limits of principles in AI ethics: Towards a focus on tensions. Proceedings of the 2019 AAAI/ACM Conference on AI, Ethics, and Society, 195–200. DOI: 10.1145/3306618.3

Wipro. (2022). Sustainability Report.

Wipro. (2023). Annual Report.

Wood, A. J., Lehdonvirta, V., Graham, M., & Hjorth, I. (2019). Good gig, bad gig: Autonomy and algorithmic control in the global gig economy. *Work, Employment and Society, 33*(1), 56–75. DOI: 10.1177/0950017018785616

World Health Organization. (2019). ICD-11: International statistical classification of diseases and related health problems. https://icd.who.int/

World Health Organization. (2022). *Guidelines on mental health at work*. https://www.who.int/publications/i/item/9789240053052

Wrzesniewski, A., & Dutton, J. E. (2001). Crafting a job: Revisioning employees as active crafters of their work. *Academy of Management Review, 26*(2), 179–201. DOI: 10.2307/259118

Yadalam, T. V., Gowda, V. M., Kumar, V. S., & Girish, D. (2020, June). Career recommendation systems using content based filtering. In 2020 5th International Conference on Communication and Electronics Systems (ICCES) (pp. 660-665). IEEE.

Yin, R. K. (2018). *Case study research and applications: Design and methods* (6th ed.). Sage.

Younas, M., & Bari, M. W. (2020). The relationship between talent management practices and retention of generation 'Y' employees: mediating role of competency development. *Economic Research-Ekonomska Istrazivanja, 33(1), Vol. 33, No. 1*, pp. 1330–1353.

Yu, J., Yuan, L., Han, G., Li, H., & Li, P. (2022). A study of the impact of Strategic Human Resource Management on organizational resilience. *Behavioral Sciences (Basel, Switzerland)*, *12*(12), 508. DOI: 10.3390/bs12120508 PMID: 36546991

Zarvijani, S. A. H., Moghaddam, L. F., & Parchebafieh, S. (2021). Acceptance and commitment therapy on perceived stress and psychological flexibility of psychiatric nurses: A randomized control trial. *BMC Nursing*, *20*(1), 239. DOI: 10.1186/s12912-021-00763-4

Zhao, H. A. O., Wayne, S. J., Glibkowski, B. C., & Bravo, J. (2007). The impact of psychological contract breach on work-related outcomes: A meta-analysis. *Personnel Psychology*, *60*(3), 647–680. DOI: 10.1111/j.1744-6570.2007.00087.x

Zidan, H. M., & Al-Loumi, A. K. (2024). The impact of strategic alignment in enhancing organizational immunity through strategic agility: A survey study in Kirkuk education directorate - Iraq. *International Journal of Research in Human Resource Management*, *6*(2), 167–185. DOI: 10.33545/26633213.2024.v6.i2b.214

Ziede, M. L. (2020). Human Resource Management and Sustainability Linkages: Building Theory From Functionalist and Interpretive Paradigms. Doctor Thesis, *Università degli Studi di Pisa*

Zimmerman, B. J. (1990). Self-regulated learning and academic achievement. *Educational Psychologist*, *25*(1), 3–17. DOI: 10.1207/s15326985ep2501_2

Zito, M., Cortese, C. G., & Colombo, L. (2019). The role of resources and flow at work in well-being. *SAGE Open*, *9*(2), 1–12. DOI: 10.1177/2158244019849732

Zuboff, S. (2019). *The age of surveillance capitalism*. PublicAffairs.

Zuboff, S. (2019). *The age of surveillance capitalism: The fight for a human future at the new frontier of power*. PublicAffairs.

Zuiderwijk, A., Chen, Y. C., & Salem, F. (2021, July 1). Implications of the use of artificial intelligence in public governance: A systematic literature review and a research agenda. *Government Information Quarterly*, *38*(3), 101577. DOI: 10.1016/j.giq.2021.101577

About the Contributors

Ricardo Marcão, PhD, MBA, PMP, works at the intersection of project management, finance, strategy, grand strategy, and healthcare innovation. He has hands-on experience across Pharma, MedTech and medical devices, IT, and professional services. At Feedzai, he serves as a Senior Project Manager, leading international programs that use AI to fight financial fraud and support business expansion. Ricardo's work connects corporate strategy with international policy, showing how geopolitics, economic strategy, and competitive intelligence shape decisions in business and government. Born in Évora and based in the Lisbon area, he earned a degree in Computer Engineering from Instituto Superior Técnico, an MBA in the US at Broward College, and advanced studies in management and finance. He is currently pursuing postgraduate studies in Grand Strategy and International Relations at Harvard University. Across roles, he has led practical transformations: deploying gamification frameworks to improve engagement and sales, modernizing consulting practices in Pharma and MedTech, and building a risk-control model that lifted project margins by about 20 percent. From 2022 to 2023, he steered global CRM initiatives for leading pharmaceutical companies, aligning efficiency across different markets. Ricardo is the author of Business Plans with Artificial Intelligence (Generis Publishing, 2025) and Planos de Negócios com Inteligência Artificial (Editora d'Ideias, 2025), two hands-on guides that integrate AI into opportunity assessment, market sizing, forecasting, and execution governance. He also edits several IGI Global volumes: Design, Development, and Deployment of Cutting-Edge Medical Devices, Evolving Strategies for Organizational Management and Performance Evaluation, and Enhancing Engagement with Gamification: Education, Business, and Healthcare Perspectives. As an academic, editor, and international speaker, Ricardo has published on strategy, innovation, and performance. He is an Assistant Professor at ISLA Santarém - Polytechnic University, where he coordinates MBA, postgraduate, master's, and higher technical programs, mentoring students at the crossroads of business, technology, and governance. He serves as Chairman of

SCIP Portugal and is active with APMP NYC, PMI Portugal in Porto, and PMI South Florida, contributing to communities focused on competitive intelligence, project delivery, and policy-aware strategy.

Vasco Ribeiro Santos (born 1986 in Caldas da Rainha, Portugal) is a Portuguese professor, consultant, and author specializing in tourism, hospitality management, and service excellence. He is Professor Coordinator at ISLA Santarém and Founder & CEO of VRS Hospitality Consulting, a firm focused on consulting, team training, and mentoring for hotels, restaurants, catering, food and beverage, commercial aviation, and corporate events. He holds a PhD in Business Sciences with a specialization in Marketing from Fernando Pessoa University and a PhD in Tourism from the University of Seville. He completed postdoctoral work in innovation management applied to luxury tourism at the University of Aveiro and further postdoctoral research in ethical marketing in luxury hospitality. Vasco also earned a Habilitation (Agregação) in Management from Universidade Europeia, and previously completed a degree in Hotel Management and a master's in Tourism Marketing and Promotion at the Polytechnic of Leiria's School of Tourism and Maritime Technology. In academia, he serves as an integrated researcher at NECE – Research Centre for Business Sciences (University of Beira Interior) and as a collaborative researcher at GOVCOPP (University of Aveiro) and CITUR Leiria. He is also Editor-in-Chief of the International Journal of Digital Marketing, Management, and Innovation (IJDMMI), published by IGI Global. Vasco is an EQAVET expert for ANQEP, an evaluator for the Erasmus+ National Agency, and a founding member of the National Tourism Platform (Plataforma Nacional de Turismo) and AMETUR – World Association of Wine Tourism. His main research and professional interests include luxury and sustainable tourism, wine marketing and wine tourism, ethical marketing, employer branding, and the application of artificial intelligence and innovation in tourism and hospitality. He is the author or coordinator of several books, including Cortesia, Etiqueta & Protocolo na Hotelaria de Luxo, Etiqueta Moderna, O Anfitrião Modelo, Gestão de Empresas com Pessoas a Bordo, Gestão de Pessoas no Lazer, Animação Turística & Eventos, Diplomacia nos Negócios Internacionais, and Planos de Negócios com Inteligência Artificial.

Filipa Martinho is a Portuguese psychologist, higher education professor, and researcher in human resource management and tourism/hospitality. She is an assistant professor at ISLA Santarém – Polytechnic Institute, where she teaches Human Resources Management and serves as President of the Pedagogical Council of the School of Management. She is also the Erasmus+ Institutional Coordinator at ISLA Santarém, working on international partnerships and academic mobility. Filipa holds a degree in Applied Psychology and a master's degree in Health Psychology, both from ISPA – Instituto Universitário de Ciências Psicológicas, Sociais e da Vida, in Portugal. Her research focuses on human resources management, employer branding, employee motivation and commitment, knowledge management, and the intersection between ethics, sustainability, and tourism/hospitality. She is coauthor of several indexed publications, including Strategic Talent Management: The Impact of Employer Branding on the Affective Commitment of Employees (2020), Generation Z and Key Factors on E-Commerce: A Study on the Portuguese Tourism Sector (2020), Determinants of Internationalization as Levers for Sustainability: A Study of the Portuguese Pharmaceutical Sector (2021), as well as studies on ethics and sustainability in hospitality employer branding, in both journal articles and book chapters.

Isabel Reis is a Portuguese higher education professor and researcher specializing in human resource management, talent management, and employer branding. She is an Associate Professor at ISLA Santarém – Polytechnic Institute, where she is Director of the School of Management, President of the Technical-Scientific Council of the School of Management, and a member of the General Council. She also coordinates the Project Support Office and is actively involved in inclusion and interculturality initiatives on campus. She holds a PhD in Management from the University of Évora and both a master's degree and a bachelor's degree in Human Resource Management from ISLA Santarém. Alongside her academic work, Isabel has significant professional experience in the management and coordination of commercial teams, internal staff training, institutional business development, strategic business planning, and performance evaluation. Isabel is a researcher at CEFAGE – Center for Advanced Studies in Management and Economics (University of Évora). Her main research interests include human resource management, employer branding, people development, recruitment and selection, and digital transformation in HR processes. She is author and coauthor of several indexed publications, including work on employer branding as a talent management tool, digital transformation in recruitment and selection, ethics and sustainability in hospitality employer branding, onboarding processes, gamification, and people management in tourism and services.

***

Beatriz Batista holds a degree in Business Management and is a master's student in Human Resource Management at the School of Management of the Polytechnic Institute of Tomar, Portugal. Her main research interests include Human Resources, Management, and Sustainability.

João Farinha Dean of the Management School at ISLA Santarém – Polytechnic University, President of the Technical-Scientific Council of the Management School, and Member of the General Council of ISLA Santarém – Polytechnic University. He also heads the Projects Development Office, where he promotes institutional innovation and development. Prof. Dr Farinha holds a PhD in Management and a Master's degree in Marketing from Universidade Europeia, and is currently undertaking post-doctoral research in Management, specialising in Leadership and Knowledge Management, at the University of Beira Interior. With over 30 years of academic and professional experience, he serves as both Lecturer and Programme Director for several key programmes, including the Higher Technical Professional Course (TeSP) in Commercial Management and Sales, the Bachelor's Degree in Business Processes and Operations Management, and two MBA programmes: the MBA in Commercial Management and Marketing, and the MBA in Strategic Thinking Development. An active researcher, Prof. Dr Farinha collaborates with research units such as GOVCOPP (University of Aveiro) and NECE (University of Beira Interior), and serves on the editorial boards of several esteemed academic journals.

Gigi G.S., an Associate Professor at Saveetha School of Management, SIMATS, Chennai, has over 17 years of experience in academia. She holds a B.Sc. for her undergraduate degree, followed by an MBA for her postgraduate studies. She completed her Ph.D. in Management, with a focus on employee engagement in the IT industry. Additionally, she is UGC NET qualified. Her teaching philosophy revolves around creating an inclusive and dynamic learning environment where students are encouraged to engage critically, helping them develop practical skills that are applicable to real-world business scenarios. She has also been actively involved in service activities both within the university and the broader academic community. She has contributed to various departmental committees, mentored students, and volunteered for professional organizations such as the Rotaract Club and UBA. Through these efforts, she has aimed to support and further the missions and goals of the institutions she has worked with. In addition to her teaching and service roles, she has guided three research scholars for their Ph.D. and served as a RAC (Research Advisory Committee) member for eight Ph.D. scholars across several universities. In recognition of her academic excellence and community service, she has received several awards. Additionally, she has participated in, presented at, and published numerous articles in both national and international conferences.

Carlo Galveias is a professor at ISLA Santarém Polytechnic University with experience in the area of Marketing, Digital Marketing and its derivatives.

Vishal Jain currently serves as a Professor and Dean of Accreditation, Statutory Compliances & Institutional Development at the School of Engineering & Technology, Vivekananda Institute of Professional Studies - Technical Campus, New Delhi. His previous roles include Professor at Sharda University, Greater Noida, and Associate Professor at Bharati Vidyapeeth's Institute of Computer Applications and Management (BVICAM), New Delhi. Dr. Jain has actively participated in various academic governance bodies, including the Faculty Board, Board of Planning and Management, Executive Council, Academic Council, Curriculum Development and Review Committee, and Academic Audit across multiple higher education institutions. He collaborates with Kuala Lumpur University of Science and Technology (KLUST), Malaysia, Lincoln University College, Malaysia and the Research Institute of IoT Cybersecurity at National Kaohsiung University of Science and Technology in Taiwan for research initiatives. He has supervised three Ph.D. candidates, with two additional scholars currently pursuing their degrees under his guidance.

Miguel Ângelo Medeiros is a business growth and strategy leader with extensive experience in business development, go-to-market execution, brand strategy, and operational excellence across international markets. His work focuses on scaling organizations, building high-performance commercial models, and aligning revenue, marketing, and operations to drive sustainable growth. He holds academic training in Psychology (BSc and MSc in Clinical and Health Psychology) and Business Management, allowing him to integrate behavioral science with strategic and operational leadership. This dual background supports his work on organizational performance, employee engagement, internal marketing, and productivity, particularly in modern hybrid and high-growth work environments. Miguel has led international expansion, key account development, and growth initiatives across multiple industries, applying data-driven strategy and human-centered management to improve both business results and workforce effectiveness. His research and professional interests include absenteeism, internal communication, motivation, leadership, and performance optimization in hybrid organizations. He currently works with innovation-driven companies, helping them design scalable go-to-market strategies while fostering resilient, engaged, and productive teams.

Arpita Nayak is currently serving as an Assistant Professor, offering courses in management. She completed her Ph.D. in management from the KIIT School of Management. Her MBA and strong interest in Human Resource Management (HRM) led her to pursue further studies in HRM. Her passion for talent management inspired her doctoral research on "A Comparative Study on Talent Management in Private and Public Manufacturing Industries in Odisha." Dr. Nayak has presented research papers at both national and international conferences and has published articles in SCOPUS-listed journals. Over the years, she has taught a variety of subjects, including Human Resource Management, Principles of Management, Business Studies Management, Tribal Entrepreneurship, and Organizational Behaviour. In addition to her academic career, she also has several years of corporate work experience.

Nuno Nogueria is a faculty member and Dean of the School of Engineering and Technology at ISLA Santarém, Polytechnic Institute. He is also a visiting lecturer at the Lusofonia Polytechnic Institute. A Senior Electrical Engineer, with specialization in Industrial Engineering and Management and Business Management, and a Senior Occupational Health and Safety Technician. He holds a PhD in Health, Disability, Dependency and Well-being from the Universities of A Coruña, Murcia, León, and Salamanca, and a DEA in Occupational Hygiene, Health and Safety from the University of León. He earned an Integrated Master's degree in Electrical and Computer Engineering from NOVA School of Science and Technology I FCT NOVA, and a Bachelor's degree in Industrial Electrical Engineering from ISLA Santarém. He also holds the title of Specialist in Management and Administration, awarded through public examinations at IPLUSO, ISEC Lisbon, and IPMaia.

Lidiane Rodrigues de Oliveira is a certified professional trainer and organizational development specialist with a background in Business Administration and Human Resource Management. She holds a Bachelor's degree in Business Administration from the Pontifical Catholic University of Goiás (Brazil), recognized in Portugal by the Catholic University of Portugal, and is currently completing a Master's degree in Human Resource Management at ISLA Santarém. Her professional experience includes executive roles in corporate and healthcare organizations, where she worked with human resources, compliance, organizational development, leadership training, and quality management. As a certified trainer (CCP – IEFP), she has delivered more than 7,400 hours of professional training, combining academic knowledge with practical organizational experience. Her research focuses on workplace happiness, person–organization fit, organizational culture, burnout, and servant leadership. Her Master's dissertation examines the mediating role of person–organization fit in the relationship between organizational culture and employee well-being.

Maria de Fátima Pina holds a PhD in Mathematics from the University of Coimbra and the University of Porto. She is an Adjunct Professor at ISLA Santarém and an Integrated Researcher at ISR - UC, Institute of Systems and Robotics of the University of Coimbra. She is Member of the Portuguese Mathematics Society,

Member of the Portuguese Automatic Control Association and Member of the Information and Technology Research Centre of the ISLA Santarém Research & Development Unit. Her current research interests include interdisciplinary areas, such as, Control Theory, Data Science, Dynamical Systems, Computer Vision, Robotics, Social Sciences and Medical Engineering.

João Reis is a final-year student in the Bachelor's degree program in Business Process and Operations Management at ISLA Santarém. His areas of study include Management, Leadership, processes, efficiency, and others. João has an academic and scientific spirit of curiosity and discovery, having already participated in several national and international scientific-academic projects.

Bruno Barbosa de Sousa is a distinguished academic with a Ph.D. in Marketing and Strategy. He graduated in Business Management in 2006 and has since held various academic positions. Currently, he serves as a Professor Coordenador at the Polytechnic University of Cávado and Ave (IPCA), Portugal and has previously lectured at the University of Minho (Portugal). Bruno Sousa is a researcher at the Applied Management Research Unit (UNIAG) and the Center for Research, Development and Innovation in Tourism (CiTUR), both in Portugal. Bruno Sousa's research focuses on diverse areas including marketing and strategy, sustainable development, tourism behavior, organizational performance and niche marketing. He has authored several books and numerous book chapters, along with contributing to prestigious journals such as Current Issues in Tourism; EuroMed Journal of Business; Annals of Leisure Research; Journal of Cultural Heritage Management and Sustainable Development; Tourism Management Perspectives; Wine Economics and Policy; Journal of Hospitality and Tourism Insights; Journal of Tourism, Heritage & Services Marketing; Journal of Organizational Change Management, among others. https

Mohammed Umair is a seasoned academic and corporate professional with over 16 years of teaching experience and 5 years in the corporate sector. Currently serving as a senior faculty member at the School of Business, St. Joseph's University, Bangalore, he specializes in Finance and Taxation for undergraduate, postgraduate, and MBA Executive programmes. Drawing from his professional background with leading MNCs, he seamlessly integrates industry insights into academia. Recognized for his student-centric approach, he has authored multiple textbooks, published research in journals, and presented at international conferences. He holds a Doctorate in Behavioural Finance. He has also contributed to academic leadership as Dean, Strategic Advisor, and member of key restructuring, recruitment, and admissions committees. He has also chaired curriculum committees, supported quality initiatives, served on statutory boards, and handled various student support an development roles.

Christian Zhelev is an associate professor at the University of National and World Economics in Sofia, Bulgaria. His scientific research area is Marketing.

Index

A

B

C

D

E

T

W

www.ingramcontent.com/pod-product-compliance
Lightning Source LLC
LaVergne TN
LVHW081535300926
849161LV00006B/1442
9798260021781